BUDDHA IN YOUR BACKPACK

BUDDHA IN YOUR BACKPACK

EVERYDAY BUDDHISM FOR TEENS

FRANZ METCALF

Illustrations by Monk Song Yoon

Seastone

BERKELEY, CALIFORNIA

Published by:
Seastone, an imprint of Ulysses Press
P.O. Box 3440
Berkeley, CA 94703
www.ulyssespress.com

Printed in Canada by Transcontinental Printing

10 9 8 7 6 5 4 3

Library of Congress Cataloging-in-Publication Data
Metcalf, Franz Aubrey
        Buddha in your backpack : everyday Buddhism
for teens / Franz Metcalf.
        p. cm.
        ISBN 1-56975-321-0 (alk. paper)
        I. Title.

  BQ4570.S6 M47 2002
  294.3--dc21   2002032245

Editorial and production staff: David Archer, Claire Chun,
  Lily Chou, Devon Watts, Alice Riegert, Keith Riegert
Cover Design: Susan Burig
Interior Design: Leslie Henriques and Sarah Levin
Cover and interior art: Venerable Monk Song Yoon

Distributed in the United States by Publishers Group West
and in Canada by Raincoast Books

C^ONT^ENTS

PART TWO: Everyday Buddhism

acknowledgements

In a work such as this one, an author needs serious help. I received it.

The whole team at Ulysses/Seastone was mobilized and vital in the process of creating this book from the very beginning (starting with the title—thanks, Lynette!). I want especially to thank "my" intern, David Archer, and "my" editor, Richard Harris, who read the manuscript with such attention and compassion. And thanks also to Susan Burig, who came in to contribute the part we're all not supposed to judge books by. Finally, deep bows to Buddhist artists Song Yoon Sunim and Brian Barry. The monk Song Yoon Sunim did the penetrating art you see here, and Dharma Teacher Barry brought it to us. You are all totally swell.

Several wise people read the manuscript, in addition to those who had to. They get extra credit and my sincere thanks: Claire Gilpin, Andy Howk, Keith Riegert, Leslie Henriques, Professor Dan Capper, and Nina Ruscio. How much better this book is for your efforts!

I want to thank those who opened up this book to the lives of teens. Carmi Rodriguez, Celinda Pearson, Roger Ipswitch, Allan Light, and the students at Polytechnic School for giving me early guidance, and Bridget Fonger for opening the doors for me. Leon

Martell and his students at Culver Academy for a fun time and good ideas. Noriaki Ito and the Occidental College Meditation Group, especially Ty Thompson, and Eddie Chaidez for wise advice and stories. Rinban Ito (again) and Janet Ito of Higashi Honganji Temple, Los Angeles, for introducing me to the young Buddhists there who aided me. Zachary and Emma Seward for being my trusted first cultural interpreters. Alice and Keith Riegert for being doubly insiders: teenagers and publishing mavens. Your critique and support were invaluable to me.

Most importantly I want to thank Buddhist teens Tashi, Eddie, Eric, Ty, Jason, Mika, Gaku, Kayla, Claire, and Andy for sharing their lives and their Buddhism with all of us. Thanks to Andy Howk and the members of the Teen Buddhist Sangha at topica.com for treating this old fogy so well.

I must echo what Sir Isaac Newton said about himself—and if it was true for him, it's 108 times true for me:

> To myself I seem to have been only like a boy playing on the sea-shore, and diverting myself in now and then finding a smoother pebble or a prettier shell than ordinary, whilst the great ocean of truth lay all undiscovered before me.

With the great ocean of dharma before me, I have found so little! Yet, thanks to my good fortune and so many bodhisattvas, I am blessed with these pebbles and shells. They are what I have; I offer them to you.

INTRODUCTION: YOU AND THIS BOOK

> Studying the Buddha Way is studying the self.
> Studying the self is forgetting the self. Forgetting
> the self is being actualized by all things. Being
> actualized by all things, your body and mind as well
> as the bodies and minds of others drop away. No
> trace of realization remains and extends endlessly.
>
> ZEN TEACHER DOGEN

Teenage life (like other parts of life, but even more so) is really hard. You have to be a daughter or son, a sister or brother, a grandchild, an extended family member, a goof-off, a hormonally deranged adolescent, a student, a citizen, a worker, a "future leader," a part of the ecosystem, a psycho-spiritual being, a human person. You have to be all that. It takes some doing. This book can help. Being a teenager is an astonishing amount of work. You know that, but this book will show how deep that work is and how you can make it deeper. Your teen experience is so central to what Zen Buddhists call "this great matter of birth and death," that to be fully awake to your teenageness is to be a genuinely spiritual person.

Buddha in Your Backpack can be your Buddhist guide for dealing with that deep, important, spiritual stuff that also happens to be the seemingly regular, everyday, even sordid stuff of your life. It's a spiritual guide even when it's talking about homework or sex. And it's a practical how-to book even when it's talking about the Buddha's awakening or some meditation practice. This book will show you that there's a genuinely spiritual dimension in every aspect of your life. Using the tools of Buddhism, you'll learn how to hold an awareness of that dimension of life from moment to moment.

Okay, but why use Buddhism? Because Buddhism is focused right on you, right on your experience *in this very moment.* You are the center of attention. *You* are the one who makes Buddhism real. And Buddhism can help make *you* real, too. Buddhism is about reality because it grows from the real life of a real person, the Buddha. He taught a way to find deep happiness, a way that still works now. It can work for you. That's why people care about the Buddha. That's why I wrote this book, and that's why it's worth a look.

Maybe somewhere along the line you learned how amazing Buddhism is. If so, you already suspect it can help you in your life, right now, if you knew how to apply it. You're right. Or maybe this is the first Buddhist book you've ever picked up and Buddhism is a total blank to you. You might think this book is about some Indian guy who lived 2500 years ago. You might think Buddhism is like some other religions that seem to focus on the founders and ignore you. If Buddhism were like that, it wouldn't matter to me, and I would never have written this book for you. But Buddhism is totally not like that.

Buddha in Your Backpack is about you and your life. It's also about the Buddha and his life and his teachings. There's a lot about the Buddha and Buddhism here, but it's always information you can use. In this book we don't worry too much about the Buddha; the Buddha can take care of himself. We use his teaching to help you.

The Buddha would be fine with this. One of the central Buddhist *sutra*s, or sacred writings, says that at the end of his life the Buddha told his followers, "The teaching and the rules I've given you, after I'm gone these will be your teachers." And 2500 years later, they still are.

So you can read this book to learn about that amazing man, the Buddha. You can read this book to gain more awareness of a big part of our new, global culture. You can read it so you'll have wise words to drop on your friends at parties. You can read it to learn something about the most flexible and down-to-earth religion ever. These are all excellent reasons to read this book, but the main reason to read it is to bring Buddhist wisdom into your everyday life.

This book is about exactly that: everyday reality. Or you might say it's about everyday spirituality, since in Buddhism what is real *is* what is spiritual. There's no gap, no difference between the sacred and the profane. Your happiness, your fulfillment—they're right here and this book will help you realize them. Someone, sometime, has probably told you that you're going to look back on these as the happiest years of your life. Don't worry: it's not true. I swear, my teenage years were *not* the happiest years of my life. Sure, there were some *days* that were great, but *years*, no way. I needed this book when I was a teenager. It's a bit late for me, but at least it's here for you.

teen spirituality

The most important struggles of being a teenager—growing into your adult body, adult society, and adult life, all of which require awareness, insight, and patience—are the very struggles of being a spiritual seeker. The everyday experience of being a teenager can be a genuinely spiritual experience, and so you are a spiritual seeker. If that sounds conceited to you, consider this: right now you are creating yourself, and that's the most important thing you'll ever do. You don't have to call it spiritual, Just respect it.

What *is* religion? What *is* spirituality? These things are notoriously difficult to define, but here's a short answer. Religion is a multidimensional system of ritual, myth, doctrine, ethics, social and material forms, and sacred experience. There is no one "right" religion; instead there are literally thousands of systems through which people relate to the sacred, giving meaning and order to human life.

Spirituality is the individual person's relationship with the sacred. It's an inner experience, so it can vary from person to person even more than religions differ from one another, yet spirituality, too, must always grow from certain unchanging truths. Some people find their spirituality through traditional religion. Others experience it through nature, art, science, or love.

As a teen, your spirituality is intense because of what you experience and because you live so close to that experience. No matter how you try to hide from your own experience, drugging yourself with TV or books or video games or even actual drugs, these attempts to insulate your-self only show how powerful your experience is. In your teenage years, you have many fundamental experiences for the first time:

✦ You become morally self-aware and have to make moral choices on your own, thinking for yourself. You stop simply accepting the rules of your parents or your church; you don't always even accept the laws of your country. Instead, you look to the principles behind these rules and decide whether those principles are valid. Once you take this step, the world will never be the same.

✦ You look to join new communities, based on principles of honesty and justice as you've recently come to understand them. These communities usually grow from religious roots. You crave the solidarity of belonging to a group that shares your values completely, whether it's a gang or a church— even though you may later come to see the hypocrisy in them and grow disillusioned. Because of this, teenagers are the most likely people to convert from one sect or religion to another. Also because of this, when teenagers find a new religion, they can get intense about it.

✦ You acquire the intellectual capacity for formal reasoning—the ability to think about thinking—which allows you to be aware of your own awareness. This experience is literally a mind-blower, since it opens up your consciousness beyond the space of your skull. You open up to the sacred, whatever is sacred to you. This experience, too, can transform your whole world.

✦ You experience your body changing and see your parents growing older. From this evidence and your new self-awareness, you deduce the inevitability of old age and death. The sudden consciousness of your own mortality can strike with such force that you feel vertigo.

✦ You may begin to search frantically for some kind of meaning in a life that must end in death and loss. If no worldly answer seems to transcend death, you have to consider cosmic answers. If you were raised in a religion, you may turn to it now in a powerful new way. Humans can't live without meaning. Most teens discover that the old meanings of childhood don't work anymore. Some teens must find new meaning in life, or it is simply not worth living anymore. You need meaning to face death.

✦ You become a sexual being, whether or not you act on it, and so face the greatest physical pleasure, intimacy, and temptation in life. Sex is profoundly spiritual. It's only considered non-spiritual in religions that deny the sacredness of the body. Buddhism (the Buddhism I teach, anyway) is not one of those. The power of sexuality may be dangerous, but it is surely spiritual.

✦ You begin to enter into romantic relationships and discover the very center of your life—the marvelous interweaving of the physical, the emotional, and the transcendent that is love. Even the most casual crush takes you out of yourself in a way that hints at the ecstatic freedom of genuine love. That's the goal of Buddhism: ecstasy.

Do you see yet that you are a spiritual being? If not, maybe it's because you don't like the word "spiritual." I wish there were a better word in English, but this is the best we've got. It's a word the Buddha almost never used. He didn't teach in those terms. The Buddha always brought people back to their own everyday experiences. Were they happy, or were they clinging to desires or views that made them unhappy? It always turned out to be the latter. Then he would help them let go of the desires and views that were causing their pain and lead them toward calm . . . toward insight . . . toward nirvana!

The Buddha did this by affirming people's everyday experiences, both external and internal. He was always directing people back to their minds, asking them to be aware of their ever-changing mental states. So he would always be very matter-of-fact about their circumstances, both inner and outer. He counseled people to concentrate their attention on the present moment—a strategy that is perfect for you, too, right now. He focused on the practical, not the airy or religious. So does this book. Don't worry about "spiritual" or "not spiritual." Whether you choose to see yourself as a spiritual being doesn't matter. You just have to see yourself as a serious one.

You're experiencing changes, and you're going to keep changing. As the Buddha taught, there's no unchanging "you," so there's no single and final identity for "you." We live in the real world, and to be comfortable here we need an evolving identity. We all work on this our whole lives, but we totally focus on it when we're teens.

So there, you're on a sacred journey. Your reality and your path through it is a sacred path—if you become conscious of it. This book will help you do exactly that.

what's in this book?

We begin by looking at the life of the Buddha. We follow him as he grows up and begins to question who he is and what he wants to become. He rebels totally against his parents, rejecting the identity they try to force on him. Instead, he goes off on a painful search for himself. Sound familiar? I hope your relationship with your parents is better than the Buddha's, but I'm sure it shares some patterns with his. The path of the Buddha is not so far from your own. His questions are your questions.

We then explore the basics of the Buddha's teachings and the religion that grew from them. For over 2500 years Buddhism has grown and changed, and it's changing now more than ever—though always remaining firmly rooted in the Buddha's insights.

In Part Two we look at typical scenes and troubles in teenage life, applying Buddhist wisdom and, as we do, learning to change. Buddhist wisdom can teach you new ways of seeing yourself and your world that will help you to be happier. As we pay special attention to exactly those things that matter—school, body image, identity, sex, all that—you'll learn that adopting a Buddhist perspective is pretty simple. Not easy, but simple. It does require some serious work . . . okay, to be honest, a lifetime of work. But, hey, no commitment is necessary now and the first steps can take you a long way in a short time.

Part Three is called "Taking a Buddhist Path." The "path" is the classic metaphor for Buddhism. The Buddha saw life as a path, and this remains the classic metaphor of Buddhism. The path has no end, so what matters is simply taking steps along it. Part Three lays out the basic steps. Of course there are things that can go wrong on the way—both inside and out. Sorry, but Buddhism is not an escape from reality. It is an escape *to* reality, which includes disappointment and pain. I give you tips on avoiding inner roadblocks (like resistance) and outer roadblocks (like prejudice) as you walk the path.

Part Three also tells you how to get started in meditation, a traditional Buddhist practice proven to help your body and mind, regardless of your religious beliefs. After teaching basic meditation techniques, it gives you a whole series of spiritual exercises you can begin to practice on your own. You don't need a teacher for these; all the guidance you need to get started is right here. These exercises act as reminders of what we and this world are really about. See which ones work for you. If you decide to continue farther along the path, they will help you make basic Buddhist practice part of your own day-to-day routine.

An ancient Zen text says, "What counts is right now; it doesn't take a lot of time. Everything I tell you falls away . . . just get this and you'll be the real person who's left home, free to spend a fortune every day." In an online teen magazine, Catherine D. quotes a Baci candy wrapper that says, "Many people live happily without knowing it." Same message.

Finally, if you want to keep following a Buddhist path, "Many Paths, Further Explorations" will help by giving you pointers on how you can move forward and learn more. It gives resources—including many websites, like the one for this book: www.buddhainyourbackpack. net—for learning more about the forms and practices of Buddhism. Buddhists are not all the same, and not all Buddhist centers or groups will be right for you. "Many Paths" can help you choose wisely.

This book offers a new way to look at your life and all the little (but crucial) things in it. It's not about making you into a Buddhist. Frankly, I just don't think that's important. Maybe there are some Buddhists who would be shocked to hear me say that, but at least one agrees with me: His Holiness the Dalai Lama, the highest authority in Tibetan Buddhism and the most famous and respected Buddhist leader in the world today. He says there are plenty of Buddhists, no need for more. People should continue to be whatever they are.

The Dalai Lama says we all should just get happy! The goal of life is happiness, and whatever path leads you to deep and lasting happiness is the path you should follow. It doesn't have to be Buddhism; it can be any path with heart. In fact, it can be several.

Whatever your path, this book can teach you something. It can open your eyes to your remarkable life and opportunities. It will help you use Buddhist ideas to become happier. And it tells you where to look if you want to discover more. But remember, your choices about what to believe and how to see the world are your own. If anyone tries to take your religious freedom of choice away from you, that person must not trust you to choose for yourself. And it's hopeless for them to try to prevent you, anyway, because those choices can never truly be taken away. They are your true freedom. Buddhism and this book should add to it. So be free and maybe go create some happiness.

PART ONE

B^UDDH^A AND B^UDDH^ISM

Someone asked, "What do you mean by the true Buddha, the true dharma, and the true path? Will you please explain them to us?"

The Teacher answered, "Buddha is the simple pu-rity of mind. Dharma is the radiant illumination of mind. The path is the clean light that can never be hindered. These three are actually one, yet remain mere names without essence."

ZEN TEACHER LINJI

WH̱O W̱AS
THE ḆUDDḪA?

 ### the buddha's world

The Buddha was not born "Buddha." He had to *earn* that name. It means "awakened one," and so is not his given name but an honorific title bestowed to show respect. Even devout, traditional Buddhists don't call the Buddha "Buddha" when they're talking about his life before his awakening. They call him a *bodhisattva*, which means a "being of awakening," or one who is far along a path of enlightenment but not yet at its end. Or they call him by his name: Siddhartha Gautama of the Shakya clan. After his awakening, they call him the Buddha, the Blessed One, the Lord, or Shakyamuni Buddha (which means "Buddha, the Sage of the Shakyas," because there is more than one Buddha, but more on that later).

Although he surely had wonderful innate talents, at first the young man who would be Buddha seemed a most unlikely person to follow a spiritual path, so for now we'll call him by his first name, Siddhartha.

Siddhartha was born around 500 B.C.E. in what is now Nepal, in the foothills of the Himalayas, the greatest mountains on earth. His culture was highly civilized even then, and his father was a *kshatriya* ruler, a noble, something like the king of a tiny country. The Shakyas, his family, were rich and powerful. As their firstborn son, Siddhartha was a great blessing to them and heir apparent to the kingdom. But there was a complication. According to legend, when Siddhartha was born a prophet foretold that he would become either a great king, turning the wheels of the world, or a great religious teacher turning the wheel of truth.

As you might guess, his parents were pretty clear on what *they* wanted their son to be. They wanted an heir and a king, and they were determined to make sure they got one. It didn't take a prophet to know what kind of a childhood Siddhartha would have.

Siddhartha grew up in ancient India, a culture that placed a huge importance on *dharma*, or duty. Young people wore their complicated social and religious responsibilities like heavy robes. They simply had to learn and accept their particular duties, which depended on many factors—most importantly sex, age, class, wealth, and family connections. Not so different from today, but much stricter.

Although he had great advantages, Siddhartha had no freedom at all. From the moment he was born, his job was to learn how to be a king. He'd have as much power and wealth as he could want, as long as he learned his place and did what his parents told him. The prophecy motivated his parents to push him even harder to keep him on track.

So they did for many years.

 ## siddhartha's long childhood

A complex myth surrounds the conception and birth of Siddhartha. You can read it elsewhere in detail. For example, check out the introduction to the Jatakas, the stories of the Buddha's lives before he was the Buddha. Here I want to introduce you to the real person, Siddhartha, as near as we can know him.

Siddhartha was the son his parents had longed for. But soon after his birth, his mother died. This was Siddhartha's first experience of sadness and frustration, the only one he was to have for a long while. Legend says his aunt stepped in to raise him, but the loss must have changed Siddhartha, though he could not remember it. Grief also must have changed Siddhartha's father, who surely wanted even more to keep his son close, since he was the living connection to his lost wife. This just raised the pressure on Siddhartha to be worthy of carrying on the family name.

We can imagine Siddhartha's childhood without believing the whole myth or all the "facts" of his early life. Yet that myth illustrates the social pressures we do know were on him. It tells the story so strongly, let's use it as a starting point for developing a new understanding of the problems he faced as the local "rich kid."

The myth says that King Shuddhodana, Siddhartha's father, created a series of opulent palaces for the young prince. These were designed for two purposes: first, to give Siddhartha all the pleasures of childhood and opportunities to learn his role in life, and second, to prevent Siddhartha from seeing the sadder side of this world, for the king was determined to avoid the possibility that the prince might encounter something that would make him doubt his destiny. The palaces were thus stately pleasure domes designed purely for entertaining and educating the prince and fulfilling his every need.

Sounds great, doesn't it? Yet the palaces were also places Siddhartha couldn't leave. They were designed to bind him in chains of gold, hostage to his own perfect but predetermined future. Their bars may have been graceful, but they were still bars.

So Siddhartha grew up magnificently, his life full of devoted attendants and doting parents. His aunt had come to love him as a son, and his father was greatly proud of him. But though they were attentive to his every desire, they were also demanding. Siddhartha had to excel at everything—and he did. After all, even though he didn't realize it yet, he was a bodhisattva, a Buddha-to-be; of course he was great at everything. He was also fantastically brilliant, and handsome, and talented. You know the expression "he had it all"? Well, Siddhartha did.

Eventually, Siddhartha finished his schooling. Then his parents picked a woman for him to marry, as was the custom at the time. Even now, around the world, most kids get married while they're still teenagers and never go to high school, let alone college. They need to work all the time just to survive. It was like that in Siddhartha's time, but his work was learning to be king—which included taking a wife and having a son and heir to pass his kingdom on to one day. His father expected Siddhartha to produce the next generation's king. (Sorry, queens didn't count.) So Siddhartha got married and, still living in the palaces, got his wife pregnant.

siddhartha discovers the reality of the world

Each of us reaches a point where childhood ends. Even if our parents are not ready for it, we are. We have to grow up. It's not necessarily about wanting to, and it's not about making everyone happy, even ourselves. It's just how things are. Siddhartha had reached that point.

Most versions of the myth say the crucial events happened just as Siddhartha's wife was about to give birth. Siddhartha's father was planning to retire to the forest soon to pursue spirituality, and Siddhartha was about to take up the task of being king, so he wanted to see his kingdom. So far, his father's efforts to protect Siddhartha from reality had worked. Siddhartha had only seen a sanitized, prettified, "G-rated" version of his kingdom. His view of India as the "happiest place on earth," however, was not to last.

Maybe it started with Siddhartha stretching his princely responsibilities. Maybe he wanted to inspect the army he was going to command. Maybe he wanted to meet some of the subjects he was supposed to rule. Or maybe he was just going to hang out at the park.

Some versions of the myth give this park explanation, though you have to wonder whether Siddhartha was just *saying* he was going to the park, when in fact he was going somewhere else with his "friend who had a car" (though in this case it was a horse-drawn chariot). Who knows where Siddhartha and his charioteer Channa *really* went? Siddhartha was a good kid, but not perfect.

However it happened in history, the myth tells the essential story. Siddhartha got off the tour route and saw "the four sights" that changed his life and the history of the world. Seeing them, he began to grow up. Up until this point, Siddhartha had been brilliant, but he was also ignorant. Now his eyes were opened. Now we can truly begin to identity with him.

Siddhartha first saw a person stooped and bent, gray and enfeebled. Of course that person was old, but Siddhartha, having never seen such a thing, asked his friend, "What is *wrong* with that person? How come he's all creepy like that?" Channa told him. Shaken and appalled that human life should come to this, Siddhartha wanted to go home, but his eyes were just starting to open.

On this trip or the next, Siddhartha saw the second sight—a person pale with disease, wracked in pain. "That person is sick," his friend had to confess, "it happens to all of us." To Siddhartha, so naïve but so pure and compassionate, this was shocking news.

Maybe you're already expecting what comes next, but Siddhartha, having lived so long in such blissful ignorance, could not. Of course he saw the third sight: a person lying still, skin livid, borne slowly, surrounded by mourners. Perhaps he thought this person merely terribly ill, but he learned now of death. He learned that the dead would never rise again, no matter how the world might wish it.

Now, we know Siddhartha was smart, and when he saw death he immediately asked: "Will this happen to you, to everyone I love, even to me?" And Channa, being a real friend, told Siddhartha the truth, "Yes, Siddhartha, we all must age, sicken, and, yes, we all must die, even you."

This was the most terrible revelation of all. The end of this process of sickness and aging would be death, inevitable and irrevocable. Siddhartha realized his whole life was based on ignorance. He had been sheltered beyond imagining, and now his shelter was gone. All his pleasures, the fair pavilions alive with musicians and dancers, the banquets and costly wines, the dancing of his beautiful courtesans, even the love of his wife, all fell to nothing in the face of the pain of life and the finality of death. His former life was over. He returned to his palaces, but now they were prisons.

In myth, life is sharpened to perfect clarity. There are no confusing details or backward steps; there's none of the vagueness that we all face in our own lives. Yet our lives are like Siddhartha's. That's the whole point of telling you this story. Being a teenager is all about breaking out of the chains of our childhoods, just as Siddhartha did. And this is true even if, like him, you don't really want to break your chains of gold. You may think your parents are overprotective; perhaps they are. Like Siddhartha's, they love you and they have great aspirations for you. They can't protect you quite as well as Siddhartha's did, but the fact is, no protection works in the end. Life (and death) breaks in, even if you don't break out.

And what about that fourth sight?

siddhartha discovers himself

Siddhartha's childhood ended when he saw the first three sights. You could say he became a teenager when he saw the fourth. It was then that he realized he had to be his own self. He couldn't be the person his parents imagined he would be. I bet you know the feeling. Here's how it happens in the story.

Siddhartha, depressed from seeing the reality of human pain, went out again into the kingdom. Maybe he was looking for hope. Maybe he just had to get away from his parents. By now he must have felt they were crushing him, forcing him to be what *they* wanted, even lying to him to keep him obedient. He knew their lies grew from love, but they were still lies. Like anyone just discovering the world, Siddhartha hated lies; he longed to find some truth.

This time, Siddhartha saw something very different from the first three sights. He saw a man, thin, poor, wearing rags—but not pitiful. In fact, this man seemed to have a kind of peace, or at least a sense of purpose that everyone else he saw lacked. The man didn't have youth or power or money or looks, but he somehow didn't seem to care. He was a holy man, an ascetic, someone who had realized the pointlessness of pursuing a life of pleasure when sickness and age and death were the only results. Such a person renounces the hollow pleasures of the world in exchange for a life of poverty and spiritual struggle. In some versions of the myth, Siddhartha talked to this man and, though the man did not have the answers, Siddhartha knew he couldn't avoid the questions any longer. He couldn't stay in the palaces; he had to find his own answers. He decided he would renounce his world, like the holy man.

Being a good son, he first went home to his father for permission. Of course there was a scene. Siddhartha said he was a changed person and in fact was already separated from the world; he *had* to become an ascetic. But the king said no. He explained, no doubt a bit arrogantly, that Siddhartha was "too young" to be making a choice like this. Siddhartha had to wait; he had to grow up first. His father called Siddhartha thoughtless and foolish and told him he didn't really know what he wanted. Only *he*, the father, knew what his son really wanted. Siddhartha was just a boy and couldn't be trusted to make the right choice. He had to stay home and do his duty. It was time for his *father* to retire. Siddhartha could only withdraw from the world a whole generation from then, when his hair had gone gray and he had seen his own son's son. Yes, then it would at last be time for him to renounce the world—as it was for his father that very night.

Hearing his father's words, Siddhartha knew his wife had given birth to his son that day. Acutely aware of the great pressure on him to abandon his dreams and stay at home, he named his son Rahula, which means "hindrance." That night, as he went to look at his wife and child, he was deeply torn.

Now let's step back from the myth for a moment and try to feel what Siddhartha must have felt when he gazed at his wife and newborn son. He must have loved them. He came from a loving home, and though he was pushed to marry, he had been able to choose his own bride. He surely loved her. And having received his parents' own love despite the death of his mother, he must have immediately felt love for his son. Yet in this terrible conflict he couldn't deny his own character and experience. He had seen aging, sickness, and death, and he knew his wife and son would experience all three. No matter how much he loved them and wanted to stay with them, there was only one way he could really save them—and it was also the only way he could honestly be himself. He had to leave them and follow a spiritual path. He had to seek a cure for the suffering of the world.

That night, with everyone else at court asleep, Siddhartha left home to begin his journey to wake up.

You might find it hard to imagine doing what Siddhartha did: renouncing everything you are and everything you have to go find yourself. But Siddhartha was just doing much more intensely what we all do in our lives. He was saying goodbye to childhood and accepting the burden of being an adult. For him, that burden was spiritual: finding an answer to *dukkha*. (That's Sanskrit for "trouble," "disappointment," or "suffering.") Even if our burdens today aren't as heavy as Siddhartha's, we still must bear them. We, too, must renounce who we are so that we can become the individuals we are called to be.

The first step in growing up is to take responsibility. This is not hard when you know why you must do it. In fact, taking responsibility at home can actually be enjoyable because it demonstrates your competence, commitment, and love.

The next step is much harder: admitting to yourself and the world that the limits of childhood, which protected us from the inevitable sufferings of life, just aren't working anymore and have to go. This is hard for everyone—for parents as well as kids.

If you're like most people, you focus on yourself: how hard it is to be recognized as ready for freedom, how hard it is even to *ask* for freedom when that freedom might itself be painful. Siddhartha saw suffering and asked for the freedom to face it. It would have been so much less painful to just say, "Yes, dad," and go back to the pleasure palace. Yet Siddhartha chose real freedom, not fake pleasure.

What choices do you face that are similar? For one, there's the freedom to spend your own money. When you start spending money it means you have to start earning money. Even if it's an allowance, you still have to earn it, and that's hard. It requires facing up to budgets, chores, jobs, time conflicts, and a whole host of adult problems.

Wouldn't it be easier to just stay home and live for free? In some ways, yes, but in the big picture, no. Choosing to stay at home means choosing to be no one. And no one wants to be no one, or even hang out with no one. You face growing up and away from your childish safety.

At the same time, your parents must face giving you the freedom to fail, to get hurt, even to die—exactly what Siddhartha's parents tried to shield him from. They thought if he never saw these dangers, he'd never have to face them. But no parent, however well-meaning or powerful, can protect a kid from the basic reality of pain in this life. How hard it is for parents, who have managed to maintain this beautiful lie for so long, to let go of the kids they love and and risk their getting hurt in the wider world. You need to understand the resistance they must feel to this. Letting them know you understand their feelings is a huge step toward helping them understand their own feelings—and yours as well.

 ## siddhartha grows up

When Siddhartha snuck out in the middle of the night, he vowed he'd never come home until he had found the answer to suffering. Not just his own suffering, but the whole world. His goal sounds lofty, but after all, this was the Buddha-to-be. He left the city, cut off his hair, and gave his clothes to a passing beggar. St. Francis, another rich boy who turned his back on his parents' world many centuries later, actually stripped naked in the town square and walked away from his father. Siddhartha did much the same, and even today some ascetics in India wander around naked. After his grand exit, he headed off into the forest to live an austere existence with other ascetics. He wanted to strip away his old self and any trace of indulgence from his life.

When Siddhartha exchanged his old life for new, he quickly became the foremost practitioner of meditation and renunciation. He learned everything he could from a series of teachers and kept moving on. From the Buddha myth we learn of the many pleasures he gave up and the many practices he perfected. According to the myth, Siddhartha achieved the deepest *samadhi*, or absorption in meditation. He ate meals of one grain of rice, one sesame seed, one jujube fruit, one pea, one bean. You could see his back ribs when you looked at him from the front, some say, and when he scratched his belly he could feel his spine. Of course, we may not believe all the old legends, but it's pretty clear Siddhartha spent years in these efforts, and his successes gained him a small group of followers.

The self-indulgence of Siddhartha's youth was far behind him. Six years of self-denial went by, and he still didn't find the answers he was seeking. I won't burden you with the details. His life must have been a horrible combination of difficult and dull, yet, despite all that work, he was no happier than before. After passing out from hunger and exhaustion enough times, he must have realized he was killing himself. He had succeeded in his attempts to fit in with the ascetics—but what had he gained? He was the ascetic version of cool, but he was miserable. After six years he realized that extreme self-denial didn't hold the answer either.

So Siddhartha turned away from asceticism as he had turned away from family wealth. Instead, he chose to follow a new path, the middle way between the two extremes. The myth tells us that in taking this path, Siddhartha was bitterly rewarded: he lost all his friends. They thought he'd given up the struggle. They couldn't see that it was they, trapped in endless self-denial, who were going nowhere.

With new strength from eating real food, Siddhartha vowed that he would sit beneath a tree and meditate without moving until he achieved awakening or else dried up and fell apart. This would be the final effort. He looked deeply into himself and saw his desires and his ignorance. He sat all night, deepening his meditation and sharpening his insight. Finally, as the morning star came into view, his mind opened to the reality that no separate Siddhartha really existed. His desires

and suffering vanished along with the illusion of his self. He had come to full understanding of this world and human experience. He was enlightened, awakened, liberated. Siddhartha had become the Buddha.

Vanishing into the formless and free
The mind is through with desire and
dukkha.

DHAMMAPADA

the buddha's long life

The Buddha (we can finally call him that) sat in bliss. He had no need to do anything; he was truly free. But soon enough he faced a choice: should he just blissfully fade away, or did he owe something to the world? He decided he would try to share his wisdom with the rest of us, hard as that might be. Out of compassion, Buddhist scriptures tell us, he began to teach.

Just to show you that even for a Buddha things are not always easy, one scripture says that the first person the Buddha met after his awakening turned away. The Buddha appeared radiant, and the fellow meeting him asked if he was a god. The Buddha said he wasn't a god or a regular person: he was a Buddha, an awakened one, the latest in a series of great spiritual teachers. The fellow stood there a moment, said something dubious like "uh-huh," and went on his way. Not an impressive start for the man who was supposed to turn the great wheel of truth and teach the world.

The Buddha didn't give up, but when he met his old followers again, they ignored him. They sat there trying not to look at him or talk to him, but the Buddha was just beaming, and they couldn't do it. They broke down and listened to him as he told them what he'd discovered. This is the well-known "First Sermon" of the Buddha, called the

"First Turning of the Wheel of Truth," which sets out the basic principles the Buddha would expand upon for the rest of his long life. As you read this book, you'll see how these basics come up every day in your own life.

From his first five followers, the Buddha's students slowly multiplied over the decades of his teaching. They increasingly looked to him as not just a teacher, but the leader of a growing organization. During these perhaps forty-five years, how did the Buddha actually see himself and what he was doing? Did he always feel certain he was doing the right thing? Was he always happy with his choices?

Buddhist texts do not answer these questions. They simply show the Buddha as a perfected person. He could never have entertained doubts or been unhappy, they suggest, because he was too all-knowing and too perfectly calm. For the rest of his life after his awakening, the texts portray the Buddha as essentially a changeless living icon—an image that is alluringly beautiful but also hard to identify with. It contrasts deeply with the way the texts portray the man we've been following through life so far.

Up to his moment of awakening, we've been able to see right into Siddhartha's struggles, his outer conflicts and his inner hindrances. We can see ourselves mirrored in his life and sometimes recognize his qualities in ourselves. Once he becomes the Buddha, the Blessed One, we can no longer see into him so clearly. We lose contact with Siddhartha, who is no more. In his place we find only traces of the man who disappeared into the Buddha. The texts speak eloquently of how the Buddha worked tirelessly to help humankind reach happiness and peace. They describe his composure, his wisdom, his compassion, his patience, and all the other good qualities he possesses (and he's got them all). In the end, however, these descriptions remind us of how we *want* to be, not how we normally *are*.

The Buddha is so exalted, so unfailingly superior to any conflict or crisis, that the scriptures no longer bother with the story of his life. In fact, there isn't much story to tell. Once he broke through to awakening, he apparently didn't change much. Why would he? He was free and devoted to teaching the truths he had uncovered. He never retired; again, why would he? He taught until the moment of his death because he was doing what he was meant to do. He had found his real identity. He had fully grown up.

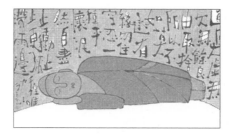

WHAT IS BUDDHISM?

When you first seek the teaching, you think you're
far away from it. But the teaching has already
come to you; you are immediately your true self.

ZEN TEACHER DOGEN

As the track of a bird in the sky does not exist,
as the shape of a dream, an illusion, a mirage, an
echo, a remembered shape, and the image of the
moon in water are unreal and ungraspable, so a
fixed dharma, a set order of dharma, is unreal
and ungraspable.

PERFECTION OF WISDOM SUTRA
IN 18,000 LINES

We've followed the story of Siddhartha as he grew up, found himself, and, finally, found awakening. But we haven't explored what that awakening was. So far we've seen the story of a person; now we'll see the story of a religion.

Don't worry, I won't give you a history of Buddhism. There are many dull accounts of this history and a few not-so-dull ones—check out the books and websites I recommend in "Many Paths, Further Explorations." For now, let's get right to the living center of Buddhism: what the Buddha saw, felt, and taught to his disciples. We'll also look at the continued growth of Buddhist ideas beyond what the Buddha himself taught, for wisdom didn't stop when the Buddha passed into final nirvana. Not at all. When humans really get something and then really strive to teach it, sometimes the student *goes beyond* the teacher. As a teacher, I know this happens all the time. There's a Zen saying that any teacher whose students don't surpass him is a failure. The Buddha was not a failure. As we'll see, his teachings have grown and deepened—and are still doing so.

you can't break the laws of physics

Now that you've read this far, you know something about the Buddha and his spiritual search. He set out to make an end to the pain, frustration, disappointment, and suffering of life. Buddhism teaches that he finally did make an end to those things, but not in the obvious way of ending the worldly causes of these troubles. No one can put an end to them, not even a Buddha, not even a god. They are inseparable from the things that cause pleasure and joy; they are woven into the fabric of the universe. There is no life without death, no love without loss. As a "take-no-prisoners" Buddhist text puts it:

> Everything together falls apart.
> Everything rising up collapses.
> Every meeting ends in parting.
> Every life ends in death.
>
> UDANAVARGA

Any person who cares about the world and other people tries to put things together, to build up what is collapsing, to postpone parting, and to avoid death. These efforts make life meaningful and beautiful. But every person who has a brain knows no amount of trying will ever finally prevent things from falling apart, collapsing, parting, and dying. We're all subject to the laws of physics, including the second law of thermodynamics that says that energy tends to flow from concentration to diffusion. As the Buddha put it, "All component things decay." In other words, over time, any complex system, such as our complex bodies, created from millions of energy transfers, will break down, come apart, and fall to ruin. There's no stopping it.

Buddhism teaches a terrible truth. Whatever we cherish, we shall lose, and there's simply nothing we can do about it. This may sound profoundly depressing at first, but it's not. It's simply the truth. It's what we all know already but don't always want to examine. It's what the Buddha saw when he left the palace. It's reality. The question is: What do we do about it?

The need to act now is the central insight for those of us who aren't sure what to believe about the afterlife or our eternal souls (if we have them). It is perhaps the most important thing that can be written in this or any book: Whatever we believe about the great issues of life and death, we have to act now, in this very moment.

The immense cosmos comes down to *right here*. The whole history of time comes down to *right now*. Terrible endings will come, yes, but that makes no difference at all right now. What matters right now still matters, right now. Think, feel, and act in this moment, responding honestly to each experience. This is life and what we make of it.

You can use up a lot of energy trying to break the second law of thermodynamics, but that's not going to get the job done. You can't break the laws of physics.

Okay, then . . . what *can* we do? Just lay down and die right now? No, very few people try that. The Buddha certainly didn't. In spite of everything, we find life sweet and want more of it. There's a trick almost all of us use: we *pretend* that we can break the law, stop time and decay, keep things just right all our lives, and live forever. We *know* this is a lie but we love to do it anyway. Amazingly, we somehow manage to ignore the feebleness of this pretense almost all the time. We lull ourselves into dreams of amusement and hope.

When people are successful at pretending, they sometimes become happy, but of course it can never last. When times of real decay and loss come, pretending fails and they have to face reality without preparation or practice. You've probably witnessed examples of this; they are obvious and painful. It's pretty clear that, over the long run, this trick just doesn't work.

But not everyone resorts to tricks. Not everyone needs to pretend. When he realized the whole world around him was pretending, Siddhartha left home to find something real. Other spiritual seekers have done this since the beginning of

> As a younger person, you haven't been practicing this dream trick as long as your parents and teachers have, so you probably see through it more easily. If you try to awaken them from their dreams, they usually are mighty displeased. Tough situation. Honesty is not always your best tool.

humanity and still do it today. After they discover life beyond dreaming, some return and invite us to wake up, too. Siddhartha was not the first Buddha. There have been many and there will be more to come. Buddhism has always taught this.

The Buddha found a way to end trouble by waking up to what really causes it. He saw a third option that would keep working even while everything falls apart. Not impossible efforts to stop the process. Not doomed efforts to deny it. Instead, he saw before him the liberating path of accepting it. He recognized the truth of impermanence and made it the cornerstone of Buddhism.

Impermanence is all around. As one teen wrote,

"I've got this huge feeling of sadness that everything I have will go one day. I was looking at all the things in my room and thinking that one day I won't have this room and the things in it. I was also looking at photos in my album and feeling sad because I know my whole family will change. People will die, we'll move on, and it won't be the same. I end up thinking it would be better for me not to have so much stuff cos the pain of losing it will be so great. I guess this is exactly what the Buddha was talking about: attachment. This is dukkha, so I must focus on non-attachment. Then I might be able to accept the impermanence of things. . . ."

The Buddha accepted impermanence openly. He could do this because he saw what it really meant. And this brings us to the astounding truth at the core of awakening.

The Buddha's truth is astounding not because it's complex or brilliant. It's astounding because it's so unsuspected, yet follows so directly from the idea of impermanence we've just been talking about. Here it is:

There's no enduring self that suffers.

That's it. Simple. Astounding. Maybe we should pause here. Yes, stop reading for just a minute and sit with that idea. Shut your eyes and breathe in and out, slowly, easily, for just a minute as you let it sink into you. Go on, mark the page and set the book down. Experience how you feel with that idea. I'll wait.

Okay, welcome back. How did that feel? This is one strange idea, isn't it? We'll get back to it in a moment, but right now let me tell you that you just meditated. Ha! You thought you were just sitting? The great Japanese Zen teacher Dogen Zenji says that "just sitting" is the highest form of meditation. Congratulations. Nothing to it. (In several ways.)

Now back to the central truth of Buddhism.

explaining
the astounding thing

"Well, it's no use *your* talking about
waking him," said Tweedledum, "when you're
only one of the things in his dream. You
know very well you're not real."

"I *am* real!" said Alice, and began to cry.

"You won't make yourself a bit realler
by crying," Tweedledee remarked: "there's
nothing to cry about."

THROUGH THE LOOKING-GLASS

"There's no enduring self that suffers." Let's connect
this central truth back to the problem of decay and the
trouble it causes. Decay is impermanence. Dukkha—the
Buddhist term for suffering, trouble, pain—comes from clinging to things in the face of their inevitable ending. The
Buddhist choice, when faced with decay or loss, is not to
worry about it. Just let it happen, because it's not happening
to you. *There's no you for it to happen to.*

Here comes the tough part: understanding how it is
that there's no you.

The Buddha was a philosopher, so from time to time in
the *sutras* (the Buddhist scriptures), when he's teaching some

egg-headed type, he will attempt to show by various means the logical fallacies of the notion of the self. But neither you nor I is really that egg-headed. (I got a Ph.D. at the University of Chicago, and believe me, I met some folks there who were *scary* smart. I figure we'll let them read other books.) Instead, let's start by breaking down what we are, what our personal "I" really consists of.

In a famous passage from the classic Buddhist text, The Questions of King Milinda, a monk is talking with the king and trying to explain exactly this idea of not-self (in Sanskrit, *anatman*, literally not-self). The monk uses the simile of a horse-drawn chariot, but to make it more relevant, let's use a car. Same idea. As the monk might ask if he were around today: What is the car? Is the axle the car? Is one or all of the wheels the car? Is the engine block the car? Are the airbags the car? And so on.

Of course the answer is no, none of these things is the car. The "car" is merely a convenient container word for this set of systems that operate together in a way that, for a time, constitutes a car. But in reality there are only the systems; there's no actual car. If we were to replace each part, one by one, we could completely rebuild the thing. (If you've ever rebuilt an old clunker to drive, you know what replacing the thing one piece at a time is like. You've also discovered that buying the parts for a car costs something like twenty times the cost of the whole car. This is an example of dukkha.) If you replaced every part, would it be the same car? Not physically. And you can't really say that it would be the same car because you would use it the same way. That's just its use, not its essence. That would be like saying that another person kissing your boyfriend or girlfriend is you, because he or she is doing the same thing you do. (There's another example of dukkha.)

This brings us to the self. Just as there is no car, there is no self. Take you, for example. Are you your liver? Your heart? Your skin? Your blood? Such things are constantly changing. They can't be you if you want to claim that you are a permanent thing. Let's cut to the chase: No part of you is you. Even your mind, which is what's left when we've discovered the various parts of your body are not you, is impermanent. Your thoughts are constantly arising and passing away. Even your consciousness itself was simply not there before you were born. It didn't exist. And after your death? Gone again. In fact it's gone when you fall into deepest sleep. It's gone even during the day in those micromoments between thoughts. There are times when your very you-ness dissolves into a grainy mess of mere perceptions and apperceptions fleeting across a field of consciousness which itself disappears when it's not active.

There's a charming passage in an early sutra that lists the questions it is foolish to dwell on:

He may ask, "Did I exist in the past? Did I not
exist in the past? What was I in the past? How
was I in the past? What was I that led to me being
as I was in the past? Will I exist in the future? Will
I not exist in the future? What will I exist as in
the future? How will I exist in the future? What
will I be that will lead to me being as I'll be in the
future?" Or he may be confused about right now:
"Do I exist? Do I not exist? What am I? How am
I? Where have I come from? Where am I going?"

MAJJHIMA NIKAYA

We've gotten pretty close to those kinds of questions
the Buddha told us to avoid. So let's stop with this simple
statement: we search for a self, an "I," and we fail to find it.
Our very self is an illusion made up of tiny grains of sense
and memory. It's a useful illusion when, say, we need to
decide quickly whether it's worthwhile to apply the brakes
and save our butts when an accident happens right in front of
us. (That's why you should never tailgate: if you do, there's
not enough time to cobble together a self to slam on the
brakes before impact potentially ends all future opportunities.) It also comes in handy when your boyfriend or
girlfriend is back and *someone* has to kiss him or her. But
useful as the self may be, in the final analysis, it doesn't exist.

Well, okay, you don't exist. What do you do now?

If you don't exist, then you can't do anything because there's no "you" to do it. Here comes another crucial Buddhist concept: the Two Truths. Ultimately, you don't have a self, but on the everyday level, you *do*. The Buddha wasn't stupid. He knew that on a conventional level it's useful to talk about cars and selves and boyfriends as if they exist. But on the ultimate level, they don't exist as separate and enduring things. All there is, really, is a wonderful, ever-evolving network of interrelationships. For linguistic reasons that we don't need to worry about here, Buddhists usually call this interrelatedness "emptiness" in English, but we might better translate it as "openness." Everything is open because it only exists in its relationships with other things. In other words, we exist only in our relationships, which are always evolving. So we might say that the self exists, but only in the context of the dance it's doing with other selves.

Can you say that you and I exist? Ultimately, you can't. But you can say that our relationship as author and reader exists. Your mind is playing with thoughts that I once had. I exist for you because I wrote my thoughts down in this book and you're now reading it. Your reading it makes me exist. You create me. Thanks!

All things are like this.

where do you go now?
number one

The idea of having no self may not seem appealing. I admit, it freaks me out, too, sometimes. But I've come to see the up side to it. You'll find it right in the Buddha's first teachings. Here it is:

> If there's no self, there's no one to feel the pain of impermanence and attachment. There's no one to get frustrated, angry, disappointed. There's no one to feel loss and no one who has to die. Imagine.

If I can manage to live on the ultimate level and the conventional level at the same time, then I can live free from my self and my experience of decay. Sure, things and people will fall apart, but I don't need to pretend they won't, like everyone else does. And I don't need to struggle against nature for letting this happen. I'll just accept change naturally, since decay is change and leads to things we know not of. I'll accept it because I don't have a self or an ego to protect, and because I know that what exists now must vanish to make way for what is to come. It's the cosmic dance.

The Buddha's astounding idea is our invitation to the cosmic dance. The Buddha is your prom date. He's wearing

Thanks to Claire Gilpin
for this joke:
Q: Why can't Buddhists
vacuum in corners?
A: Because they have no
attachments!

the latest style of robe and arrives with a lovely lotus flower corsage for you. He sweeps you off your feet with suave lines like "You're nobody 'til somebody loves you," or maybe "You're so pretty; what was your original face before your parents were born?" He's on time to wake you up from your dream and give you the chance to find genuine happiness and fulfillment, the kind that comes from dancing. The Buddha knows how to move on the cosmic dance floor. When we dance with the Buddha—in fact anytime we dance well—we'll be doing the right thing and we'll be happy without even trying.

where do you go now?
number two

Joining the cosmic dance: that's the goal of Buddhism in four words. If it's a bit too airy for you, the Buddha spent 45 years teaching clear and detailed cosmic dancing lessons. He gave hardheaded directions to make this liberation happen in our lives. In the 2500 years since, some brilliant, sincere, and sometimes funny people have spent their whole lives trying to make it even clearer, so we can get this freedom into our thick heads. They've shown us the way; we just have to follow it. See if you can follow my lead.

Buddha's first dance partners were the five ascetics who had followed him when he was practicing austerities. Their reception of him was charming because of the way they opened their minds to him. Their first reaction was to cling to their prejudice, believing that Siddhartha had abandoned serious religious practice and so could not possibly be worth listening to now. Yet, seeing him, they had to admit that he looked better. So they decided to listen after all, and as he started his teaching he must have made them better, too.

The new Buddha first told them that going to the extreme of self-indulgence was harmful. It was vulgar and useless. It led to suffering, not liberation. This was just what they wanted to hear. Perhaps, they thought, Siddhartha had come to his senses and would return to lead them. But no, after telling them this quick bit of good news, the new Buddha immediately showed he was no longer

At the time I wrote this book, a big American chain of clothing stores was featuring T-shirts with Buddha on them and the caption: "Buddha Bash: Get Your Buddha on the Floor." Is that unbelievably insulting to Buddhism? Or is that kind of cool? I don't know, do you?

Siddhartha. He told them that going to the extreme of self-denial was harmful. It was painful and useless. It led to suffering, not liberation.

What the Buddha was telling the ascetics was that their *whole lives were a total waste of time.* All their self-denial was for nothing—worse than nothing, in fact, since they had actually weakened and harmed themselves. Here is where I imagine them getting really pissed off. They're doing serious religious practice, and some young guy comes around and shows them up. Then he leaves to go have fun, and now he comes back and insults them. Who the hell is this guy? Who does he think he is?

Well, of course that was the first question the Buddha was ever asked, and he answered that he was "awake." Something in his awakened smile must have held his pissed-off old followers there long enough to hear his core teaching:

The right way is the "Middle Path" between
indulgence and denial, between all extremes.

The "Middle Path" means Buddhism. It's also called the "Eightfold Path" because it consists of right view, right intention, right speech, right action, right livelihood, right effort, right mindfulness, and right meditation. Fill your life with these eight right things and you are on the way to calm, to vision, to awakening, to nirvana.

The Buddha then moved right into his famous Four Noble Truths: they're the reason why we need to follow the Middle Path. They are the foundation of Buddhism, and they're simple.

SIMPLE TRUTH #1: *Life is full of dukkha.*

People usually translate dukkha as "suffering," but it also means disappointment, dissatisfaction, frustration, anguish, affliction, discontent, displeasure, unhappiness, misery, melancholy, sorrow, grief, woe, heartache, vexation, discomfort, disquiet, mortification, distress, pain, and trouble. We have many words to express this feeling, which is so common, so close to our hearts. Each of these words captures a part of it, but none captures it all. So in this book we'll stick with the original word, dukkha, and know it means all these things and more. It is the truth we all experience. We might not have thought of the other three Noble Truths, but dukkha doesn't need much explaining. Life is no picnic. Our pleasures are great, but they are never enough and they always end. No power on earth can prevent this. Our desire always outstrips our satisfaction. Dukkha happens.

> Don't think the Four Noble Truths are easy. They're not easy; they're simple. Easy and simple are totally different things.

SIMPLE TRUTH #2: *The dukkha we feel comes from our desire.*

We feel dukkha simply because we want certain things to happen and others not to. That's the story of our lives. It's also the reason there's never a happy ending to our life story. We never reach a place of contentment because we're always wanting more. We can't rest. We're always moving forward into the next episode— and it had better be a *fun* one.

You say you don't need a lot? You say you'll be okay once you get this much or that much? Maybe so (though I doubt it), but you'll still be wanting more because once you get it you'll want it to continue. And if it doesn't continue, you'll want it back. There's just no end to wanting until you realize you need to step off this wheel. This applies to our very lives. You say you don't need anything, you'd be happy as a beggar, you have no desires? But you still want to be you. You still want to live. Again, there's just no end in sight—until you are ready to see things differently.

SIMPLE TRUTH #3: *There's a way to see things differently and end this dukkha.*

Go on, the Buddha taught: turn the whole world upside down. When you realize that there's no self to satisfy, you won't have to satisfy it. That's it. Dukkha stops.

It's well known among the Buddhist crowd that the Buddha denied that the self was either eternal or annihilated at death. He could deny both because there *never was* a self. The self is not destroyed at death because it was never there to destroy. This works for desire as well: Buddhism does not say we have to give up desire. Desire is all about someone wanting to control things. But what if there fundamentally *is* no "someone"? Then there can't be any desire either. Desire is a natural part of the illusion of the self. If we see through that illusion, desire ceases to control us.

Does this mean you won't feel hungry when you spend your lunch money on a movie and can't eat? No, you'll still feel hungry, but that physical sensation does not have to cause you dukkha, not if you can fully accept it. That sensation is healthy. It's the right thing to feel when you've made your choice and seen the movie. No problem, no dukkha.

Even an extreme case like the pain you might feel if you weren't quite quick enough with the brakes and crashed into the car you were tailgating—it's still not dukkha if you can accept the pain as natural and right. Accepting it takes away the wrenching desire to make it different when you can't. When the desire goes, the dukkha goes. Even the pain of death—yours or that of someone you love—is not dukkha until you make it dukkha. Of course, facing an extreme case requires extreme equanimity. Most of us will never get to the place where losing a friend doesn't create heartache. But accepting the loss is still right and still leads away from dukkha. Just because you can't imagine reaching the end of the path doesn't mean you shouldn't *start*. There are rewards along the way, not just at the finish.

SIMPLE TRUTH #4: *Following the Eightfold Path, you move away from desire and away from dukkha.*

Like the others, this truth is so clear, so short, so sweet. The power of all these truths comes from their simplicity. They are the engine driving Buddhism. Their power drove the Buddha to teach his students, and it drove them to teach theirs. It drove the teachers to deepen the teaching in India, in Sri Lanka, in Burma, Thailand, Laos, Indonesia, in China, Vietnam, Korea, Tibet, Japan—and now the West. It drives me to deepen my knowledge and help you deepen yours.

This last truth leads us right into the Eightfold Path. As we look at the Eightfold Path and what it means to walk it, we'll be looking at this unending process of learning, teaching, changing, and deepening.

oh, so it's really not about where
we go—it's about going there

Right. It's about going there, and that means it's
about the path. That's why Buddhism is called the "Middle
Path." In fact, in that first teaching to the five old followers,
the Buddha never talked about "Buddhism." That really
might have sent his followers away. Instead he talked about
just what I'm talking about, and he said they were the same
thing:

> O monks, what is the middle path, which gives
> insight and knowledge, and leads to calm, to
> vision, to awakening, to nirvana? It is the noble
> Eightfold Path: right view, right intention, right
> speech, right action, right livelihood, right effort,
> right mindfulness, right meditation.
>
> SAMYUTTA NIKAYA

In this chapter, we've examined the basic insights of the
Buddha. Now we'll look into their embodiment: walking the
path. This is where every student of Buddhism needs to put
his or her effort. Helping direct us in walking the path is
where Buddhist teachers have been putting their own efforts
for 2500 years.

We don't need to know the details of the five *skandhas*, the mental/perceptive heaps our selves fall apart into, to understand "not-self" and feel better. We don't have to remember the twelve links in the chain of *pratitya samutpada*, or interdependent co-arising, to see that all things are interwoven and cause each other ceaselessly. Realizing Buddhahood depends on becoming a Buddha in this life, not studying up on abstruse philosophical doctrines. You've already made it through the toughest philosophy in this book.

> Note: Like all things worth doing in this life, fulfilling these vows is hopeless, yet not certain.

Even keeping the Eightfold Path straight in your head is not important. There's a story that the Buddhist scholar, D. T. Suzuki, who opened so many in the West to Zen, sometimes forgot one or another of the eight factors of the path when he was lecturing. He said don't worry, it's not important.

But I just said following the path is the whole of Buddhism. It's where our genuine effort needs to be. How could it not be important?

Suzuki (and I) never said that following the path is not important; it's everything. You just don't have to know which part you're following when. Ideally, all the parts should be happening at the same time anyway. Still, let's begin at the beginning and take the factors in their traditional order.

Right speech, right action, and right livelihood go together. They form the ethical part of the path; they're all about doing the right thing. Practicing them is the bottom line of being Buddhist. It should be the bottom line of being human, or at least *trying* to practice them should be. Buddhist tradition has developed them into the "five precepts" we all should live by. (Mahayana Buddhists have a few more, but all Buddhists share these five.)

ONE: I vow not to kill, or even harm, things needlessly.

TWO: I vow not to take what is not mine.

THREE: I vow not to engage in harmful sex.

FOUR: I vow not to lie and harm through words.

FIVE: I vow not to harm my mind with intoxicants.

Making these vows is nice. Actually trying to live up to them is what being a Buddhist is all about.

You don't have to be a Buddhist or make these vows to learn from this book. This book is not about taking precepts. It's about what Buddhists do, and it's about applying Buddhism to your life. Buddhists try to follow the Eightfold Path, and that means following these precepts. You do what you want.

Right effort, right mindfulness, and right meditation are the second group, concerned with training the mind. Right effort means putting our energies into being happier in the deepest way—in other words, not having selfish desires, doing harm, indulging bad habits, all that crap we humans do. Right mindfulness means checking in with ourselves to make sure that we're aware of our feelings and that we're honest about those feelings. No more denial, no more pretending to be happy or angry or in love or bored when we're not. Finally, right meditation is letting thoughts drop away and simply being in the moment as it evolves. It's a beautiful thing, and, for most of us, *unbelievably* hard.

Because it's so hard, Buddhists have spent thousands of years working out new ways of meditating that might work for you. There are dozens of techniques, from sitting in graveyards to having sex. Some are totally simple (" sitting"); some are intricately complex (that sex meditation, by the way, is one of these. It's a real "don't try this at home" kind of thing). All of them, though, come down to this: helping us see through the illusion of the self. It's in meditation that the Buddha was awakened, and it's in meditation that we have the best chance of being awakened ourselves. Meditation burns away the illusions that keep us unhappy.

I mentioned " sitting." As I said before, that's Dogen Zenji's highest form of meditation. Let me now ask you the big question about it: When we're just sitting, not harming anyone, not pursuing desires, embodying the Eightfold Path, who are we? Here's the really brain-shaking answer: We're Buddhas. Yep, that's what Dogen says: We're Buddhas. Explaining that brings us to the next part of the path.

Right view and right intention form the wisdom aspect of the path. Right view means seeing through all illusions—such as the separate self. Some Buddhists argue that any mental formation, including any doctrine, is an illusion, so true right view means having no fixed view at all. It's about accepting the now and dealing with it appropriately. Right intention means wanting to follow the path and intending to grow your wisdom and compassion, the two great Buddhist virtues. When you intend these things and have the right view, then when you meditate why *wouldn't* you be a Buddha? At least for those few minutes you're sitting there, you're a Buddha. Give yourself a bow.

Then get on with your life.

PART TWO

EVERYDAY BUDDHISM

When mind is original, the
    world is original,
Neither form nor
    openness.
As for form—pay
    no attention to it.
As for openness—
    don't hang on to it.
You're not a saint
    or a sage,
Just an everyday person,
    doing everyday things.

LAYMAN PANG

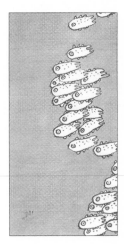

You know the saying "Been there, done that." But when it comes to situations of conflict or confusion, we're more likely to look back and wonder, "Been there, why'd I do that?" The aim of this central part of the book is to show how Buddhist ideas can guide you from "why'd I do that?" to "did the right thing." My conversations with teens revealed a whole range of situations where Buddhism can help. They fall naturally into a few basic categories: Homelife, Your Body, School Issues, The Opposite Sex and You, Finding Yourself, and Big Questions.

Real-life situations don't always fall neatly into one category. In fact, life is pretty insistent on throwing everything together at once. Not to worry. Principles and practices that work in one simple situation will work in other, more complex ones. Buddhism is a surprisingly simple way of life. Unless you get into its amazingly complicated philosophy, Buddhist wisdom comes down to a handful of really practical ideas and techniques that we can learn to use every day.

HOMELIFE

Young man, the child should act toward
the parents in five ways, thinking:
    As they supported me, I'll support them,
    I will do their work,
    I will keep the family traditions,
    I will earn my inheritance,
    I will give to charity in honor
        of my family.

Young man, parents show compassion
to their children in five ways:
    They keep them from doing harm,
    They encourage them in doing good,
    They train them for a profession,
    They set them up for marriage,
    When the time comes, they give them
        their inheritance.

DIGHA NIKAYA

becoming who we are

Of course the first place we begin to become who we are is in our families. This process starts even before birth. Consider your life before birth: when you were in the womb, you were in relationship. You may not have known it then, but your mother and you were *really close*. Even for the first year or so after you were born, you only existed in relationship with another person—your mom or whoever gave you the most care. As psychologist D. W. Winnicott used to say, there is no baby without a mother and no mother without a baby. They just don't exist apart from each other.

Since then you've been discovering who you were, separate from—but related to—others. That's why you were such a pain when you were two. You were discovering what was you and what wasn't, and you were discovering there really were other people and they couldn't be magically controlled by you. Bummer, but you got used to it. In fact, realizing that was the key to your being able to really relate to others. They were just like you, with feelings and everything. Amazing! You had to test them and you really did test your parents. Did they really love you? If you hurt them, would they still come back? Could you create your own rules? Who was the boss? You found out.

As a teen, you're figuring yourself out all over again, in relationship with your family as well as a whole variety of other people. From a Buddhist perspective, the relationships *are* you. There is no you, separate from them. This is why you care so much about them. The Buddha wouldn't have any problem with that. He would remind you, though, that ultimately you are not the "you" in any one of these groups. You are boundless.

Our society doesn't force you to absolutely decide your identity. It lets you play around, try different things, and see what works for you. In fact, these experiences *create* the you that goes on to try new things. But meanwhile, you do have to accept some greater responsibilities. If society is cutting you slack and letting you try things, you also have to cut it slack and do what you need to do—maybe by working, maybe by keeping your grades up, or maybe by helping others who don't have this fantastic privilege. That's the price of freedom, and sometimes it seems to take away the freedom. Don't worry—the freedom is still there. The freedom of youth can't be taken away because it's the freedom of time. You can experiment because you have plenty of time to start over. No one who matters will think you're a failure just because you found out an identity didn't fit and had the courage to try another.

For the Buddha, the freedom of youth lasted until *way* after his teens. You might say he was a late developer. He was hanging in pleasure domes all the way through his teens and into his twenties. In ancient Indian tradition, this was his "Student Stage." Only with marriage did one enter the "Householder Stage," adulthood. But the Buddha extended his play into that stage as well. He was a big, overgrown teenager. He didn't really make a choice about his life until his great rebellion in his late 20s. When Siddhartha did finally make a choice with consequences, people saw him as anti-social, but he saw himself as going beyond the merely social sphere. He saw his role as actually *changing* society. To do that he had to take a role outside society, at least for a time. This is the choice many true leaders make. It takes vision and courage, and often it takes the experiments of your teenage years as a foundation. Siddhartha had to go through different phases before finding his true identity, being Buddha.

Have you ever heard anyone say about you, "He (or she) is just going through a phase"? Isn't that maddening? Of course you're going through a phase. So are they! What do they think, you come pre-made and ready to heat like a burrito? Siddhartha went through "phases" as a spoiled prince, a husband, a new father, a humble renunciant, and a hot young *sadhu* (spiritual seeker) before he became who he was longing to be. He went through selfishness at home, then

depression after seeing the first three sights, then a lot of conflicted emotions with his groups of meditators, then a true
effort to think for himself—and only then did he become the
Buddha. Yet that last part could never have happened
without all the other parts that came first.

We are all like the Buddha. We all have that Buddha
identity inside, and we'll find it when we've sifted through the
failures and found a "path with heart."

(over)protective parents

Almost all kids feel their parents are overprotective. Becoming aware of the restrictions parents
put on you is one of the very first signs of growing up. You
may have begun to feel this even before you became a
teenager.

In one sentence, being a teenager is about growing
from a family member into a world member. Like any one-
sentence description, it's overly concise, but it gets to the
heart of things. You don't stop being a family member, but
you see yourself and prove yourself in a larger sphere.

Becoming a citizen of the world sounds a bit grandiose,
but that's exactly what you're doing. It happens slowly. You
begin to act in a larger context, and of course it totally makes
sense that you're the first one to see it. If you see it first, it

means your parents don't. And if they don't see it, they won't *act* like they see it. This means you'll very likely be wanting to widen your sphere before they're ready to let you, which leads to tension and sometimes conflict.

Tension and conflict are different things. Tension tends to cause conflict, which then tends to cause more tension, and so on. But though things start with tension, they *don't* have to progress to conflict. This is Buddhism in a nutshell: becoming mindful of your situation, inside and outside, so that you can act with power and freedom. Let's see how Buddhism helps with tension about parental rules.

You want few rules. You want great freedom, even danger. You think you can handle things. On the other hand, your parents want many rules. They want less freedom and danger. They think *they* can handle things. This is a situation of tension. In fact, it's a situation of unavoidable tension. What to do?

Buddha would say, open your eyes to the larger picture. You are growing, and you're going to make mistakes. In fact you need to make mistakes—that's how growing gets done. Or at least that's how things look from your center of the picture. But yours is not the only center; there are others. In this case the most important other center is your parents'. From their center, they are doing their best to provide a safe environment for their child to grow. That's their responsibility, and it's also an expression of their love. Their rules are their way of protecting their child from harms the child might not even imagine. Children need this protection while they're growing; that's how life goes on.

So the situation is more complicated than it first appears. Now here's the Buddhist kicker: *all things are like this*. All things are more complicated than you might first think. Becoming mindful of this lets us hold the tension between the different centers of this picture. That way you don't have to break the tension through conflict. Instead, you accept it. No one side is fully right or wrong in some objective way—not even *your* side. The tension in your relationship with your protective parents is inseparable from your growth and their love, and it comes from those two things. Both your own growth and your parents' love are beautiful things, and that means the tension is beautiful, too. At least that's how it looks on a really good day, when the tension is low. See it that way one day, and it's easier to see it that way the next. That is practice. That is wisdom. Welcome to nirvana.

Here's part of a conversation I had with a Buddhist teenager:

Him: "You can look at anything in a negative way."

Me: "In marriage, for example, we do this a lot."

Him: "This is true in relationships. I can perceive what I did in a different way. Say I cleaned

someone's room for them. I thought they'd be
happy. But they were upset because they felt I
took control from them."
Me: "Where's the Buddhism there?"
Him: "For every action there's a reaction. So I
stepped into their space and there was a reaction.
[With Buddhism] I can see where they're coming
from. We can come to a compromise."

Changing anyone is enormously hard. Changing parents
is even harder, but you're going to want them to understand
you and adapt to your way of living your life. Here's a tip
that comes directly from the openness I described in the last
paragraph: Show them how your choices make you happy.
Make choices that reveal a deep sense of ease and happiness
in your life. If your parents love you (and almost all parents
do, even if they don't always seem to), they'll see this and be
more inclined to accept your choices. Trying to change them
with your words, however forceful, won't get the job done.
They'll listen, but they won't change. This is different; this is
giving them a chance to change *themselves* to encourage a
happier you. Though you cannot change them directly, you
can use their own values—their wanting you to be genuinely
happy—to change them so they're willing to accept your
happy-making choices—even the ones that conflict with theirs.

This almost sounds sneaky, but it's not. It's simply being honest and making positive choices. It could also work as a trick in the short run, though there are no guarantees. This I do guarantee: Nothing sneaky works as well as this in the long run.

As I hope you can see, the benefits of mental opening go beyond what you feel. Here's another practical benefit: If you show your parents that you have the capacity to see this kind of nuance, and you accept that it means living with rules, you are going to impress them with your maturity for sure, and they are going to *relax the rules*.

It's a paradox. (That's not a problem for you, is it? I didn't think so.) Start the process, and they will pick it up. Sure, there may be some lag time while they do their own mental opening, but they'll come around. If you want to suggest that you're seeing things from their perspective so that they might try to see it from yours, that's okay. Just don't *tell* them to. That wouldn't be respecting them or seeing it from their perspective. Buddhism has been clear on this for 2500 years: Always embody the change you wish to see in the relationship. You want growth in the relationship? Start it yourself.

You are a complex, growing individual and should be respected as such. Parents can be slow to catch on to this, simple as it is. If you react to their slowness by being angry, stubborn, and uncooperative, they'll tell you you're acting

You're going to see that a bunch of Buddhism is DIY: changing from within. It's like the joke where the Buddhist asks the hot-dog vendor to "Make me one with everything!" Ha! But there's more, and starting changes ourselves reminded me of it. After the hot-dog vendor makes the Buddhist one with everything (!), the Buddhist gives him five bucks, waits, and finally asks, "Hey, how 'bout some change?" And the hot-dog vendor says, "Change must come from within!" Ain't it the truth. Stay alert for times your adversary wisely and compassionately starts change from outside. Don't hold your breath, though.

like a child and do not deserve respect. Unfortunately, they'll be right. You must embody the change while they catch up with this new, complex you. Paradoxically, parents can be blind to your struggles and eagle-eyed for your failures. (Parents will testify that teenagers are like this, too.)

The trick in creating a new familial identity is to remember that fluidity is a good thing. The very fact that parents treat you sometimes as a child, sometimes as an adult, means their relationship with you is flexible enough to grow. You need to develop and display a new identity at home—that of a thoughtful and responsible teenager. You'll work to accomplish this, but a teenager's identity also includes making mistakes and even occasionally making intentional choices that are bad ones. It's all part of the process of growing up. When no rehearsals are allowed, there are bound to be mistakes. Buddhism acknowledges that and says just learn from them. Look at the Buddha: He made plenty of mistakes. He only got his dad to approve of him after he was awakened—at the age of thirty!

Do I need to tell you that this principle applies to *all relationships*?

 ## evolving family relationships

Think of your evolving role in your family as an always-handy way to practice philosophy. Oh sure, sounds like fun, you say? Well, think about it some more: Your family role is constantly making you practice philosophy anyway, so you might as well make it productive for everyone involved.

Your family role keeps on contrasting *you,* the ultimately free person who can't be frozen in time or even fully known, with *you,* the individual person who has interests, friends, rules, and responsibilities. When you add time into this equation, things get even more complicated because that second person is always evolving. There's a genuine philosophical question of who you are.

Buddhism helps by constantly asking: "Who am I?" Remember how we compared the person to a car? Ultimately the car has no identity—not in its parts, the way it was made, or the factory or showroom it came from. Its identity is more like what it does, where it goes, how it moves forward in relation to people. Like a car, we're not our parts, our growth, or our homes. We're what we do with other people, and this is always new, always moving forward. Yet we are also like that car in all its parts. It can't go anywhere if it's stuck in the shop.

Your role as a teen is constantly evolving. It's a continual struggle with others to break out of the boxes people put you in. Everyone does this to everyone else, but you'll see it most clearly with your parents. When you want to be free, you're thinking "ultimately." Like a car that can't be defined, you're a process. You're where you're going. You're movement. You're change. You can't be pinned down. When parents (or other people) try to label you, they're thinking "conventionally." They're saying you're like a car that needs gas, oil, insurance, and careful driving because it's the sum of its parts and its functions.

When it comes to cars, it's pretty obvious that both ways of thinking are necessary. Shouldn't it be at least as true with you? You're more complicated than a car, right? That's why I invite you to think of this from a Buddhist perspective. On the ultimate level you're a boundless process. On the conventional level you're a person with limits. You're stuck with this philosophical tension, so why not practice philosophy?

Hold both levels of truth in mind. Your mindfulness of the tension between these ways of thinking reflects some subtle Buddhist thinking. The philosophy part isn't important in itself; what's important is the openness this mindfulness gives you. Mindfulness will help make being in the family acceptable by acknowledging both levels of being you.

failure

Don't be afraid to fail in your parents' eyes. Your parents know you sometimes experience failures when you're learning new and worthwhile things. They let you fail when you were learning to stand and walk. They were right to do this, even though it caused you pain, because it was the only way you could learn to stand on your own two feet. Well, they need to let you fail now for the same reason. It's the only way you'll learn to stand on your own two feet, so to speak. It's the same process. You can tell your parents this when they are smothering you and preventing you from learning. But remember, back when

Ever hear that old joke: "Your life is a test; it is only a test. If this had been your real life, you would have been issued instructions on what to do." Ah, if only! On the other hand, who wants to be told what to do?

you were learning to walk they could let you fall because you were only hitting the ground from toddler height. Now you might be hitting the ground from the equivalent of a bungee jump (or maybe a *real* bungee jump).

Buddha failed for a long time, and Buddhists are constantly failing in their practice and their lives. Go back to the definition of Buddhism as the Eightfold Path. Is Buddhism achieving the goal? No, it's the journey there (especially because "there" is just here, fully realized), and while Buddhists are journeying they're constantly failing. But, as any Buddhist teacher will tell you, this is no problem. Practice, fail, change, fail some new way, practice, fail—it just goes on. Zen Buddhists recite this:

> All the evil karma I've created, due to my
> beginningless greed, hatred, and ignorance;
> born of my action, word, and thought; I now
> witness openly and fully.

They recite this because they've made mistakes but are trying to let them go. As the Aussies say, "No worries, mate." Just start again.

divorce

I write these words knowing that more than half of my readers come from broken families. I mean this two ways. Families where there's been a divorce are often called "broken families." Yet some families where there has not been a divorce are broken families, too. They are families where the parents can no longer find intimacy with each other. (I'm not talking about sex here. If anyone ever told you that sex was intimacy, they were confused.) As a kid, life may be harder in a family like this even than in a family where there's been a divorce.

Being a teenager in a broken home is tough. It means you've seen fights. You've seen failure. You've seen what was beautiful turn to bitterness. Maybe you've lost confidence in love between partners, and now you just can't talk to your parents together anymore. You may see your dad (or sometimes mom) much less often than you did before. You may be angry with one of them for messing things up.

Buddhism teaches that all these things are natural. Please allow yourself these experiences and feelings. There is nothing wrong with your feelings, even bad ones, about divorce or a broken home. Think back to dukkha, the First Noble Truth. Life is full of dukkha—pain, disappointment, frustration, trouble—because people always want things to be perfect. It's natural that you want your parents to be together and happy. Give yourself some credit for wishing happiness to others. It's just as natural that you lack the power to make this happen. So you feel dukkha. Paradoxically, the first step to freeing yourself from this dukkha is to allow yourself to have it. Remember, Buddhism is about waking up. You can't free yourself from dukkha while you're denying it.

This step may last a seriously long time. When you're feeling bad, remind yourself that it's okay to feel bad about what you've lost, but be careful not to confuse that feeling with others that don't apply. For example, don't feel bad that you have been abandoned by a parent who's moved out. You have not been abandoned. One of your parents left because they couldn't live together; it's not because of you. If you doubt me, just ask them. I bet they'll tell you they stayed under the same roof longer than they thought they could just because *they didn't want to leave you.*

> A one-parent home that's always been a one-parent home is *not* broken. This kind of home is whole and can be perfectly healthy. Homes with two mothers or two fathers are also whole and healthy. Even homes where a parent has died can still be whole, not broken. It's all about the love.

You don't have to choose between your parents. Each of them may feel abandoned by the other. They may try—even unconsciously—to get you to side with them against the other. That might give you a sense of comradeship with each while you're with them, but it will lead to a terrible sense of splitting in the long run. Instead, Buddhism teaches you to use right speech. You don't need to criticize one parent who's badmouthing the other. You just want to keep yourself from participating. When the Buddha encountered such situations, he maintained a "noble silence." Try it. You don't have to defend either parent against the other's accusations; just don't chime in. Change the subject, or even find a way to leave the room. If you can do that without anger, your parent will come to understand it. If you do feel anger, acknowledge it before you try to respond. Let it come to a place of control before you open up the conversation, if you must. And if you do, remember that there's no way you're really going to change your parent, so be clear about what you need to express in the conversation. Perhaps it's simply that you feel pain when this kind of badmouthing occurs. This approach allows room for your parent to change, if he or she can. It also applies when you're parents are together, but fighting. They may try to bring you into the fights. You don't have to go there. Ask yourself if going there is right speech. If not, then right speech is being quiet. Embody that for your parents.

Here again, openness of mind lets you see things from the other's perspective. When one parent has left home, perhaps the other is worried that *you'll* abandon them, too. Ah, but this might be exactly the same worry *you* have—that they'll abandon you! Such feelings are often unconscious, but that doesn't stop them from giving you pain. This worry is unnecessary dukkha. Shed it like a snake sheds its dead skin.

the other kind of parents

Not all teens face overprotective parents. Some parents are closer to Missing in Action. This is a tougher problem, but in a way it's simpler. It means you're facing your identity crisis with fewer models to follow. You need to find yourself, much like Siddhartha did.

Siddhartha fled home. Some teens have to do this as well. If this happens to you, perhaps you'll be able to go back, but even then you're beyond your parents. Siddhartha's parents actively tried to imprison him, to stop him from ever becoming more than they were. Perhaps yours didn't seem to care enough to do even that. Either way, inside, you're on your own.

This is freedom. It's not a punishment, it's not a blessing. It's just freedom—the chance to make something of yourself. Whatever painful situation this freedom arises from, it remains pure and untainted if you can see it that way. Your life is your responsibility; your freedom is your power.

Buddhist monks are free from their families and most of them start as teens. The scriptures teach monks to think of themselves as free to wander like a rhinoceros, unbound and perfectly in the moment, without malice and without regret. Like a monk, you have a real chance at liberation.

Your first step will be liberating yourself from your parents—not outside, but inside. A few pages from now I talk more about this, but here I want to offer a few words to any reader who feels harmed by parents or other figures in the past. Letting go of these figures is hard for everyone, but if they really did harm you, you've got a lifelong challenge here. Buddha would smile on you and say try not to think of them as your family at all. Think of them, instead, as the messed-up people they are.

Start with your wish for your own relief from pain and expand it to others. As you need happiness, so do all beings— even your parents. If you feel sad for yourself because of your pain, imagine how much pain *they* experience. They have to deal with their own problems and struggle to raise a child at the same time. They just don't have the strength. You can be angry about their harmful choices, but you can also be compassionate for them in their weakness. Feeling pity for others, even those who harm us, embodies Buddhism's greatest virtues: wisdom and compassion. In doing this—only in doing this—can you finally be free from anger and fear.

 ## siblings

Many teens I've talked with mentioned brothers and sisters as a problem, especially if a sibling seems somehow favored over them. Nichiren, the Japanese Buddhist reformer, wrote, "If a couple has seven children and one gets sick, though they love each child the same, the parents think most about the sick child." Doesn't seem fair, does it? Jesus made a similar point when he spoke about the prodigal son—a constant screw-up, but when he returns home broke and debauched, his father gives him a big welcome-home party. The "good" siblings who had stayed home with the family weren't too thrilled with *that*. The same way, it's liable to grate on you if you consider yourself a good kid, yet you see your sibling getting all the attention.

To deal with this situation, first get some perspective on it. Parents don't love you more or less than your sibling who's getting more attention. They love you *differently*. Perhaps your sibling is sick in some way—maybe physically ill, as in Nichiren's story, or maybe emotionally troubled, as in Jesus' story. As Nichiren says, the Buddha thinks about evil people just like parents who think most about their sick child. Jesus' God is the same way: God throws a party to welcome back the lost sheep, but seems to ignore the ones who never strayed. This does not mean Buddha or God or your parents love you less when you're being good. It means they are *forced* to show their love in obvious ways to others who are not being good.

Think about the way they actually show that love. Think about the type of attention troubled siblings in fact get. It's almost always a pretty mixed bag. Seriously, is that what you want? And what about those siblings themselves? Do you want their troubles? Is that a good price to pay for the attention they get?

Buddhism calls you not to compare what you're getting with what others are getting. There will always be people who seem to get more than you, whether it's siblings or the president's kids or whoever. Let me repeat: This is *always* going to be true. Buddha suggests you rethink things. If your complaint is that there is *always* this unfair situation, then you've created a *permanent* unhappiness. Oops. Buddha was constantly asking people he taught, "Does this make sense? Does this lead to calm, to ease, to happiness?" And they always had to admit, well . . . uh . . . no.

Look to your own self, your own relationships. This is where happiness exists already—and also where dukkha exists already. This truth applies to more than just rivalries. Take fault-finding. Many people want to find fault with the world. They see in the world the root of their own frustration, anger, depression, or sadness. But our feelings are always our own doing. This is true in general, and it's even more true about seeing faults in people. Where do you see faults the most? In your siblings, of course, because deep down they are so much like you, even if they're radically different on the surface.

What's so remarkable about fault-finding is that it's actually useful. Not useful because we can change others by informing them of their faults (something that almost never works) but useful because the faults you find in siblings are so often your own faults projected out where they're easier to see. It's like that old joke where the guy loses his keys in the dark in the driveway but looks for them under the streetlight because it's so much brighter there. Same thing here. Faults are so much easier to see in obnoxious siblings. So when you become frustrated with a fault in a sibling—or anyone else—use the opportunity to look inside. Take a breath and turn the microscope around. Look for that fault in yourself. If it's bugging you *out there*, expect to find it *in here*. Things *in here* we can change. So make something useful out of your siblings' faults; use them to help yourself.

letting go of family

We started talking about family relationships with a look at becoming a teenager, so let's close with un-becoming a teenager as you get ready to go off on your own. Eventually, to become yourself, you need to let go of your previous roles. That includes your family role. It must change, no matter how comfortable it was or is. You have to let go of your parents; they do not control you, and your old ways of being with them won't work anymore when you leave home. They won't even *prepare* you to leave home.

To function with freedom and pleasure in the world, you need to accept yourself and find a sense of identity. To find that sense of identity, you need also to accept your roots, your family, where you came from. When you accept that your family did their best, you can move on. That doesn't mean you have to believe they were the best family in the world, just that they were the best family they could be, given their limited abilities.

Acceptance of your parents even allows you to see them in yourself without having to *be* them. Much as you love your parents, you don't want to become them; you want to become yourself. There remains a continuity: Your self still owes a lot to your parents. It is exactly that continuity you need to acknowledge. Physicist Isaac Newton (who was not a Buddhist, by the way) said of his discoveries: "If I have seen further it is by standing on the shoulders of giants." You will see farther than your parents if you've been wise enough to stand on their shoulders. In seeing farther, you are insepara- ble from those who raised you, but you are also free from their perspective. You have to let go of them to make your own discoveries.

By seeing things this way, you're using Buddhism to help yourself. You can be free from your past, even though it's inseparable from you. Of course it's tricky. It's why monks and nuns give up their past identities completely. They try to start fresh, but we householders—that is, all of us out here in the big world—have to accept our continuity with the past without letting it trap us. Remember to ask yourself who you are. You *come from* a past, but you *are* what you do right now. This applies in so many areas of your life: your career choices, your educational choices, your politics, even your love life. Maybe especially your love life.

The fact is, you can't be fully intimate with another person if unresolved issues with your parents get in the way. You can only be intimate when you're really *with* someone, seeing who they are and feeling what they feel. Trouble is, that is extremely hard to do. To be honestly and intimately with another person requires several things, all of which are in short supply. I'll say more about these things later. Here I'll just mention one: Intimacy requires privacy. Not external privacy—though that sure helps. I mean internal privacy.

If you're too wrapped up in your parents' relationship and your relationship with them, then when you try to have your own relationships you bring your parents right into the room with you. Way too crowded. You'll be doomed to relive your relationship with them instead of creating new relationships that are truly your own. It's a well-known psychological truth: Without effort, you create relationships

much like those you learned in your family. If they were good relationships, creating new ones is easy for you. If they were bad relationships, you have to put in the effort to take charge and change things.

To get your parents out of the room, say goodbye to them. Accept your parents and what they've done with you—*even if you don't like it*—so you don't have to bring them into your new relationships. As in so many parts of life, acceptance is crucial. It's easy if family life is relaxed. It's hard if family life is conflicted. Again, it's a matter of emptiness or openness: letting your parents be who they are, and letting yourself become who you will become. Zen Teacher Linji wrote:

> Whether inside or outside, whatever you meet, kill it! If you meet a buddha, kill the buddha. If you meet an ancient teacher, kill the ancient teacher. If you meet an awakened person, kill the awakened person. If you meet your parents, kill your parents. If you meet your family, kill your family. Then you'll be free at last, untangled, able to go where you want.

Notice that Linji mentions people we respect or love. So what does he mean by killing them? He means getting them out of the room. He means untangling yourself so you're free to be you. Linji's killing is never physical, no matter what angry fantasy you might have! Even anger leaves you bound up. Only openness lets you go where you want.

SCHOOL ISSUES

Every morning Ruiyan would call out,
"Teacher!" and he'd reply, "Yes!"

Then he'd say, "Be awake, be alert!"
and reply, "Yes!"

"From now on, don't be fooled by
anyone!"

"Yes, yes!"

WUMENGUAN

Just as self-discovery sometimes led to fights when you were two or three, it leads to fights when you're 12 or 13. In your early teens, you need to find a sense of who you are outside the family as well as inside it, which is why peer groups are so important. Your friends, clubs, cliques, and even gangs give you a chance to be with others like you. They let you see yourself through the eyes of others and fit into that image. As you go through middle school and into high school, being the same as everyone else may become less important. Your identity in your peer groups becomes more individual as you get clearer on what makes you "you." This takes time, work, honesty, and insight.

Siddhartha's privileged experiences at school were no doubt much different than yours or mine. Yet there are striking parallels between the future Buddha's education—inside and outside the classroom—and yours. Siddhartha chose his new identity and really got into it, but even then it didn't work for years. He tried to fit in and he was successful on the outside, but he wasn't fulfilled. He was like a new girl in school who manages to get into the coolest group and hang out with the queen bees, but realizes she isn't happy. Many of us don't have the strength to change our minds and our identities when we're trapped like this. Siddhartha did. He saw that he was stuck in a group that cared too much about how they looked and not enough about how they acted—and got out. He left and went from one group to another until he realized that *no* group was going to make him cool *inside*. Realizing that, he found his identity. He had a snack, sat down, and realized unexcelled, supreme, perfect enlightenment.

Finally, these relationships in cliques and in school are *impermanent*. Even a long-lasting social situation in school will last only a few years and then be over, gone, done. But *you* will go on growing and changing. Like Siddhartha, you'll pass through many groups and outlast them. When a situation is a problem, remember, it will pass.

 ## drama

A girl told me about her middle school, "It's like they need a new drama every day!" This got a big laugh and a chorus of nods and yesses. What is this pressure to dramatize?

School is where you spend most of your time as a teen. You spend much more time there than with your family, so it's often at school that you have to work out who you are and aren't, who you want to be with and who you don't, what you want to do and what you want to avoid. There's a learning curve, and just like learning to play a video game or drive a car, it takes experience. This is where drama comes in. It provides more intense experiences, so more learning happens. Of course, these experiences aren't always fun.

Here's what Buddhism tells us about the most common drama, cruel comments: "Surely a person is born with an axe in her mouth, and she cuts herself with it when she speaks foolish words."

You know just what the Buddha is saying, don't you? We all do it, teenagers and adults alike, though maybe teenage girls do it the most! I love my wife beyond words, yet too often I end up hurting her with words, and as soon as that happens, her pain becomes mine. Not only because I feel pain for her, whom I've hurt, but also because she hurts me right back. We both end up using our mouths like battle axes, with predictable results, until we shut up. I'm sorry to tell you that shutting up takes a while. I'm happy to tell you that it does happen, and it happens faster as you practice.

As a teenager, I really did not know when to stop. People asked me to "be honest," so I was. Once in that mode, I cared more about full disclosure than about other people's feelings. My axe would keep swinging until it cut up everybody in sight with the truth. Yes, it was truth, but it was also foolish and hurtful. It's not hard to be cruel with the truth, and it's not helpful, either. When we do it, we're going directly against the Buddha's advice.

If truth can be foolish, lies and gossip are worse. I was never a good liar, but I can gossip pretty well. When our words stray toward lies or gossip, then *all* of them are foolish. It's even worse than foolish honesty. There's really no excuse for it.

Fine, fine, shut up already! you may be saying by now. Don't do that too-honest thing. Okay, let's get to some more positive advice from the Buddha. He didn't just talk about foolish words, he also talked about wise ones. The principle here is right speech, one of the three parts of Buddhist morality I told you about in Part One.

Following the words of the Buddha, here's how to practice right speech:

> If it's not true, not beneficial, and disagreeable,
>> don't say it.
> If it's not true, not beneficial, and agreeable,
>> don't say it.
> If it's true, not beneficial, and disagreeable,
>> don't say it.
> If it's true, not beneficial, and agreeable,
>> don't say it.
> If it's true, beneficial, and disagreeable,
>> know when to say it.
> If it's true, beneficial, and agreeable,
>> know when to say it.

Follow that advice, and you can't go wrong. You'll find yourself talking less and saying more. Your chatter will stop, and the quality of your conversation will increase. People will start to take you more seriously. They'll nod their heads when you talk. When there's a debate about something, they'll come and ask you what you think. People will start saying things about you like "Still waters run deep," or "Her speech is silver, her silence golden," or maybe just "Wow, pretty smart."

The two great virtues of Buddhism are wisdom and compassion. To follow the advice of the Buddha, you need both. You start with wisdom, which tells you what's true and beneficial. Those are the things worth saying. Wisdom's not something you need to learn; it's something you have and sense inside. In fact, sometimes you have to *un*learn things to get in touch with wisdom.

> This business about unlearning is literally true. I "knew" much more in high school than I do now, and I went to grad school for eleven years! Real learning turns answers into questions. Answers stop you. Questions let you grow.

Take a moment to see things from a Buddhist perspective. Consider others. Think long-term. Remember that satisfying short-term desires will never make you deeply happy or satisfied with life. Take a breath. Look inside where it's quiet. Meditate on it. This is the way to wisdom, whatever your individual situation is.

Sometimes you won't be sure what the "truth" is. That's good. Becoming aware of what you don't know is a sure sign of wisdom. The Zen teacher Shunryu Suzuki wrote a beautiful book called *Zen Mind, Beginner's Mind.* In it, he tried to tell us to keep "beginner's mind," the mind that's not full but always open and ready to receive. That's real "Zen mind," too; they're the same.

When you aren't sure of the truth, you don't have to speak. When you really *are* sure you have something true and beneficial to say, unleash your second virtue—compassion. Compassion helps you know when to say what's true, because compassion is all about the other person, not about you. It's not even about what you have to say, however true it may be. Compassion looks into the other person, the listener, and feels whether the time is right for that person to hear your truth. *You* don't matter. The truth doesn't even matter if the person is not ready to hear it, because they *won't* hear it. With compassion, it is the other person that matters.

Feel the situation from the other person's perspective. Feel their feelings. Feel their needs. If you do this, you'll know when they need to hear something agreeable and when they're prepared to hear something disagreeable. Naturally the former happens about a hundred times as often as the latter. You can't let this frustrate you, though, because there's just no point in trying to tell people things they can't hear. Have patience.

Did you know that patience is one of the "ten perfections" in Buddhism? Well, it is, and it can be tough to achieve. Patience is another thing that follows from compassion, because compassion opens you up to accept your failings and everyone else's. With that acceptance comes patience, the ability to be calm while things work themselves out.

Speaking of calm, you may not feel calm when you keep quiet, especially when you're surrounded by people who are saying mean or small-minded things. If that happens, you need to become aware of those feelings and ask yourself whether hanging around those people is worth it. Either you'll find yourself saying mean things, too, or you'll feel frustrated because you don't say them. Just ask yourself whether it's worth it. There's no right or wrong answer. Buddha is not telling you what to do, and neither am I. Just ask the question.

 ## cliques and bullies

These phenomena are obviously related to the "drama" of wrong speech. It's in cliques that most wrong speech at school gets said. Bullies always use wrong speech, though they often focus more on wrong action. Buddhism offers different approaches in dealing with both of these things.

When you're on the outside, cliques can act like group bullies, picking on you because you're different. But the strange thing about cliques is that when you're *inside* them, they're totally different. Being in a clique provides you with a sense of identity. It makes you feel safe, understood, and just like everyone else. We *need* this as teenagers—and, in fact, all our lives—so I'm not going to condemn cliques. In fact, Buddhism itself can be viewed as a clique. Even within Buddhism there are cliques—the different schools of Buddhism, the clique of monks and nuns, and the ultimate clique of awakened teachers.

Buddhism has always insisted we choose our cliques wisely. Look at how they treat outsiders. Are they compassionate to others? They don't have to always be doing kind things for others. They don't have to be charitable organizations. We're talking about groups to hang with! The question is, are they at least neutral toward outsiders, or are they cruel? No matter how cool a clique seems, if it's cruel, that cruelty will rub off on you. Hang with the pigs and you start to stink. As the Buddha says:

> Though you're good,
> if you stay with evil people
> people think you're one, too.
> You get a bad reputation.
> The people you make your friends,
> the ones you stay with,
> they're the kind of person you become
> because being together leads to being alike.
>
> ITIVUTTAKA

Choosing to hang with good people will make you a better person without your even trying. Take advantage of that.

Being with good people who aren't hung up on it will also help you accept others who are different. In fact, *everyone* is different. A Buddhist teen told me that Buddhism

> . . . has helped put an end to my habits of oftentimes judging others because they didn't have what i had, look like me, or hang out with my friends. And among my friends, i have begun to change the way i act toward those that are different from me, and with my example, they see that, hey, ya can still fit in and treat others well. In fact you get more friends from it. What a novel idea. ;)

Then again, there are people who seem to delight in being cruel. I'm going to assume you are not that kind of person. If you were, you wouldn't be reading this book. You certainly wouldn't have gotten this far! You may hurt people from time to time, but we all do this, and it does not make you a bully. A bully is someone who is so unhappy with himself that he takes his sadness and anger out on others. Bullies do not feel bad when they do this—not consciously, anyway.

It's in how you act with people weaker than you that you discover your true character. This is where you're really tested. Do you feel bad when you hurt weaker people or animals? If so, that's good. Let your bad feelings make you aware of your actions. Many times you experience these feelings without knowing why at first. Don't be afraid of them. Look into them. Let your feelings lead you back to their roots. If you discover that they come from harming another person, don't get angry or depressed—that would be harming yourself! What good would that do? Instead, just make a mental note that you've discovered an action that leads to harm. Consider not repeating it. Consider telling the person you hurt that you've made this discovery. But you don't have to do that, and of course there's the question of whether they are ready to hear it. That's how right speech works.

Now, what about dealing with real bullies, the ones who hurt you on purpose? I don't even know if "bullies" is a strong enough word for some of these people. Bullies grow into toughs, creeps, gangstas, even killers, but let's just call them bullies. Here's the first Buddhist tip: You are *not* going to change them. If they were ready to be changed by a passing encounter with you, they'd already have changed. If they are so messed up that they've become bullies, all you can do is act wisely and hope they catch on. The first part of acting wisely is not dealing with them.

If *they* choose to deal with *you*, you may get hurt. This is simply the truth. It has happened to me, to people I love, to everyone. One teenage friend of mine got sent to the hospital by a gang of bullies last year. He wasn't trying to change them. He was just in the wrong place at the wrong time. It was like being in a house on fire. He simply got out as quickly as he could. Sometimes it can be done by running away, other times by hitting the ground. Trust your instinct for protecting yourself. Most bullies don't want a fight. They're all about maximizing power over you. If you fight back, they may look for easier targets. Still, if they're looking for a real fight, you can be pretty sure they're choosing to fight because they know they'll win. After all, they've had more practice than you. You're in a house on fire; just get out. You'll have burns. They'll cause pain. I have no magic Buddhist cloak to protect you. Buddhism is not about magic. It is about taking away dukkha, about getting happier.

When you've got burns from a fire, you experience the pain, but you don't complicate it by being angry at the fire. Bullies are like fire. Being angry with them is like being angry at fire because it burns. It only adds to your dukkha. Give it up. Move on. Fires happen, and bullies hit people. Move on. That's the real Buddhist wisdom here.

In her diary, a Buddhist teen wrote:

*I often feel as if I'm living my life as if I'm still being
bullied. But now I feel so uplifted. I found some
photos of the girl who used to bully me, and instead
of feeling really small when I looked at her, I was
able to rise above it, and I can see that she is just a
human being like me and she is trying to be happy
in the best way she knows how. Sure, I hated how
she made me feel, but now I feel more connected to
her—I know we all have the same Buddha-nature
deep down. So now I can be mindful about it and
not let my emotions cloud my mind whenever I
see her.*

She took inner action and changed her situation.
Buddhism allowed her to rise above it. You can take outer
action as well, but that's your choice to make. It's not any
kind of obligation. You might tell a bully to grow up, though
probably he or she never will. You might get the authorities
involved in telling the person to grow up. You can ignore him
or her. You can try to teach the person by example. If you
choose this last course, do this as a lesson for yourself. That
way you're sure of not wasting your time. Be mindful when
you're with a bully: What is the lesson? Facing fear? Seeing
anger? Who is learning? Is anyone?

homework

I can't tell you how many teens have complained to me about their homework. It's a major source of real pressure—not so much because you can't do it, but because there's too much of it. I've heard more than once that teachers fail to take students' lives outside school into account when they assign homework. What to do?

It comes down to a time-management issue because your feelings and actions with respect to homework are not going to change the amount your teachers give you. Perhaps you should think of your teachers like bullies! They are just going to be there, and you're going to have to make the best of the situation. In fact, this is a basic Buddhist message: Make the best of things. When it comes to homework, that means managing your time wisely.

People in high school and, these days, even middle school operate under tremendous time pressures. You've got more to do than you have time to do perfectly, so you learn to cut corners. But 2500 years of Buddhist wisdom says "you can't cut corners on learning, and to learn you have to concentrate." Yes, you might have to spend less time studying than you feel you need. Make that choice if you must. But when you're studying, really *study*. Concentrate. It is possible to be quick without being hasty. How? By focusing your

mind. Buddhists (and many other people) call this concentration. Practice it enough, and you can achieve "one-pointed
mind" and sink into an advanced state of deep and peaceful
meditation. But that's not what you're after here. Right now
you just need concentration on your homework.

Try this exercise for a moment when you sit down to
do homework. Begin by putting away other concerns and
issues. If they arise, acknowledge them, accept them, and
then clearly put them away. You can return to them later;
don't indulge in thinking about them now. Don't pretend
they don't exist—don't explore them. Instead, concentrate on
a simple visual object or on your breathing. Let it fill your
mind easily and slowly. Then come back up to normal consciousness and move directly into your homework. This is
not a full meditation, just a way of harnessing concentrative
power—which is exactly what you need for homework.

Some people think that homework is boring and that's
why it's hard to do. Okay, so it's hard to do. You still have to
do it. Here's the thing, though: Clinging to the view that homework is boring automatically makes it boring because it doesn't
let you experience the homework, only your prejudice against
it. That's foolish behavior because you still have to sit and do
it. Buddhism offers another way of thinking about boredom.

"If you find one thing boring, you'll find everything
boring." That's Zen Teacher Dogen's way of thinking about

it—a total reconception of boredom. (Dogen is always blowing us away with his reconceptions.) Boredom comes from the inside out, not the outside in.

Why are you bored when you're bored? Because you are building a wall between yourself and your life. Sure, some things are more interesting than others, but literally *anything* can be interesting if you are prepared to do the work to make it so. By contrast, when you're bored, it's because you are actually boring yourself and the world. Think of "boring" as a verb, not an adjective. Boring doesn't mean "dull." To be boring means to be sucking the life out of your own life. What a terrible thing to do to yourself. If you feel bored, ask yourself why. Sit quietly and let the answer rise up from within. Don't go looking for it, just let it rise up. What will come is an awareness of the thing you'd most prefer to be doing, or the anger you feel because you're stuck here, or the conflict you have with your teacher who assigned your homework, or maybe just how hungry you are. Whatever it is, it's not part of the situation outside; it's part of the situation inside. This means you can let it go if you have the mental discipline. When you acknowledge your feeling, you begin to gain power over it. Don't indulge it, just acknowledge it. Then you can return to your outer situation with more energy.

grades

The stated purpose of school is to teach you knowledge and skills to succeed in society. In middle school and high school your learning is measured by your grades. That's not a good measure of the most important things you learn in school, but grades do (very crudely) measure your academic progress, so you and other students tend to care about them.

Grades are an external standard for measuring internal progress that can never be adequately expressed in a way that teachers can evaluate. For this reason, grades are crap. But your internal goals, such as getting into college, might depend on getting good grades, so grades are important crap, and you should care about them and preserve both sides of this tension.

Your desire for high grades is a desire for something genuinely good. This kind of desire can still lead to dukkha, so it's still dangerous, but it's not inherently harmful. As long as you can keep working toward your desire without getting attached to its achievement, you're fine.

Easier said than done, right? In fact, working toward what you want without getting attached to the outcome is the practical goal of Buddhism, so don't expect total success.

Nevertheless, some success is not only possible, it's practically certain if you can simply remember that achieving your goals (like college) is not going to totally satisfy you. Real satisfaction comes when you're moving forward on the path, fully experiencing the present moment of that progress. Be proud of your grades as lasting manifestations of your journey, but remember that the movement itself is what matters most.

A Buddhist teen told me: "If you just sit there all day, if you sat your whole life, you'd be unsuccessful; you wouldn't achieve anything." You need a balance of acceptance and goals. I wondered if that balance comes from Buddhism. She said, "It may be something I've always had, but Buddhism has made me aware of it."

YOUR BODY

Followers of the way, the Buddha's truth doesn't require heroic efforts. Just be normal, without trying to act any special way. Shit, piss, put on your clothes, eat your food, and lie down when you're tired. Fools laugh, but the wise know what I'm saying.

ZEN TEACHER LINJI

We've talked about identity in the external world. Now let's talk about identity inside your own body. Of course environment, body, and mind can never be fully separate. The outer environment, the physical body, and the inner world mutually co-create each other. Still, it's useful to separate them now and then for the sake of getting a clearer look at each one. Just remember that in real life they are all bound together in a thoroughly Buddhist way.

Personal identity grows from our senses of our bodies. We start from that core and move out from there. We begin moving outward at birth. In fact, our very early sense of personal self is hardly separate from the whole of our experience. We really don't know where our bodies begin or leave off. Most people don't remember the mysteries of infancy, but you can see them whenever you watch a baby's wonder at the movements of its own hand or its own mother. Over the years you've learned that your main physical boundary is your skin. Inside is "you"; outside is "the world." But this rule is a bit fuzzy. When you eat food, for example, does it become "you" as soon as you put it in your mouth? And is it "you" when it's about to emerge again from your other end? If you say no, I can understand . . . but then how do you explain how people grow? In fact the food you put in yourself really does become "you." You turn it into your very body.

Okay, back to identity. You learned early in life that "you" are roughly your body. But over time, bodies change. You soon learn that you're growing up. In fact most kids are in a hurry to do so, especially around age 10 or 12. If you're in a hurry, be happy: Kids are reaching puberty earlier than ever in history. Girls are getting their periods 18 months earlier than a hundred years ago, and boys are reaching their full height at about 18 instead of 24 as they did even just fifty years ago.

Still, it takes a while, and the changes are never perfect. You hit puberty, ready to become that perfect, long, lean, hardbody you see in ads. For about 98% of people, that doesn't happen. You may not have cared much about this when you were younger, but you *really care now*. And while you're caring so much, your body is changing so fast you don't know what's what.

Did you know that often the first sign of puberty in boys is swellings behind their nipples? Neither did I until it happened to me. (It freaked me out, but it goes away in a few months.) This sort of thing happens constantly to teenage bodies and you may not be any more prepared for it than I was. Some changes are cool, but others will disturb you or seem to take way too long in arriving.

Everybody has to deal with the constant changes in their bodies. When you're a teen, these changes also mean constant changes in moods and abilities. You're almost always out of balance with your body. Just when you get used to being one way, it's gone. This is good Buddhist training for life, but it's tough and it can be embarrassing when you don't control your body the way you want to.

This struggle to adapt to your constantly changing body brings up the whole huge issue of what's usually called "body image"—in other words, your sense of your physical identity, your view of yourself. There are two troubles with body images. First, as I mentioned earlier, most all of us don't look like the image we want. We all have to deal with the fact that our bodies are not perfect. They have design flaws. Sometimes they don't function exactly right. And they're quite varied. Even other species of animals can easily tell us apart. We may not have the perfect image we desire, but most of us come to accept what we've got to work with. We're able to do this because as we go through our teens we find that others accept us. That makes all the difference. And we can fine-tune our bodies once we accept them as our raw materials.

The second trouble with body image comes when your own image of yourself doesn't match what others see. Everybody is a little like this. You may feel that you're pudgy or scrawny, or some anatomical part is too small (or too big), even though others tell you it's not true. In itself this isn't a problem. The problem comes when the images diverge too much and you lose the ability to believe that others' images of you are likely to be about right. When everyone says you're really skinny and you're the only one who thinks you're fat, and you just can't believe them, then it's a problem. You're not living in the real world. You're clinging to something you want to believe—even though you hate it. If you then diet (or binge and purge) to try to lose weight, you can harm or even kill yourself. All this is most un-Buddhist.

Even if we don't get to this place, we all can understand it. We all want to improve our bodies and our body images.

We all want to feel a true sense of physical identity with ourselves. We want to be the free and happy body we imagine. Boys want to be tall and buff. Girls want to be curvaceous and toned. Putting effort into becoming these things is just like putting effort into becoming our social selves. Eating light and working out is right and healthy. Just remember, if you're not enjoying the effort itself, the goal is probably not worth working toward.

puberty

I'll level with you, Buddhist texts don't talk much about puberty. In fact, most religions tend to ignore this enormously vital physical experience. In a large sense, though, puberty is about two things: change and desire. Buddhism talks a great deal about both.

Change is one of the three fundamental qualities of everything. The other two are dukkha and anatman (no-self), the "astounding thing" at the core of the Buddha's awakening. Change is the central fact of being a teenager. During these years, everything keeps changing—most of all you. It's sometimes said that in seven years every cell in our bodies will have been replaced, so we're totally new, not the same person we were seven years earlier. I don't know whether that's really true, but it might as well be. By the time you reach age 20, you are utterly changed from the person you were at 13. It may be that your mind is even more changed than your body, but your body keeps its change right in your face.

Of course you begin long before puberty. Your greatest period of change is in the womb, and the next greatest is in the first three years after that. But in those years you have no sense of being a self that is constant. You have no feeling that your body endures. So the rapid pace of change doesn't bother you. You flow with it. Watch a baby or toddler reveling in its changing. They *love* it. By the time you reach, say, eight years old, though, you've developed a sense of self you begin to think of as lasting.

Puberty throws that out the window. Sure, you grow during those years right before puberty, but puberty doesn't just make you a bigger version of yourself. It actually changes your *brain*. After that happens, you just aren't the same person anymore. Science and the Buddha agree on this. Puberty brings you face-to-face with change, revealing that great irony: Change is the only thing that lasts.

When puberty hits, you'll think things, feel things, and want things that never even occurred to you before. I actually remember thinking as a kid, "I'll *never* care about girls." I really meant it. I couldn't imagine a single situation in which girls would hold any interest for me. They didn't rate. It wasn't that I tried to ignore them or hate them; they just didn't matter. Then puberty hit. All of a sudden girls were vital. There was a time one summer when the mystery of girls seemed to be *everything* to me. Most of us get over this stage, but for some boys it never seems to end. Same with girls, just in subtler ways.

I had no way to process this sexual transformation. For example, no one told me about sexual dreams. For boys these sexual dreams might lead to orgasms. But if you've never had an orgasm, how do you know what one is? I remember dreams where I had these very pleasurable sensations, but heck if I knew what they were! In fact, to be totally honest, I *still* don't know what they were. I figure they were orgasms, but who knows? Back then I wondered, I was confused, and I had nowhere to look for answers.

I'm telling you this personal stuff because it's exactly how things are with puberty. You just don't know what's happening next. Even a textbook on sexual development won't answer all your questions. You have to learn your own experience from the inside. It's about change, and it's also about pleasure and desire. Other than that, you just have to wait and find out.

How can Buddhism help you face this double whammy of change and desire? It can help by fitting your body experience into a non-judgmental, spiritual frame. Buddhism teaches that change and desire are natural states of human beings. We are constantly changing and constantly desiring things. So the first thing Buddhism says is "Relax, you are totally normal. Your body is normal, and your experience is normal. Nothing is wrong with you physically or spiritually when you feel these things."

Buddhism's simple acceptance of your experience as normal goes a long way toward making that experience better. Then Buddhism goes farther; it says the change and desire you're experiencing are making you feel dukkha because you want stability in your body and you want fulfillment of your desire. This dukkha is natural, too, but you don't have to have it forever. If you can let go of your wants, you'll also be letting go of your dukkha.

We've been talking about puberty as a general thing. But maybe now it's time to talk about some of the problems that puberty leads to. For these more specific problems I'll be able to give more specific techniques for dealing with dukkha.

 ## imperfection

None of us is fully happy with his or her body. No doubt a thousand years ago teens wished for nicer bodies. This wish is normal—but our society is not normal. Perceptions of "normal" and "attractive" are not the same everywhere; they change and they can be manipulated.

A recent survey showed that 27% of girls felt pressured by the media to have "perfect" bodies. Hello, *no one* is perfect!

We are imperfect people with imperfect bodies. I can't even begin to list my many imperfections, and I'm actually pretty lucky with my body. Yet we're told we're unattractive if we don't conform to a particular norm. The scary part of this is that if we're all bombarded with enough propaganda at an early enough age, we actually will begin to become unattractive to ourselves and others, because our views of what is attractive will change to conform to the unattainable "norm."

One reason these norms are so *un*-normal is so we'll all be forced to strive ceaselessly to reach unreachable standards. This insures a never-ending flow of cash from us to the providers of beauty, whether they're clothes sellers, make-up sellers, or body-part sellers.

What would Buddha say about that? I bet you know, but just to make sure, I'll spell it out. It perfectly embodies (so to speak) the First and Second Noble Truths. Here we have dukkha (First Truth) because we desire (Second Truth) to become perfect. But perfection is by definition impossible to reach or maintain, and the sellers know it. They keep you running after what you can never obtain, like a hamster on a treadmill.

Girls feel their imperfections more, and they spend bigger bucks and go to more desperate lengths to make up for them. But boys may be catching up. Could pumped-up toy action figures lead to boys feeling inadequate, as Barbie dolls and photos of supermodels lead to girls feeling fat? Will boys "need" to take steroids like girls "need" to get breast implants? Even now *millions* of teens start smoking to help them lose weight—getting addicted to a harmful substance to help pursue an impossible quest to be what they can never be. It's a good thing the Buddha died before that started. He'd be disgusted. Take back your body from the marketing machine!

Zen Teacher Linji wrote,

> As long as you can't shut up the ceaseless activity of your mind, you are trapped up the tree of ignorance. . . . But if you can shut up your mind you'll enter the place of the clean, pure body . . . taking any shape you want, feasting the truth and the bliss of meditation, and making the world lucid with your own body's light.

Step off the hamster wheel of desire. Jump down from the tree of ignorance. Linji taught that *this very body* is the Buddha. *Your* body. Every body is perfect in its particular way. You don't need perfection if you already have it.

thinness

It's not your fault if you want to be impossibly or unhealthily thin. In a recent survey, more than two-thirds of girls admitted that magazine models influence their idea of what they want to look like. But those same girls have only a one in a hundred chance of being as thin as those supermodels. So two-thirds of girls think they are too fat and almost all women think they weigh more than they really do. The top wish of young teenage girls is to be thinner.

These girls are ready and willing to do what they must to get there. Methods can include make-up and dieting, but also starving themselves or binging and purging. In one study, one out of six college women admitted they binged and purged. Guys don't admit it, because they think this is a female thing, but guys definitely binge and purge, too. *The Zen of Eating* (Ronna Kabatznick, Perigee, 1998) takes this issue of food and makes a whole book out of applying Buddhism to it. I'm sure it's well worth reading if this issue is an issue for you, because for people with eating disorders, the stakes are very high. You can permanently ruin your body if you get too thin—even when *you* think you're not.

Better to use Siddhartha as your supermodel. He knew all about fasting. In fact, he got skinny as a rail. He did this because he thought it would make him look spiritually good, and in a way it did. But it also prevented him from doing anything else. He got weak and couldn't even meditate well. (And it's not as if meditation takes a lot of physical energy.) When he realized what he was giving up to be so thin, he simply started eating again. He made a choice between fitting into an image that was harming him or finding some balance and strength and enjoying life again. For him the decision was easy—and it should be easy for you, too. This decision became the basis for the Middle Path and Buddhism itself. In terms of eating, the Middle Path is the path between harmful gluttony and harmful starvation. The Buddha could not have been clearer about this. When he finally ate some brain food after years of starving efforts, he immediately became awakened! It's no coincidence. Echoing Siddhartha's experience, Zen students sometimes eat a kind of rice porridge much like what Siddhartha ate just before his awakening. Before eating they chant:

> Porridge is effective in ten ways
> To aid the student of Zen.
> No limit to the good result,
> Consummating eternal happiness.

YM magazine has recently changed its policies to stop doing diet stories and start using models whose body types are more like its readers'. Will it help? It sure can't hurt. How can you help yourself stay normal in the face of all this? Here are some psychological tips paraphrased from *BodyLove: Learning to Like Our Looks and Ourselves* (Rita Freeman, Ph.D., Harper & Row, 1988), with Buddhist comments after each one:

1. Listen to your body; when you're hungry, eat.

The Japanese Zen Teacher Bankei once said, "My miracle is that when I'm hungry, I eat, and when I'm tired, I sleep."

2. Be realistic about your likely size due to your genes and history.

What is real is what is valuable. What use is some body you'll never have?

3. Do regular and enjoyable exercise, however much you weigh.

The Buddha got regular exercise, as Buddhist monks still do. They go out every morning, walking for hours on their begging rounds. The Buddha did this until he was eighty!

4. Expect changes in your weight and your shape, following your normal weekly and monthly cycles.

"Expect changes"—the very essence of Buddhism!

5. Accept yourself; forgive yourself; be gentle with yourself.

Loving kindness begins with yourself. Wish yourself well, then expand this throughout the universe.

6. Ask for encouragement and help from friends and family when you're stressed out.

No one is an island; let your peers know where you are and what you need. This is what prayer is all about, after all, whether it's Christian or Buddhist or whatever.

7. Decide where you want to spend your energy: pursuing the "perfect body" or enjoying your life.

There's a lot of talk in Buddhism about the bodies of the Buddha—the Truth Body, the Bliss Body, the Manifestation Body. Some Buddhists go around questing after these things, to worship them or become them or something. They're like girls who are always on a diet for the perfect body they'll never enjoy. You like thin? Check out that skeleton—ooooh, sexy. Meanwhile, listen to Linji: "Looking outside for some Buddha body with form—this is totally unworthy!"

 ## sleep

You need more sleep. This probably comes as no surprise. Just about all teens I talk to agree.

There are so many duties, options, activities, entertainments, responsibilities, practices, reviews, study sessions, parties, dates, vacations, and who-knows-what-else, that the choice becomes live or sleep. That's why we have the expression "I'll sleep when I'm dead." In fact, too little sleep makes you feel dead even though you're still moving. As the Dhammapada, one of my favorite Buddhist texts, puts it, "Attention is living; inattention is dying. The attentive never stop; the inattentive are dead already." If you don't stay attentive, what's the point of going on? And you can't do that if you're too tired.

If you choose some other activity instead of sleep, but you're dozing off while you do it, you're not getting the benefit of either thing. Much better to just go to bed early once in a while. The good news is that getting extra sleep can reset your clock and bring you back to attentiveness. The bad news is "binge sleeping" (sleeping 'til 11 a.m. or so on weekends) is not good for you. It screws up your clock and makes it that much harder to go to sleep at night the next week. The fact is, we all have a "circadian rhythm," a daily clock that keeps us up at certain hours and knocks us out at others. As a teenager, your rhythm probably keeps you up past 10 p.m., even if you can't keep your eyes open while doing homework before dinner. (It's not your fault! But you might try doing the homework *after* dinner instead. Really.)

You may not have much choice about when you wake up. Most high schools start between 7 and 8 a.m., so most high school students are not getting the nine hours of sleep they ideally need. Yes, nine hours! If you can't change when you wake up, you have to change when you go to sleep.

Here's where you can take a Middle Path between cramming everything in and blowing everything off. Doing everything is a bit like the Buddha's early life: too indulgent. Doing nothing is like his period of austerity: too denying. You want to find the middle ground between the two. Flexibility is the key. Respect your body and its wisdom. If it's telling you that you've got to sleep this weekend, then sleep this weekend. You'll never have a better advisor than your body when it's telling you what it needs. (Notice I didn't say "what it wants." It's not always so wise about that!)

 ## your mind

By the time you reach the end of your teens, your body will have stopped changing so fast. Then it will be easier to develop a stronger sense of physical identity. Your body will continue to change—this is the nature of all things—but the changes will be slow enough so that they will no longer challenge your sense of self. You'll have an enduring sense of what you are physically, and from this sense of *what* you are, you can refocus on *who* you are. With that in mind, next let's turn to who you are mentally.

Earlier I wrote about no-self, the idea that an individual self/soul/spirit is an illusion. Yet I've also written about how your great task as a teenager is to *become* this illusory thing. Why should we even be talking about identity, let alone cultivating it?

This is a good example of the tension between the ultimate level of truth and the practical level of truth. Ultimately, there's no self and so no identity to find. But practically, our identity gives coherence to the evolving complex of relationships, duties, pleasures, and pains that constitutes us. For this purpose, identity matters; in fact, it's vital. We need to cultivate an identity that is social, corporal, and mental.

Think of it this way: Buddhist psychologists say "you have to have a self in order to lose it." We need the sense of self we work so hard to create during our teen years. And starting in those same years, we need to let go of that sense of self if we want to grow further and find a wider freedom. First comes gaining the self, then comes losing it.

We can't hold too tightly to our selves. Just as our bodies change and our images of them are never accurate and always out of date, so our minds change, and our images of them are equally unreliable. Wise people know this, even very young ones:

"Who are *you?*" said the Caterpillar.

This was not an encouraging opening for a conversation. Alice replied, rather shyly, "I—I hardly know, Sir, just at present— at least I know who I *was* when I got up this morning, but I think I must have been changed several times since then."

"What do you mean by that?" said the Caterpillar, sternly. "Explain yourself!"

"I can't explain *myself*, I'm afraid, Sir," said Alice, "because I'm not myself, you see."

ALICE IN WONDERLAND

On the foundation of our bodies, we build the structures of our minds. As our bodies change, so do our minds. In fact, recent MRI scanning research on teenage brains has shown that they are physically changing all through the teen years. They are refining their structures and the way they use those structures. They might even process information in the late teen years using different structures and skills than in the early teen years. So is it fair to expect teens to have a truly coherent sense of mind or spirit when their brains are changing so fast? No, but is it fair to *ask* them to develop a coherent sense of mind or spirit? Yes. Teens wrestle with questions of mind, faith, and spirit every day. It's exactly the right time to do this.

your brain

Brain science has recently found that during the teenage years the brain changes more than we previously imagined. Imaging studies have shown that the brain grows in size a great deal just before adolescence and then spends the teen years figuring out how to use that new gray matter—particularly the prefrontal cortex, the part of the brain that thinks ahead and is wise and clever. During your teen years, you need to teach the brain how to think; in doing so, you exercise it. The rule is "use it or lose it." The parts of the brain you exercise are the parts you keep for the rest of your life. What you think about becomes your future. The Buddha would agree. Consider the opening lines of the Buddhist book I recommend to new students, the Dhammapada:

> All things come at first from mind.
> Mind creates them, mind fulfills them.
> Speak or act with tainted mind,
> You'll drag around a cart of pain.

> All things come at first from mind.
> Mind creates them, mind fulfills them.
> Speak or act with lucid mind
> And joy will follow like your shadow.

The more you practice lucid mind—that is, the more you try to be mindful, compassionate, and wise—the easier it gets. In fact, the whole process becomes second nature. Buddha knew your brain was doing this. That's why he said that all things come from your brain, and exercising good thinking makes good thinking stronger. Wise Buddhists have been teaching this principle for thousands of years, but you don't have to take their word for it. Now it's science. Believe who you want, just start exercising your mind.

Do you want to pump up your resentment muscle or your compassion muscle? Your video game muscle or your soccer muscle? It's totally up to you. Just remember, the pain or joy you're creating is right behind you. As one teen told me, "If you look at things in a positive way you're more likely to come up with a better outcome. If you're thinking of the negative you may end up with nothing."

THE OPPOSITE SEX
AND YOU

> Evil people are trapped by sex, but others turn it
> into a way to gain freedom from entrapment here.
> Passion binds the world, yet passion also frees it.

HEVAJRA TANTRA

 ### desire and enjoyment

Some say that Buddhism forbids enjoyment. This is simply not true. Even the strictest forms of Buddhism allow taking pleasure in harmless things that don't lead to further desire. Buddha never said pleasure was not pleasing. He merely said that for most of us, pleasure is ringed round with pain, and that the fulfillment of desire does not satisfy the ongoing desire itself. To give you an idea of different views of pleasure in Buddhism, here are two quotes.

Leaving behind delight and pain,

cool and calm, lacking nothing,

victorious over the world, all worlds,

He's the one that I call holy.

DHAMMAPADA

Eat, drink, and indulge the senses!

SARAHA

The first quote is an early Indian teaching. The second is a later Tibetan one. They both show how the Buddha teaches us to enjoy ourselves. Does the Buddha allow pleasure? Of course. True enough, there have always been Buddhists who say no, you must utterly turn away from pleasure because pleasure is ultimately groundless, fleeting, and unsatisfactory. But *this* Buddhist says it's still pleasure. We can enjoy it for what it is, just as we should experience all things for what they are. "Fleeting" does not mean "unpleasant." Go ahead: love it. And while you're at it, love love itself. You can even love sex.

We value what is rare. Good experiences are rare in time. They come late and pass quickly. For that reason, we should enjoy them *more*, not less! Wouldn't it be sad if a person could find no joy in the green of summer simply because it must quickly pass away? The Buddha would join in this sadness. He would say, "Rejoice, just don't cling." So what do you say? Let's enjoy our passing fancies!

 ## equality

Most societies have a lot of rules about spending time with the opposite sex. Sometimes these rules are meant to prevent people from having sex or getting preoccupied with it. Sometimes they're meant to protect men from "pollution" by women, who are seen as impure. Sometimes the rules don't have reasons anymore, they're just brainless extensions of some tradition of separating men and women. Modern Western society is pretty open compared to most other societies. Buddhist societies have been more divided. In fact, Buddhism needs your help.

How can you help? Well, I'm glad you asked. The Buddha was amazingly egalitarian compared with his own society, which was characterized by gross gender inequality. He accepted women's rights and women's achievements in Buddhism. His fight for women's rights was only excellent, not perfect, but the Buddha is not the final authority here. As I see it, the Buddha was only the first awakened Buddhist in recorded history. He had insights into the core nature of humanity and the human world. He saw that people are only prevented from being Buddhas due to layers of wrong thinking and years of wrong action, which have turned into the bundles of habits and prejudices that we call our selves. When we free ourselves from our selves, what is left? Buddha might say "nirvana," the free play of the Buddha nature. And what does this have to do with women's rights? Everything.

Free play of the Buddha nature means real freedom that we all share equally. It means no boundaries—not for men and not for women. In fact, on many levels there *are* no men or women; these gender forms are mere appearances. In several ancient Mahayana Buddhist sutras, men and women change into each other—an illustration of the shallowness of gender differences. Free yourself from them!

The idea that we all share the potential for the Buddha nature means something for each of us. It means we are the Buddha's manifestation on earth, right now. All those who have moved the Buddhist tradition forward, deepened it, clarified it, have the potential to be as authoritative as the original Buddha. (In fact, Siddhartha Gautama claimed *he* was not the original Buddha, either. He said he had *re*discovered the teaching, claiming that there were Buddhas before him.) It is in our power—and thus our duty—to bring the tradition up to date. We must free it from itself, just as it frees us.

Treating the opposite sex as equal is a realm where you can do exactly that, showing older Buddhists that young Buddhas can hang out together without collapsing into a heap of sex or ritual pollution or whatever the older people fear. This can be your offering to the tradition and your way to move it forward. You can make this offering whether you're a full-time, Asian-American Buddhist from a traditional family, or just experimenting with a Buddhist idea here and there. You've got the Buddha nature. Just show its free play where sex and gender don't matter. If there are—or should be—no boundaries between men and women, then you should feel free to hang out with people of the opposite sex.

dating

Dating is not a problem for most teens. *Not* dating, *wanting* to date, *worrying* about dates— *these* are problems. An actual date itself usually just happens. No one wants to be told what to do on a date, so I'm not going to give you Buddhist dating advice. Instead, I'm going to offer a smart way to approach the whole process.

Dating is the discovery of how you relate to another person. It's exciting for several reasons. There's the charge of sexual attraction. That's pretty obvious. More than that, there's the mystery of exploring the other—and even more, the double mystery of creating a relationship together. All this alluring complexity from just spending time together. Amazing!

Why do I call dating a "double" mystery? And why is it so alluring to us? It's "double" because the process of a date reveals an unknown other person, and it also reveals the unknown *you*. In the Buddhist view, everything is open, including the self; what really exists are *relationships between* things or selves. So dates are a powerful place where you come into existence. Dates are all about relationships. Ultimately, relationships *are* the people in them. You exist *in* the date. On the conventional level, as a relationship evolves, you come to know not only the other person but also yourself.

Humans are born to be in relationships. In fact, people die if they're not in relationship with others from the very first. Like everybody, you have a deep need to form partnerships with others, eventually pairing off and creating new humans with whom you will have new relationships. It's your biological nature—and your Buddha nature. "Naturally," then, it means you want to date, and you feel frustrated when you don't get dates or when your dates go badly. As the Buddha would tell you, chill out. Of course some dates go badly. What do you expect, to find the perfect partner when you're 16? You haven't even found *you* at 16 (or 13 or 19).

The central focus of being a teenager is the process of discovering yourself and creating your relationships. To do so, you learn by experimenting, which means being with different people, seeing what you create together and in each other. If you haven't gone on any bad dates, you haven't been experimenting widely enough. Keep trying. They say the Edison Company tried 100 different light bulb filaments before they found one that worked. It was only because of those other failed experiments that they knew the last one was the right solution.

Be honest with yourself and your dates. Since dating is about discovering yourself as well as the other, you have to be honest. Otherwise you're actually creating a false self, and you cannot be happy when you are false. Lie, especially to yourself, and you lose both your freedom and your identity. It's a loser's game.

You have to be honest before your dates, too. You have to be honest in picking your dates. Choosing people to date based on what others think or how you and another person might fit together in other people's eyes means you're creating yourself based on other people's ideas. This is literally bogus: fake, shallow, and useless. Don't worry about finding the "perfect date." The perfect date for you is one you grow with, so he or she is not perfect until you're actually growing together. Pick your dates based on your own sense of yourself and them, how you feel *inside*. Your guts are honest, even when they're vague or confused. Who says honesty is always clear? *Lies* are often clear, but they're still lies. Honesty is sometimes muddled, but it's still honesty. So be real: no games with yourself, no games with your dates, no games with your reputation or your image.

You probably feel the strong drive to speed up the process. Maybe you don't really want to hurry up and get married and make babies, but people frequently act like it. Buddhism invites you to ask yourself where your sense of urgency comes from. Is it perhaps a blind push you don't need? Instead, relax into being right where you are. That's how your Buddha nature manifests itself in your activity right now. There's no other place you need to get to. In the final analysis, there's no other place you can even be, because all other places are illusory. Enjoy the present moment—the *only* present moment.

Think about where this long process of romance and sex and babies leads to. Keep going with that story—it leads to sickness, old age, and death, just as the Buddha saw. Why are you so anxious to get there? What's your hurry? What's wrong with right here, right now? That date you're fantasizing about won't satisfy your drive to get on with the process, and even if it did, where would it lead you? True satisfaction comes from accepting your drive for what it is—something that can never be fulfilled and *doesn't have to be.* The Buddha showed by example that you don't need to date to be a great person, a helpful person, a wise person, or a happy person. Dating doesn't make you happy; it only answers your dating drive for a night. What makes you happy is what you bring to the date, or what you have at home, or what you share with friends. It's what's in you already.

 ## having sex

Don't be fooled by people who tell you that having sex is not important or that your body is not ready for sex. Your sexuality is blatantly there and needs to be accepted. You don't have to have sex—far from it—but you *do* need to accept the truth of your body.

Reliable sources say that about two in five teenagers are sexually active by the ninth grade. Over half are having intercourse when they're 15 to 19. Innumerable books about teenagers ask why the age for having sex keeps getting lower. They worry about this. Frankly, I have to ask why *not*? The age for having sex has always been younger than it is now, except for a brief and anomalous few generations that happened to come right before yours. We humans are physically constructed to have sex in our teens—even our early teens if our bodies are ready. Only our minds lag behind, and one main reason they do is that our society doesn't help our minds catch up to our bodies.

Catching your mind up to your body is especially tough for teens who aren't certain whether they want to be with boys or girls. You normally find your sexual identity before you have sexual experiences. But how can you find that identity without having the experiences that teach you about yourself? It's not so bad when the society says be one way and you are. It's hard when it says be one way and you're not sure you can be. This paradox can be cruel.

Buddhism can offer you some support. The Buddha taught that *all* sex caused dukkha. He didn't seem to think heterosexuality was any better than homosexuality or a combination of the two. Gay, straight, bi, transgender, the Buddha doesn't care and he doesn't want you to feel bad about who you are. What would be the use of that? The Buddha taught insight and acceptance. Find who you are and accept it, in sex as in other spheres. Desire is the same, whatever position you view it from.

Don't get me wrong. I'm not trying to convince you that 15-year-olds should be having actual intercourse. It's not my role to tell you what to do, much less judge your behavior. That's not what Buddhism is about—not my Buddhism, anyway. But being halfway awake, I *am* going to face the reality that teens *are* having sex. And if you're having sex, *you had better be using contraception*—preferably condoms, which also help prevent sexually transmitted diseases (STDs). This bit of advice can make you happier for the rest of your life.

Buddha says put on the condom! Seems like it should be really obvious, but the average time between first having sex and finally using birth control is a whole year, so apparently a lot of people are not listening. A year! Meanwhile, one in five girls gets pregnant in her teens. What is happening here?

Part of the problem may be simple ignorance. Buddhism can help in overcoming ignorance, hatred, and greed, the roots of dukkha. They all grow from selfishly ignoring the way things really are. So let me try to be a good Buddhist by dispelling some ignorance.

Maybe you're thinking to yourself, "No one tells me how this whole sex thing works. I'm just guessing, and I'm embarrassed and so I'll keep it hidden. If it's part of my hidden life, it can't affect my regular life." There's nothing like buying condoms at the market to make you feel *totally revealed*! The trouble is, what's hidden absolutely *can* affect the rest of your life. It happens all the time.

A large majority of teens say they feel uninformed about how to use contraception. Here are two condom tips that no one gave me.

FIRST: Practice with one. The first time you need one is not the ideal time to try putting on a condom for the first time. You want to be cool when you do this thing with an audience, so just practice once beforehand. It's really easy, but practice may make the difference between feeling comfortable and using one when it counts, or feeling awkward and not using one. That could save your life, your partner's, or the life of the fetus you don't create. Practice.

(Extra tip: If you're not a guy, you can put the condom on your partner. In that case, you don't need to practice first, because the guy doesn't expect you to have done it before.)

SECOND: Not to get too graphic, but a guy usually gives out a drop or two of semen after he gets hard, long before he has his orgasm. There are *plenty* of sperm in those drops to get a girl pregnant. Put that condom on early. Don't screw around with penetration before that thing goes on. Condom first, then penetration. Ladies, are you listening? Did you know about those drops? Well, now you do. Insist on condoms. If a guy is not willing to put himself in a condom at the right time, he's definitely not worthy of putting himself in your precious body.

(One more extra tip: Ladies, buy the condoms yourself. Then you don't have to listen to lame excuses by lame guys. If you're strong enough to have sex, you're strong enough to buy condoms.)

What does all this have to do with Buddhism? Everything. This, along with every other totally engaging, intense, important activity in your life, is Buddhist practice. Being responsible, having sex that doesn't harm you or others, is number three of the five precepts: "I vow to strive not to engage in harmful sex." If you're a teen having sex, contraception is a part of fulfilling that vow. It's part of living out your Buddha nature.

Sex can also be a place for spiritual practice. It is where desire, attachment, love, compassion, and wisdom all come together. Good sex, practiced with compassion, without attachment, without the goal of fulfilling desire, is genuine spiritual practice. This is why a few high-level tantric Buddhists have sex in ritual ways: to test themselves and see whether they can do something so emotionally dangerous without falling into increased dukkha.

But let me say this: no tantric sexual practitioner is a teenager. In fact, no teen I've ever known has ever engaged in sex that was spiritual practice or that didn't on some level lead to increased dukkha. Teen sex seems to shape you, rather than you shaping it. Even though you use condoms, it still controls you. You don't really choose it; you're in its grip, ensnared in attachment to desire. Ah, dukkha!

And that's just the male perspective. Most boys say they are glad they had sex the first time. But the large majority of girls feel conflicted or actually sorry they did it. Remember this basic Buddhist truth: The experience of sex will never satisfy the desire for sex. Not when you're a teenager, not ever. Putting the risks and second thoughts together, it's clear the vow not to engage in harmful sex almost certainly means not to engage in sex *at all* as a teen. I'm not saying you can't do it, I'm just saying the Buddha has warned you.

Bottom line: When thinking ahead about sex, consider whether you really are choosing it freely. If not, it's controlling you and will cause you dukkha. And when you really are about to have sex, be mindful of your body and the bodies of others. Protect all sentient beings. Use condoms.

pregnancy

Teenage pregnancy, a really heavy subject. You get hit over the head with it in school, so I'll be brief. Buddhism has no problem at all with contraception. The best contraception is verbal contraception—when a person says "No." The second best contraception is condoms—used right.

Why condoms in particular? Condoms are more Buddhist than other forms of contraception because they help stop the spread of STDs, so they reduce dukkha. Buddhism is not about morality; it's about trying to reduce dukkha in the world. Buddhism is in favor of doing whatever reduces dukkha, and part of that is avoiding getting sick or having kids when you're still a kid.

In other societies, where teenagers are trained to grow up fast and take on adult responsibilities, teen pregnancy is no problem because these teens are already accepted as adults. But in our rich societies today, where teens are in the enviable position of not being saddled with real responsibility until after high school, college, or even later, teens are not yet trained to be ready for parenting. It's practically automatic that having a baby as a teen leads to dukkha. Teen mothers miss out on so many of the great things of youth, trading them for kids that they can still have later. As for teen fathers, think about the unbelievable cars they could be driving if it weren't for those child support payments. Girl or boy, is that a bargain you want to make? Again, it's not a moral thing—it's about making mindful choices.

> The early Buddhist suttas insisted that birth automatically leads to dukkha, since life was so full of it. But life is pretty darn good here and now; I'm not sure most teens would agree life is dukkha, anymore. On balance, life is good until pretty late in the day.

love

Ah love! Yes, there's always that possibility! Legend tells us that the Buddha himself got married when he was a teenager and that he loved his wife dearly. Yet in the end he left her and his son. Why? Because he found that his real identity did not lie in being a prince or being married. Sadly, he found out only after his early marriage, so it caused many tears. The Buddha's advice on love would echo his experience: Find yourself first, then decide whether romantic love is for you.

Love within the family is a given. It's the foundation of all other loves. As an old Buddhist sutra says, "It is hard to find a living thing who hasn't been your mother some time in the past." Our love for our mothers should radiate out to all beings everywhere. With romantic love, though, things are trickier because our love for our mothers is so solid, so trustful (even when we're not getting along) that we do not doubt it, become jealous, or find it running dry. Yet with romantic love, we do all these things, and it happens faster with teenage love than with older love.

So what should a person do? Give up on love? For some the answer is yes, but not for most. Some may find that the process of looking for love is too filled with dukkha to be worth taking part in. The Buddha felt that way, and Buddhist monks and nuns make the same choice even now. Most of us, though, feel that love is well worth the effort it requires and the inevitable dukkha it creates. For most of us, the key to love is realizing that it will not complete us—we are complete already. With that in mind, we can make choices that reflect our real interests and the interests of others.

Here's one example:

i recently went through my g/f cheating on me with my old best friend. She was sorry and it was a mistake that she made. My initial response was to kick her out the door and never look back, but with the Buddhist view now part of my life, i chose to sit on it. Literally. i sat down and meditated to sort out those feelings of love, and in the process discovered that my anger was more towards my old friend than her. Although the trust issue remains, we are well on our way to working it out. Without my Buddhist practice of meditation, i can honestly say i would have made the wrong choice, and broken up with her.

This teenager is taking the time to really see things clearly. For him, meditation made the difference. He was able to accept his feelings, separate them, and make a choice that minimized dukkha and maximized future happiness. You can, too.

FINDING YOURSELF

Master Tushuai Yue asked three questions of his students.

Avoiding confusion and seeking the hidden is just to see essence. Right now, where is your essence?

Only knowing your essence can you be free of birth and death. When you're dying, how will you be free?

Being free of birth and death, you'll know where you're going. When your elements fall apart, where do you go?

WUMENGUAN

friends

Self-discovery through dating and love doesn't happen so much in our early teens. We first begin to find ourselves in our teens through friendships.

Friendship is fundamental to Buddhism. Even for monks and nuns, friendship is central. The *sangha*, the organization of monks and nuns, is a big group of friends, and among them each person has a "preceptor," or close spiritual mentor literally called a "good friend."

According to the Buddha, good friends are the first prerequisite for walking a spiritual path. He says, "Having good friends is the whole of the holy life." Good friends means friends who are good for you and who are good to you. Such friends are the Middle Path, the way to true happiness, so choose your friends wisely. As with cliques, so with individuals: They rub off on you. Since you create yourself in relationship, your friends are inseparable from your future.

Now turn this idea around for a minute. As a friend, you have responsibilities. A scripture says "When someone goes wrong, it is right for his real friends to move him, even by force, to do the right thing." Intervene. You can't just walk away when you know that the right thing to do is to save your friend. Of course there will be times when you don't know it. Don't kick yourself when you don't figure it out until too late; no doubt your friends are just as good at keeping things hidden as you are. But when you do know, you need to act. This kind of love can be tough to give and tough to take. But it's still love.

 ## peer pressure

A lot of ink gets spilled about "peer pressure" in the teen years. Although it's usually viewed by adults as something bad, it can just as well mean something good. In groups we find support to become different from our parents and discover ourselves. Group solidarity gives us power. It can also give the rest of the group power to pressure us. What can you do about bad peer pressure?

The Dhammapada (a text I've quoted several times) says "If on the path you don't meet your equal, it's best to travel alone. There's no fellowship with fools." Peers are your best friends and your worst enemies. It's not people who hate you and fight you that are likely to corrupt you; it's bad partners and friends. When your peers pressure you to be less than you are, you may have to decide between being with them and being by yourself. It may be a lonely choice, but you can't avoid it. It's the kind of choice you may not have had to make before you were a teenager, but now you might as well get comfortable with it. You'll have to make these choices for the rest of your life. Don't feel too bad; the fewer fools you're around, the fewer fools you'll meet. When you turn away from peer pressure, you strengthen your self and your own abilities. As you continue to make strong choices, they'll get easier.

Gangs are just very strong peer groups. They've always been around and they always will be. The trouble is, they're more powerful now. Many gangs have gotten involved in drugs, and where there are drugs, you'll also find money and guns. If the Buddha were around today, he would tell you he didn't care about the details of drug money or guns. He would remind you that you join a group, whether it's a clique or a gang, because it helps you find your identity. The real issue is whether a group you choose to get involved with is doing something that increases dukkha in the world. If it reduces dukkha, other people are likely to call it a "group." If it's neutral, they call it a "clique." And if it increases dukkha enough, it's a "gang." Find a group that helps you reduce your dukkha, one that does not harm others, steal, have harmful sex, lie, or encourage you to hurt yourself or others with drugs.

drugs

The Buddha's advice about drugs was clear: Don't do them. In fact, that's one of the five precepts for avoiding dukkha. In the Buddha's time, of course, people didn't have high-tech substances like ecstasy or crack. In his part of the world, they didn't even have tobacco, but they did have alcoholic beverages as well as other mind-altering substances that were widely used by shamans and cults, so we can be sure the Buddha knew what he was talking about.

You might think that *some* drugs *don't* harm you. I can relate to that—I mean the belief, not that it's true. I'm a practicing Buddhist and I drink wine and I consider it a pretty harmless passion. So maybe I'm not always a good *Buddhist*, but at least I drink good *wine*. If I'm offered or receive bad wine, I usually find a nice way of avoiding it. Drinking wine has enriched my world. It does not cause me dukkha, and I don't *need* it. I'm in charge of my drinking. I'm not afraid to let people know about it. But it took a while to get to this place.

I remember drinking wine one afternoon as a teenager. I was a senior in high school with a strong interest in theater, and I was supposed to perform in some comedy sketches that night. But I had chores to do, and one of them was to transfer some jug wine into individual bottles. It turned out that there was just this *little bit* of wine in each jug that didn't fit into the bottles. So guess what? I drank it. And surprise! I somehow got drunk. I totally didn't see it coming; it just happened. But once it did, I had to face the consequences. I took a nap—shut my eyes for a few minutes. When the phone rang, it was three hours later, and the director was calling my house, desperate to find me. Where was I? I was on in fifteen minutes! Well, I jumped up and ran toward the door . . . and then it hit me: *I was still drunk!* So I missed my first sketch entirely and wobbled through the rest of the show trying to hide my total embarrassment as well as the fact that I was still messed up. I was moping backstage, really ashamed, when the director burst in and said, "You asshole, you just missed another entrance!" By feeling so sorry for myself, I had actually created a whole *new* problem. It started with drinking but progressed to a whole new level of bad choices.

So much for that miserable night. Judging from all the statistics that are published about teen substance abuse, chances are you have gotten drunk or high and will again. For the most part, you probably enjoy it and think you're controlling it. But as my own story shows, even when drugs seem harmless, they are a powerful force that you cannot always control. Yes, even wine.

Again, as with sex, I'm not making a moral issue out of drugs; neither was the Buddha. The point of the precepts is to help you avoid dukkha. Avoiding drug abuse is a precept because it sneaks up on you, and once it does, it can already be out of control. Some people *can* use drugs safely, even spiritually, as some religions do. But playing with intoxicants is like playing with fire. It feels like a cool game that you control. Then it burns your house down.

downward spirals

My miserable night offers a good example of how we can sink into a downward spiral once something goes wrong. I'd gotten drunk and missed an entrance, but that was in the past. I had made it to the theater and was able to go on with the show. Things could have gotten better then, but I made them worse by choosing to identify with my failures rather than my possibilities.

We all tend to wallow in our failures when we lose confidence in ourselves. Teens may be even more prone to it than older people. Something goes wrong, causing us to question our own worth. Then one thing leads to another in a vicious cycle. Awareness of our failure cuts the legs out from under our resolve to succeed. We get depressed. We begin to see our failure as who we are, and that awareness keeps us stuck there. In contrast, Buddhism teaches that an awareness of how bad things are should be exactly what causes us to change.

Sure, teens make bad choices and always will— like adults. The trick is to avoid trapping ourselves in them. Let's say you've made a bad choice and have lost something you cared about. It's natural to wrap yourself up in your misery and hold tightly to the one thing you have left—your bad choice. "Dammit," you may say, "I lost my driving privileges because I went to a party to see my sleazy friend X, so I'm damn sure going to keep hanging with X!" Part of you knows this makes no sense. What's happening here is that you're taking your good feelings for what you've lost and transferring them onto the exact thing that lost them for you. When somebody else falls into this kind of mental trap, you're likely to see it as completely stupid. Yet you do it, too, and so do I. So does just about everybody. The Buddha says quit! Instead, look at the cause and the effect. What got you to that bad place? *That's* what you should give up, no matter how hard it is.

Depression is endemic in our culture, especially among teens. Literally millions of teens are depressed. From a Buddhist perspective, it comes as no surprise. After all, life is full of dukkha. The question is, what should you do when you're depressed?

A teen wrote about her depression,

The best and most satisfying thing to come out of all this is that I'm also far more compassionate and understanding to others. Because of my depression I have come into contact with others who are depressed and in whatever small way, I've been able to help simply because I understand. The positive feedback I've received from this has made it all worthwhile for me. In a more universal way I also feel like the depression has shattered part of my ego-self, so that now I see my suffering as part of our whole interconnectedness rather than something that is happening solely to "me." As a result I am far more compassionate and am really dedicated to removing as much suffering from the world as possible.

Another told me,

My everyday life is totally affected by Buddhism. It has to be. The 4 Noble Truths run my life. Buddhism isn't just a religion. It's a way of life. It's all the little things like loving-kindness and peace of mind. Buddhism has made me a better person. I used to hate myself, cry myself to sleep sometimes, think about suicide, and I had really low self-esteem. But I'm so much better now. I love myself! just the way I am! I deal with my problems in a much better way. I don't stress out as much. I know what's really important to me.

Although Buddhism did not cure these teens of their depression, it added richness to their lives. It helped the first see her own dukkha as part of something greater. It allowed her to feel more compassion for others and turn that compassion into action. It made the second a better person and, perhaps more importantly, a person who could accept and love herself. From that place, she could successfully *deal with* problems. Faced with the reality of depression and its causes, that qualifies as a victory.

possessions

Possessions are great, nothing wrong with them. But possessions do not make you cool, and they can trap you. Here's a scary quote:

> See them floundering after their cherished possessions, like fish flopping in a river starved of water.
>
> SUTTA NIPATA

What good are CDs or cool shoes going to do you when you're flopping in the mud like a fish? I mean, not to put it too crudely: none. They won't help at all.

Right now you're not dying; you're just being born. Can you enjoy your possessions now? Sure, enjoy them. Just don't flounder after them. You like your shoes? Wear them! You like your CDs? Play them! Buddha says yes to that. But your possession of them is just a dream because, like dreams, all things pass away. You can grasp after them, but you can't catch them. Your life is like a series of little dreams that rise and fall. Your possessions are dream-things without substance. When you wake from a dream, you don't try to hold onto dream-things. You're awake. Move forward.

ddhist monks, even now. In fact it's likely that the Buddha
d after eating some bad pork. Only in East Asia (and some
nasteries in the West) are monks vegetarian. Why? Be-
se the Buddha did not set up rules based on right and
ong. He set up rules based on helping and harming. If a
nk is offered a meal with meat in it, he can eat it. In fact,
has to eat it, otherwise he'd be harming the giver of the
l by not accepting it. There are only a few exceptions to
rule: monks and nuns cannot eat an animal they killed,
they saw killed, or one killed especially for them. We're
talking about monks and nuns here, though. Regular
dhists have always been able to eat whatever they want,
no rules.

Of course, things are different now than they were in
Buddha's time. The industrialized production of, say, the
industry, contributes to grievous harm to animals and to
whole environment. It may be that if the Buddha were
g now, he would forbid monks and nuns from eating
-raised animals.

It comes down to your personal decision about how
n you want to eat tasty animals versus how much harm
want to do to the world. It's a genuinely tough deci-
—and one you make every day. You have the chance to
this life and death spiritual decision with every meal:
eat this animal or not? Do I eat low on the food chain

BIG QUESTIONS

Because it's so intimately present, you cannot get
the truth out of your eyes. When you open your
eyes it strikes them; when you close them it's still
there. When you open your mouth you express it;
when you shut your mouth it speaks for itself. But
if you try to attain it through mental effort, you've
already missed it by eighteen thousand miles.

ZEN TEACHER DAHUI

right and wrong

Western culture focuses a great deal of attention
on morality, what is right and what is wrong.
Buddhism, by contrast, has never been all that concerned with
right and wrong. Instead, it has been concerned with what
leads away from dukkha and what leads to dukkha, what is
useful and useless, and what is helpful and harmful. So let's
switch this section title to. . . .

helpful and harmful

Now, let's look again at the five precepts:

ONE: trying not to harm things needlessly

TWO: trying not to take what is not yours

THREE: trying not to engage in harmful sex

FOUR: trying not to lie and harm through words

FIVE: trying not to harm oneself with substances

I phrased them a little differently here than earlier in this book. That's okay. They get translated and interpreted differently all the time. This is one of their beauties; they are aspirations, not rules. They are ways we strive to be, not commandments to do certain things *or else*.

Another beauty of the precepts is that they're all about avoiding harm. The first precept contains all the others, which is why it's first. Everything follows from it. The great goal of Buddhism is to minimize harm—to the self, to other people, to living beings, to the environment, to the whole cosmos. It begins inside and radiates throughout space and time. How shall we radiate it in our lives?

We constantly do harm. We're always failing to keep our promises and pay our debts, whether monetary, emotional, social, or spiritual. Don't hound yourself about such things. Acknowledge your failure, learn what harm you've

done, make it better if you can, and spend your time chastising yourself you'd have no time left to do anyth acting from hatred is not a mistake; i ing when a kid who's killed his own made a mistake. I'm so sorry." When it, went to school, and started firing mistake—he was choosing to comm his hatred and fear. We won't do any not confuse mistakes and choices in o fourth precept: not lying.

Each of us needs to acknowled to create harm in this world, even wit help it. Just in staying alive, we cause tage of other beings. For one thing, w is a good place to start examining hov

vegetarianism

Vegetarianism is on the especially teenagers. You a vegetarian for moral reasons be animals to eat them creates too mu would certainly respect this decisi though, that the Buddha was *not* a v

B!G Q̲U̲E̲ST̲I̲O̲NS

Because it's so intimately present, you cannot get
the truth out of your eyes. When you open your
eyes it strikes them; when you close them it's still
there. When you open your mouth you express it;
when you shut your mouth it speaks for itself. But
if you try to attain it through mental effort, you've
already missed it by eighteen thousand miles.

ZEN TEACHER DAHUI

 ## right and wrong

Western culture focuses a great deal of attention
on morality, what is right and what is wrong.
Buddhism, by contrast, has never been all that concerned with
right and wrong. Instead, it has been concerned with what
leads away from dukkha and what leads to dukkha, what is
useful and useless, and what is helpful and harmful. So let's
switch this section title to. . . .

helpful and harmful

Now, let's look again at the five precepts:

ONE: trying not to harm things needlessly

TWO: trying not to take what is not yours

THREE: trying not to engage in harmful sex

FOUR: trying not to lie and harm through words

FIVE: trying not to harm oneself with substances

I phrased them a little differently here than earlier in this book. That's okay. They get translated and interpreted differently all the time. This is one of their beauties; they are aspirations, not rules. They are ways we strive to be, not commandments to do certain things *or else*.

Another beauty of the precepts is that they're all about avoiding harm. The first precept contains all the others, which is why it's first. Everything follows from it. The great goal of Buddhism is to minimize harm—to the self, to other people, to living beings, to the environment, to the whole cosmos. It begins inside and radiates throughout space and time. How shall we radiate it in our lives?

We constantly do harm. We're always failing to keep our promises and pay our debts, whether monetary, emotional, social, or spiritual. Don't hound yourself about such things. Acknowledge your failure, learn what harm you've done, make it better if you can, and move on. If you were to spend your time chastising yourself for all your mistakes, you'd have no time left to do anything useful. Then again, acting from hatred is not a mistake; it's a choice. It's horrifying when a kid who's killed his own classmates later says, "I made a mistake. I'm so sorry." When he got that gun, loaded it, went to school, and started firing, he was *not* making a mistake—he was choosing to commit a terrible crime from his hatred and fear. We won't do anything like that, but let's not confuse mistakes and choices in our own lives. This is the fourth precept: not lying.

Each of us needs to acknowledge that we will continue to create harm in this world, even without willing it. We can't help it. Just in staying alive, we cause harm by taking advantage of other beings. For one thing, we eat them. Perhaps this is a good place to start examining how to live.

 ## vegetarianism

Vegetarianism is on the rise among Americans, especially teenagers. You may have chosen to be a vegetarian for moral reasons because, for you, killing animals to eat them creates too much harm. The Buddha would certainly respect this decision. I should tell you, though, that the Buddha was *not* a vegetarian, nor are most

Buddhist monks, even now. In fact it's likely that the Buddha died after eating some bad pork. Only in East Asia (and some monasteries in the West) are monks vegetarian. Why? Because the Buddha did not set up rules based on right and wrong. He set up rules based on helping and harming. If a monk is offered a meal with meat in it, he can eat it. In fact, he *has* to eat it, otherwise he'd be harming the giver of the meal by not accepting it. There are only a few exceptions to this rule: monks and nuns cannot eat an animal they killed, one they saw killed, or one killed especially for them. We're only talking about monks and nuns here, though. Regular Buddhists have always been able to eat whatever they want, with no rules.

Of course, things are different now than they were in the Buddha's time. The industrialized production of, say, the beef industry, contributes to grievous harm to animals and to the whole environment. It may be that if the Buddha were living now, he would forbid monks and nuns from eating farm-raised animals.

It comes down to your personal decision about how much you want to eat tasty animals versus how much harm you want to do to the world. It's a genuinely tough decision—and one you make every day. You have the chance to make this life and death spiritual decision with every meal: Do I eat this animal or not? Do I eat low on the food chain or not? Do I cause harm to myself in eating or not? It may not be *your* life and death, but every day is indeed a life-or-death day for something. Do carrots have feelings? Why wouldn't they?

 ## being harmful

Knowledge of doing harm is inescapable. You carry it around with you. This is a good thing.

Some people don't have this knowledge. But though they just go for what they want, you'd never want to *be* one of them. They can never be happy because they don't know what is good—nor do they know what good is. Does that make sense to you? It means they don't know what will make them happy, nor do they know what will make the world happy.

You, who *do* feel this inner knowledge, may feel burdened by it. You may think, "I know I could go to the party instead of studying with my friends like I told my parents." And then you think, "It's messed up, though, because even if I don't get caught, I'll be worried." Why are you worried? Because you know you *will* get caught. How? You will *automatically* be caught by the perfect cop: you. This sounds terrible at first, but it's actually okay because it comes directly from your awareness that you don't *want* to get away with crap. Deep down, you want *everyone* to stand up and be honest, especially yourself. This is your Buddha nature coming out. So when you feel guilty, feel proud. Your guilt proclaims your goodness.

Don't try to deny your responsibility for crap you've done, or you will separate yourself from your own nature. You may fool others, but you cannot fool yourself. The short-term advantages that denial and deception give you are eventually swallowed up by your own long-range alienation. Denial is lying, and lying contradicts reality. It takes you away from what is real. Then neither you nor the Buddha is happy. Even when the short-term benefit of a lie fills your mind, the long-term harm has already begun to affect you. Inside, you know you're becoming fake, phony, and unreal. You are dying.

 ## being helpful

Remember the Buddha's saying that practically every other living creature was your mother in a past life? Well, these days all kinds of new sayings are popping up on the net, and here's one of them from a guy named Meng at www.serve.com/cmtan/buddhism/index.html:

> Every other living creature owes me money
> in a past life.

Yes, Meng is joking. But he's also right. Taken together, these two quotes tell us that all things are interrelated. All things are profoundly wrapped up in each other. Treat them with respect, whether they've hassled you or given you birth. How we treat others is the measure of our success in life.

Consider environmentalism as an example. Buddhists have written whole books on why Buddhism promotes environmentalism. Here is the very simple reason: If every living thing was your mother at some time in the past, don't you have a deep responsibility to care for all of those things and the environment in which they live? The Buddha was an environmentalist 2500 years ago. If we want to honor his teaching, we need to be environmentalists now, more than ever. Young people are much more aware of the need for sustainability than older folks. You have something to teach them. After all, it's your future—and the future of the planet—that's at stake. Human impact on the environment must be ecologically sustainable or with our cars and air-conditioners and plastic bags we may kill our whole family.

 ## anxiety

When I was a kid, and even in college, I thought the world would soon be destroyed by nuclear war. I had nightmares of the bombs falling, and I truly did not believe I would ever grow up. That threat has receded, but new ones have taken its place.

Now teens live in fear of terrorists, or drive-by shootings, or even their fellow students. Each generation has its own demons. You may find that fear of these things affects your life directly. It seems there's always fear lurking in the background that can take the joy from your days and the hope from your future.

Note: this doesn't mean *ignoring* the outside. This whole part of the book is full of techniques for dealing with real outside situations and problems. We've all got plenty of those, we don't need to make up others.

Buddhism reminds us that this kind of general anxiety is useless. It doesn't lead to any more safety; instead it adds to more dukkha. Anxieties are like the questions the Buddha said don't lead to happiness, awakening, or nirvana. Pursuing them is a complete waste of time. Why do we continue, then? Because these anxieties and questions are ways of avoiding dealing with things that we really *can* do something about—but don't want to.

Take the energy you spend worrying about your anxieties and put it into looking inside. Let go of these vague concerns and get busy dealing with what you can change in your life: things inside you. When you take responsibility for the inside, you realize outside factors are less important. You may find that when you open up to insights about yourself—especially critical ones—your external anxieties fade away.

 ## religion

One reason I became a Buddhist is that I never *had* to become a Buddhist. Oh, that's right; I'm not a Buddhist. But I am.

I'm saying it doesn't *matter* if I'm Buddhist or if you are. Just keep doing what you're doing. The Buddha said any path leading away from dukkha is a good path. He liked the one he taught, but he didn't demand you follow it, too. Over a thousand years later, Zen Teacher Wuzu Fayan said, "What should we do? What should we do? The true offering to the Buddha is not more incense."

Wuzu doesn't need you to offer anything to the Buddha. And the Dalai Lama doesn't need you to become a Buddhist. This gives you genuine freedom. You can be Buddhist or not. Whichever it is, when a friend asks you to go to a church, try to go. Or to a synagogue. Or to a mosque. Go ahead. If you do, your true offering is making your friend happy. It's being together with people who are trying to go beyond themselves and share some peace. For the moment, don't worry about difficult beliefs, or scandals in the church, or oppression of women, or whatever is wrong with these religions. Be open to what's right about them. Share that rightness with their members. Try to be a part of spreading it. You can even be a member, too. Be it all, the Buddha doesn't mind. This is true Buddhist practice, wherever you are.

 ## thinking for yourself

People don't have to be lying to you for what they're saying to be totally wrong. A wise person does not trust everything he or she hears or reads. (Trust me when I tell you this. . . .) Whether you're hearing things from CNN or MTV or from your parents or girlfriend or boyfriend, you can't simply believe them. What to do? Think! Think for yourself!

Here's maybe the most important quote in all the Buddhist scriptures:

> Do not be led by rumor, or tradition, or hearsay.
> Do not be led by the authority of religious
> scripture, nor by simple logic or inference, nor
> by mere appearance, nor by the pleasure of
> speculation, nor by vague possibilities, nor by
> respect for "Our Teacher." When you've seen for
> yourself "these teachings are skillful, blameless,
> wise; when followed they lead to good and
> happiness," then stay with them.
>
> ANGUTTARA NIKAYA

In these famous lines from the Kalama Sutta, the Buddha says: Try it out. See if it works. Only then will you really know whether to stick with it. The Buddha is talking about spiritual teachings, but his advice applies equally to all beliefs. Don't believe a thing simply for any of the usual reasons ("because it's always been like this," "because God commands it," or "because I say so"). Believe it because it works for you.

But how do you decide whether something works for you? Is the Buddha saying, "Whatever works for you is fine; do your own thing"? People (including me, I admit) sometimes use this sutta to excuse their own indulgent lifestyles. We pick out what we like from religions, teachers, politicians, diets, friends, whatever. Then we reject the rest, saying, "I've tried it and I don't like it." We might say, "Hey, the Buddha said, 'See for yourself' if it makes you happy. Well, that part about not doing drugs doesn't make it for me, so, hey, I'm blowing it off." Uh-oh.

Let me clear this up: The Buddha did *not* say "whatever turns you on." Maybe it was Hugh Hefner . . . one of those old-timers, anyway. The Buddha said to carefully examine whether some teaching or authority or practice or belief makes you skillful, blameless, wise, good, and happy. If it does, then follow it. That's a completely different story than "whatever turns you on." The Buddha says self-indulgent pleasure is not real happiness, and it's certainly not blameless, wise, or skillful. Real happiness comes from being the whole list of good things he mentions. It's a balance of positive thoughts and actions that grows easier as you get the hang of it. It's the path, the practice, the Middle Way itself.

PART THREE

TAKING A
BUDDHIST PATH

Sentient beings are
    numberless, I vow
    to save them;
Desires are in
    exhaustible, I vow
    to abandon them;
Dharma gates are
    boundless, I vow to enter them;
The Buddha way is unsurpassable,
    I vow to embody it.

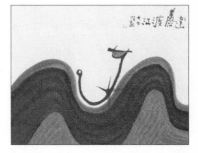

THE FOUR GREAT MAHAYANA VOWS

WHAT IS
THE PATH?

The central metaphor of life as a path, so central to Buddhist teachings, was already in wide use at the time of the Buddha. In India and all over the world, seekers have been talking for thousands of years about following spiritual paths. The earliest Christians, for example, called themselves "Followers of the Way." The "Tao" in Taoism literally means "the way." The Buddha spoke of his teaching as the "Middle Way" and the "Noble Eightfold Path." Buddhist seekers like these metaphors because they reveal an awareness of the long journey we all have toward embodying the sacred. Let's explore some parts of the Buddhist path and what it's like bringing them into your life.

the path

You don't have to become a Buddhist to take a Buddhist path. You can simply walk a few steps and see whether you like where it's taking you. You can walk on and off the path as you like. Just reading this book means you've already taken a look along the path. But that doesn't mean you have to stop exploring other paths you may want to follow. Please, continue! Buddhism, and all religions, should be about adding richness to your life, not taking it away. This book lets you stay on your own path while adding Buddhist richness to it. As one 19-year-old who had been meditating for years told me, "I wouldn't necessarily consider myself a Buddhist, but I'm practicing all the time."

Following a physical path means making inevitable discoveries and taking crucial steps. There's the eye-opening experience of seeing the path for the first time. Perhaps most important is taking that first step. There's the moment you discover you've walked far enough so that you can no longer see where you began, nor can you see where you will end up. You must simply trust the evidence of the path beneath your feet and in your view ahead. Then there's a glimpse of the destination in the distance. This does not mean you are there, only that you can contact it with your physical senses. It is made real to you in this way. Finally, for the strong and patient, the ultimate destination appears before your eyes, and the remarkable experience of reaching it unfolds. You are transformed from someone who is moving toward a destination to someone who has arrived.

Just like a pilgrim following a physical path to a sacred site, when you follow a spiritual path—especially that of Buddhism—you come to the same landmarks. First you encounter the path and see its beauty. Then you take that vital first step on the path, whether it be learning, meditating, meeting others, chanting, or any other practice—even reading this book. You reach a point where you've gone far enough that the beginning is lost but the end is not yet in sight. This is where Buddhists seem to spend most of their time, perhaps because this echoes Buddhism's emphasis on always checking back in with yourself to make sure your practice is moving you forward. The focus is internal rather than external, so it's inside that you might expect to see not only the path but also the *destination*. Many Buddhists, perhaps most of them, glimpse the destination in their present lifetimes. Zen Buddhism uses the metaphor of the clouds parting and the sun peeking through to describe that first glimpse of the destination. After a person has seen the sun once, even though the clouds return, he or she knows that the sun still exists behind them.

A very few Buddhists, now as in ancient times, are said to actually reach a place where they lastingly embody the goal of Buddhahood. Although they may not be full Buddhas

Mahayana means "Great Vehicle." It refers to the tradition of Buddhism that accepts a wide and growing range of ways of awakening. It began a few centuries after the Buddha and is the common tradition of Buddhism in China, Tibet, Mongolia, Korea, Vietnam, and Japan.

in the sense of being teachers to the world, they bring the full presence of the Buddha into their lives and selves. They are both Buddhas and at the same time normal people like the rest of us. In fact, in the Mahayana view, *every human is a Buddha already*, so being truly "normal" is being truly Buddha. But this works only when people accept themselves as fundamentally not-selves, always not alone, connected to and responsible for *everything*.)

where the path leads

The goal of the Buddhist path has been debated since the time of the Buddha himself, so you'll get different answers to this question depending on who you ask. What follows is a sampler of Buddhist views on the subject of where the path leads.

Every Buddhist (well, almost every Buddhist; some Buddhists, like some of everyone else, are really weird), says the goal is to be like the Buddha. It's a powerful and alluring goal, but it's not something that many Buddhists expect to achieve—or even attempt—in this life. Owing to the difficulty of realizing full awakening, for some the goal of Buddhism is to be reborn as a monk in their next lives. They think of this as a reachable goal, since it's a stepping stone to becoming a Buddha. Reincarnation as a monk means the freedom (in a future life) to spend all one's energies on making even more progress on the journey toward awakening. Many Theravada Buddhists consciously adopt this strategy for their next birth. (Of course, to get reborn as a monk you have to do some good things in this life now.)

Pure Land Buddhists in East Asia adopt a similar strategy to the Theravada. This form of Mahayana Buddhism also views the goal of awakening as nearly impossible in this life, so it relies on the power of Amida Buddha—another Buddha, this one a compassionate, celestial figure—to help its followers be reborn in the Pure Land in their next lives. Living in the Pure Land makes awakening vastly easier even than being a monk here in this world.

Some Pure Land Buddhists, especially in Taiwan and Japan, believe in a different version of the Pure Land. They don't think of the Pure Land as somewhere other than

Theravada means "Way of the Elders." It refers to the tradition of Buddhism that focuses on the classical ways of awakening. It is the common tradition of Buddhism in Sri Lanka, Burma, Thailand, Cambodia, and Laos.

here and now. Instead they see it as something only one thought away, which they create in their minds and lives every instant—if they can. For them, the goal of Buddhism is to turn this sad world into the Pure Land itself. Naturally, this may take a while.

Then there are the Vajrayana Buddhists, who take the fast-track to awakening. They believe they can achieve the goal of Buddhism—the liberation of the mind, the bliss of oneness with the cosmic body of the Buddha—before they die. Of course, many long and arduous practices lead toward this noble goal.

Vajrayana means "Diamond Vehicle." It refers to the tradition of Buddhism that focuses on the relationship with one's teacher and a variety of symbolic practices, including deity meditations and tantric practices. It is the tradition of Tibetan Buddhism, but is also practiced in the rest of the Himalayas, China, Korea, and Japan.

Zen Buddhists claim several things—not always consistent ones (they're famous tricksters). They believe that their teachers are Buddhas, awakened ones, and in fact that *everybody* is already Buddha and there's nothing to teach anyone. "This very mind is Buddha; ordinary mind is Buddha." (I'm not making this up, several teachers really said this.) Their goal is to realize the true nature they already have, their intrinsic awakened state. This realization is like getting out of bed in the morning. We are sooooo tired and we sooooo want to close our eyes again, but, hey, the griddle is hot and it's time to move on to breakfast. The goal here is to be really awake (or awakened), and be happy to cook, eat, or whatever.

Finally, all the Mahayana and Vajrayana traditions agree that no personal goal in Buddhism can be separated from the ultimate goal of awakening all sentient beings. Some Theravada Buddhists talk this way, too. Here we need to help every single living thing realize Buddhahood. This is the bodhisattva ideal: embodying selfless effort to save all beings. Let's just say this is a long-term project.

Okay, enough of this tour of Buddhist soteriology (the fancy word for how people view life and death and what we should do about them). The distant goals of Buddhism don't really matter except to orient and inspire us in the present moment. What matters right now is what we *do* right now, what we *think* right now, how we *feel* right now. And, thank goodness, on this practical level, all the traditions of Buddhism agree on certain basics. Most fundamental of all is the idea that it all comes down to happiness.

The Buddha says over and over in the sacred writings that he's a doctor, come to make us feel better. In fact, he has come to take away the disease of dukkha. He's all about making us happier, getting rid of trouble, pain, and suffering. Simple.

I used to be all hung up on getting "enlightened." Now I don't even like the word. Sure, it's attractive, it's spiritually sexy, but so what? The Buddha didn't teach how to get enlightened. He talked about finding calm, peace, and equanimity. Sometimes he went so far as to talk about liberation. Liberation from what? From dukkha.

I ask you, what is enlightenment? You might have a lovely and exalted answer. Here's mine: Enlightenment is that thing that distracts me from doing the real work of my life— waking up to reality so I can be happier. If we're focused on waking up instead of getting enlightened, then whether we're Buddhists or not is less important. Teens I've talked with are wise to this. One wrote,

The life of compassion and understanding that you begin to integrate into your world really becomes inseparable. In other words, there is no saying where my Buddhist half begins and my other teen nature ends; they are interwoven nearly completely. I guess you just can't live a life of compassion and not become mixed with it like that. In a way it's wonderful!

wisdom and compassion

 Buddhism's two great virtues, wisdom and compassion, blend together. They're inseparable, like all good Buddhist things. All forms of Buddhism agree that humans' work in this world is to embody these virtues. That's what Buddhists mean when they speak of taking a Buddhist path.

Wisdom comes first, because compassion flows from it. The essence of Buddhist wisdom is that we are "not-two." All beings are not-two, not separate, not independent, not free, not alone. Notice how we like some of these adjectives ("not alone") and dislike others ("not free")? That comes from our ignorance of this wisdom we're seeking. We feel independent and free, and we like that. But if we were truly free and independent, we would also be truly lonely, truly rootless, and truly isolated. We surely don't want *that*. The reality is that we are completely enmeshed in a web of relationships that extends to all living things. In fact, it extends to all acting things and all things that have relationships. That includes everything in our biosphere and perhaps beyond. In an ultimate sense, it's all us. It's all me. It's all you. That knowledge is the root of all Buddhist wisdom. The fundamental meaning of taking a Buddhist path is deepening our wisdom—and acting like it.

Here is where compassion comes in. If we are all "not-two," how can we help but be compassionate? Look at the very root meaning of the word: compassion means "to suffer together." If you feel dukkha along with another or others, they are yourself in a fundamental way, so *of course* you'll be compassionate toward them-and-you. You won't be able to help it. You will naturally act with compassion just as you naturally act with hunger or sleepiness. It is simply the process of awakening. The trick is to keep the process going during times when old habits of selfish thinking resurface.

As I say, all forms of Buddhism agree about wisdom and compassion. Different forms of Buddhism have different ways of advising us and guiding us toward more wisdom and compassion. For example, one teen described her practices with animals:

> We free fish or crabs or crickets. If a lama is around, cool, but it doesn't have to be a Buddhist thing. It's just a let them go thing. . . . We need to have compassion for everything. Just because things are not cute and fuzzy doesn't mean they don't have a right to live.

She actually rescued a *rat* she found near her home and nursed it back to health. It clawed its way out its little hospital three times, and each time she found it again and kept nursing it. Eventually it was strong enough to survive on its own.

On another level, wisdom and compassion form the foundation for the four great Mahayana vows. The first vow says, "Sentient beings are numberless, I vow to save them." Why? The vow grows from compassion, and compassion grows from the wisdom that all those beings are no different from you. They're not separate from you. You will be saved only when all of them are. Perhaps you don't even need to vow this. It's simply how things are.

 ## being buddhist: the path itself

So far you've been looking at how you can orient yourself to the path: searching for it, finding it, and taking a look ahead at where it's going. Now let's move on to walking it.

> Just as a pot without a stand is easy to upset, but a pot with a stand is hard to upset, so a mind without some kind of stand is easy to upset, but a mind with some kind of stand is hard to upset. What's the stand for the mind? The Noble Eightfold Path.
>
> SAMYUTTA NIKAYA

The path keeps you solid. It keeps you going the right way with your feet on the ground. You remember the Eightfold Path we talked about earlier in this book? To see how each step on the path leads to the next when you're actually walking it, consider the eight factors in the traditional order.

Right view and *right intention* are the wisdom section of the path. As wisdom leads to compassion, so right view and right intention lead to following the ethical aspect of the path. It all begins with seeing things from the Buddhist perspective. Right view is seeing that there are actions and the fruits of actions. Your actions, including mental actions, and their fruits form your life (and lives) to come. Luckily, this idea is not so different from the basic idea of cause and effect most of us grew up learning. The Buddhist word is *karma*, but don't get hung up on that. Buddhism asks you to admit that you are responsible for what you do and realize that doing what's right is not merely a burden but an endless opportunity to change your world for the better.

Right intention then follows naturally. In fact, right intention is where compassion fits into the Eightfold Path. Right intention is the resolve to renounce selfishness, to be free from hatred and harm, and to do good for all the world.

Right intention leads inevitably to the next section of the path: morality. With right intention you immediately start to practice *right speech*—avoiding lying, badmouthing, abusing, or chattering sorts of talk. Speech is just the beginning, though. The Buddhist path integrates all aspects of life. A good Buddhist also practices *right action*—the avoidance of killing, taking what's not yours, and engaging in harmful kinds of sex or other amusements.

Further, you have to think seriously about your work. The next step on the path is *right livelihood*, which means not doing work that harms the world. If harmful amusements you do just for fun are wrong, surely harmful work you get paid for is wrong, too. You can't just say it's your employer's responsibility. It's yours, too. If you're a corporate executive enriching yourself while the company's stock is going down the tubes, or if you sell bogus travel packages to old folks, forget about using the excuse that your boss told you to do it. Maybe you just flip burgers that only exist at the expense of raped rainforests and toxic runoff from polluted, silt-choked rivers and then clog the arteries of people who should have lived longer lives full of love. Perhaps it's the only job you could get. Okay, but maybe it's time for some serious introspection about how you can actually help the world and get paid for it, too.

The third sequence in the path involves cultivating the mind and deepening your practice. It begins with *right effort*—simply the effort to *be* Buddhist and *do* what's wise and compassionate. Right effort crosses the border of inside and out. It's in your mind but also in your actions. Right effort is the engine that drives your progress on the path. It's the transition from the ethical section of the path to the inner cultivation section. Yes, it takes work and energy. It doesn't just happen. You have to choose it and do it, and you have to make the choice and the effort about 108,000 times a day. Okay, maybe only 108, but I'm not kidding, it could really be 108 times a day. That's why it's called Buddhist *practice*. You keep *practicing* it every day. And, yes, it does get easier.

Right mindfulness simply means being aware. Most people are easily distracted from what's right in front of them. They get hung up in their fantasies, their concerns, and their fears. The challenge is instead to be mindful, awake to the ongoing relationship between our inner and outer states. Being mindful means not judging things but remaining aware of them and our reactions to them, whether they're inner thoughts, physical sensations, external situations, or whatever. Mindfulness is open. It has room. Imagine the open and relaxed mind of the Buddha himself: accepting all things even as he also tried to make them better. Being mindful is pretty close to being like the Buddha.

Last is *right meditation* or concentration: focusing the mind down to one point, helping it calm down so there is no stress—or even no thinking at all. Although meditation is its own element of the path, it adds to all the others.

MEDITATION

With enough practice, you become Buddha;
With enough water, stone wears out.
Thick heads can too be cracked.
People only think their hearts have hardened.

SHIWU

"Meditation is when you can clear your mind."

"It's not a certain activity. It's anything that causes me
to focus on that and nothing else. It's a drive to focus."

"[It's like watching a sunset.] It's not that you're trying
to obtain anything through the sunset. It's just there."

QUOTES FROM
TEENAGE BUDDHISTS

what is meditation?

Seems like it should be an easy question, but it's like asking what is love. There are so many aspects of it, so many perspectives on it, and so many ways to experience it that meditation doesn't lend itself to being reduced to one quick answer. The best I can do is this: Meditation means ways of making the mind understand itself.

I don't mean "understand" in an intellectual way, like the way a neuropsychologist understands patterns of brain activity. That's an understanding of facts but not an experience of inner knowing. Buddhist understanding starts inside and recognizes what is happening right here, right now, in our heads. Meditation helps you understand how and why your mind moves and thinks and wants by letting you see these things as they happen.

And meditation goes beyond this. You start with the rest of the Eightfold Path—or any other wise and compassionate way of being, such as other religions provide. When you then add meditation, you gain the power to change your mind. Literally. You can change how your mind works. Why change your mind? The usual reason is to get happier. When you use the tool of meditation to unlock the processes of your mind, you can reprogram yourself to get rid of greed, ignorance, and hatred, replacing them with calm, satisfaction, wisdom, love, and joy. Who wouldn't want that?

So why doesn't everyone meditate? Two main reasons. First, some people are taught that meditation is somehow un-religious and makes one susceptible to the influence of evil powers. I'm not kidding; this is the official position of the Roman Catholic Church as I write this book. This is such a fundamentally ignorant and harmful view it is best I don't say anything more about it. I don't want to get into wrong speech!

There's also a more understandable reason people avoid meditation: It can be really hard. Meditation is hard when we're resistant to it. Sometimes our minds don't want to let go of our hard-won sense of solidity and selfishness. We've been working on that sense of self since we were tod-dlers, and on some levels it's necessary for survival, so we cling to it. We also resist meditation when we'd rather have external amusement than internal happiness. This may sound stupid, like something nobody would ever want, but *most of us feel like this all the time.* Think about yourself honestly. Given a choice, don't you always feel immediate desire to do the most exciting, fun thing? If so, join the club; you're a human being.

The trouble is, that search for amusement and excite-ment never fully succeeds. In the end it always fails completely as we die. It cannot be the path to happiness. Real happiness is internal and it comes from changing your mind after learning how it works. Meditation can get you there because it reveals the workings of your mind and lets you fix them.

Because of their personal resistance to meditation, and because it takes time, energy, a quiet space, and a bit of knowledge, most people in the world don't meditate. Even most Buddhists don't meditate, and a person can be an excellent Buddhist without meditating. Yet most young people interested in Buddhism do meditate, and they're right to. For many people it provides the single strongest push forward on the path.

There's something immediately obvious about concepts like right speech and even right effort, but meditation is another story. It goes against all the thought habits most people have cultivated over their whole lives. Yet meditation produces immediate, positive results across the whole spectrum of body and mind. If you try it yourself, you'll quickly discover that meditation can produce benefits for you that range from eliminating stress to getting better grades. It may even help you wake up.

calming meditation

The many methods of Buddhist meditation all boil down to two main types. The first type is *samatha,* or calming meditation. It's not about putting your-self to sleep. That's not meditation; it's not even calm—think of how active your dreams can be. Samatha is more like concentrating your mind. This concentration is not like con-centrating on a math problem or on driving. That's much too active and linear. Here, concentration means focusing thoughts on one unchanging thing, not for the purpose of doing anything with it, but simply to let it fill your whole mind. Samatha calms the mind further and further until it reaches a place of true rest and ease called *samadhi.* (If sa-matha and samadhi sound alike, it's because they come from the same root, meaning "peace.") Buddhism shares this general type of meditation with other religions, especially Hinduism. When Siddhartha practiced meditation and self-mortification with the renunciants in the forest after he left home, he was working toward ever-deeper immersion in open and quiet meditative states. He was doing samatha meditation.

When doing samatha, you start by concentrating on a visual or mental object. You try to develop a one-pointed mind, free of the hin-drances of ill-will, laziness, greed, and other such feelings. You purely

> Other religions *do* have meditative paths even though they may call them by other names. As examples, contemporary Christianity has "centering prayer," and Islam has "*dhikr*," the repetition of the name of God.

concentrate on the object. After much practice, you can even let the object go and concentrate on internal experience. As you do so, your concentration strengthens, your calm deepens, and you find yourself more and more able to achieve this state each time you sit down to meditate. The process is not just some dry skill you acquire; it's enjoyable in a way that touches you more deeply than normal fleeting pleasures. Samatha gives you a foundation you can stay with as you look at the action in your mind. That looking is the other type of meditation.

insight meditation

"Insight" is the usual translation of *vipassana*, which literally means "clear sight." Buddhism attends to insight more than other religions do in their meditative paths.

When doing vipassana, you don't strive for calm. Instead your objective is insight. You look right into your mind to see how and why it's doing what it's doing. You begin to see how one thought leads to another and how an attitude or desire leads to a natural reaction that may or may not be good. When you see that actually happening in your mind, it really hits you: you need to change, and you have the power to do it. That power is the strongest thing in the world, and it's in you now. Insight meditation puts that power right in your hands.

Is it possible to get this power without meditation? Sure it is. Great spiritual people throughout time in all cultures have tapped into this power, and most of them were not Buddhists. They gained insight without Buddhist meditation, and so can you. Of course, each of them was a one-in-a-million person with fantastic powers of intellect, awareness, compassion, and mental discipline. Have you developed all those qualities? If not, maybe try meditation.

HOW TO MEDITATE

What is sitting meditation? In this teaching, sitting means in all circumstances and without any obstructions to avoid active thinking. Meditation means manifesting the clarity of the original nature.

THE PLATFORM SUTRA

The instructions that follow will let you do real meditation right away—if you make the effort. It's a great start, as well as a crucial step on the meditative path.

Yet I am not a meditation instructor. I am only a beginner like you, and my instructions here and all through this book are just the barest beginning of teaching. If you keep following the Buddhist path, you'll need to learn more about such matters as the pitfalls of meditation, the pride that can strike you and the frustration that can weigh you down. You will almost certainly need a teacher you can actually talk with and share stories with—someone who really knows meditation and who really knows you—to guide you as you move forward. This book can't talk with you as you make progress. If you keep meditating, keep learning more as you do. You can start online, where you'll find some great meditation instructions. Eventually, though, unless you're one of those one-in-a-million people who are spiritual virtuosos, you will want your own teacher.

For now, here are two basic meditations you can do in different situations. One meditation you can do anytime, anywhere. It's quick enough so that other people won't even have to know you're doing it, so it's really handy when you're out in public, where doing anything obviously Buddhist and religious would be too weird.

The second technique is a full meditation that includes an element of samatha and an element of vipassana. It's the meditation I do myself, so I can tell you what I've discovered about it. Each of these two meditations has the potential to change your mind. They form the basis for several of the exercises you'll find later in this book.

secret meditation

In this simple meditation, you use your breath as a way of guiding your mind to a new place. It takes just a few breaths—sometimes just one! There is something deeply calming and enjoyable in following the breath. It changes your experience of the world right away. One breath can make the difference between anger and pity or frustration and acceptance.

Here's how it works: At any moment—even this one, right now, so let's practice—put your focus on your breathing and let yourself enjoy the act. That's it; that's the whole thing. Nothing could be simpler, but I'll give you a little more coaching.

The first step in this quick meditation is taking your focus away from *doing* anything. That's why it's easiest to sit when you're meditating. Before you try to meditate while moving, practice while sitting. If you do try secret meditation while walking, running, or doing any other activity, let that activity simply happen without effort for the duration of the meditation.

Relax your body. Even if you have to continue to move, don't put energy into the moving of your limbs or positioning of your body. Just let the process continue naturally on its own. You'll find that much of what you do all day can just continue without your attention every second.

Close your eyes if possible, though you can also practice this meditation with your eyes open. Relax your eyes and stop looking at anything in particular. Let your whole visual field just be there—each object where it is, in its inevitable place. There's no need to pay attention to any one thing. When you've released looking, even if your eyes are open, there's no focus, no mental energy going out to particular objects.

Next, turn your attention to your breath. Close your mouth and feel the air moving in through your nostrils. Feel your belly push out with the air in your diaphragm. Let the belly rise; then let it fall away again. You may feel tension as your belly pushes against the intake of new air. You'll also feel tension when your belly is full of air, just before you release that air as you breathe out. These feelings are okay; let them be.

Your mind is the most important element in this meditation, as it is in all meditations. Direct your mind to the perfect and infinitely repeated action of drawing in and letting out breath. Enjoy that breath, that flowing of air in and out. There is something liberating about the breath. It's your very life, yet it's also something beyond your full control. It's so vital, so intimate, yet so free. Trying to control it just messes it up. Instead, see it, float in it, and accept it.

That's all there is to it. It takes longer to describe than to do. When you really get into this meditation, all things but the breath fall away—even you. Only the breath remains, relaxed, smooth, calming. As you meditate, your anger, worry, or whatever emotion you were feeling when you started will fall away along with all other things. What a liberation!

Does this liberation last? Of course not. This is a quick and secret meditation, after all. But "quick and secret" means you can do it before a test or even *during* one. You can do it during a date, or during a talk with someone you can't stand, or whenever. Whatever the circumstances, if you meditate you'll feel an instant freedom. You'll feel a sense of presence in the moment and perspective on the emotional charge you felt before you started. This is the power of meditation. Not only do you feel it in the moment, but the feeling also permanently puts perspective on those feelings of being trapped in emotions. In this way, the meditation points the way to a liberation that does last.

full meditation

The principles of the secret meditation apply to full meditation as well. In full meditation, though, you'll be committing to a longer time of sitting, and you'll add several crucial elements that form the foundation for more advanced meditation techniques. As a beginner, you're best off doing seated meditation until you get further advice from a meditation teacher. Seated meditation is easier to do since it's physically simpler and you're less likely to be distracted by your environment.

First, find a good place to meditate. Meditating is difficult when there are distractions. Of course there will always be distractions, but you want to reduce them to a minimum. Your bedroom may be the best place to meditate. You can just sit on your bed. Sure, it's nice to have a special meditation room where you can sit on a cushion and light incense at an altar, but none of that is necessary. It just helps you concentrate. The real power is inside. Sit anywhere.

Decide on a meditation period. You can be flexible, but it's best to decide on a period and try to keep to it every day. Maybe it'll be ten minutes in the morning, or after school, or twenty minutes before bed. Start small; don't try to do too much and get burnt out. Five minutes of meditation you do is better than half an hour of meditation you don't do. After years of practice, I can estimate how long I've meditated during a sitting. You might want to set an alarm if you've got one that sounds pleasant, such as a CD alarm that's queued to gentle music. A vibrating cell phone alarm is perfect. Put it behind the pillow you'll be sitting on. If you don't have one, figure something else out. The traditional method is to burn a stick of incense until it's out. They come in different lengths for different lengths of meditation. Or put a clock on the edge of your vision and glance at it when you think your time is up. Or just guess. No one else is timing you.

Some teachers claim that certain sitting postures, such as the lotus position, where you fold your feet up onto the opposite thighs, physically calm the mind. As a beginner, don't worry about your position. Just find a way to sit where you can stay still for ten minutes, twenty minutes, or even half an hour without fidgeting. Try putting a pillow under your butt and sitting cross-legged with one foot in front of the other—*not* with one ankle crossed over the other. This is called the Burmese posture, and it works for me. You can even sit in a chair. In fact you can even lie on your bed. Very comfortable. Sadly, it's *too* comfortable: you can easily end up falling asleep! That's why teachers don't recommend it.

Sit up straight, but not as if you were in the army; just don't slump. Slumping is not good for you, whether you're meditating or not. Lean a bit left and right, front and back, to help you find your center and sit straight up. Relax your arms and let them rest naturally on your legs. You can just put your palms on your thighs, or you can do something the Zen Buddhists do: cup your left hand in your right, palms up, so your thumb tips touch lightly. Let your arms rest in your lap. Easy.

Now you're ready to go. Take a couple of deep breaths and let them out slowly. Relax into your posture. You can close your eyes or keep them half-way open. Halfway open is the Zen way, and I encourage you to try it. It helps keep you alert but not distracted by what you see. You may want to face the wall, again as some Zen meditators do. Facing a blank wall is calming. Let your head look slightly down, close your mouth, but don't clench your teeth. Relax. (Have I said that before? Well, it's key.) Your body is meditating . . . but what do you do with your mind?

Try this: Once you've taken your two or three deep breaths, just breathe normally and count your breaths in your head. Count "one" when you breathe in, "two" when you breathe out, "three" when you breathe in, "four" when you breathe out, and so on up to ten. Then start again with one. When you lose the count—I say "when" because you *will*—go back to "one." Let your mind be filled with the count. Let other thoughts drop away. Simply count to ten over and over with the breath. Sound easy? It's not.

> There are way more forms of meditation than I can mention in this book. A young Buddhist told me about an unconventional one: *"Sometimes, playing basketball is my meditation. Sometimes in meditation I'm more flooded with thoughts than at home. But in basketball I get this rush, I forget about everything. It's meditation for me. I'll write a better paper after playing basketball. . . . When I'm playing, I'm thinking without thinking. It's like saving someone's life. You just do it."*

In fact, facing this not-easiness is the great work of meditation. Counting the breaths is a challenge few people ever fully master. Sometimes you can't even make it to ten once in a whole meditation! Don't let that bug you, though. What's the point of making it to ten? Nothing. The point of the meditation is to calm the mind enough to be able to see how it works. When you gain the ability to see your own mind, you gain the opportunity to change it. So the counting is about focusing the mind. It's a form of calming meditation. Of course that focus leads to your being able to observe the workings of your own mind, so it's also a form of insight meditation.

Does this sound too basic for you? Not nearly as exotic as you imagined meditation to be? Don't be fooled; it's the real thing. There are other techniques with more bells and whistles, but the real work of meditation all comes down to the practice of calming and seeing into the mind. The form of meditation I've described here is one of the purest forms that do both. It has a richness that you won't soon exhaust. Even highly advanced Zen practitioners come back and do this same practice and learn from it. As I say, it's the real thing.

FINDING
YOUR OWN PATH

It's best if you get rid of everything and be open and ordinary. Truly feel freedom from the conditioned mind and see all things as dreams and illusions. Be fully open, reacting immediately to the actual moment. This will give you the true support enjoyed by all awakened Buddhist householders.

As your abilities allow, you'll help all beings so together you enter the simply flowing sea of our original nature. Your life will thus not be wasted.

YUANWU

sangha: buddhist community

There's one more ingredient to really being a Buddhist. In fact, in traditional Buddhist countries it's the sine qua non. It's joining a Buddhist community, a sangha. There's the sangha of monks and nuns, who have given up the world as the Buddha did. But there is also the wider sangha of other folks on the Buddhist path. Traditional Buddhists have local temples just as Christians have local churches, and they go to those temples with others just as Christians go to church with others. These communities are their sanghas, groups of people who support each other in following the Buddhist path.

I've left this for last because, for people who are just learning about Buddhism, sometimes joining a sangha is the last step in the process of entering the path. For such people—and I am one—what matters most is our own relationships with the teachings, the practices, and ourselves. We have to get fully comfortable with following a Buddhist path before we would consider becoming a member of a temple or meditation center.

We treasure our freedom to experiment, but for it we pay the price of not having the support of others who walk the path with us. This is a heavy price because, as the Buddha taught, having good friends is the whole of the holy life. If we don't have friends to walk the path with, do we have any spiritual life at all? Of course we do. We have our own friends. Even if they're not Buddhists, as long as they're true friends, they walk the path with us. If we are honest with each other, they will support us and we will support them as we face dukkha and work toward realizing who we truly are.

Buddhist teachers have compared the sangha to a tumbler full of stones: as they rub each other, they wear down their rough edges. If you are a lone young Buddhist, your work is to make the whole world your sangha. Then you make everyone your teacher, and you let all things soften your edges. Doing this, you make everyone your "good friends" and so your everyday interactions are the "whole of the spiritual life."

Perhaps you have no desire to join with Buddhists. You may not even think of yourself as a Buddhist. That's fine. You may find the same kind of spiritual sharing at your church or with your family, without joining an official Buddhist sangha. Still, if you don't find that sharing, and

I want to suggest one middle ground. There's an online community called the Teen Buddhist Sangha. You can join them and gain the support of good friends without having to know anyone or know anything about Buddhism. They'll welcome you and answer your questions and help you when you're down. That's a real sangha, even if it isn't "official." Check "Many Paths, Further Explorations" for instructions.

your path takes you toward becoming a Buddhist, you'll want to consider a sangha.

Whether you're with friends or traveling solo, there are sure to be rocky stretches on your path. Like all spiritual paths, the Buddhist one has its twists, its steep places, and its rough patches where you'll stumble and fall. You'll likely encounter two sorts of difficult spots: internal ones and external ones.

 ## internal troubles

When you face your inner world you'll discover that, as in the outer world, not all of it is beautiful. Buddhism is all about seeing the way things are, and that includes seeing how you are. You'll find that you are resistant, lazy, and undisciplined. You may also be indecisive, arrogant, mean-spirited, wimpy, and full of other character flaws, but *all* human beings are resistant, lazy, and undisciplined.

Since we're all like this, the first thing to say about such troubles is to not worry about them. For instance, don't be mad with yourself because you're resistant to meditating. This anger is a clever way your mind continues to resist: If you get angry with yourself, you're likely to hate the whole meditation experience and stop. It's one of life's little ironies.

Don't be mad. Accept that you are resistant and then just keep meditating. That's what I do after so many years!

Deal with your other inner troubles the same way. You're lazy. So? You get up for other things, and you can get up to meditate. You're undisciplined. So? You don't always do your homework, but in the long run you graduate high school. Let your practice be the same way. Accept indiscipline, but keep working as consistently as you can. Your discipline will improve. That's how changing your mind works.

If you are prone to anger, you might want to try *metta* (loving-kindness) practice (look for it in "Practical Exercises"). If you're arrogant, try reading Shinran's *Tannisho* or Shunryu Suzuki's *Zen Mind, Beginner's Mind* (see "Many Paths, Further Explorations"). If you're indecisive, read Zen collections and, more importantly, look inside for that part of you that knows without thinking. Zen Buddhists call that your true nature. It's in there. You may just have to uncover it slowly. While meditation will help, mindfulness in each instant of daily life is the real challenge.

Buddhism has antidotes for all our faults. They are usually the hardest practices for us exactly because they change our resistant minds. Buddhism is not one of those religions that says, "If you just do this one thing, all your troubles will melt away." It's a long path toward calm, peace, and happiness. Enjoy the journey.

 ## external troubles

If you do take the Buddhist path, you'll eventually encounter someone who thinks you are horribly misguided, perhaps even dangerous. It may happen right away. Your own family may not understand you and your practice. Let me offer a couple of strategies for you.

First, unless you've already joined a temple, taken the precepts, and gone for refuge in the Buddha, the dharma, and the sangha, tell them *don't worry, you're not a Buddhist*. That should help, and it's true. If you're just reading this book or doing some meditation or trying to apply the Buddha's life to your own, you are not a Buddhist, you're just using Buddhism in your life. It takes a long time before you somehow "become" a Buddhist. I still don't know if *I'm* a Buddhist and I've been at this for fifteen years.

Second, remember that other people's prejudices are not your burden unless you choose to carry them. Their actions may restrict your life, but their mental states do not have to weigh you down. In fact, dealing with the prejudices of others is a perfect opportunity to practice compassion. The classic Indian text, the Bodhisattvacharyavatara (*The Way of the Bodhisattva*), says

Even lacking compassion for all
Who, following their imbalanced passion,
Try to hurt or even kill me,
The last thing I want is anger for them.

Whether you're facing parents who don't understand and think Buddhism is some kind of black magic, or you're facing school authorities who think prayer is good but meditation is cult activity, or friends who think Buddhism is weird—in fact, whenever you're facing anyone who just doesn't get it and reacts with aversion to any part of your Buddhist path— let it roll off. You can learn from your enemies. They provide a means of spiritual practice for you, which is a gift even though they don't intend it as such. Accept their gift: Be compassionate toward them in their blindness.

That's the spirit to maintain whenever anyone hassles you or harms you. That's the spirit the Dalai Lama embodies for his people as they suffer real genocide at the hands of the Chinese government. If he can keep that spirit in those conditions, you can keep it in yours. If someone tells you Buddhism is satanic, don't argue. Just show them that it isn't. Buddha would do exactly the same thing, and so would Jesus. *Be* peace. Turn the other cheek.

Once, when I was talking about Buddhism and Catholicism with a couple of older teens, they described two

I quote Hamlet a couple times there. If you haven't read it yet, you soon will. It's great. Why? Because Hamlet is this totally honest guy dealing with huge family issues. Sometimes he acts loco, but all the time he's asking (in Shakespeare's brilliant language) exactly what the Buddha asked, exactly what you're asking: Who am I? How do I treat people? Where do I fit in?

strategies they use to keep peace between those two religions in their lives. Their approaches might work for you, and they certainly apply to other forms of Christianity and to other religions.

First, one teen told me: "You don't have to denounce Catholicism to be Buddhist. Think of it as going to school. From that perspective, you're just learning things, and they're things from outside the Church." If you can learn from high school, you can learn from Buddhism. Neither one needs to threaten your religion or any religion.

Second, the other student told me: "The way I deal with it is to say to my friend [a devout Catholic] that there is much in common between Buddhism and Christianity. There are underlying principles shared by both religions." This is absolutely true: Buddhism and Catholicism share much more in common than they disagree on. People who tell you otherwise are distorting the truth. You might wonder why—but you don't need to find out.

Troubles don't just come from people; you have "to face the slings and arrows of outrageous fortune." Your life is, and always will be, full of troubles, challenges, and frustrations. This is what the Buddha meant when he said life is dukkha. You need to face these "thousand natural shocks" just as you face your internal troubles and people troubles.

We covered many of these situations in Part Two, but what will you do when you find more we didn't get to? You'll have to improvise. To improvise you'll need to have a kind of spiritual foundation, an inner feeling of strength, knowing you can handle things. Buddhist practices develop that strength, especially practices you do not sitting. This book has given you explanations, insights, advice, stories, and meditations. Now I want to give you something new: a whole variety of practical exercises, exercises that strengthen your spirit, just as other exercises strengthen your body.

PRACTICAL
EXERCISES

    Although there are many crucial practices of
the body, be relaxed and comfortable and stay free.
Everything's covered by that.

    Although there are many crucial practices of
speech, like breathing exercises and reciting mantras,
be quiet and remain mute. Everything's covered by that.

    Although there are many crucial practices of mind,
like concentrating, relaxing, projecting or dissolving it,
and focusing on insight, everything's covered by just
letting it rest naturally free without effort.

PADMASAMBHAVA

All the many forms of Buddhism agree that Buddhism needs to be embodied. You need to try to be a Buddha on a practical level. Even the forms of Buddhism that emphasize meditation say that meditation begins on the cushion, but ends everywhere. They mean you begin meditating in the simplest, easiest fashion, but you try to extend your meditation into your daily life. In the end, your entire life *becomes* a meditation.

Life-as-meditation may be some way down the road, but once you can practice the two meditations I described, you can try some new practices that begin to take you down that road. This is real Buddhism in real life. This is not reading; this is not thinking; this is *doing*. To get you started, here are some exercises I've done. Try them out and see which ones work for you. This is taking a Buddhist path.

 ## praising the buddha

For millions of Buddhists around the world, chanting praise of the Buddha is the primary form of religious practice. Among converts to Buddhism, meditation is more popular, but don't neglect praise. Here's the simplest and most central chant of all:

Namo tassa bhagavato arahato
sammasambuddhassa
(Praise to the blessed, the worthy,
the fully self-awakened)

This phrase is in Pali, the language of the Theravada scriptures, and it's traditional to chant it in that language. You can write down this phrase so you get it right when you chant it. If you have a Buddha image, chant this praise to it. If you don't, don't worry; visualize the Buddha instead. You may want to bow before and after you chant. You can do any kind of bow you like, or none at all. But I encourage you to bow, because it physically expresses what you are verbally expressing in this chant. If you do, try bowing three or even nine times, and do them slowly. Three and nine, traditional Buddhist numbers, put you in the right frame of mind.

When you are ready, look toward the altar or your inner image and chant "Namo tassa bhagavato arahato sammasambuddhassa" three times. It will get easier as you practice; in fact, soon it will roll off your tongue. Let the sound be soft, not harsh. Let the pitch be low, not high. As you chant, let your mind go with it. *Be* praise.

Perhaps you don't feel grateful for a Buddha outside yourself, someone exalted and blessed already. And the fact is, such a Buddha doesn't really need your praise anyway. Look through the words. Give your praise to all that is blessed, worthy, and self-awakened, even your own self. Praise the part of the universe and you that has become awakened to its own nature. That indeed is worthy of praise and support as it strives to grow.

 ## nembutsu

Nembutsu means "name of the Buddha." More specifically, it refers to the repetition of the phrase "Namu Amida Butsu," which means "Praise Amida Buddha." Pure Land Buddhists repeat this to encourage themselves to give up personal focus and rely on the power of Amida Buddha to help them on the path. This particular version of the phrase is Japanese. The Chinese version sounds like "Namo Amito Fo."

Such reliance on a power other than your own may seem in tension with the meditation you've read about here. Perhaps, but tension does not mean contradiction. Tension can be creative. After all, where would we expect to encounter the power of Amida other than in our own success at being better people? In the end, being better is the goal, isn't it?

Try practicing the nembutsu. I often repeat this phrase when I'm driving and I see an animal that has been killed on the road. This use might be new, but it is in harmony with the traditional spirit of the nembutsu, which is often repeated for the benefit of other beings. It is such a quick prayer or chant that you can do it in two seconds.

Repeat the phrase a few times to get used to it. Then keep it in your backpack (so to speak) and take it out when the right moment comes. If you step on a snail, for instance, you may feel queasy and need a bit of strength yourself. Take out that "Namu Amida Butsu," repeat it, and send your sincere hope out into the universe.

When saying the nembutsu, putting your hands in the prayer mudra may help you set your intention to open yourself up to a power greater than your conscious mind. You don't have to understand it; just be open. Even Shinran, a great Japanese Pure Land teacher, wasn't sure whether the practice worked or whether it was the best practice. He just knew it was what he could do, so he did it. You can do it, too.

om mani padme hum

This recitation, done so often in Tibet, means several things. Even the sources explaining the simplicity of this *mantra* (sacred chant) are pretty esoteric themselves. The syllables don't have a literal meaning. The simplest translation that makes sense is "Praise to the Bodhisattva of Compassion." (This Buddha is named Avalokiteshvara in Sanskrit, and Chenrezig in Tibetan.) The bodhisattva of compassion will exist as long as there are living beings to save. Vajrayana Buddhists believe he is presently embodied as the Dalai Lama.

Mantras, or sacred sounds, work best when said correctly. The Sanskrit version should sound like "Ohm Mahnee Pahdmay Hum" for Americans. The Tibetan pronunciation sounds more like "Ohm Mahnee Pehmeh Hung." You may say it either way.

Saying the mantra is another practice you can do anytime, anywhere. You should do it aloud, not just in your head, so unless you're in a crowd of Tibetans, it's easiest to do it someplace where you can be alone. Try it while sitting in your meditation spot. Sit comfortably and take several deep breaths. Let your mind rest and your thoughts flow out with your breaths. Then begin reciting the mantra.

It's not necessary, but it adds to the power of the mantra if you visualize Avalokiteshvara as you recite, so it may help to close your eyes for this practice. You might visualize the bodhisattva of compassion outside or inside your own body as you recite the mantra. In any case, the bodhisattva's heart is surrounded by the mantra and radiates light in all ten directions—in other words, everywhere. There are pictures of the bodhisattva online that are better than any description I can give you. Do a search. For now, you can visualize the Dalai Lama or try just visualizing the words spinning around your own heart and their light radiating out through space. Using yourself makes sense because chanting this mantra is believed to remove impurities from you as you do it. In the end, we become bodhisattvas ourselves.

 ## bowing

When you bow to the Buddha, what are you really doing? Who are you really bowing to? Buddhist bowing disturbs some people because they think it's bowing to a god, a person, or even an idol. You know who the historical Buddha was, but bowing to the Buddha is not bowing to that person, to God, or to anything at all outside yourself. Bowing to the Buddha is bowing to awakening itself, the universe's true nature, which you yourself share.

The simplest Buddhist bow is to put your hands together in the prayer *mudra* (position), palms and fingers touching, fingertips in front of your chin. Now bend from your waist. You are bowing.

More beautiful is the full bow, where one touches the floor. If you have a Buddha image, or bow in a temple, or just feel like it, it is appropriate to bow this way. There are many variations; I'll describe the Zen style. First, bow as above, but then bend your knees and drop them to the floor so you're kneeling. Now sit down on your legs and lean forward so your head comes toward the ground. As you do, separate

your hands so your arms point forward and let them rest on the ground from the elbows on, with your palms facing up. Lower your head all the way and let your forehead touch the ground. As you do this, raise your palms a few inches into the air, a gesture that symbolizes raising the Buddha above your individual self.

The sequence is very smooth and easy once you've practiced it. More important, though, is practicing the idea of bowing to the Buddha, to the future, to something greater than yourself.

 ### *kinhin*

Perhaps you envision meditation as something completely peaceful and still. Not always. Meditation is a tool for calming and concentrating the mind any time, any place. Sitting meditation comes first because it's easiest, but there are other kinds. One of the most important is walking. Now that you've tried sitting, try *kinhin*, a Zen form of walking meditation.

Sit down and begin meditation as you've learned to do. After five minutes or so, when you feel you are calm, slowly stand up. If your legs are asleep, uncross them and let them wake up first. Falling down is not usually a good form of meditation!

Once you're upright, place your hands close in front of your chest, with your left hand in a fist and your right hand resting on it, your right palm and fingers covering your left fingers and back of your hand. Let your elbows stick out naturally. Keeping your eyes half open or a bit more, begin to walk around the room—very, very slowly.

The object is awareness. Be aware of the complexity of movement in simple walking. When the weight transfers from your trailing leg, the heel of your leading leg touches the ground, your weight comes down on this leg, the ball of your foot and toes lower, you press down on this leg and prepare to lift your trailing leg. Then you balance on the leading leg, bend the knee of your trailing leg, lift that heel, and swing it forward into the air. You're committed then; you're falling, and the ground is there to catch you every time. Each step is like this: trust and embrace, your balance, your foot, the ground, gravity, a dance.

Don't think about it, just experience it. You will find not thinking about it very difficult at first. You may take pride in your movement when it's smooth and graceful. If you're beaming with pride or thinking too much, remember that you're just walking—no reason to get puffed up. Relax your thoughts and let your mind calm down.

If you can manage this slow kinhin, try speeding it up, letting your arms relax and swing normally. Try doing kinhin

outside. Eventually you'll be able to bring kinhin awareness into normal walking. It's the first step toward bringing meditation into your whole active life.

fast walking meditation

In Japan kinhin is done *really fast*. It must feel good after a long session of sitting meditation. You're probably not doing whole days of meditation like Zen monks do, but you might want to try this during finals time or some other time you've been sitting too long and need action.

The meditation techniques we've talked about so far are usually done indoors. For fast walking meditation, it's best to have a large space to walk in. Unless you live in a big house, it will be easier to practice outside. The back yard is often good, since you won't run into anyone there, and no cars will run into you. Plan your route before you start the meditation. Walking around the perimeter of the yard is good. Try to stay on flat ground.

Sit in meditation for a few minutes until you can follow or count your breath without getting lost too often. Stand slowly. You can take the same posture as in kinhin, or you can let your arms hang normally at your sides. It is a bit harder to do with arms hanging because they'll begin to swing. Don't let it bother you, just let it happen naturally. Next, start walking. Keep your eyes half open so that you can see where you're going, but don't focus on any one thing. Don't risk tripping and falling over, just don't get hung up on what is in your field of vision.

Start slowly for a few breaths. Once you're moving and able to return your mind to breathing, you can pick up your speed to a normal-to-brisk pace. Remember, you are still meditating. You may be tempted to start thinking, to look around, even to stop at an interesting place such as the fridge or the basketball hoop. These are thoughts. Don't follow them. Let them fall away. Return your mind to meditation. Tougher here, isn't it? You are expanding your meditation farther into your life. You can practice fast walking meditation anytime you walk.

grace

And now for something completely different. We've mostly dealt with difficult stuff in this book. What about good stuff, like food? Hey, be happy! Here's a way to express that happiness: a Buddhist way to say grace.

In the Christian tradition, grace is the free giving of God to the world. It's also what Christians call the thanks given to God for one of God's gifts, food. Grace goes both ways. Buddhists, too, give back gratitude to the world for its gifts. Here's my version of the thanks given before everyday Zen meals:

> We give praise to the Three Treasures
> and are grateful for this meal.
> Innumerable labors bring it to us,
> the gift of other living beings.

Alone or even for your family, say this blessing or make up one of your own and extend your grace to the labors and lives that come to you in the form of food. As you speak, bring to mind the web of life we are one strand of, the web that sustains us, the web we are unraveling. Apart from that web, no food, no you.

 ## mindful eating

This exercise can be surprisingly intense. Begin by choosing a meal when you'll do this practice. It is best to choose a meal when you'll be alone because you'll find sensory mindfulness so much easier to do in silence. Choose what you'll be eating, perhaps fixing yourself a sandwich. You don't want to have to plan or decide much during the meal.

Start being mindful with the preparations. For instance, when you open the refrigerator, what do you feel? Notice the astonishing array of things in that fridge. Pick your ingredients. Feel their weight. How do they smell as you open them? If you're slicing something, just slice it. Don't think ahead, no need, this is easy. Just do what you're doing. Feel the change in the knife as it cuts through a tomato. Look at the fantastic patterns in the lettuce. There is so much to notice. Let it in.

As you eat, use all your senses. How does the food feel as you chew? Can you smell your soda? Can you hear it? Do you appreciate the burn as it goes down your throat? Are you seeing your food or looking away? Do you feel the weight of the food in your stomach? When are you full? Do you keep eating after that?

Look inside as well. Are you feeling desire? When do you expect to feel pleasure? Later, do you feel that pleasure? Does it come when you expected it? Do you feel greed for your food? Do you feel you need to finish it? Are you grateful? There is so much to learn from the simplest meal.

mindful driving

Teens die on the road all the time. So do adults, but teens are in even greater danger. Here's a meditation that might help you understand why.

Try an awareness meditation while you drive. You'll need to do it when you're driving alone or when no one expects you to talk to them. It is vastly easier to do in a quiet car. Turn off the music. Sit up straight but comfortably and hold the wheel with both hands (like you're supposed to). Drive within the speed limit, and let go of your thoughts other than those arising from the immediate experience of driving.

Observe what you see and hear and feel. Don't dwell on any one thing; move on to the next. Notice the *unbelievable bunch of stuff happening*. Driving is one of the most engaging, dangerous, fast-paced things you'll ever do. Yet most drivers normally only halfway pay attention to it, which is insane.

Let your mind fill with the actual, "right now" experience of just driving. Amazing intensity: the texture of the road's shoulder, the speed of oncoming vehicles, the sensuous vibration of the tires. It's like a video game—*but it's real*. When you truly concentrate on driving, the speed limit is as fast as you can handle. It's plenty. Mindful driving is the same as good driving. No time for talk or music, and no need for them, either.

Driving meditation gives you an unexpected gift: the beauty of the road. You'll find yourself noticing the color of flowers, the character of a building, smoke from a chimney, who knows. What surrounds you every day is overwhelming, and when you're driving, it comes that much quicker. Last time I did this, I got an extra bonus: I had the joyful view of a cop passing me on a lonely road at night *when I wasn't speeding*. Now *that* is traffic school!

beginning metta practice

Metta means "loving-kindness." It's a state of mind based on compassion in which you radiate good thoughts for others. Ideally, we humans would remain like this all the time. Realistically, we need practice. Here is a first step.

Sit down in whatever meditative posture feels good to you. In this meditation especially, be kind to yourself, be comfortable. Take several slow, deep breaths and let your outside concerns fall away. When you are able to follow the breath, begin to repeat to yourself, silently,

> May I be free from hatred
> May I be mentally happy
> May I be physically healthy
> May I live in peace.

If you want something shorter, just repeat "May I live in peace." Let a sense of metta toward yourself fill your mind. It is an emotion more than a thought. It is a state of mind more than an emotion. Let metta fill your meditation for as long as you can sustain it easily. Don't press yourself too hard. Remember, you are being kind to yourself. When you are ready, take a few quiet breaths and come out of meditation.

This is the beginning of compassion, the foundation of love. Let it fill you with energy. You must be kind to yourself to sustain kindness to others. Go ahead.

extending metta practice to others

After you've set the foundation of metta practice by sending metta to yourself, take the next step: Send it to someone else.

The classic instructions wisely say to try sending metta first to someone you feel extremely positive about, someone you love and respect. Pick the person you feel strong love or respect for and have minimum conflict with. It might be a parent, teacher, coach, or religious figure. It is best to have this person not be sexually attractive to you, so you don't mix metta with desire. Don't worry about the choice. Just choose a person and try the exercise. If you find yourself conflicted, start again with a different person.

Begin as you did with the first metta exercise. When you can follow your breath, silently start repeating to yourself the metta recitation you did then. When you feel a real sense of metta toward yourself, you are ready to extend it to another. Now change the "I" in your phrase to the person's name. Thus,

> May (name) be free from hatred
> May (name) be mentally happy
> May (name) be physically healthy
> May (name) live in peace.

Feel the same positive, supportive feelings you beamed to yourself; simply send them to the person. Visualizing that person in your mind might help, but the meditation is not about visualization; it is about sending metta. Try to keep your concentration on the feeling itself. Repeat it as long as you can sustain your metta easily. When you're ready, let your mind quiet and come out of meditation.

You may find this *easier* than sending the metta to yourself. I do. It's a sign that you have plenty of metta to go around. Good. Send it on.

extending metta practice further

Now that you've sent metta to yourself and a loved one, how about trying something harder? Send metta to a neutral person you don't really care much about.

Begin as you did with the first metta exercises. When you can follow your breath, start repeating to yourself, silently, the metta recitation. When you feel metta toward yourself, extend it to a loved one, changing your silent phrases accordingly. Then, when you again feel the same positive and supportive feelings, send them to that person you feel neutral about, again changing your phrases to incorporate his or her name. Continue the repetition as long as you can sustain your metta easily. When you are ready, let the mind quiet and come out of meditation.

This time you may find it more difficult. It is harder to feel unbounded good will for someone you just don't care about. But if you practice metta, you will find yourself starting to care, at least for the time you're practicing. You'll eventually be able to do this meditation in places that might otherwise fill you with frustration or dislike—airports or Department of Motor Vehicles offices, for instance. You can change the phrases to apply to "everyone here." You'll feel better, and it can't hurt the people around you, either.

taking metta to the limit

The most difficult place to take metta is to people you dislike or even hate. This meditation will help you dissolve that hatred, which is a poison for you just as much as for them. No one says you must like your enemies, but Buddha teaches that hating them destroys you.

Begin as you did with the other metta exercises. When you can follow your breath, start silently repeating to yourself the metta recitation. When you feel metta toward yourself, extend it to a loved one, changing your silent phrases accordingly. When you again feel metta, send it to a neutral person, again changing your phrases appropriately. Finally, when you feel the same positive and supportive feelings for the neutral person, extend your metta to a person you actually dislike. It may help to visualize that person as a small child whom you love as a parent. Continue the repetition as long as you can sustain your metta easily. Don't worry if this is not very long. When you are ready, let the mind quiet and come out of meditation.

This is of course the most difficult metta practice. You may feel that reciting "May (hateful person's name) live in peace" is giving an advantage to your enemy. Perhaps so: It gives them the advantage of an end to hatred. In fact, that advantage extends to you as well. If this practice wears you down, don't do it. After a metta meditation you should feel strengthened, not depleted. If you don't feel genuine metta as you practice with a person you dislike—or any person, for that matter—go back to directing the phrases to yourself for a time. Don't be in a rush. You have a lifetime to perfect your metta.

intoxicants

Don't get me wrong, I am not saying young people should take mind-altering substances. A couple things I do know: doing so is illegal, tied to a harmful money trail, and potentially harmful to selves and others. Still, people are going to do it; minds want to be altered. Buddhism is a mind-altering substance, too, so I also know that altering the mind is not a bad thing if done with awareness. If you're doing drugs, even alcohol, at least do them with awareness.

Whether you're drinking or getting high or whatever, be mindful of your mind. Let part of your mind ask these questions and witness the answers. How do you feel before doing this drug? Are you anxious? Are you doing it for you or others? Do you feel in control of your thoughts? Are you nervous while taking the drug? Are you excited? Are you impatient? What is lacking in your mind that makes you want to change it?

When you are high, are you in control of your thoughts? How have they changed? Is your sense of self different? If so, what *is* your self? Are you a different person when you're high? If so, do you like this new person and what he or she does? Look at who you're with. Do you like them and what they are doing?

Altering your mind with drugs can be a bit like meditation: If you look inside, you can open yourself up to places
you didn't know were there. But not everything about you is
good, so be ready for those places, good or bad. Be alone and
safe or be with friends—real friends—and safe. Don't judge
yourself too much, and don't hide from your own size: You
are large; you contain multitudes.

 ## fantasy

Like the practice with drugs, this is not a meditation. It is a mental exercise informed by Buddhism.
It's one everyone can do because everyone fantasizes. Sexual
fantasy is one of the most common kinds, but it works with
other fantasies as well. Fantasy is an active part of sexual life.
In Buddhism it's the mental part of sex that really matters, so
fantasy is a fundamental part of your sex life.

When you notice yourself fantasizing, remain mindful
of it. Are your fantasies realistic? Is it pleasurable to fantasize,
or do you feel the pleasure will only be in making the fantasy
real? What if that never happens? How does your fantasy fit
in with the Four Noble Truths, with desire and dukkha?

Is your fantasy romantic, physical, or both? If not both,
do you feel that it is incomplete in any way? After a fantasy,
however long or short, do you feel good or cheap or excited

or depressed? Do you feel you were wasting time or experimenting with the future?

Ask these questions of yourself during and after the fantasy. Don't stop fantasizing, and don't judge your fantasy. Let it happen, but try to ask the questions with part of your mind. Fantasy teaches us much about our lives. Buddhism teaches that we are all asleep and our lives are like fantasies. It also teaches that thoughts change reality. The Sutta Nipata says, "The world is led around by mind." So learn your mind and let your fantasy lead you well.

 ## death

This (the exercise, I mean) is not for everyone. Do it only if you feel like it and have someone to talk to afterward if you need to.

Sit comfortably in meditation. Begin following your breaths. Don't count, simply follow. Try to be conscious of your breath as life itself. Feel your breath; it *is* life itself. When breath stops, death begins. Now imagine that this series of breaths is your last. Feel the space between your breaths. After you've breathed out, everything slows down. Rest in that space. Lengthen that space. Feel the slowing. Imagine it continuing. Imagine your very last breath.

It will happen eventually. Are you ready? Imagine that your last breath is here. Feel the slowing lengthen and death begin. Feel your answer to the question: Are you ready? What comes to mind? Observe your emotions and thoughts. Is there struggle or fear? When you are calm—or, more likely, when you can't stand it anymore—let the thoughts go. Follow the breath. Come gently out of meditation.

Then think about your answers. If you weren't ready to die, what taught you that? What do you still "need" to do? What are you actually doing to get there?

bring a friend

Do a simple meditation—the one you feel you can share most easily with a friend—and do it with that friend. Don't do anything fancy; I recommend the simplest sitting meditation. Don't play guru, just share the experience.

Plan on an hour for this. You'll need fifteen minutes or so to settle down and teach the basics of the meditation to your friend. Then you'll need ten or fifteen minutes for the meditation, then twenty or thirty minutes more to talk about it and get back your regular life. You can face each other, but that can be distracting. It's easier to face apart or face the wall.

During the sharing, try to be equal. You are both beginners. Your friend may be curious or bored or worried or enthusiastic. They may love this or hate it. Let them have their feelings. Meditation is not about judging. Neither is Buddhism. Really listen to your friend. This is a great chance to learn from another person whose questions may help you focus your own. It is also a chance to share something real with a friend. As the Buddha said, that's the whole of the spiritual path.

FARTHER DOWN
THE PATH

You're now about done with this book. I hope you'll come back to it to refresh yourself by looking back at Buddhist principles and practices that help you. This is just a beginning, of course, yet it points the way far beyond where it must leave off. Every issue raised in this book applies to every person who tries to incorporate Buddhism into his or her life. We are all walking the path together, and both we and the path continue endlessly.

> A new monk came to Teacher Xuansha and asked where he could enter the truth of the teachings. Xuansha said, "Do you hear the sound of the local stream?" The monk said yes. Xuansha said "Enter there."
>
> ZEN TEACHER XUANSHA

APPENDIX

MANY PATHS, FURTHER EXPLORATIONS

One who sits on top of a hundred-foot pole
may have realized something, but not full reality.
On top of a hundred-foot pole, one must step
forward to manifest the whole body everywhere.

WUMENGUAN

Having read this book you're a bit like the person on top of the hundred-foot pole. You've gotten somewhere, but you'll probably want to step forward eventually. That can be scary, so I've created this appendix of many sources for your own exploration of Buddhism. I lay out the territory so you can find your own path. If you begin from these sources, your path will be rooted in Buddhism, yet your path will remain uniquely your own journey. This is what I mean by "many paths." There are many journeys to be made. I hope these sources deepen yours.

All the following sources carry my personal recommendation. I have checked them and from what I see they teach the dharma. Not every one will speak to you, though, nor have I read every page of every source. As the Buddha taught: Try them out and see what works for you. Don't worry about the rest.

a book about the buddha (and more)

There are many versions of the Buddha's life available on the net, but they are all relatively short and most come from the particular perspective of one or another Buddhist school. You can start with any one, but if you want to really learn something about the Buddha, his world, and his teaching, check out Karen Armstrong's *Buddha* (Penguin, 2001). Ms. Armstrong carefully works through the details of the Buddha's life, separating fact from myth (as much as possible). Doing so, she also provides an introduction—a good one—to the Buddha's teachings. Her book is the best current foundation for those of you who want to begin your exploration of Buddhism from the perspective of history.

After the death of the Buddha, things become more complex and books reflect this. For histories of Buddhism, you have two choices. You can read histories of the various branches of Buddhism written by scholars, or those written by the branches themselves. For the basics, from a scholarly perspective, I recommend the articles in the *Encyclopedia of Religion* (Macmillan, 1989). These will probably tell you all you want to know, but if you want more they all have bibliographies. Since there are too many articles to list, I'll leave it to you to check the index. Everything important is there and you can look things up by tradition, by country, by important figures, by practices, by concepts, etc. Your local college or city library should have a copy of this encyclopedia.

books about the dharma

More likely you're less interested in books that tell you the history of Buddhism and more interested in books that tell you the teachings of Buddhism. If so, there are dozens of excellent ones on all aspects of Buddhism's teachings and practices. I'll recommend a few, covering each of the three major traditions of Buddhism (and a couple of other important topics).

First, for a focus on the basics of Buddhism—the practice of mindfulness right now—please read Steve Hagen's *Buddhism Plain and Simple* (Tuttle, 1997). Hagen cuts away the overgrowth and reveals the simplicity of the Buddha's insight and path. For an immersion in the harmonious stew of Buddhism, you cannot beat Roger Corless' *The Vision of Buddhism* (Paragon House, 1989). A scholar and a Buddhist, Corless is careful and informed, but frees the tradition from the dryness of academic models. He sees it for what it is, in all its variety and wonder. This is a delightful place to begin further exploration. And, for a thorough but fun drive-by of Buddhist history and practice, Gary Gach's *Complete Idiot's Guide to Understanding Buddhism* (Alpha, 2002) makes a good read and a good resource.

The Theravada Buddhist path is well-summed up in Bhante Henepola Gunaratana's *Eight Mindful Steps to Happiness* (Wisdom, 2001). Here Bhante (that means "venerable monk") Gunaratana lays out the whole Eightfold Path from a Theravada perspective. Clear and balanced. The monk Walpola Rahula's classic *What the Buddha Taught* (Grove Press, 1959) still gives a fine introduction to the core Theravada teachings. As a contrast, you might want to look at a contemporary book by someone specializing in vipassana (insight) meditation. Ayya Khema has written several, including her classic, *Being Nobody, Going Nowhere* (Wisdom, 1987). Look also for books by Sharon Salzberg, Jack Kornfield, and Sylvia Boorstein; they're all good.

Mahayana Buddhism is so complex and varied, no one book can fully describe it. Still, here are two books I can wholeheartedly recommend. First, I love Taigen Daniel Leighton's *Bodhisattva Archetypes* (Penguin Arkana, 1998). Leighton, who is both a scholar and a Zen teacher, guides us through the rich world of Mahayana bodhisattvas, their virtues, and the practices associated with them. In so doing, he brings Mahayana to life and into our lives in a way no one else quite does. If you really want to get into the details of the development of Mahayana and the subtleties of its myriad doctrines, get a copy of *Mahayana Buddhism* by Paul Williams (Routledge, 1989). If you want more than Williams gives you, you'll have to get a Ph.D.

On Vajrayana Buddhism (also sometimes known as Mantrayana Buddhism, Tantric Buddhism, or Tibetan Buddhism), a nice starting place is the work of His Holiness the Dalai Lama (HHDL for short), the foremost spiritual leader of all Tibetan

Buddhists and one of the most respected people in the entire world. HHDL has written many books now, on his tradition, on the psychology of Buddhism, on being happy, etc. From the early classic, *Kindness, Clarity, and Insight* (Snow Lion, 1984), to the new *How to Practice* (Pocket Books, 2001), all HHDL's works are filled with lucid wisdom and genuine compassion. For deeper exploration of the Tibetan tradition, dip into John Powers' *Introduction to Tibetan Buddhism* (Snow Lion, 1995). It's complex, but it really answers your questions. Finally, for a treatment of the Vajrayana approach to both life and death, read Sogyal Rinpoche's *The Tibetan Book of Living and Dying* (HarperCollins, 1992).

Since my own field is Zen Buddhism, I can't help mentioning a couple of Zen books for you. I find Robert Aitken's *Taking the Path of Zen* (North Point Press, 1982) a lovely and practical introduction to doing Zen yourself. Aitken, an American Zen teacher, writes with uncommon dignity and clarity in this book and his others, all of which are worth reading. For the ideas and history of Zen, I recommend going right to the collections of Zen texts; try the Wumenguan first. For a very honest and powerful view of Zen practice, read Shunryu Suzuki's *Zen Mind, Beginner's Mind* (Weatherhill, 1970). This book has rightfully become a Buddhist classic, especially for people just starting practice.

Finally, though they don't constitute a school of Buddhism, women are playing an unprecedented role in contemporary Buddhist practice. Their new roles raise new questions for the religion and for every Buddhist practitioner. An excellent introduction to women's roles in contemporary Buddhism is *Buddhist Women on the Edge*, edited by Marianne Dresser (North Atlantic Books,

1996). A good treatment of the history and prospects for Buddhism's relationship with women is *Buddhism after Patriarchy*, by Rita Gross (SUNY Press, 1996).

buddhist texts

Buddhist sacred writings have been translated and collected many, many times. Your local library will have at least a couple of these collections, perhaps more. These writings, especially the sutras (the teachings of the Buddha), are the taproot of Buddhist wisdom, reaching back to the Buddha himself. This makes them the most important reading you can do on Buddhism. There are so many of them, you may feel bewildered. Here are a few recommendations.

The basic Theravada texts are contained in collections called Nikayas. Libraries may have these, hopefully in the recent translations published by Wisdom Publications. Try to find these, since they are so much easier to read than the old versions. Another wonderful Theravada text is the Dhammapada. It's part of one of the Nikayas, but you can find it on its own. Because it's all short sayings and verses, it's fun to read; a perfect start. It's also the easiest Theravada text to find.

Many of the most important sutras from the Pali Canon are online at www.accesstoinsight.org/canon. These writings are absolutely central to Theravada Buddhism, but they're vital to Mahayana and Vajrayana Buddhism as well. Not only that, this site gives you many other writings, commentaries, explanations, and search engines. It is *the* place to begin a serious exploration of Buddhist texts.

Access to Insight is wonderful for Theravada texts, but it is strictly Theravada. There are no Mahayana texts there. For Mahayana texts, there is no one comparable url, nor are there standard collections in print (like the Nikayas). You have to look for different sutras. To begin, look for these and see how you like them: the Lotus Sutra and Vimalakirti Sutra (especially in Burton Watson's translations); Shantideva's beautiful *Way of the Bodhisattva*; the *Tannisho*, by Shinran; the *Record of Lin-chi* (translated by Watson again); and *Moon in a Dewdrop*, by Dogen (collected by Kazuaki Tanahashi). These are just a bare beginning, but they are among my own favorites.

In addition to single sutras, you can find excellent anthologies of Buddhist texts across the whole spectrum of the tradition. Other collections focus on one school or another and so can give you more depth. When you find a school that you like, definitely seek out its texts. This is best done at a library or a truly good bookstore where you can look through books before buying them. Over time you'll find the kind of texts that speak to you. It's a journey of discovery.

zen autobiographies

Dozens of people who discovered Buddhism as adults have written autobiographies of their experience. For some reason, most of these seem to be by Zen students. Some are best after you've learned more about Buddhism; some make wonderful introductions to Buddhism at the same time as they entertain you with real stories. My favorite of these is the story of Janwillem van de Wetering, a Dutch man who goes to Japan to live in a Zen monastery, then comes to

America. He's written three books and all of them are laced with his ironic humor and his great honesty. He punctures nearly all the inflated Zen myths you may have heard. Start with his first; it's called *The Empty Mirror*. The other two are *A Glimpse of Nothingness* and *Afterzen*. St. Martin's Press has recent editions in paperback.

Here are three other good ones: I loved reading David Chadwick's extremely funny account of his time in Japan, studying and working, called *Thank You and OK!* (Penguin Arkana, 1994). Peter Matthiessen's *Nine-Headed Dragon River* (Shambhala, 1985) is great and critical, but a bit advanced; read another Zen book first. Alan Lew's *One God Clapping* (Kodansha, 1999) is the embracing story of a Zen student rabbi. Yes, you can be a rabbi or a Catholic priest or nun, or whatever, and still be a Zen teacher.

books especially for you

If you liked this book, you will surely like and learn from two other recent books written by and for young Buddhists. First, *Blue Jean Buddha*, edited by Sumi Lounden (Wisdom Publications, 2000), is a collection of stories by Gen X Buddhists about their experiences growing up or becoming or trying to grow as Buddhists. By the time you read this, a new volume may be out, about actual teenage Buddhists. How bad could that be?

Whatever your practice, I highly recommend Soren Gordhamer's *Just Say Om!* (Adams Media, 2001). Gordhamer, using his own experiences, gives you a really down-to-earth guide to Buddhist practice and life in general for teenagers. It's a great companion to this book. I especially like the way Gordhamer helps you through problems in meditation but also with big questions. Check it out.

buddhist websites

Here are five superior starting sites for exploring the Buddhist web:

www.ciolek.com/WWWVL-Buddhism.html
Dr. Ciolek's site has a serious flavor. Excellent for linking to history and texts. No graphics, so really good for slow connections.

www.dharmanet.org
Like Dr. Ciolek's site, this has a more analytical quality, and thus excellent links to a huge range of study sites. Great for learning about various forms of Buddhism and their history. This site has the best links to meditation centers in the U.S.

www.buddhanet.net
This one has a Theravada emphasis, is best for non-U.S. readers, annotates links nicely, and organizes itself more around practices and traditions. Great for learning about Theravada traditions, including many forms of meditation.

www.tricycle.com
This site is the online presence of the slick-but-good Buddhist magazine, *Tricycle*. It looks much better than the other sites, lets you search for dharma centers, read past

articles and interviews, and, most importantly, has an extensive teaching section, introducing many aspects of Buddhism and Buddhist practice. Very open and balanced.

www.beliefnet.com

Look up Buddhism here for a lively collection of all sorts of things. Good interactive staff here—plus those other religions you may be curious about.

You'll see, from hitting those sites, that there are more Buddhist websites than the mind can conceive. This is wonderful if you're far from a library or temple. It's also wonderful because you can sample Buddhism on your own, without making a big production out of it.

Thousands and tens of thousands of Buddhist centers, temples, lineages, and followers have websites. Among all these sites you will find cool ones, informative ones, weird ones, pretty ones, all sorts. These sites are not organized; you just have to explore to find them. To give you an idea of how different these sites can be, here are just a few I like. Remember, these are just a taste. Go find your own, after all, there are many paths. . . .

www.accesstoinsight.org

I mentioned this one already. The great source for Theravada scripture. It also has good meditation instructions.

www.buddhajones.com

This is the funniest Buddhist site I've ever seen. Provocative, visual, topical, excellent.

www.kagyu.org

Here's an excellent Vajrayana site. It gives good background
and an especially detailed introduction to meditation
practices.

www.robertaitken.net

This is the site for Robert Aitken Roshi, an elder statesman
of American Zen. It includes many of his talks and writings
and gives the flavor of this feisty and venerable teacher.

www.bpf.org

This is the Buddhist Peace Fellowship, a group devoted
to decreasing dukkha in this world through national and
international programs for peace. They are the good guys.

www.syzenart.com

Here's the site for the art of Song Yoon, the Korean monk
who did the paintings in this book. See them online in living
color. Beautiful and true!

www.buddhainyourbackpack.net

It's the site for this book, where you'll find more stuff you
can use to make your life happier: articles on teen Buddhism,
new bits by me, links to especially happening sites, etc. Plus I
hope you'll hit the site to talk with other teens interested in
Buddhism and to ask me more questions about your life and
practice. Come on down.

sanghas where you live

Since I don't know where you are, I can't recommend any Buddhist temple or center in your area. Even if I did know, there are now literally thousands of places to choose from just in the U.S. With so many choices, you really need to decide for yourself what kind of Buddhism might be right for you.

If you would like to visit a Buddhist temple or meditation center, here are some suggestions:

1) Look up your area using the directories at buddhanet.net and dharmanet.org. See what you have to choose from. If you live in a large city, you may have two or three or even ten or twelve choices from different Buddhist traditions. Go to their websites. Get a feeling for them. Email them and see when they welcome visitors. If you visit, be prepared to be honest and to ask questions.

2) Check out "Buddhist" under "Churches" in your local Yellow Pages. Sounds strange, I know, but many Buddhist organizations list their numbers there. Before the net, this was the only easy way to let people know your center existed. Call several places, tell them you're interested, and see how they respond. If you are honest, you deserve honesty in return. If they give it to you, they're worth visiting.

3) To help you get a feeling for the sort of Buddhism that interests you most, look through *How the Swans Came to the Lake* (third revised edition, Shambhala, 1992) by Rick

Fields. Fields provides a vivid history of Buddhism in America and so lays out the landscape of Buddhism as we find it in America and elsewhere outside Asia. His book tells human stories and can help you find a school or tradition that works for you.

4) Think about joining the Teen Buddhist Sangha. They're a great group. They're supportive, yet there's no pressure since it's online-only. They helped me with the book, but more importantly they help each other with their practice and their lives. Members come from many different Buddhist traditions all over the world and I know they're in your area, since they're as close as your keyboard.

Go to http://members.aol.com/_ht_a/Howky523/index.htm, where you can learn about the group and follow the instructions to join if you think it's for you.

Once more: These suggestions are just first steps. Not only can't I show you the whole path, I don't *want* to show you the whole path. I want you to find your own, whether it's Buddhist or not. I wish you well!

WHERE THE QUOTES COME FROM

Here are references for the quotes you've read in this book. I give you these so you can track down the one you enjoyed and read more.

In the following, classical Buddhist texts have no quotes or italics around them. These texts were listed by title in the book and all of them are traditionally attributed to the Buddha. Buddhist works with single known authors were listed by author's name in the book; here they have quotes around their titles.

introduction

p. xi   The epigram on the way is from Dogen Zenji's "Genjo Koan" ("Realizing the Koan"). Dogen is the greatest thinker in the history of Zen Buddhism; this short talk beautifully expresses his provocative thought. Tough but worth any time you give it.

p. xiii   The Buddha's advice to his students for after his death comes from chapter 6 of the Mahaparinibbana Sutta, which forms section 16 of the Digha Nikaya. That sutta (means the same at sutra) describes the last weeks of the Buddha's life. The Digha Nikaya is one of the great collections of the Buddha's teaching collected in the Pali Canon, the sacred scriptures of Theravada Buddhism. These scriptures are also shared by Mahayana Buddhists.

p. xxii   The Zen quote on being free and real is from section 14 of "The Record of Linji," the amazing collection of his talks and stories from Zen Teacher Linji's life. Linji (also spelled Lin-chi) and Dogen are my favorite Zen writers, for totally different reasons. Linji pulls no punches; he's totally honest that he has nothing to teach. You've got to love that.

p. xxii   You can find Catherine D.'s quote at http://TeenInk.com/Past/2002/May/WhatMatters/Headlines.html in her piece called "Headlines."

part one

p. 1   The epigram on Buddha, dharma, and path comes from section 20 of "The Record of Linji." This is about as clear as he can make it for us.

p. 18   The exclamation of the Buddha on awakening is from the Dhammapada, verse 154. If you've never read a Buddhist text, I suggest starting with the Dhammapada. It is indispensable.

p. 23   The first epigram for "What Is Buddhism?" comes from the "Genjo Koan," by Dogen.

p. 23   The second epigram comes from section 11 of The Perfection of Wisdom in 18,000 Lines, an early and fundamental Mahayana sutra.

p. 25   The "take-no-prisoners" quote is from the Udanavarga, an early Theravada sutta, section 1.22.

p. 25   The quote on things decaying comes from the Digha Nikaya, section 16.6. There we find the Buddha's last words: "All component things decay. Keep striving mindfully."

p. 30   The conversation between Alice and Tweedledum is naturally not a Buddhist text at all; it's from *Through the Looking-Glass*, by Lewis Carroll. But perhaps we could call it a Buddhist text; it just didn't happen to be *written* by a Buddhist. Anyone who questions what the self and the world are can learn from Lewis Carroll.

p. 33   The convoluted set of questions on existence is from sutta two in the Majjhima Nikaya, another of the great collections of suttas in the Pali canon.

p. 43 The Buddha's description of the path is from the Samyutta Nikaya, section LVI.11. The Samyutta Nikaya is yet another of the great collections of suttas in the Pali canon.

part two

p. 49 The epigram is from "The Record of Layman Pang," a Chinese Chan (same as Japanese Zen) lay person who stayed in the everyday world but was just as awake as any Zen teacher.

p. 51 The quote on young people and parents is from the Digha Nikaya, section 31, the Sigalavada Sutta, a piece sometimes called the Buddhist guide to ethics for householders—everyone who's not a monk or nun.

p. 70 Nichiren's quote on parents paying attention to the sick child is from his short essay, "Winter Always Turns to Spring." He was a firebrand, a wild and prophetic Japanese monk, but he knew human nature.

p. 75 That intense quote on killing comes from "The Record of Linji," section 19. Linji's words have freaked out non-Zen people for a thousand years. You know better.

p. 77 The quote on the teacher is from Wumenguan 12. That's case (or chapter) 12 from the collection Wumenguan (usually translated as *The Gateless Gate*). This is one of the major collections of Zen stories. You can find it in many translations. Very alive!

p. 79   That saying about the axe in your mouth is from the Sutta Nipata, verse 657. The Sutta Nipata is one of the earliest collected sets of teachings by the Buddha, and so likely is one of the most reflective of what the Buddha really taught

p. 81   The text on when to speak is not quite a quote, but a paraphrase from sutta 58 of the Majjhima Nikaya.

p. 85   The quote on being with good or evil people comes from the Itivuttaka, verse 76. This collection is another one of the earliest in the Pali canon.

p. 91   Dogen's quote on boredom is from "Gakudo Yohin-shu" ("Guidelines for Studying the Way"), a great little essay on how to orient yourself in sincere Zen practice.

p. 95   That kickass quote on pissing and eating and sleeping is from section 13 of the "The Record of Linji," by that good ol' irascible Zen teacher.

p. 104 The quote on the clean, pure body is from section 19 of the "The Record of Linji." Can you tell I think he's great?

p. 106 The *gatha* (verse) on porridge is the version chanted by the Diamond Sangha, a Zen Buddhist group with centers all over the world.

p. 107 The quote from the Japanese Zen Teacher Bankei on eating and sleeping is from a story about him. Many of the greatest sayings in the Zen tradition are passed down in stories.

p. 108 The quote from Linji on the Buddha body is from section 19 of "The Record of Linji." Where else?

p. 109 The quote on attention comes from the Dhammapada, verse 21.

p. 112 The conversation between Alice and the caterpillar is from *Alice in Wonderland*, by Lewis Carroll, another Buddhist text by that great non-Buddhist.

p. 113 As if you didn't know, the verse on mind that opens the Dhammapada is from the Dhammapada, verse one!

p. 115 The quote on sex and passion is from the Hevajra Tantra, section 1.9. This is a Tibetan text teaching the path of using desire to defeat desire. A powerful practice, but a difficult and dangerous one as well. This is *not* something to try to practice, maybe even understand, on your own.

p. 116 The quote on leaving delight and pain behind is from the Dhammapada, verse 418.

p. 116 The opposing quote, on indulging the senses, is from section 24 of the "Dohakosha" by Saraha, a legendary Tibetan tantric teacher. Indulge your senses, yes, but only when you're simultaneously following a moral path.

p. 130 The quote on other living things being your mother is from the Samyutta Nikaya, section XV.14. Other Buddhist sources echo this idea. Lovely thought, isn't it?

p. 132 The questions of Master Tushuai Yue are from Wumenguan, case 47. Tough questions, and only you can answer them.

p. 133 The quote that good friends are the whole of the spiritual life is from the Samyutta Nikaya, section XLV.2.

p. 133 The quote saying friends should intervene when necessary is from the Jatakamala, section 20.23. The Jatakamala is a rich collection of stories of the bodhisattva in his previous lives before he was the Buddha. He's the hero, of course, but he's not always a religious figure.

p. 134 The quote on traveling alone is from the Dhammapada, verse 61. Don't all these quotes make you want to read the Dhammapada yourself?

p. 141 The quote on fish (us!) floundering in the water is from the Sutta Nipata, verse 777.

p. 143 The quote on the truth being *right here* is from a letter to Liu Yanzhong by the great Chinese Zen Teacher Dahui. Dahui was talking about *you*, by the way, not just Mr. Liu.

p. 151 The quote on the true offering by 11th-century Chinese Zen Teacher Wuzu Fayan is from "The Record of Fayan," a collection of his words much like "The Record of Linji" is a collection of Linji's.

p. 152 The quote on thinking for yourself is from the Anguttara Nikaya, section III.65. People quote this passage all the time because it expresses a wonderful freedom in Buddhism, a freedom not found in all religions: the freedom to think.

part three

p. 155 The epigram, The Four Great Mahayana Vows, is recited every day by millions of Buddhists around the world. It expresses the great desire and effort to realize the dharma in this life, along with all other living things.

p. 162 The Zen quote on ordinary mind was perhaps originally said by Zen Teacher Mazu. Look for it in the Wumenguan, case 30.

p. 167 The quote from the Samyutta Nikaya comes from section XLV.27.

p. 171 The poem from Shiwu comes from his collection, "Mountain Poems." Shiwu embodied the Zen and Chinese poetic tradition of living as a recluse, close to nature. If you like this poem, read more. Also check out the poems of Hanshan, another Zen hermit.

p. 178 The quote on what meditation is comes from The Platform Sutra, a Zen text falsely attributed to Huineng, a great teacher in the early Chinese Zen tradition. It's a Zen classic, whoever wrote it.

p. 187 The long quote from Yuanwu, on being ordinary and empty, is from his collection, "Essentials of Mind." Yuanwu is best known for the Blue Cliff Record, another one of the major Zen story collections.

p. 192 The quote from the marvelous "Bodhisattvacharyavatara," by Shantideva, is chapter six, verse 38. We can all learn much from this text, written for us living in the world, dealing with anger and compassion and love and hate.

p. 196 The quote on crucial practices is from the Tibetan teacher Padmasambhava's "Dakini Teachings." Padmasambhava is the root teacher of all forms of Tibetan Buddhism and is revered there almost as much as the Buddha himself.

p. 217 The quote on mind is from the Sutta Nipata, verse 1.39.

p. 220 Xuansha's quote on entering the path is from "The Record of Xuansha." What do you hear, now?

many paths, further explorations

p. 223 The epigram on where you go after stepping off the hundred-foot pole is from Wumenguan, case 46. Don't watch your step—watch the world.

OTHER SEASTONE TITLES

EINSTEIN AND BUDDHA: The Parallel Sayings
Thomas J. McFarlane, Editor   Introduction by Wes Nisker
Einstein and Buddha reveals how modern science and ancient
Eastern thought lead us to the same deep truths.
Hardcover. $19.00

JESUS AND BUDDHA: The Parallel Sayings
Marcus Borg, Editor   Introduction by Jack Kornfield
Traces the life stories and beliefs of Jesus and Buddha, then
presents a comprehensive collection of their remarkably similar
teachings on facing pages. *Trade paper. $14.00*

JESUS AND MUHAMMAD: The Parallel Sayings
Joey Green, Editor   Foreword by Dr. Sayyid M. Syeed
Introduction by Dr. Kenneth Atkinson
Presents for the first time parables of Jesus and the parallel
ethical teachings of Muhammad. *Trade paper. $14.00*

MUSIC OF SILENCE:
A Sacred Journey through the Hours of the Day
David Steindl-Rast and Sharon Lebell
Introduction by Kathleen Norris
A noted Benedictine monk shows us how to incorporate the
sacred meaning of monastic life into our everyday world by
paying attention to the "seasons of the day" and the enlivening
messages to be found in each moment. *Trade paper. $12.00*

THE TAO OF THE JUMP SHOT:
An Eastern Approach to Life and Basketball
John Fitzsimmons Mahoney   Introduction by Bill Walton
Much more than a book about basketball, *The Tao of the Jump Shot* describes how to move with grace, prize every action and experience the beauty of life through the simple act of getting a ball through a hoop. *Trade paper. $9.95*

WHAT WOULD BUDDHA DO?:
101 Answers to Life's Daily Dilemmas
Franz Metcalf
Much as the "WWJD?" books help Christians live better lives by drawing on the wisdom of Jesus, this "WWBD?" book provides advice on improving your life by following the wisdom of another great teacher—Buddha. Not just for Buddhists, *WWBD?* is for anyone looking for spiritual direction and help in navigating through contemporary society.
Trade paper. $9.95

YOU DON'T HAVE TO SIT ON THE FLOOR:
Making Buddhism Part of Your Everyday Life
Jim Pym
You Don't Have to Sit on the Floor explains how to make Buddhism part of daily life while being true to one's customs and beliefs. The author draws on his own experiences being raised as a Christian to show how opening the way for East to meet West can enrich our lives. *Trade paper. $12.95*

To order these titles or other Seastone books call 800-377-2542 or 510-601-8301, e-mail ulysses@ulyssespress.com or write to Ulysses Press, P.O. Box 3440, Berkeley, CA 94703. There is no charge for shipping on retail orders. California residents must include sales tax. Allow two to three weeks for delivery.

about the author

Franz Metcalf did his Masters work at the Graduate Theological Union, and received his doctorate from the University of Chicago with a dissertation on the question, "Why Do Americans Practice Zen Buddhism?" He currently works with the Forge Institute for Spirituality and Social Change, co-chairs the steering committee of the Person, Culture, and Religion Group of the American Academy of Religion, and teaches college in Los Angeles. He has contributed reviews and chapters to various scholarly publications and is review editor of the *Journal of Global Buddhism*. He's the author of *What Would Buddha Do?* and co-author of *What Would Buddha Do at Work?* If you want to learn more about Franz (and other Buddhist things), check out www.buddhainyour backpack.net.

about the illustrator

Illustrator Monk Song Yoon is a Korean Zen monk-artist. Be sure to check out his homepage, Zen Art by Monk Song Yoon, at www.syzenart.com.

Responding to Global Warming

To the memory of Arthur Shercliff
Professor of Engineering
at Cambridge University

Responding to Global Warming

The Technology, Economics and Politics of Sustainable Energy

by
Peter Read

Zed Books Ltd
London & New Jersey

Responding to Global Warming was first published by Zed Books Ltd, 7 Cynthia Street, London N1 9JF, UK and 165 First Avenue, Atlantic Highlands, New Jersey 07716, USA, in 1994.

Laserset by Idiom, Plymouth
Cover design by Andrew Corbett
Printed by Biddles Ltd, Guildford and King's Lynn

The right of Peter Read, the author of this work has been asserted by him in accordance with the Copyright, Designs and Patents Act, 1988.

A catalogue record for this book is available from the British Library

US CIP data is available from the Library of Congress.

ISBN 1 85649 161 7
ISBN 1 85649 162 5

Notes and References

Supernumerary numbers in the text of this book refer to references cited in the notes; supernumerary numbers followed by an asterisk refer to substantive notes--all of which are located at the end of the relevant chapters.

Contents

Tables

Figures

Acknowledgements

My chief debts are to my mentors in engineering and economics. Arthur Shercliff – to whom this book is dedicated and whose untimely death was such a loss to Cambridge engineering – suggested I get into alternative technology at a time when I was finding Whitehall a little frustrating. Richard Layard suffered me kindly at the LSE, as a student mature to the point of over-ripeness. I also learned a lot in Whitehall, perhaps more from Ray Willmott than most, and at the Open University where I am much beholden to Godfrey Boyle. In the last dozen years I have been lucky to work at Massey University where my research interests have had ample rein. In particular I owe much to the indulgence of my colleagues in the Economics Department, most of whom teach more hours than I, and to the generosity of the arrangements for study leave.

Late in the preparation of this book it turned out that I had more to say than budgeted for. I am very happy to acknowledge the generous support that was forthcoming at short notice from Tasman Forestry Ltd., from the Maruia Society, and from Massey University. This coming together of business, environmentalists and academia in New Zealand is particularly apt to the message of this book, which in part is that the environmental problems of today cannot be resolved by confrontation. Rather must industry enlist, in joint endeavour with non-government activists, to work out ways of using the market to resolve these problems. It is fitting that Tasman Forestry Ltd. should be involved, given their past achievements in this area – particularly through their commitment to the Tasman Accord with the Minister of Conservation and with environmentalists groups, including the Maruia Society. This has seen their holdings of native forest protected throughout New Zealand and a habitat preserved for the endangered Kokako. I hope that, from my academic ivory tower, I have provided an analysis that points the way to similar joint endeavour, albeit on a wider canvas, in relation to the difficult problem of global warming and that, through the framework provided by the Rio Earth Summit, it will help governments to join together in levelling the playing field for such an endeavour, one that has for too long been tilted against the environment, and against hopes for our grandchildren's enjoyment of it.

In the process of developing this book I am indebted to many who have been kind enough to read different parts of it. In particular to David Lomax, editor of the *National Westminster Bank Review,* where some of this material first saw the light of day, and Mick Common, who helped me to understand that this is not just a problem in environmental economics. *For my family, who put up with me, no words can suffice.* Of course nobody named or unnamed above can be held in any way responsible for what I have made of their wisdom and help.

Palmerston North

Glossary

avtur	aviation gas turbine fuel
b.a.u.	business as usual (scenario)
bbl	barrels (of oil)
BIGSTIG	biomass integrated gasifier steam-injected gas turbine
BTU	British thermal unit
CBA	cost benefit analysis
CFC	chloro-fluoro-carbon
CNG	compressed natural gas
CoP	Conference of the Parties to the FCCC
DCT	dedicated carbon tax
EGE	enhanced greenhouse effect
EJ	exa-joule (1,000,000,000,000,000,000 joules)
FAO	Food and Agriculture Organisation (of the United Nations)
FCCC	Framework Convention on Climate Change
GATT	General Agreement on Tariffs and Trade
GCM	general circulation model
GDP	gross domestic product
GEF	Global Environment Facility (of the World Bank)
GIS	geographical information system
GJ	giga-joule (1,000,000,000 joules)
GREENS	global redevelopment with energy environment sustainability
IIASA	International Institute for Applied Systems Analysis
IPCC	Intergovernmental [scientific] Panel on Climate Change
kW	kilowatt (1,000 watts = 1,000 joules per second = 1.34 horse power)
kWh	kilowatt-hour (3,600,000 joules)
LPG	liquid petroleum gas
MW	megawatt (1,000,000 watts)
NES	nuclear estate with small-holdings

North countries	OECD member countries ('rich' countries)
OECD	Organisation for Economic Cooperation and Development
OPEC	Organisation of Petroleum Exporting Countries
PJ	peta-joule (1,000,000,000,000,000 joules)
ppm	parts per million
QUAD	quadrillion (1,000,000,000,000,000) BTUs
R&D	research and development
RSA	Republic of South Africa
SERI	Solar Energy Research Institute, Golden, Colorado
South countries	non-OECD member countries (see North above)
SOTER	soil and terrain survey
TAO	tradeable absorption obligation; also, implicitly, tradeable (net) absorption obligation
TCAD	tradeable carbon absorption obligation
UNCED	United Nations Conference on the Environment and Development

Preface

At one time there seemed to me to be nothing very original in this book and that there ought to be dozens of people equally competent to write it. I had been in the habit of waking up early and saying to myself 'Why on earth don't they get on with it and put the stuff back underground?' After that I asked around and found nobody else seemed to be thinking on those lines. Having spent most of my working life on energy questions of one sort or another, I found that rather surprising. Anyway, that question was the origin of the 'making coal' idea, which plays a minor part in these pages, but which was what got me going.

It seemed to me that the broad scheme which I develop should be obvious to anybody who knows a bit about energy technology and who has a training in economics to go with it. However, a number of people who have read some of the draft tell me it is not at all simple and I must take their word for it. But the individual components are pretty basic. The scientific content is accessible to anyone who paid attention at school. Energy technology seems to me to be a matter of general knowledge, but there I may be projecting my own experience. The economics starts near the beginning and doesn't go very far.(It could go further, and my most recent work, currently submitted to academic journals for refereeing, claims that the 'least cost theorem' of Chapter 6 is incorrectly applied to the economics of climate change—a result which strengthens rather than weakens the message of thisbook.) The political dimension raises the greatest problems in terms of the practical application of the scheme, but its understanding requires no more than a broad familiarity with the serious media.

If there's a spark of originality as regards the individual components of this response strategy, it lies in the economic instrument I have devised for making it happen, if the politicians are inclined so to do, which I call the Tradeable Absorption Obligation. For the reasons stated herein, I believe it to be an improvement on other ideas, such as theTradeable Emissions Permit with Absorption Offsets, but as with most advances, if it is an advance, it is a pygmy dancing on the shoulders of giants. So I think that the complexity of the book comes from the inter-connectedness of its components. And that aspect is, I suspect, why politicians and their advisers, who are largely trained to think from the perspective of a single discipline, have been making rather heavy weather of the whole global warming problem—or, rather, of the threats of climate change.

I have written 'threats' since it now appears that my speculation towards the end of Chapter 2 may not be too far wide of the mark. Taking the

Greenland Ice-core Project results together with some mathematical modelling of the North Atlantic linked ocean and climate system, both reported in *Nature* in July 1993, it seems possible that increased levels of greenhouse gases may cause the global climate system to revert to Ice Age conditions rather than to the extreme warmth that has more generally roused concern. For the GRIP results suggest that, away from the conditions of the last 10,000 years, the climate system has prehistorically been far more unstable between benign and glaciated states than the experience of history suggests. Indeed, the experience of history may have occurred precisely because of the unusual stability of the climate system over recent millennia, with its consequent potential for agriculture and for human settlement and civilization to develop.

Thus the advocacy of this book, outlined in its second sentence, takes urgency from the latest advances in scientific understanding.

1. Introduction

This book is a work of advocacy as well as scholarship. What is advocated is that the remaining years of this century should be used to take preparatory steps that will make it possible, if need be, to get control of global warming at acceptable cost in the opening two decades of the next. The method of advocacy is to demonstrate the practicability of such a long term strategy from the technical, economic and political perspectives. It is intended to give impetus to hopes that the problem of global warming can be dealt with by a collaborative effort worldwide.

Such hopes were somewhat dimmed prior to the second United Nations Conference on the Environment and Development (UNCED)[1]* held at Rio de Janeiro, in June 1992 – what came to be called the Earth Summit. This was because the preparatory work towards the two agreements that were initiated there, the Framework Convention on Climate Change (FCCC) and the Convention on Biological Diversity, was surrounded with much bickering and procedural wrangling – symptomatic of deep-seated disagreements.

Surprisingly, perhaps, to those whose memories stretch back to American leadership in environmental matters, the USA managed to cast itself in the role of principal villain and declined to sign the Biodiversity Convention. But it did, in the event, sign the FCCC (described in Chapter 9) after late stage redrafting that resulted in a document remarkably different from what had been under development through most of the negotiating process.

Gone were proposals for legally binding commitments to specific targets, with the focus on emissions of carbon dioxide (the principal greenhouse gas). And newly drafted were political commitments, hopefully effective, to aim for comprehensive targets on all greenhouse gases and to take account of absorption of greenhouse gases, as well as emissions ('sinks' as well as 'sources' in the jargon).

In the wrangling, most parties were taking up prepared positions from which to protect perceived national interests. Of the Earth Summit itself it was remarked that it turned out to be mainly about money and sovereignty.[2] So it is naive to suppose that, with the Rio Conventions in place, those which signed each will disinterestedly exert themselves in solving the shared global problems to which they respectively apply. In this book, concerned as it is with the response to global warming, biodiversity takes a back seat, save for occasional remarks drawing attention to ways in which the response towards climate change advocated herein can also have beneficial impacts on biodiversity.

The aim will be to show how common interest may be found amongst nations in dealing with global warming, a problem which arises mainly as an external environmental effect of the workings of the energy market as it currently operates. Common interest arises because, it will be shown, the collaboration of the South [3*] is needed for any strategy for dealing with global warming to be effective, and because the low-cost strategy advanced in this book will not only impose rather modest burdens on the North but also serve to improve prospects for development in the South, including the transfer of energy technology achieved through a 'polluter pays' mechanism.

The collection of ideas which constitute this strategy I call the GREENS [4*] concept, standing for Global Redevelopment with Energy Environment Sustainability. Global since that is the perspective required, and redevelopment, because it involves change in the developed North as well as in the less fortunate South, and because the idea of sustainability implies that there cannot be an unending supply of greenfield sites. Energy Environment Sustainability involves weaning the commercial energy system away from its mother's milk of fossil fuels (and progressively onto an adult diet of biomass raw material and other renewable sources of energy) as existing plant becomes due for retirement. GREENS includes an economic device that enlists the industrial muscle of energy firms to manage such a transition. The GREENS acronym is used throughout this book to mean the set of ideas and actions that it is advocating.

The rest of this chapter is devoted to setting the scene. This involves firstly trying to see why policy towards global warming got into something of a muddle, after which we state briefly a broad argument as to how the muddle can be sorted out, secondly, seeing how people with different backgrounds perceive the problem and, thirdly, to outlining the broad perspective from which the way ahead is mapped out in this book.

Apart from Chapter 10, where some conclusions are drawn, the rest of the book comprises three sections. Chapters 2 and 3 provide an analysis of why a precautionary response is appropriate to the global warming issue and a methodological approach for rational precaution. It should be noted that a rational precautionary approach may be quite expensive, e.g. in time lost on precautionary activity which could otherwise be spent producing pleasurably consumable goods. In a sense this message gets overtaken in Chapters 4 and 7 where the technological and economic aspects of the problem are discussed in an apolitical context. Since most people have a basic understanding of natural science but not of economics, Chapters 5 and 6 fill the gap with a thumbnail sketch of the neo-classical economic theory which underlies most economic reasoning. Given a timely start and providing the land requirement can be met, as is most probably the case, it emerges that both the technology and the economics of responding to global warming are, from a global perspective, much simpler and more inexpensive than many people have hitherto thought.

However, global warming presents an 'externality' upon the world market system. This externality, and the requirement for globally effective policy that arises from it, is no less real because of uncertainties, e.g. as to the possibility of climate 'jumps'. Or – if unprecedented greenhouse gas levels do not cause a climate 'jump' but, as may be more likely, cause substantial long-run climatic change due to a higher global average temperature – there may at least be uncertainties as to the cost of the damage. Requiring a global policy solution means collaboration between nations towards securing a sustainable climate future and that, unlike the technological and economic aspects, is difficult, as is discussed in Chapters 8 and 9. Thus the point in arguing for a precautionary approach to decision taking is to reinforce politicians and bureaucrats in their efforts to overcome these difficulties, and the efforts of those who influence the political process through the media and lobbying activities.

Misunderstanding, Uncertainty and Conflict

The deep-seated disagreements that have been mentioned have obscured the true nature of the global warming problem or have reflected a misunderstanding of it. Perhaps misunderstanding has been due to disinformation put around by those with an interest in business as usual. Most likely, however, it is the compartmentalised nature of analysis, in relation to a problem which requires an inter-disciplinary approach, that is to blame.

For whatever reason, the problem had, until the last-minute changes to the FCCC, been seen in terms of the very difficult business of reducing *gross* emissions. However, as we shall see in Chapter 2, it is the level of greenhouse gases in the atmosphere which causes global warming, so that more absorption is just as useful as less emission. And it is a relatively simple business – given a sufficiently long timescale for a technological transition of the industrial energy system – to reduce *net* emissions. It is very much easier to greatly increase absorption than it is to greatly reduce gross emissions.

In a work of advocacy, one must be careful not to mislead. It is not certain that there is a global warming problem and, if there is, it is almost certainly not due exclusively to commercial energy activities. But it will be argued that precautionary action should be taken until we are certain there is not a problem, that commercial energy activities almost certainly have a lot to do with it if there is a problem, and that it is by changing our commercial energy activities, in a deliberate and gradual way over the next few decades, as discussed in Chapter 4, that we can most surely and cheaply deal with the problem.

Depending on the results of scientific research into climate change over the next decade or so, these uncertainties will be resolved in the direction of greater or less concern about global warming, which is attributed to anthropogenic additions to a variety of greenhouse gases: carbon dioxide (the most important),[5] on the increase largely because of the cumulative burning of fossil fuels; methane mostly from agricultural sources; nitrogen oxides mainly due to vehicle exhausts; and the CFCs (chloro-fluoro-carbons) used in refrigerators and aerosol cans.

In such an uncertain world, any action carries an 'option cost', that is to say the loss of later opportunities forgone as a consequence of the irreversible choice that has been previously made. The preparatory process of 'getting ready' that is advocated here constitutes a process of 'learning by doing'[6*] which will enable policy to be modified in the light of new information as it comes forward. Its option cost is the loss of living standards that results from using resources in this way rather than continuing with business as usual whilst 'waiting and seeing'. On the other hand, business as usual carries the option cost of being unprepared if science comes forward with a call for urgent action.

It will be argued that, if we become sure that there is no problem, the cost of having taken these preparatory steps unnecessarily (the loss of the option of waiting and seeing) would be small. Indeed, they may yield net benefits in terms of fuel-wood plantations left to grow to maturity, and available to meet demands for commercial timber products in lieu of further exploitation of native forests. If on the other hand we do nothing for 10 to 15 years (losing the option of getting ready) and then find that the problem is in fact very urgent, the cost of action begun then may be very great. In other words, 'a stitch in time saves nine'.

From the point of view of net emissions, carbon dioxide is certainly the most important greenhouse gas since it is the only one that we know how to absorb – by the man-made production of biomass, i.e. growing more plant life, which absorbs carbon dioxide from the atmosphere in its basic process of photosynthesis. Mostly this book looks at the problem of stabilising the level of carbon dioxide in the atmosphere. But if uncertainty about global warming is resolved in the direction of greater rather than less concern than currently exists, it may be necessary to think in terms of anthropogenically reducing the level of carbon dioxide in order to compensate for rising levels of the other greenhouse gases.

Yet the FCCC negotiators did not, until the last minute, address the question of absorbing carbon dioxide but focused instead on reducing gross emissions and the technical problem of measuring them. The technical problems of measuring absorption had not been addressed before the Conference, an omission that could not be put right in a smoke-filled room off Rio's Copacabana beach, since defining how to measure absorption also requires time-consuming negotiation. So the FCCC is very much a framework, leaving much to be filled in, and what matters, and what this book addresses, is what happens after the Earth Summit.

This is not to put down the significance of that event, or to detract from the importance of politicians agreeing to take specific action, however inadequate, as a long-run response. If no FCCC had been signed there would be no basis for regular meetings of the signatories (or Conferences of the Parties as they are called in the FCCC) to negotiate improvements to it. But, rather than the technical content of the FCCC, it is the spirit in which debate was conducted, and the political will that emerged, which signifies.

The example of the Montreal convention on ozone-destroying CFCs gives the lie to the cynics who claim that international collaboration is a hopeless endeavour. However, global warming presents a much more difficult problem. With CFCs, the major players in the industry had already developed alternative products and expected to do well out of the elimination of the older CFCs where they no longer had control of the market.[7] Alternative products to fossil fuels do exist but major energy firms have no control of that market. One of the features of the proposals discussed in this book, implemented through a Tradeable Absorption Obligation[8*] (TAO – see Chapter 7) is that it provides a framework for a continuing major role for existing energy firms, thereby anticipating one of the prospective sources of resistance to effective action.

However, the major cause for despondency amongst those concerned about global warming is the perception that effective action would be so prohibitively expensive that politicians will choose to do nothing about it until too late. This perception arises from the same misunderstanding which beset the FCCC negotiating process – from ignorance or disregard of the potential of alternatives to fossil fuels. Without such alternatives, effective action – taking the form of reduced usage of the fossil fuels which are the major source of man-made greenhouse gases – seems to require both a dramatic change in lifestyles in the North and a farewell to hopes of economic growth in the South.

Thus the option costs have been perceived in terms of costly, premature and, possibly, impracticable, targets on the rate of gross emissions. Accordingly, the cost of precautionary action has been wrongly perceived to be great and the benefit from low-cost learning by doing has been ignored. This has led to the adoption of conflicting policy positions: between North and South; between some Northern countries with a big stake in the existing energy system and others more affected by pollution; and between those groups concerned for the environment and future generations and others concerned more with development in the South and the fate of the currently impoverished.[9]

The first of these disagreements is of course why environment and development were linked together in the United Nations Conference. This linkage has had little directly to do with global warming previously, although, as mentioned above, the concept advanced in this book does result in a direct economic link. So far there has been only political linkage rooted in the North-South debate over the failure of industrialised nations to ensure that their economic success is adequately reflected in progress amongst the less well-off.

Some rich nations felt that some poor countries saw the Earth Summit as a platform to castigate the North for sins of commission and omission in the history of development assistance. They were concerned that the proposed FCCC could have become an instrument for extracting a high price from the rich countries in exchange for poorer countries' co-operation in measures to protect the environment and to secure its future use on a sustainable basis.

These feelings in the North are paralleled by poorer countries' beliefs that global warming and other problems with the environment have been caused by rich countries, are of no immediate concern to the South and are for rich countries to deal with at their own expense. Some take a stronger view, which has been lucidly articulated by Malaysian Prime Minister Dr Mahathir bin Mohamed. Speaking in Caracas in November 1991, he said, 'We are told that the South must curb its aspirations and its approach towards development so that mankind's, i.e. the North's, enjoyment of the good life is not threatened. Against all accepted codes of ethics, the poor are being told, and indeed coerced, into paying for the well-being of the rich.'[10]

The second disagreement, internal to the North, originally saw the USA, Japan and the UK opposed to continental Europe and Australasia, but latterly saw the USA in a more isolated position. In the end the USA agreed to the final version of the FCCC but, if the better appreciation of the option costs towards which this book points does not see a further shift in the USA's position, the notion that its government is captive to fuel industry interests – implicit in the view that the misunderstandings have sprung from disinformation – will gain force.

The third disagreement is quite simply resolved in the approach advocated in this book which, subject to land availability and to concerns considered in Chapter 9, yields technology transfer and development in the South as an integral aspect of a sustainable future for all achieved through responding effectively to the global warming problem.

The Argument of This Book

It is by now plain to the reader that I am arguing that the perception that effective response must be very costly is incorrect. This claim challenges the orthodox analysis of economists as embodied in, for instance, the proceedings of the 1990 Rome Conference,[11*] which set the tone for most subsequent economic analysis of the problem, and for much policy analysis. Broadly speaking, those analyses take the technological possibilities as given by current practice whilst the basis of our claim lies in recent advances in two areas of alternative energy technology research, and one advance in mainstream energy technology.

Studies of intensive biomass production using short rotation silviculture show that land availability is unlikely to be a severe constraint. Developments in fermentation technology indicate that liquid fuel produced from woody biomass is likely to be competitive with gasolene from petroleum by about the year 2000, i.e. at the time it is needed. Leading edge technology electricity generation using gas turbine prime movers is better adapted to sulphur-free biomass fuelling than it is to coal.

These advances suggest that, although not quite economic at the present time, only a small penalty would be involved in achieving control over the net rate of carbon dioxide emissions (i.e. emissions less absorption) through the progressive adoption of these technologies over the next few decades. They would show net benefits *vis-à-vis* a business-as-usual future featuring rising costs of fossil fuels (in addition to the benefit of effective control over global warming) by around 2020.

Thus the basis of the strategy advanced in this book is both technological and economic. It is embodied in a scenario for the substantial transformation of commercial fuel supply to reliance on biomass (specifically fuel-wood grown intensively and converted to usable fuel products near where it is grown) that is first sketched out at the end of Chapter 4. But the implementation of this response affects different nations differently and therefore raises problems in the field of political economy which are made difficult by the legacy of attitudes derived from the history of North-South relations. Given the unpredictability of political processes, a political plan cannot be worked out in the way that the economics of technological change can be. But it is possible to consider the negotiating process that would mediate its achievement, and to chart a course through the difficulties, and it is to that task that the latter part of this book is addressed.

The key requirement is that the North recognise its responsibility, through the history of its industrialisation and the technologies that have fuelled it, for the situation that has arisen. This requirement is accepted in the FCCC, where the greater ability of the North to pay for whatever response is needed is also noted. Such a response must entail the transfer of efficient and sustainable energy technology to the South, where the bulk of new demand is anticipated. The TAO provides a vehicle that enlists the commercial energy business to this end, so that North consumers pay for the South's development – what in the jargon of FCCC negotiation is coming to be called 'joint implementation' – with minimal involvement of governments.

Even so, the implementation of the GREENS strategy involves some conflicts of national interest and their resolution is considered both from the national perspective and in terms of the work that lies ahead for the institutions set up to implement the FCCC. It presents a formidable task for statesmen and for the officials who serve them. Whether the FCCC was signed by some in cynical expectation that the task would prove too great, but that the political pressures required a futile gesture, we cannot know. The lesson I draw in these closing chapters is that, with the overall cost greatly less than has generally been perceived, and with the development of the South helped rather than hindered by the process, the formidable political task can be managed.

Doing that may point the way in other areas. For the problem of sustainability facing future global development, outlined in the Brundtland Report *Our Common Future*,[12] is not simply one of coping with global warming. Whether failure to do anything about that problem would lead to climatic catastrophe we will hopefully never know for sure. But that there is some limit to the number of people who can live on this planet, and that it is inversely related to the per capita impact each makes upon the environment, seems beyond doubt.

Whether that implies also a limit to per capita consumption, or whether alternative, non-environmentally damaging directions for improving our standard of living will evolve, is more open to question. But the introduction of sustainability considerations into the direction of human development requires a change of course to a system that has immense internal momentum. For that change to be enforced by a painful, possibly fatal lesson from nature, rather than the attempt made to bring it about by conscious effort, would be a dereliction of this generation's duty to posterity.

The redirection of immense momentum requires either huge force in a sudden damaging crunch, or moderate force applied consistently over a long time. To manage such a global-scale change of direction is a challenge to world statesmen, suddenly released from preoccupation with the Cold War. Whilst there are no short-term electoral victories to be won from successes in meeting that challenge, neither were there in the Cold War. Rather was it seen as politically suicidal to pander to totalitarian communism.

So, equally, must it become suicidal for politicians to deviate from working for the common good of a viable posterity. For that to happen there must be the same public commitment to our common future as there has been to the maintenance of liberty. That commitment requires continuing with the education of the electorate which has been so great an achievement of environmental pressure groups and the media, however cranky some of their campaigns may at times seem to be.

Different Perspectives

Economists and engineers

It is perhaps worthwhile taking time to understand why it is that well intentioned analysts come up with very different solutions when trying to answer the question of how much it is going to cost to deal with global warming. Two quite different modes of thought are involved when engineer/scientists and economists address themselves to advising politicians on this question. Economics has been said to be about 'making the best of things' whereas an engineer has been characterised as 'a person who can do for a nickel what any fool can do for a dime'.

Unlike science, economics cannot learn from the results of repeated experiments. Economists rely on rationalising the unrepeatable history of economic events, often projecting their own analytic rationality onto the behaviour of individuals in the market. They deduce that the 'invisible hand' of market forces leads to efficient results, with rational behaviour causing production to be as cheap as possible given the available technology. If you say to them that there are better (cheaper) ways of, for instance, producing cabbages, they will ask you why it is not being done, why is it that profit-loving business people are not in there producing cabbages more cheaply and underselling the current producers.

Modern economists recognise that there are costs involved in acquiring information, and in getting into a business where others are already engaged, costs which explain the slowness with which new technologies diffuse into the productive system. They also recognise that most technical advances can only realise their potential within a system different from the existing, so that a technological shift involving a chain of technical advances may be activated by the innovation which constitutes its final link. But their instinct is nevertheless to rationalise the optimality of the status quo and they are very clever at it. As one of the best of them once remarked, 'It is ...a reflection of our sense of values ...particularly the preoccupation with brain-twisters ...that ...economics is guided much more by logical curiosity than by a taste for relevance. The character of the subject owes much to this fact.'[13] Technology is boring to most economists. It is much more interesting to construct enormously complex models of the global economy, and to predict the impact of stupendous levels of carbon tax than it is to study the humdrum details of the way in which well-known (but, at present price relativities, little used) biomass-based technologies can penetrate the commercial energy market.

An engineer, however, is trained to acquire empirically testable information when faced with a problem and to come up with an answer: if it's cheaper than continuing to bear with the problem well and good, if it's not, then its 'back to the drawing board'. It is this constant striving to improve on the status quo – sometimes altruistic, sometimes motivated by the sheer pleasure of problem solving, and often spurred on by profit seeking – which sharply differentiates the engineer from the economist. It is the engineer's improving approach which offers hope that the problems set by an increasingly complex and interactive global society can be satisfactorily resolved in the context of a decision-making framework that takes prudent account of our uncertainty, or even plain ignorance, regarding many aspects of our situation.

The two disciplines tend to give different answers because engineers employ a 'bottom up' approach which involves new technologies, or putting together known technologies in a different way, and thus alter the productive possibilities available to the economy. Economists, taking productive possibilities as given, solve the problem in a 'top down' way, using some model of the economy as a whole and seeing how it would have to alter its behaviour in order to reduce carbon emissions.

By a model of the economy is meant an abstraction, usually in the form of a set of mathematical equations representing those parts of economic theory which pertain to the problem, with the equations 'calibrated' by reference to past behaviour. The behaviour of the model may reflect the behaviour of the real world only rather loosely but this approach has the advantage that it can take account of the complex system effects that follow from a change to one small part of it, whereas the engineer's problem-solving approach is perforce partial and local.

To an economist, since the economy has always shown a close link between energy use and production,[14] and since energy use within modern technological experience has always been closely linked to fossil fuel use, which means carbon dioxide emissions, there must be a strong linkage between carbon dioxide emissions and economic activity. Within the familiar range of price variation, substitution for fossil fuels in the production process has been rather small and the economist's expectation is, therefore, that abatement of carbon dioxide emissions must result in a corresponding loss of production.

Production in an economy is conceptually quite clear but its measurement as Gross Domestic Product (GDP) is a little bit murky. One way of thinking of it is as being equivalent to the payments made to the owners of all the inputs to production (wages to workers, rents to landowners and royalties to landowners who are lucky enough to be sitting on minerals such as coal and oil, interest [15*] to the suppliers of finance for capital investment and profits to entrepreneurs and risk takers). Note that nobody pays mother nature for her inputs, such as clean air. The substitution of effort for mother nature's bounty – cleaning up atmospheric pollution – means more work for the same output, i.e. a reduction in the real wage. If human inputs are regarded as fixed, a reduced real wage means less production, less for people to consume and, therefore, a reduced standard of living – in short a very costly business. 'Bottom up' analyses,[16] on the other hand, usually show the cost of reducing carbon dioxide emissions to be small, or even not a cost at all but a benefit.

The two disciplines come together in cost benefit analysis (CBA) in which economists' rules are applied to evaluate the system effect of a particular change proposed by an engineer. Indeed, after a methodological caveat in Chapter 3, this book in essence takes its departure from a rudimentary cost-benefit analysis of the impact of the technological advances mentioned above (intensive fuel-wood production, gas turbine power generation and ethanol fermentation from biomass) on the assumption they are applied on a global basis.

A precautionary perspective

However, even if the result of that analysis were considerably less attractive than it turns out to be, it is argued herein that precautionary steps to anticipate the possible climate effect of rising carbon dioxide concentrations should still be taken. One reason for this, amongst others to be discussed later, is that CBA is only properly applicable when a project under consideration is small in relation to the economy as a whole, so that the penalty from being wrong is not very great. This is clearly not the case for a unique decision like global policy towards global warming.

For it to be argued – as it has been by one economist writing for the *Economist*[17] – that because climate affects only agriculture, forestry and fishing, which constitute only 4 per cent of US GDP, then the damage is likely to be insignificant even if global warming occurs, is really rather silly. One may as well say that, because the air we breathe makes no contribution to GDP, we can quite easily do without it. Furthermore it demonstrates a certain insularity of approach given that the bulk of the world's population can far less easily do without 4 per cent of their income than can affluent US citizens.

More importantly, most of the poorer countries are far more dependent upon climate than for a mere 4 per cent of their output. Subsistence farmers are 100 per cent dependent upon climate. In relation to a single, global and essential asset such as climate, a much more cautious decision-taking framework than CBA is needed. Accordingly we shall, despite the attractiveness of the rudimentary cost-benefit results that have been mentioned, be maintaining a precautionary perspective.

History and attitudes

That there is little justice in this world provides scant consolation to the underprivileged, be they individuals oppressed by their boss, ethnic or religious minorities by their local majorities, or impoverished nations that have gained little from the process of industrialisation. Governments in the South are informed, more often than not, by dependency theories of the development process.[18] Such theories hold that the advance of more developed countries is at the expense of the less developed and that the capitalist system substitutes economic power for military power in a neo-colonialism that took over when old-style empire ended.

There is no need, in this book, to take a position on that confused and confusing debate. History cannot be re-run and it must be accepted that, on account of their relative lack of economic progress, many less developed countries hold resentful attitudes towards richer countries. That is a legacy which the past imposes on the present and which has the potential to frustrate future North–South co-operation. Whatever the validity of dependency theory, the reality is that the adjustments entailed by the Third World debt crisis have fallen more heavily on the debtors than their creditors. Thus the attitudes which the South brings to the debate have their roots not only in the North's responsibility for the problem but also the inequities of recent experience. Finding solutions to global warming along the lines of the GREENS concept, cannot depend upon its imposition by powerful nations, nor upon its acceptability to all nations, but must build on partial consensus through a combination of political wisdom and economic power intelligently applied. The result may be partial and incomplete fulfilment in the early stages, but hopefully with regional and/or bilateral arrangements anticipating its eventual global coverage.

The imposition of an energy technology transformation by force of arms is obviously ridiculous, and its imposition by economic power – for instance trade sanctions – would be counter-productive in relation to some of the major players in the game, most notably coal-rich China. (Turned in on itself by external economic pressure, China would have no reason to refrain from using its vast resources of cheap coal.) Nor can reliance be placed on consensus, open as it is to obstruction by individual nations seeking to gain leverage for ulterior purposes. It would not do, for instance, for global or regional agreement on GREENS to be held up by, say, Syrian conditionality related to the resolution of its dispute with Israel over the Golan Heights.

Some countries would gain more from the operation of GREENS than others and some, most notably coal-rich countries in the first instance, would lose. The argument that would certainly be made by such losers that happen also to be less developed, is that rich countries have got where they are by using up more than their fair share of the atmosphere's capacity to absorb carbon dioxide pollution. A response from rich nations that they got where they are today by their own enterprise and that the whole world benefits from the fruits of economic prosperity would fall on deaf ears.

That the alternative energy technologies described in Chapter 4 are not much more costly than the fossil fuel technologies they can replace, maybe even cheaper in some circumstances, is a help in practical terms. It is a help because it means that the burden falling on rich countries becomes one that is manageable within current perceptions. Thus an effective response, in line with a precautionary perspective, does not need to wait until the public has been educated into an acceptance of energy price increases, or international financial transfers, that are currently unacceptable. Upwards of 30 per cent on bulk fuel prices, spread over a decade or so, and more in the North than in the South, is not going to cause riots in the streets, while the shift of an increasing proportion of international energy trade away from traditional fossil fuel exporters will break few hearts. On-going flows of government-to-government expenditures connected with the institutional arrangements for making GREENS work would be well within the scale of the aid programmes to which we have grown accustomed.

Such arrangements can provide a basis upon which the political will for collaboration in dealing with global warming may be built. But to succeed with the South it must address the Third World debt problem. Many outside the South would regard doing something about this problem as desirable in its own right, if only for the health and stability of the world financial system. However, without some such ulterior pretext as is being suggested, it is an action which it is difficult to undertake on account of the precedent which such debt relief provides to potential debt defaulters in the future.

Even with some such accommodation of this kind to lubricate the general arrangements needed to implement GREENS, it remains the case that there are some South countries that have vast resources of cheap coal – and indeed that its cheapness arises in part precisely because they are less developed and pay low mining wages. Of course almost all countries have estimated but unproven fossil fuel resources of some sort, but account needs to be taken only of those proven resources which are cheaper to exploit than turning to renewable GREENS technologies. Thus, in achieving partial consensus involving at least those South countries which are in a position to seriously vitiate the effectiveness of GREENS, there are two separate problems to be faced.

One is the general problem facing all countries of meeting energy demands arising from the development process. GREENS potentially carries rich rewards for South countries that are in a position to provide a venue for the large-scale growing of fuel-wood on behalf of rich nations. To the extent that GREENS leave other countries somewhat better off than they would be under present prospects of having to import increasingly costly oil, then they do not present a substantial difficulty.

However, the second problem, resulting from past use of fossil fuels by already rich nations, gives rise to the need to compensate those South countries that are already using their own resources of cheap fossil fuels to get their development moving.[19] For the operation of GREENS to be effective, either these countries, including India and China, must be persuaded to forgo the benefit of using these resources or compensating absorption of carbon dioxide must take place elsewhere in the globe. Inevitably, the second problem imposes a burden, mainly on the North, until such time as the countries have been re-equipped with an energy supply system that leaves them with no incentive to use their coal reserves in a manner that vitiates the overall scheme.

A Way Forward

For the lines of solution advocated in this book to be plausible a way forward needs to be found that does not require a huge and unrealistic revolution in consumers' economic behaviour. One dimension of our politico-economic subsidiary theme is to trace out, therefore, a path for change that is feasible in a democratic society.

This path involves the transformation of the world's commercial fuel system onto a sustainable basis, relying on biomass for its main raw material. For the remainder of this century this involves 'getting ready', as opposed to 'waiting and seeing'.[20] In the decades thereafter, it can, unless nature holds in store some truly dreadful surprises, put the world economy in shape to get global warming under control by 2020 – and get greenhouse gas levels where we may want them to be by around the middle of the next century.

Getting ready means intensive research into the capability of the global land supply to produce suffient biomass and into the process of adapting the global energy system to a sustainable fuel resource. It also means 'learning by doing', or action research, by way of pilot schemes and trial developments worldwide, and the creation of the human resources and institutional structures needed for such a transition. Policies that may need to be raised to a very high level of application can be initiated at a low level and escalated at a more or less rapid rate depending on the news which is forthcoming from the climatologists.

However, it is a path that cannot be followed very far without the collaboration of many nations, and not to its end without the willing involvement of the majority. Achieving this requires the developed countries to give a lead and to accept what I call the 'burden of history' in a new relationship with less developed nations. The burden of history lies in the recognition that cheap fossil fuels, to the extent they have not already been used up, can no longer be used heedlessly. The possibility of that coming about depends upon our leaders developing sustained statesmanship. However likely or unlikely that may seem, the viability of the political path that we propose should not be muddled up with the feasibility of the technological and economic message which provides its basis.

The political path is one that could pioneer a path that may have to be followed in dealing with the many other problems thrown up by the dominance of nature by homo sapiens. It is a path that may enable the world to turn away from the eventual ecological disaster foreseen by some. At the very least, it may provide a pattern for piecemeal responses to the problems that can arise in an increasingly interdependent world.

This path may be followed in an untidy and muddled way, through initiatives by individual countries such as New Zealand, through bilateral and/or regional arrangements, or under a global agreement negotiated through the good offices of the appropriate United Nations agencies. One can only hope that statesmen seize the opportunity. But if they fail, we can – to return to our technological and economic basis – be confident that it will not be because the task is technically impossible or, even, economically very painful.

Sustainable energy at practicable cost

That the sustainable energy path outlined in this book eventually shows net benefits in the direct cost of delivered energy does not, of course, mean that fuel prices will be at or below their present level in 2020. Fuel prices will rise in real terms (i.e. exclusive of the effect of inflation) because it is getting harder and harder to find and extract new supplies of oil, and because the huge reserves of the Middle East will give preponderant market power to suppliers in that region.

Furthermore, by competing with oil and limiting its market, the alternative technologies mentioned above could prevent oil prices rising as much as they otherwise would. So the eventual cost saving may appear less real than it is. With apparently endlessly rising oil prices in the late 1970s, the motivation for initiating the research into new energy technologies which has now borne fruit was indeed cost saving. In terms of the original objective, however, the research has not, with the mid 1980s drop in oil prices, been a great success. But, as is so often the case with research, there has been an unexpected pay-off. Certainly, when it comes to cutting net carbon dioxide emissions, these technologies are winners.

By achieving a transition, over the next two to three decades, to sustainable fuel technologies based upon intensive biomass production – and its gasification for modern gas turbine-based power generation, together with chemical processing into ethanol for the portable fuels needed for mobility – we can achieve effective control over the rate of carbon dioxide emissions and, over time, reach a desired level of carbon dioxide concentration in the atmosphere. As far as existing energy extractive industries are concerned, this means more or less doing away with burning coal and, to a lesser extent oil and natural gas, over the next few decades.

But implementation of the idea of Tradeable Absorption Obligations (TAOs) will ensure that the traditional fuel companies will remain the major operators in the energy market, but based upon fuel-wood[21]* (or, more generally, biomass) as the raw material. The idea of more or less doing away with coal, of limiting oil extraction, and of devoting vast areas of land to intensive fuel-wood production of course raises questions of acceptability and credibility which are covered in detail in later chapters. We need merely note here that the land requirement does not seem to be so great, in competition with food production, as to present an insuperable obstacle over the next few decades.

As has been said, the real problem is not the rate of emissions of carbon dioxide into the atmosphere, but the level of carbon dioxide concentration. This is rising because fossil fuels emit carbon dioxide without providing any mechanism for its recapture. However, biomass fuels absorb carbon dioxide during the plant's growth process so that, on a net basis, and over the duration of the growth and use cycle, first absorbing and then emitting, it leaves the carbon dioxide level unaffected.

But the notion, advocated in some quarters,[22] that the global warming problem be solved by creating 'carbon sinks' – to drain carbon dioxide out of the atmosphere as fast as the man-made sources (principally fossil fuel burning and tropical forest burn-off) pour it in – will not do. This is because it provides only a temporary solution; the sink will fill up because there is not enough land available to do the job that way.

To absorb carbon dioxide at a given rate, long rotation tree-growing, which is what would best provide such a sink, takes three to five times as much land as short rotation intensive fuel-wood production techniques. However, tree-growing that is partly justified for other reasons – to combat soil erosion or provide windbreaks for instance, in addition to a variety of amenity and conservation values, or as long-term commercial afforestation that carries the side benefit of reduced logging in virgin forest – can certainly help boost the initial rate of recapture ('sequestration', as it is called) of carbon dioxide from the atmosphere. This could be particularly valuable if scientific advice points to the necessity of actually reducing the level of carbon dioxide, prior to establishing a sustainable energy system designed to stabilise it.

With intensive fuel-wood production using short rotation techniques such as coppicing, which involves cutting the tree crop at frequent intervals to get rapid regrowth from rootstock left in the ground, something has to be done with the crop. It would swamp the market for conventional timber, assuming it were of commercial quality, and the only answers to this disposal problem would be either to bury it or to use the wood as fuel.

The static 'carbon sink' concept is thus replaced by a dynamically sustainable carbon fuel cycle which can, with care and some degree of international collaboration, do the trick. Biomass-based fuel technologies therefore provide the basis for a renewable and sustainable energy system provided, however, enough land is available for growing the fuel-wood. As we shall see, this seems likely to be the case. Furthermore, when burned efficiently in modern equipment, fuel-wood is virtually free of both the sulphur and nitrous oxide emissions which bedevil the use of fossil fuels.

Effective control of carbon dioxide levels in the atmosphere therefore means a very far-reaching technological transition for the world's energy industries. The investment needed to achieve such a transition appears likely (on the basis of estimates related to the New Zealand case described in the Appendix) to average about 10 per cent extra on raw energy prices over about 25 years, peaking at no more than 20 per cent around 2005.[23] (We discuss the problems of treating New Zealand as a microcosm of the world in Chapter 7, but may claim such costings do make GREENS a politically realistic prospect, given that concerns regarding global warming will thereby be met.)

If climatological research eventually shows that it is necessary to reduce the level of carbon dioxide in the atmosphere – perhaps to compensate for rising levels of other greenhouse gases that cannot so easily be absorbed by human action – that also can be done, but at greater cost. The greater cost would be substantial once fuel-wood production exceeded the amount that could be absorbed in the energy sector, since there would then be no offsetting benefit from the savings resulting from reduced fossil fuel extraction.

On the other hand, if claims that global warming is not happening – or alternatively is on balance actually desirable – turn out to be true, the cost of having begun the new energy policy are negligible: the relatively small amount of coppiced land involved in the 'learning by doing' phase can simply be left, allowing the trees to grow to maturity for eventual commercial use.

Essentially, these new technologies change the global warming problem from one which can at best be mitigated, or one to which the globe must perforce adapt, to one which can be controlled to the benefit of the natural environment and of this and future generations. In contrast, the current perception amongst politicians and their advisors is that energy prices would need to increase by 100 per cent to achieve only a 20 per cent reduction in carbon dioxide emissions by 2020.[24] That perception is based on the assumption made by economic analysts, taking current fuel technology as given, that the solution to the problem must simply be by deterring emissions. They calculate that a high carbon tax is needed in order to deter fuel consumption and induce higher efficiency in use. Of course, such a tax would yield huge revenues that could be used to offset other taxes and so is not properly regarded as a cost. Nevertheless, such a huge price increase would be highly disruptive (and unpopular, given the slow and small effect that it yields).

The difference between that scenario and the scheme outlined in this book is twofold. Firstly, the revenue from the (quite modest) fuel price increases we envisage is fed directly into the development of the alternative fuel-wood based technologies, thus affecting both the demand side and the supply side of the energy market. Secondly, our scenario is focused on net emissions, rather than the gross emissions which provide the focus of the current perception.

Other technologies and economising behaviour

It should be mentioned that the particular technologies described here are emphasised because they are known and practicable. They may thus be regarded as 'backstop technologies', a term used by economists to describe a technology that can be used if nothing better is available and which accordingly places an upper limit on the cost of doing whatever it is that the technology does. Almost certainly better technologies will become available, or improvements made to those described, in which case the approach which is advocated will be less costly (or more beneficial) than claimed above. Thus, in general, references to fuel-wood should be taken to mean fuel-wood or some other better source of biomass. Similarly, references to the utilisation technologies mentioned above are to these or to some other better utilisation technologies based upon using biomass raw material.

And the focus on sustainable fuel technology based, in general, on biomass does not mean that other, non-fuel sustainable energy technologies are left out of account. We shall refer to technologies that make use of wind, waves (and indeed solar energy save when stored as biomass fuel) as ambient energy technologies. Each of these can find a specific niche in a sustainable energy system – windmills where it is windy, solar water heating where it is sunny, and so on. How big a niche depends upon their economics in competition with biomass fuels at the price levels that obtain.

In addition, the price increases that are forecast to take place in any case, together with the modest additional cost increases arising from the progressive adoption of sustainable backstop technologies, will induce economising behaviour in all areas of energy supply and demand. Such behaviour (encouraged by public interest policies to break down the barriers of ignorance and prejudice which currently inhibit it) is anticipated in the cost estimates reported above.

This has been done by making the simple assumption that the 'business as usual' scenario, against which the 10 per cent cost increases are measured, will involve unchanging effective demand for fuels. Growth in final end use (resulting from continued growth of economic activity) will thus be met by increased use of ambient energy technologies and vigorous economising behaviour between the mine head, the refinery gate, or the fuel-wood coppice and the final end use, be it cooking or motoring.

To sum-up, rising final-user activity will be met partly by continued use of fossil fuels – only a very small part if climatologists demonstrate that the global warming problem is very urgent. The gap that is created will be filled partly by economising behaviour and partly by ambient energy technologies. Whatever part of the gap remains still unfilled would be supplied by sustainable fuel technology based on fuel-wood or other biomass.

Neither ambient energy systems nor economising behaviour, including for instance the adoption of more efficient power generating plant and the more widespread use of diesel engines in motor vehicles, are greatly dwelt on in this book. This does not mean that they are regarded as unimportant – quite the contrary – but that it would overburden the text to elaborate on all the multifarious ways in which such ambient energy technologies and economising behaviour will find a place.

The focus in this book, on biomass technologies for providing the raw material supply for a sustainable fuel system, is therefore not intended to imply that they are the only technologies that will play a part in dealing with global warming. Rather the message is that biomass technologies provide an assurance that all the effort that will be going into using ambient energy and into economising behaviour will not be wasted on ineffectually mitigating a possibly catastrophic climate change but can form part of an effective global programme for dealing with the problem.

Global redevelopment

The best places for intensive fuel-wood production are the hot and wet tropical regions that have seen so much destruction of primeval rainforest since World War Two.[25] One effect of implementing the environmentally sustainable energy future proposed in this book could therefore be a shift in rich country spending towards impoverished Third World countries, in the form of wage income to workers in fuel-wood production and processing. This shift could do much to relieve the Third World debt problem which threatens the stability of the North's financial markets, as well as relieving the poverty which is the root cause of malnutrition and famine in the South. Thus our proposals might also yield a new and more equitable pattern of development as well as a remedy to the global warming problem.

However, a note of caution is in order. The poorer countries have complex and precarious patterns of dependence on the soil which are better understood within the discipline of social anthropology than market-oriented economics. For rich countries, or commercial organisations based in rich countries, to go barging in with vast cash flows on the scale of current payments for OPEC and other oil supplies, in order to grab millions of hectares of land for growing trees to fuel the profligate energy demands of the rich, is a prospect that rightly raises both panic and derision amongst those with experience of land use problems in the South.

Panic, because a new colonialism based on corporate rather than sovereign power is conjured up with the peasantry further deprived of land for their traditional and subsistence farming becoming dependent on low wages in the new fuel-wood plantations to meet the necessities of life. Ground down by competition in a global biomass market, a Malthusian vision of a new plantation slavery is invoked.

Derision is another reaction because experience of tropical agriculture shows that such 'top down' enterprise in developing countries, which does not mobilise the knowledge and ingenuity of the people on the ground in a way that meets their own needs and aspirations, is doomed to failure.

To what extent the resistance of the South in the skirmishing that surrounded the negotiation of the FCCC is based upon such apprehensions, and to what extent they are based upon opportunism directed at extracting the maximum advantage from environmental concern coming from the rich, is hard to say. In the main, most probably the latter, since the notion of forests as carbon sinks, still less the concept advanced in this book, was not well enough established to loom large in the negotiating process. But certainly they are apprehensions that should concern anybody from a rich country making proposals that imply an extensive new use of land in poor countries.

Fortunately it is not necessary to use such land during what remains of this century since, in the first place, 'getting ready' does not require very large areas, but only a good number of demonstration projects in a variety of settings sufficient to establish the commercial practicability of GREENS and to provide experience and training opportunities. Secondly, sufficient woody waste material is currently unused – and sufficient under-utilised land exists for fuel-wood cropping in the rich countries – for the process of conversion to a fuel-wood based energy system to go quite a long way before any land in the hot wet parts of the planet need be used.

How the South, however, can become aware of its comparative advantage in fuel-wood production (and learn to resolve some of its development and economic problems by selling this new 'invisible export' of pollution clean-up services to rich countries) is a complex matter. It may be resolved in different ways in different countries, under the aegis of institutions set up under the FCCC, as is considered later in this book. However, the prospect remains that such a desirable outcome can, with wisdom and foresight, be brought about by implementing the GREENS concept – that is to say the coherent body of ideas presented in this book – thus benefiting both rich and poor countries in the coming decades, as well as handing on an atmosphere made safe for future generations.

Acceptability and credibility

Apart from the disagreements that have been mentioned between rich nations and poor, quite other disagreements exist, and much closer to home, to entrap the would-be reformer of our energy system. Indeed it sometimes seems in advancing the GREENS concept that the twin navigational dangers have grown together, leaving no passage between the Scylla of conservative industry pouring scorn on the notion that fossil fuels – oil in particular – might ever be dispensed with, and the Charybdis of certain environmentalists disappointed that a technical fix might be found for their longed-for ultimate obstacle to continuing economic growth.

It should be noted there is nothing in logic or economics which says that an input which was used in an outmoded technology should not become used again later on. Economists familiar with the 'capital re-switching' debate [26] will be aware of the possibility that even a complete technology which became outmoded because of a falling cost of capital can become preferable once more if the cost of capital falls even further. Certainly it cannot be argued that because biomass – old-fashioned wood burning – became outmoded with the progress of the industrial revolution, then it can never, with new technologies and circumstances, become viable again. We are not envisaging a return to smoky carcinogenic open-hearth wood burning, or to charcoal technology, but the use of biomass in modern, efficient and clean burning applications.

Nor does a zero – or even negative – growth path seem to be a sensible component of a practicable approach to a sustainable energy future. Apart from the damage that would result from a crash stop to the immense economic momentum referred to previously, a moral difficulty arises. For zero growth would condemn billions of the world's people to a no-hope future since there is no prospect of rich nations sharing their standard of living with the less well-off. Greater equity between nations can only come about by the less well-off growing more rapidly than the rich, with the latter comfortably enough off to accept slower growth.

Nor can the prospect of the motor car's demise be taken seriously. Clearly it is out of place in congested city centres, and the growing recognition by even rightist politicians of the need for public transport that works [27] – in the sense of being willingly used by the bulk of inner city travellers – is a hopeful sign that this particular kind of economising behaviour will yield significant emissions reductions in many places. But few people would seriously doubt the immense convenience yielded by Henry Ford's invention of the mass-produced auto.

Although a GREENS strategy posits no such implausible assault on consumerism, it remains somewhat difficult to be optimistic about its being taken seriously, given the record in energy-related matters of successive US administrations in the 1980s. However great one's admiration may be for the USA, it remains the case that the Reagan era, heralded by the symbolic dismantling of solar panels from the roof on the White House, brought in a most foolish and damaging episode in US energy policy.[28*] Damaging, in particular, in its retreat from the economising behaviour of other nations – epitomised by the continued production of 'gas-guzzling' autos that were unsaleable outside the USA.

One must hope that the Clinton Administration, amongst its many other preoccupations, will take a new look at US energy and environmental policy and see the wisdom of adopting more intelligent approaches. In this context a GREENS approach to tackling global warming problems becomes particularly apposite, and hopefully more likely to be seriously considered.

Notes

1. This is the first of a regrettably large number of abbreviations and acronyms which occur in this book, some my own I fear, which are gathered in a glossary at the end.

2. *Economist*, 13 June, 1992, p.12.

3. Fashions change as regards what to call countries that are not amongst the OECD group of industrialised nations. I generally adopt North for industrialised and South for undeveloped, under-developed, less developed, developing countries.

4. This acronym is not intended to convey any political platform – a concern for the environment is common currency amongst all modern political parties. Rather is it in the spirit of maternal admonitions to "eat your greens up dear, because they are good for you" ('greens' being British colloquial for green vegetables).

5. IPCC, 1992, p.72.

6. A key phrase (Arrow, 1962) in the development of economists' appreciation that the history-free workings of the 'invisible hand', which we come to in Chapters 5 and 6, provides a poor basis for considering technological progress.

7. *Economist*, 16 June, 1990, p.24.

8. In some earlier presentations of these ideas, this was called a Tradeable Carbon Absorption Duty (TCAD). But I discovered that some audiences take the word 'duty' to mean a tax, as in Excise Duty, whereas what is intended is a responsibility to ensure that actual physical absorption takes place at the expense of the energy firm incurring the TAO – and hence at the expense of the consumer

whose spending choices are the ultimate cause of greenhouse gas pollution. The 'C' (for carbon) is dropped since the idea is in principle applicable to other forms of pollution. And absorption can be on a net basis, so that a firm can discharge its obligation by paying for some other firm's (or some other country's – particularly 'South' country's – emissions to be reduced. An increase in net absorption is the same thing as a decrease in net emissions, which is the aim of the policy.

9. Morisette and Plantinga, 1991, p.2; Simonis, p.106.

10. Mohamed, 1991, para 9.

11. Now available in *Global Warming*: *Economic Policy Responses* edited by Rudiger Dornbusch and James M. Poterba, which makes conveniently available the papers discussed at this landmark conference held in October 1990. These include the paper by Hirofumi Uzawa which is taken up in Chapter 8 of this book. An introductory essay by Andrew Solow, a non-economist, on 'Is There a Global Warming Problem?', concludes that the debate should not be about scientific facts and uncertainties but over how to respond to them given that an 'immediate' emissions reduction by 75 per cent would cause 'massive economic dislocation'. It was a landmark because it was the first occasion when leading figures from the economics profession were brought together to discuss global warming. As such it set the tone for subsequent economic thinking on the subject and, although we advocate a different mode of analysis in Chapter 3 of this book, the importance of quantification, and of cutting the policy coat to suit the cloth of resources available for meeting competing ends, cannot be doubted.

This approach has been identified most closely with the work of William Nordhaus, who has developed several models of global warming, the first (with Gary Yohe) as early as 1983. His essay for the Rome Conference, on *Economic Approaches to Global Warming*, mentions his estimate of 0.25 per cent of US GDP as the calculable damage cost of a doubling of carbon dioxide levels, elsewhere bumped up to the range 1-2 per cent to allow for less easily quantified aspects (Nordhaus, 1991). In Economic Approaches Nordhaus prioritises policies as, first, to research climate change in greater depth; second, to develop new energy technologies with low greenhouse effects; third, to adopt 'no regrets' conservation policies that more or less pay for themselves; and fourth, carbon taxes.

Perhaps the most surprising thing about this book, and the trend of mainstream economic opinion formation which the Rome Conference set in motion, is the contrast it provides with the profession's reaction to the previous bout of environmentalist concern following the publication of *Limits to Growth* (Meadows et al, 1972) shortly before the first UNCED and the first OPEC oil price hike in 1973. Then the profession jumped in to proclaim the adaptability of the economic system, the implausibility that any input is technically essential, the opportunities for substituting alternatives for oil and the existence of 'backstop' technologies which would always be available to come to the rescue if the growth process began to get stuck. With global warming, however, the profession has been proclaiming the difficulty in adapting to a non-carbon future, the near-essentiality of fossil fuels, the absence of backstop technologies, and the great cost of responding to global warming in terms of a slowing of the growth process.

12. Brundtland Commission, p.49 *et seq.*

13. Sen, 1970, p.33.

14. Webb and Ricketts, 1980, p.15.

15. Not actual interest on all loans in the financial sector, but notional interest on the finance needed to fund investments in physical plant and other capital, including human capital such as the acquisition of productive knowledge.

16. Darmstadter, 1991, p.8.

17. *Economist*, 7 July, 1990, p.19.

18. Harrison, 1988, p.70 *et seq.*

19. The most important amongst these low income fossil fuel rich economies are China and India.

20. Manne and Richels, 1992, Chapter 4.

21. The *Oxford English Dictionary* cites Cobbett's *Rural Rides* (1885,vol.I p.361, "There is a good deal of fuel-wood") but not wood-fuel, woodfuel or fuelwood.

22. Myers, 1989, p 76.

23. Read, 1991, Table 2.

24. Dean and Hoeller, 1992, Chart 2 and Hoeller et al, 1992, Tables 4 and 12.

25. World Bank, 1992, p.57.

26. Ahmad, 1991, pp. 183 and 246.

27. Norris, 1992; Department of Transport and Department of the Environment, 1992, Annex D.

28. Now, it seems, on its way out with the new administration's proposals for substantial energy taxes that will begin to bring US energy prices – and in due course no doubt, US energy efficiency – in line with its competitors and better reflecting 'the real cost of energy' (Hubbard, 1991) but still falling short of an appropriate response to the threat of global warming.

2. The Fragile Climate System

It is ironic that, no sooner had we begun to breathe easier over the dread prospect of nuclear winter, than we were plunged into fearful contemplation of global warming. The apparent opposites of nuclear winter and anthropogenic enhancement of the greenhouse effect, EGE,[1]* are linked by a common factor, which of course is the fragility of the thin layer of air which surrounds the only world we have for living and breathing in. This fragility was revealed by early versions of the general circulation models (GCMs) of the global climate system used to analyse the likely environmental impact of a nuclear holocaust,[2] and now available in more sophisticated versions for studying the effects of greenhouse gases.

It is a fragility that has long been familiar to those who have studied the relationship between climate and major volcanic eruptions. The most spectacular of these in modern times took place at Krakatoa in 1883 when the island of that name all but disappeared off the map in a violent eruption. The vast quantity of ash thrown into the stratosphere by that event resulted in spectacular sunsets for several years following and in unusually cold weather – poor summers and hard winters. Similar effects, on a less noticeable scale, followed Mexico's El Chichon eruption in 1982 and Mount Pinatubo's in the Philippines in June 1991.

Crying Wolf?

To many casual observers it must seem that the doom-mongers have cried wolf once too often, especially with a sceptical strain of commentary, questioning whether EGE is taking place at all, that emanated from climatologists close to the White House of President Bush.[3] Or, if it is, whether it has much to do with human actions. Global warming may, so these commentators say, be due to natural causes or, alternatively, EGE may be just what is needed to stave off an impending ice age. Maybe so; such comment is closely in line with the view taken here, though leading to an opposite conclusion.

The title used for an early draft of this book ('What to Do About Global Warming; Even if It Isn't Happening – and Even if It Might Be a Good Thing') implied the view, analysed in the following chapter, that inaction is not necessarily an appropriate response to uncertainty. The likelihood that nothing is coming the other way at a blind bend in the road does not make it sensible to cut the corner. The bits of science that are discussed in this chapter are chosen for their relevance to a precautionary approach and leave out much that is reported at length in the authoritative work of the Intergovernmental Panel on Climate Change (IPCC).

The IPCC, which involved 370 leading scientists worldwide as participants in either formulating or reviewing their 1990 Report,[4] focused on what is most likely to happen as a result of EGE, on the basis of various scenarios regarding policy response to EGE in the decades ahead. Their predictions listed a catalogue of damaging consequences which led representatives from 137 countries at the November 1990 Second World Climate Conference in Geneva to include in the resulting Ministerial Statement a call for negotiations on an FCCC to begin without delay. In relation to the uncertainties the Statement said 'Where there are threats of serious or irreversible damage, lack of full scientific certainty should not be used as a reason for postponing cost-effective measures.' – a turn of phrase which is embodied in the FCCC.[5]

This response to uncertainty is inadequate. A precautionary approach would suggest taking extra, non-cost-effective measures, in order to be prepared for the worst, such as might result from less likely but nevertheless possible predictions. But the IPCC may have judged that politicians might not be willing to act on such a basis and may have decided to focus on a central, most likely prediction and the impact of different responses to it. In the event it has been accepted that, on these 'most likely' outcomes, action should be put in hand without delay. The scientific perspective that follows provides reinforcement of the need for action. Serious as the catalogue of likely damage is, there are even more weighty reasons for scientific concern about EGE.

For we cannot be certain of anything predicted by the climatologists – nor would they claim we should be. Their models serve to generate warnings rather than forecasts. And it could well be that global warming, if it is happening, is caused by natural rather than anthropogenic processes. However, whatever may be the cause of global warming, if it is possible to control it – through measures that enable us to choose how much anthropogenic enhancement of the greenhouse effect we generate – then control should be exercised for the common good. And until we are sure that EGE is a good thing, control should be exercised on a precautionary basis in the direction of returning towards the status quo ante, that is to say towards the atmospheric conditions that obtained under natural forces prior to this century.

The bits of science which are relevant to this message are firstly the energy fluxes that drive earth's climate system, secondly nature's carbon cycle and the impact of human action on the balance of that cycle with consequential effects on the climate system, and thirdly the concepts of negative and positive feedback which underlie the behaviour of complex dynamic systems like global climate. In discussing system dynamic behaviour we provide grounds for a precautionary 'stitch in time' approach to policy.

The Global Energy Balance[6]

The temperatures experienced near the earth's surface, and therefore our climate, depend upon a balance between the amount of radiant energy reaching the earth – almost entirely from the sun – and the amount lost to cold outer space by radiation from the earth's surface and atmosphere. Radiation has fundamental properties like a wave motion and different radiation has different wavelengths. How much energy is transported by radiation depends on how hot the emitter is. The hotter it is the more energy it radiates, with a shortening in the average wavelength of the radiation.

The sun's surface, at around 6,000° Celsius, emits intensely, mainly in the visible (white) and shorter ultraviolet wavelengths. The earth – land, sea and air, mostly around 15° Celsius – mainly emits invisible, longer wavelength, infra-red radiation, and very much less intensely. It appears blue from outer space but that is the fraction of visible solar radiation which is reflected by the oceans and transmitted by the atmosphere. The earth appears dark on its night-time side since our eyes are unable to see infra-red radiation.

The reason why volcanic eruptions have their effect on climate is closely similar to the reason why a nuclear holocaust would cause nuclear winter. Different wavelength radiation is differently affected by encounters with dust, and indeed differently by different kinds of dust. Dust in the upper atmosphere, whether propelled there by volcanic action or by nuclear explosion, prevents solar radiation reaching lower levels of the atmosphere. If it is white or shiny dust, part of the sun's rays are reflected straight out into space. If it is black or dirty dust it absorbs some of the solar radiation and warms up the surrounding stratosphere which then radiates more infra-red than it otherwise would, and in all directions, some of it into outer space.

However, that is not the end of the story since the dust might also, in principle, be expected to prevent the loss of heat from near the surface of the earth by just the same mechanisms as it prevents some of the energy in the sun's rays reaching the earth. The overall effect of dust in the atmosphere thus depends on a balance, just as the basic processes determining the earth's surface temperature depend on a balance.

The reason it is not an exact balance is because of the different wavelengths of the sun's and earth's radiation. This has to do with the mechanisms of quantum physics where interactions between matter and radiation depend sharply upon synchronism between the wavelength of the wave motion and the size of dust, or of some atomic component of the dust. Because of the possibility of synchronism or nonsynchronism, small changes can have big effects.

To illustrate this, think of the screw threads on an engineering nut and bolt as respectively the wavelength of a radiation wave motion and the size of a dust particle with which the radiation might interact. Clearly the interaction is going to be quite different if the threads are the same (strong interaction), very slightly different (interaction only with difficulty), or significantly different (the nut simply won't screw onto the bolt at all). It turns out that, although dust interferes quite well with incoming solar radiation, it has little effect on outgoing infra-red. So the earth's surface cools down a bit until, with the cooler surface radiating slightly less intensively, outgoing infra-red is again in balance with the incoming solar radiation.

The reverse is true of greenhouse gases, present in the atmosphere in small, or in some cases minute, quantities. The molecules (or discrete particles comprising bundles of atoms) of which these gases are composed, also have characteristic dimensions which, much more than the main constituents oxygen and nitrogen, interact with incoming white radiation differently than with outgoing infra-red radiation and thus affect the balance of energy fluxes which determines climate. But in the case of greenhouse gases, the strong interaction is with infra-red outgoing radiation, part of which is then returned to the earth's surface, so that the earth's surface must warm up a bit in order to radiate enough infra-red (net of what is trapped by the greenhouse gases) to balance the incoming solar radiation.

Without this effect the globe would be much colder – about 33 degrees Celsius colder on average. So there certainly is a greenhouse effect and it certainly is a good thing since without it most of the globe's surface would freeze up. The question is whether we want more of a good thing, i.e. enhanced greenhouse effect, given that the biosphere – the system of living organisms in the oceans, in or on land, and in the lower atmosphere or troposphere – has now adapted to the amount provided by nature in recent millennia. The concern is about stabilising the greenhouse effect at levels that are environmentally benign to homo sapiens and the other life forms that have evolved to occupy the planet as it is or, rather, as it was before the industrial revolution.

Energy fluxes

Having seen how quite tiny concentrations of particular substances in the atmosphere can, because of a strong interaction with incoming or outgoing radiation, have disproportionate effects on the balance of energy fluxes through it, let us get a handle on the scale of these energy fluxes.

Global energy fluxes are vast – so great that only a small enhancement of greenhouse effects (or reduction of them) is needed to have dramatic effects on the balance. Total solar radiation reaching the earth's surface is equal to about ten thousand times the rate of global industrial energy use. If it were possible for the energy flux in one direction to be stopped, the earth's atmosphere would change temperature at about 1000 degrees Celsius a year: life would cease in a week and the oceans be boiling in a month.

These energy fluxes are illustrated in Figure 2.1. It can be seen that only 51 per cent of solar radiation is absorbed by the earth's surface – which of course is mainly ocean – with 30 per cent reflected immediately by cloud tops, polar icecaps and deserts, and 19 per cent absorbed in the atmosphere before it gets near the surface. The infra-red radiant energy flux into the atmosphere in the opposite direction is 1.14 times the total solar energy flux, of which 0.15 is transmitted directly into outer space and 0.99 is absorbed, together with 0.32 received through convective and evaporative transfer, giving a total of 1.50 absorbed in the atmosphere from above or below. Of this 0.95 is re-radiated downwards (giving a total heat flux to the earth's surface of 1.46 times incoming solar radiation and hence the natural greenhouse effect) and 0.55 upwards to outer space which, with the 0.30 reflected and 0.15 transmitted directly, equals 100 per cent – just balancing the incoming solar radiation.

Thus, when an equilibrium exists, the atmosphere and the earth's surface are each in energy balance, and jointly with the earth's surroundings. Slight discrepancies in these balances lead to warming or cooling of the atmosphere, land and oceans in order to restore equilibrium, with impacts on surface temperatures and the climate. The basic radiative process is stable-heat gain, for whatever reason, leads to a higher temperature and more outward radiation until the gain is balanced out. But the balance which preserves the biosphere is far removed from the basic radiative balance and involves complex relativities between atmosphere, land and ocean, with complex variation in different places – in short the global climate system in all its half understood complexity.

The ocean deep[7]

The big stabiliser in all this is the enormous thermal inertia provided by the ocean and the polar icecaps. The average temperature of the atmosphere cannot get too far away from that of the ocean because air that is warmer than usual, relative to the ocean, reduces the evaporative transport of latent heat from the ocean (clouds do not form so easily so that some of the water vapour that has evaporated from the ocean finds its way back to the ocean with no net heat transport to the atmosphere). Thus the ocean is less cooled by net evaporation – and the atmosphere is less warmed by condensation – than normally, until the usual temperature difference is restored. Heat conduction from ocean to atmosphere ('sensible' heat, i.e. heat that can be felt or sensed) is a weaker effect

Figure 2.1 Energy Fluxes Through the Atmosphere

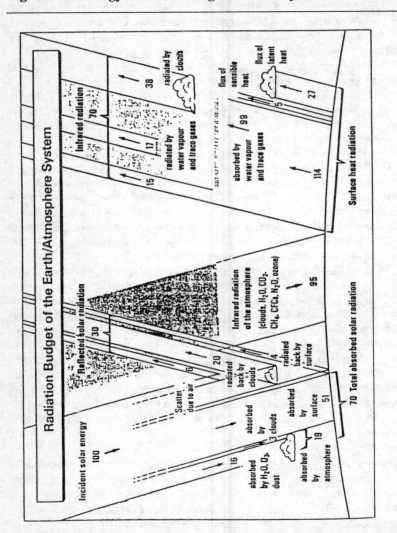

Reproduced, with permission, from page 202 of the English translation of the Report of the German Bundestag Study-Commission entitled 'Protecting the Earth' published in 1991.

than evaporative heat transport, as can be seen from Fig 2.1, but is similarly reduced if the air is warmer than usual. The steadying influence of the ocean can be appreciated from the fact that it takes as much energy to raise the top three metres of the ocean by one degree Celsius as it does to do the same for the entire five billions of millions of tons of atmosphere.

The oceans are roughly four kilometres deep. There is a catch in so far as stabilising a warming process is concerned since warming a liquid from above is a slow way to warm it through, and thus not a very effective way of cooling whatever is above the liquid. (That's why we boil water on top of the stove rather than under the grill – warm water rises and sets up convection currents that mix up the whole body of water). On the other hand it is very difficult to see an atmospheric cooling process getting out of hand, as the whole ocean's area would need to freeze over before convection processes in the ocean ceased to provide a supply of water for the rapid evaporative transport of heat into the atmosphere.

Nevertheless, even with a warming process from above, there is mixing of the upper layers of the oceans because of the waves and currents that are set up by surface wind patterns, such as the trade winds which push warm subtropical water against Florida, to be deflected into the Gulf Stream that keeps Northern Europe habitable, and the Roaring Forties which propel cold Antarctic waters up the coast of Chile. Furthermore, for as long as there remain substantial quantities of polar ice, the breaking off of icebergs and their melting into the Northern and Southern Oceans prevents the upper ocean from getting warm at all fast.

Despite evaporative heat transfer upwards, warming from above is what goes on, on average, over most of the globe's oceans – hardly surprising given that it is the deep blue oceans, covering seven-tenths of the earth's surface, which in fact absorb most of the solar radiation that reaches it. The upper kilometre of the deep oceans, together with the continental shelves, is a body of water that is warmer and less salty – and hence less dense – than the deep ocean which comprises the remaining three kilometres. Intensive cooling of the oceans is relatively localised, with the warm North Atlantic waters around Iceland, cooled by prevailing freeze-dried winds from Greenland's icy mountains, by far the most significant as regards climate.

Rapid evaporation there leads to increasing salinity and cooling and hence to substantial densification. The result is a downwards plunge of cold and saline water into the deep ocean which sets up a vast and slow convection current flowing in deep water southwards in the Atlantic – underneath the Gulf Stream and equatorial currents – eastward in the Antarctic, underneath the surface current propelled by the Roaring Forties, and northwards to rise gradually to the surface in the Indian and Pacific Oceans and begin a slowly warming contrary drift of upper ocean water, muddled up with the various windblown surface currents, back into the

South Atlantic and then, via the Gulf Stream to take the North Atlantic plunge again, some centuries later.[8]

It is thought that ice ages may have been brought about by the failure of this huge convection current, perhaps brought about by a preliminary warming phase that leaves Greenland less icy and the salinifying and densifying evaporative cooling of the North Atlantic ineffective. The higher rainfall, predicted with changing climate patterns under EGE, could reinforce the effect of melting freshwater Greenland ice in reducing the salinity of the North Atlantic.

A failure of the huge oceanic convection current could block or slow the warm Gulf Stream and precipitate expansion of the Arctic ice sheet – an unstable process since more ice means more reflection and less absorption of the percentage of solar radiation that reaches the earth's surface, hence more cold weather and more ice.[9] In short the kind of process that may have been involved in the abrupt climate jumps to ice age conditions that have occurred in pre-history.[10*]

On the other hand, very strong EGE could accelerate a retreat of Arctic and maybe Antarctic ice (and lead to a warming instability with more absorption and less reflection) before the deep ocean convection had time to stop – thus leading to the green Greenland and green Antarctica of some geological periods, with the oceans more than 50 metres higher than they are today.

The linkage between polar ice and ocean currents and temperatures on the one hand, and, on the other, the atmospheric currents (winds) and temperatures which form our climate pattern, are not at all well understood. As suggested by the idea of a stabiliser, the timescale of some oceanic events is much slower than that for atmospheric events (with polar ice changes an order of magnitude slower again). This is partly because of the thermal inertia effect mentioned above, and partly because of the much slower movement of the oceans. Even in the 'fast' Gulf Stream water takes about two years to cross the Atlantic, whereas air in a stratospheric jet stream can do the trip in less than a day. Polar sea-ice may have a shorter response time than the deep oceanic current, while the melting of thick continental icecaps could take a millennia.

From the perspective of the ocean's ability to stabilise climate change, it appears that quite a small portion of the ocean's surface can generate mixing with the deep ocean when it is being strongly cooled from above, whereas the rest of the ocean, being warmed from above, remains layered and insulated from the bottom three-quarters. If the deep ocean convection ceased, as it is believed to have in past glaciations, the stabiliser will be much less effective against either another rapid cooling to glaciation or a rapid warming that might eventually green Greenland.

Greenhouse Gases[11]

Before going on to discuss the long-term dynamics of the climate system, and the problem of knowing what is happening to it, we must look at the greenhouse gases, both naturally arising and anthropogenic, which are believed to be causing a warming of the atmosphere. As mentioned earlier, the enhanced greenhouse effect is believed to arise because anthropogenic trace quantities of these gases, like trace quantities of dust in the upper atmosphere, interact differently with incoming, mainly white, solar radiation and outgoing infra-red radiation. In addition, water vapour, the main greenhouse gas, condenses to form clouds which interact both with white, solar radiation and outgoing infra-red radiation.

We will discuss water vapour, clouds and other aspects of the impact of water on climate (apart from the stabilising effect of water in the oceans, and possible destabilising effect of failures of the deep ocean current, discussed above) later, and here deal mainly with carbon dioxide and the chloro-fluoro-carbons (CFCs hereafter) with only brief comments on other greenhouse gases. Apart from water vapour, carbon dioxide is the main greenhouse gas and is so because it is the next most prevalent greenhouse gas in the atmosphere. Other gases are more powerful, in the sense of greenhouse effectiveness, for a given standardised concentration, but are less important since less heavily concentrated.

A fuller understanding of which greenhouse gases are more important requires a dynamic analysis over future time, since different gases have different rates of dispersion (by chemical breakdown to harmless gases, or by ocean absorption) as well as different effectiveness for a given standardised concentration.[12] Dispersion rates measured by residence time in the atmosphere matter, since it is the level of concentration of greenhouse gases, resulting from cumulated emissions minus dispersion, that affects the rate of temperature increase, and because it is the cumulative temperature increase, and for how long it persists (e.g. long enough, perhaps, to halt the deep ocean convection current) that matters as far as risks of major climate effects are concerned.

Carbon dioxide

Carbon dioxide in the atmosphere is the result both of human activity and of natural processes linked with what is known as the carbon cycle. Life on earth comprises two balanced kingdoms of plants and animals, which take opposite roles in the carbon cycle. Animals consume carbohydrates as their main source of energy. Carbohydrates are complex chemicals containing mainly carbon and hydrogen. To release this energy animals breathe in oxygen from the air and 'burn' the carbohydrates in the muscles which power their movement. They then breathe out water vapour and carbon dioxide, which are the waste products of the muscular activity.

Plants consume carbon dioxide and water to make carbohydrates, in which the first stage is the process of photosynthesis powered by sunlight, with release of the oxygen needed by animals. They also respire for their energy needs, emitting carbon dioxide as do animals. Without mobility, their energy needs per ton of biomass are much less than for animals, but such is the huge preponderance of plant life over animal life that their respiration exceeds animals'. A large proportion of animal life is under the earth's surface, insects and microbes, which together with the impact of the underground portions of plants, yields soil respiration.

In fact the natural carbon life cycle comprises more carbon fixing by photosynthesis than carbon dioxide release by animals, with the balance made up by natural forest fires, accumulation of carbon-rich humus in the soil, and changes in the carbon dioxide contained in the ocean, together with geological timescale effects from the weathering of carbonaceous (chalky) rocks brought to the surface by movements of the earth's crust. Human activity adds to this carbon cycle by the combustion of fossil fuels, and the clearance of standing timber for agricultural development – nowadays mainly by setting fire to tropical jungles but historically by similar burning of the temperate forests of Europe, North and South America and Australasia.

So, as with atmospheric temperature change, related to the net effect of two energy flows that are nearly balanced, carbon dioxide concentration in the atmosphere changes in response to two flows that are also large and nearly balanced, as follows: [13]

Flows of carbon into the atmosphere: [14*]

	(billions of tons)
Deforestation burning	2
Burning of fossil fuels	5
Plant respiration	50
Soil and animal respiration	50
Diffusion from oceans	100
Total	207

Flows of carbon dioxide from the atmosphere:

Photosynthesis by plants	100
Diffusion into oceans	104
Total	204

Net annual increment	3

Given the response of natural forces to the present situation there would be an annual decrement of four billion tons of carbon from the atmosphere compared with the current increment of three billion tons. Thus human activity is shifting the global stock of carbon from below ground (fossil fuels) and on the ground (standing timber) and in the soil (by unsustainable exploitation and degradation of previously humus-rich forest soils) into the atmosphere. The principal difference between anthropogenic emissions of energy and of carbon dioxide is that, while the first comprises less than 0.01 per cent of total energy flows through the atmosphere, mankind's carbon dioxide emissions now comprise maybe as much as four per cent of the total carbon dioxide flow.

This increased flow of carbon dioxide into the atmosphere alters the location of the globe's carbon inventory which is currently believed to be made up as follows (in billions of tons): [15]

Carbon as carbon dioxide in atmosphere	720
Carbon fixed in the life cycle	2,750
Carbon in estimated fossil fuel reserves	5,000
Carbon dissolved in oceans	38,700
Carbon in ocean sediments and lithosphere	66,000,000

The stock of carbon in the life cycle includes the vast Northern (boreal) coniferous forests and temperate deciduous forests, both of which are nowadays roughly stable in size, plus tropical forests that have been declining rapidly since World War Two with commercial exploitation and burn-off for agricultural clearances. These forests cover about two-fifths of the world's land surface area and hold about four-fifths of the lifecycle part of the carbon inventory: forests dominate the dynamics of the natural carbon cycle which, given the time needed to grow, has long-term periodicity like the oceans.

As with energy flows, the oceans are, again, a huge sink into which atmospheric carbon dioxide eventually finds its way. At current atmospheric temperatures and carbon dioxide concentrations, about one-half of the additional carbon dioxide released by mankind is removed by oceanic absorption and other processes. Quite how is a bit of a mystery: it was assumed until recently to go largely into the oceans,[16] but work reported in 1990 suggested that only about 15 per cent could be accounted for that way.[17] One supposes that the carbon dioxide washed out of the sky by rain falling at sea has been included in the calculations, though I have not seen it mentioned.[18*]

That leaves around 20 per cent of emissions reabsorbed nobody knows where. Recently work has begun on growing trees in a closed environment to see how much total carbon is absorbed, below ground as well as above.[19] This is being done in a carbon dioxide-rich environment also, to see whether higher levels of carbon dioxide might become self-stabilising, with higher concentrations resulting in faster rates of carbon absorption.

An important aspect of the carbon cycle is that the ocean's capacity to dispose of the excess supplied from the land depends upon phytoplankton, micro-organisms in the oceans which photosynthesise carbon dioxide (arriving from whatever mechanism) and eventually precipitate it to the ocean floor after it has climbed the food chain of the ocean ecology. The viability of these organisms, and their ability to prevent ocean surface layer concentrations of carbon dioxide rising to equilibrium with the atmosphere, the point at which more cannot be absorbed, depends on the supply of nutrients coming from the up-welling of deep water (which is why plankton-eating whales go to the Antarctic to feed). Thus there are linkages both between the physical behaviour of the oceans and their biological content and conversely.

What is clear is that there is great ignorance about the carbon cycle, and therefore about how carbon dioxide gets into and out of the atmosphere, contributing to the uncertainties which surround the EGE. As far as proposals to be elaborated later are concerned (and given that extra carbon dioxide may need to be absorbed to compensate for rising levels of other greenhouse gases) we take the rather conservative assumption that only one-third of emissions are absorbed naturally, leaving two-thirds to be dealt with if the objective is to stabilise the level of greenhouse gases in the atmosphere.

CFCs – a cautionary tale[20]

A particularly unfortunate characteristic of this man-made trace gas is that it interacts not only with radiation but also with a very important gas which is naturally present in the upper atmosphere. The CFC gases, which are the subject of the Montreal convention, have a chlorine component which has a near perfect quantum mechanical fit with ozone molecules, so that a chemical reaction occurs between them very easily, with consequential destruction of the ozone molecules. This is the cause of the 'ozone hole' which appears over Antarctica in the Southern spring and is symptomatic of generally reducing ozone in the stratosphere.

It is the ozone in the upper atmosphere which interacts strongly with the harmful ultraviolet component of the incoming radiation from the sun, absorbing it and shielding the biosphere from damage. Unfortunately the chlorine component is not removed by its ozone destroying reaction, but merely acts as a catalyst for a process which sees two ozone molecules turn into three molecules of ordinary oxygen. Thus the impact will not diminish until the catalytic chlorine disperses, which will take a very long time. It seems likely that, even with the Montreal convention proving effective in sharply reducing further emissions of CFCs, it will take about 100 years for the CFCs already up there to disperse and for the ozone hole to be filled.

Meanwhile we and other life forms will suffer the carcinogenic consequences of increased ultraviolet radiation reaching the earth's surface, including impairment of plant productivity and food supplies. A consequence which may prove to be of significance in relation to EGE is the sensitivity of phytoplankton to ultraviolet radiation. These are concentrated in the Southern oceans where the ozone hole gives greatest cause for concern. Just when we need these little animals to be busy disposing of the rising levels of carbon dioxide absorbed into the oceans from the atmosphere, they are being killed off by enhanced ultraviolet. And maybe will suffer from reduced supply of nutrients brought up from the depths if the huge oceanic convection is slowed.

This makes for a cautionary tale, having regard to the rather meagre benefits yielded by the ubiquitous aerosol. (CFCs are used in refrigeration also, which has certainly yielded great benefits but, as with aerosols, other gases, such as propane-butane mixtures, can do that job nearly as well.)[21*] And more cautionary still, having regard to the blithe disregard for possible side effects with which industrial society took to using CFCs.[22*] But perhaps the most cautionary aspect of all is that the ozone-destroying impact of CFCs was foreseen in 1974 and measurements undertaken all over the earth of upper atmosphere ozone concentrations. The analysis of these measurements was based on an assumption built into a theoretical model of the possible CFC process, which predicted that ozone destruction would go on uniformly all over the globe and all the time. But the rapid localised destruction which causes the ozone hole is due to stratospheric ice particles that concentrate CFCs during the intensely cold and dark Antarctic winter and then release them suddenly in the spring.

The seasonal and polar tendency of ozone depletion was there in the measurements, and able to be observed long before the Antarctic ozone hole appeared. But the measurements showing this were disregarded. The computers that had been set up to process the data rejected them on a built-in assumption that readings substantially inconsistent with the theoretical model must have come from faulty instruments!

The lesson, of course, is not to despair of rational modelling but, in relation to problems where a precautionary approach is needed, to use the models to explore the bounds of what might happen, rather than to focus on predicting what is most likely.

Other greenhouse gases

On a business as usual basis, carbon dioxide is expected to contribute more than half of the greenhouse effect attributable to human activity in the next half century. Some of the other greenhouse gases (methane, nitrous oxide and ozone) arise partly from natural processes and some, mainly the CFCs discussed previously, are wholly anthropogenic. The former thus contribute to the normal greenhouse effect as well as to EGE. Like carbon dioxide, their effect on balance is to impede outgoing infra-red radiation more than they impede incoming white solar radiation.

However, the role of ozone is ambiguous because, in the upper atmosphere, it acts as a coolant by preventing incoming ultraviolet light reaching the earth's surface, whereas lower down it blankets outward going infra-red. The CFCs thus have a double effect: they both destroy ozone and act as very powerful greenhouse gases in their own right. The newer CFCs, and other refrigerants, are less damaging to the ozone but they remain about as powerful in their direct greenhouse effect. The current changeover to newer CFCs under the Montreal convention is because of the carcinogenic consequences of damaging the stratospheric ozone. Eventually the choice of commercial refrigerants may need to be determined by their long-term greenhouse impact as they leak away to the atmosphere, with a willingness to accept lower technical efficiency from refrigerators.

Of the other greenhouse gases, methane is expected to have only about one-fifth the EGE effect of carbon dioxide on a business as usual scenario, but will emerge as the most significant residual problem if measures to control carbon dioxide prove to be inadequate to handle EGE. Fortunately, to the extent such measures lead to the meticulous collection of biomass residues and their use as fuel, one of the sources of methane, rotting vegetation, would be reduced. Other sources, mainly animal flatulence (at either end as far as ruminants, the main offenders, are concerned) and rice paddy emissions, would present a more difficult problem.

Nitrous oxide (and sulphur dioxide emissions leading to the acid rain problem) would also be reduced to the extent that economising behaviour and alternative motor vehicle power systems are successful in substituting more benign biomass-based fuels for fossil fuels. However, dealing with acid rain has a down side since sulphur dioxide has the effect of whitening clouds and increasing the proportion of incoming solar radiation that is immediately reflected back into space. So its reduction, in response to the acid rain problem, leads to the greenhouse effect being somewhat reinforced. Another way of putting it is to say that sulphur dioxide is currently masking part of the EGE.

The History of Carbon Dioxide in the Atmosphere[23]

The main point that emerges is that the normal stock of carbon dioxide in the atmosphere is of the order of only 100 times the annual net flow, as enhanced by anthropogenic emissions, so that it needs only a few decades of human activity at the rate it has reached post-World War Two for the atmospheric concentration to be altered quite substantially. The important question is, then, whether this anthropogenic shift in carbon dioxide concentrations is leading the global climate system into a state which is in any way abnormal. Fortunately, our knowledge of the concentration of carbon dioxide in the atmosphere now stretches far back beyond our recent technological ability to measure it, which dates from the nineteenth century development of quantitative chemistry.

Falling snow carries with it a fingerprint of the atmosphere at the time it falls by trapping small bubbles of contemporary air as it densifies into ice. At the Antarctic icecap ice-core samples have been taken of compressed snow that has been piling up for 160,000 years, covering four ice ages and the intervening periods, of which the latest warm epoch has featured recorded history. Contemporaneous temperatures can be measured by the proportion of the isotope deuterium (resulting in 'heavy water') in the ice and cross-checked by studies of the widths of annual tree rings in ancient logs recovered from peat bogs, etc.

The age of both ice-core samples and of buried trees, and hence carbon dioxide and temperature contemporaneity, can be determined by carbon dating and other radio-isotope techniques.[24*] It has been established that there is a close correlation between higher carbon dioxide concentrations and episodes of prehistory that have been warmer than the intervening ice ages. This correlation is illustrated in Figure 2.2 in which the patterns of carbon dioxide concentration and temperature change for the last 160,000 years are superposed.

This correlation does not establish causality – mere playing with statistics never can. However, with our knowledge of the radiative properties of the various greenhouse gases, as outlined above, it is clear that carbon dioxide in the atmosphere should be expected to have a greenhouse effect. Thus, if carbon dioxide concentrations in prehistory were not wholly causal of the correlated climate changes, it is hard to believe they did not make a reinforcing contribution to whatever was causal. And even if the temperature was causal of the carbon dioxide, it is not much comfort since, with causality also running from carbon dioxide to temperature, that would simply be to set up a reinforcing vicious circle, with more heat causing more carbon dioxide and more carbon dioxide causing more greenhouse effect and yet more heat.

The answer to the important question raised above emerges with a clarity that is striking for a situation in which almost everything else (carbon budgets, polar ice, ocean currents, the ecology of phytoplankton, and the effect of changed ultra-violet radiation as we have seen; General Circulation Models, GCMs, as we shortly will see) is confused by uncertainty. Something unusual – indeed unprecedented – has been happening to the atmosphere since the industrial revolution, and specially since World War Two.

As may be seen from Figure 2.2, prior to the industrial revolution and throughout the previous 160,000 years, the concentration of carbon dioxide in the atmosphere has *never exceeded about 280 parts per million and has never been less than 180 parts per million*. However, since World War

Two, the concentration (which had been brought to about 305 ppm in the previous 150 years) has *risen to 360 parts per million and will rise to 400 parts per million by 2010*. On business as usual trends *it will reach 600 parts per million before the end of the next century, more than twice the highest level it has reached at any time in the last 160,000 years*.[25*] To take a biological parallel, it is as though a human being's systolic blood pressure, symptomatic of a cardio-vascular condition, having risen from its normal between 100 and 140 to a worrying but unexceptional 170 millimetres of mercury, were forecast to reach a heart-stopping 350, and to keep on rising!

Figure 2.2 The Prehistoric Record of Carbon Dioxide Concentrations and Global Temperatures

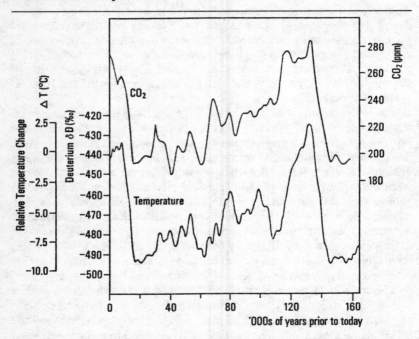

Reproduced, with permission, from page 350 of the English translation of the Report of the German Bundestag Study-Commission entitled 'Protecting the Earth's Atmosphere', published in 1989. A similar diagram in *Scientific American* for April, 1989, has an incorrectly labelled temperature scale.

The vast timescale of Figure 2.2 should be noted. At least it is vast in relation to politics, where a week has been said to be a long time. It is of course a small timescale compared with the thousand times greater timescale of geological processes, like the movements of continents on the tectonic plates which carry them, and the workings of nature's underground factory for making coal and oil. The bottom scale divisions are in tens of thousands of years, so that the industrial era is no more than the thickness of a strong pencil line, while the post World War Two phase would require extremely fine drawing to show it at all.

Such a timescale does not permit the year to year correlation of movements which might enable the record to support theories, on the timescale of the current GCMs, regarding the direction of causality between the carbon dioxide level and climate change (if it is unidirectional, which we have doubted). On the timescale of Figure 2.2, mankind has simply forced the climate system into a new regime by imposing a step jump in one of the variables which clearly has much to do with long-run climate variation.

The next question to ask is whether this unprecedented forcing of carbon dioxide levels is to be regarded as a serious matter. To answer that we will need to spend a little time considering the dynamics of complex systems, of which the changing pattern of interactions between the biosphere, the atmosphere and the ocean is a classic example. Before going on to that, however, we may note that prehistory (Figure 2.2) has seen several climate excursions which, if they occurred in the next few hundred years, would be regarded as catastrophic to society and civilization. However, they have all been downward excursions of carbon dioxide concentration and temperature, never upward beyond about 280 parts per million of carbon dioxide in the atmosphere.

These pre-historic excursions have been the periods of heavy glaciation, reaching as far south as the Alps and the US cotton belt, known as iceages, a recurrence of which would force the globe's population to migrate towards the tropics, with the loss of most existing temperate food-producing areas. These events, associated with low carbon dioxide levels, were episodes of cooling from above, in which natural convection currents, in broad areas of ocean away from the frozen poles, would have served to slow and – eventually it would seem, from the fact that we are all here – help to reverse the glaciation process.

It may also be noted that such potentially catastrophic events were associated with a quite small downward deviation of average temperature – indeed, of the same order of magnitude as the upward movements that are being discussed for the next century under the impact of business as usual carbon dioxide emissions.

An upwards temperature excursion, associated perhaps with anthropogenic forcing of carbon dioxide levels, might not be stabilised by deep ocean convection, especially if increased fresh water inputs to polar waters were to disrupt the North Atlantic driving force of the existing deep water convection current. This is not to deny that some other stabilisation process might come into play, at least for as long as there remains a substantial amount of sea ice around the polar continents – presumably such a process exists strong enough in relation to natural warming processes to explain why there has never, in the last 160,000 years, been a prehistoric 'steam age' much hotter than the present time, like there have (within the natural 100 ppm range for the period, of atmospheric carbon dioxide) been ice ages much colder.

Indeed, from our previous discussion of deep ocean currents, it seems possible that nature's response to naturally occurring warmings has been the arrest of deep ocean convection, followed by the rapid spread of the polar ice caps and the onset of an 'ice age'. On the other hand, it may be that an initial warming triggers increased polar snowfall and a larger area of polar sea ice – a bit mushy perhaps, but maybe effective in preventing the evaporation that densifies North Atlantic waters enough to drive the deep water current. Either way round, we don't know enough to be sure it cannot happen. However, it may be noted that studies of insect fossils suggest that the warming since the last ice age has not been a steady business, but has featured rapid heatings with intermittent coolings, maybe at regional rates as fast as six degrees Celsius per century in the heating phases, though not more than one or two as a global average.[26]

While this bodes well for the self-adapting capability of the global ecosystem, the globe was not at that time burdened with the activities of an advanced industrial society of six billion people, rising to at least 10 billion next century. If the natural stabilising process of the prehistoric past featured carbon dioxide levels always below about 280ppm (and especially if there are sharply reduced numbers of phytoplankton in the oceans due to unprecedented intensities of ultra-violet radiation) a warming process initiated at the present time could require some other stabilising process to halt it. There may not be one in nature.

Certainly it is the case that civilization has flourished at near the extreme upper range of temperature variation over the last 160,000 years and it may well be, as has been suggested by climatologists close to the White House, that a small EGE would be beneficial. The question which we shall address, in considering complex system dynamics, is whether we can be sure that a small one will not trigger off a big global warming, possibly an uncontrollable one.

Dynamic Systems[27]

Feedback
Before moving on to discuss complex system dynamics we must first understand the notion of 'feedback'. The idea of feedback is basic to an

understanding of complex system dynamics, in which many parts of the system influence many other parts. For instance weather affects plant growth which affects both water transpiration and the balance of the carbon cycle. But water and carbon dioxide in the atmosphere affect weather which affects ocean circulation which in due course also influences weather. And ocean circulation and weather, together with ultra-violet radiation, affect phytoplankton, which affects the carbon cycle.

All of these effects occur with different time lags and collectively comprise a complex system. The reaction of the system as a whole to an externally imposed change, or 'forcing', of some characteristic of the system – say carbon dioxide concentration – normally results in a further change of that characteristic. That reaction is what is embodied in the idea of feedback.

Complex systems, like the climate or an oil refinery, are either stable or unstable depending upon the size of the overall feedbacks within the system and on whether they are positive or negative. If the flow of oil through a refinery gets too cold, an instrument will measure the deviation in the actual temperature from that which is desired; this error signal is used to measure how much to turn up the heat somewhere so as to restore the flow of oil towards the desired temperature. This is called negative feedback because the direction of response is opposite to the direction of the deviation. Natural systems are maintained within their ecological niche by negative feedbacks – for instance we shiver when we feel cold, which warms us up, and we sweat when too warm, which cools us down.

Of course, after one response time the adjustment will not be perfect – if the feedback is negative one-half the error signal will still be one-half with further feedback of negative one-quarter and residual error of one-quarter leading to residual error of one-eighth, etc. Obviously, after sufficient time has passed, the system is as close to the desired temperature (or other target variable) as needs be. Control engineers designing an oil refinery will try to design systems with responses that are sufficiently quick, and feedbacks sufficiently close to minus one, to get the refinery back to the desired temperature before the damage caused by outside forces, say a snowstorm, gets unacceptably costly.

It the negative feedback happens to be greater than one, say minus 1.1, then the approach to the desired level of the target variable would fluctuate around it, say $+1$, -0.1, $+0.01$, -0.001, etc. in successive time periods – a process sometimes called 'hunting', like a dog chasing a rabbit scent and tending to overshoot each time the rabbit dodges.[28*] If the feedback is greater than negative two, say negative three, we are in trouble, with the overshoot so great that the error increases in each response time and consequential instability, say $+1$, -2, $+4$, -8, etc.

Positive feedback – an overall system response which acts to cause more movement in the same direction as the original deviation – always leads to instability. For instance a positive feedback of 0.1 gives successive errors of 1.1, 1.21, 1.331 (by 'compound interest at 10 per cent') to be ever further away from the desired value of the target variable. Since they are unstable, such systems exist only transitorily before shifting to a new regime which may or may not be a desirable one.

Of course, real world complex systems do not flip from one easily measured state to another on a year to year – or century to century – basis. There is no reason why the intervals over which data are collected should be the same as the natural response time of the system, and transitions may be gradual so that measurements become a series of snapshots of a changing process. Very often it may be a fluctuating or oscillatory changing process, with measurements at successive time intervals, what is called a time series, giving the appearance of a wave when plotted on a graph.

The response time may, for instance with electronic circuits, be millionths of a second, in which case the human eye perceives only the initial stable state and a second stable state. Or it may, possibly in the case of climate change, be hundreds of years, in which case the human eye may not know for a long time whether a transition to some new, possibly undesirable, second state has actually begun, or whether the system is merely responding to random disturbances which existing negative feedback processes can handle well enough to maintain the existing regime. If it commences in the midst of a lot of distracting measurement error and extraneous other changes, the beginnings of an oscillatory process are indistinguishable from the beginnings of a compound interest divergent process.

Feedbacks in the climate system

It is important to distinguish conceptually between stable and unstable global warming. Stable global warming, due to a specific cause such as a carbon dioxide concentration of .04 per cent, will result in a specific temperature rise, to a level where the climate's negative feedback processes can hold an equilibrium despite the higher carbon dioxide concentration. Unstable global warming would occur if the higher carbon dioxide concentration triggered a positive feedback process which is not operative at the lower global carbon dioxide concentrations which have obtained, give or take a few ice ages, for the last 160,000 years.

Such possible positive feedbacks are not hard to think of:

1. The polar ice caps reflect solar radiation back into space, so that, when they melt with warmer climate, the amount of solar radiation absorbed by the globe is increased, with consequential further warming of the climate system.[29] It may be that, while this process is going on, the oceans are fed with melting ice which reduces the rate of ocean temperature

rise and masks the warming that is going on. If, or when, the floating ice at the North Pole and in the West Antarctic ice sheet is melted, then global temperature increases would be more easily measured. Effectively there may be a regime change, as with a gin and tonic, which begins to become rapidly unpleasant after the ice has melted.

2. The scientists of the InterGovernmental Panel on Climate Changes (IPCC) are certain that the main greenhouse gas – water vapour – will increase with EGE.[30] During the day, water vapour condensed in clouds keeps the earth cool by reflecting incoming sunlight. During the night clouds keep the earth warm by reflecting outgoing infra-red. If more water vapour in the atmosphere results in greater cloud cover, proportionately, at night than in daytime, then we may have a positive feedback, with warmer nights and not much cooler days resulting in warmer oceans and more evaporation yielding even more night cloud.

Climatologists appear to be more concerned about whether additional cloud is formed at high or low levels. But in truth there is great ignorance about the science of clouds and the day – night contrast is easy to understand. However, it may be noted that recent work using satellite observations [31] to measure the correlation between atmospheric humidity and ocean temperature supports the hypothesis that positive feedbacks exist in the greenhouse effects due to water vapour.[32*] Warmer atmosphere causes more evaporation which causes increased greenhouse effect thus causing even warmer atmosphere, and so on.[33*]

3. Another possibility is that the large amounts of methane believed to be locked into the frozen tundras of the North, and in 'methane hydrates' in the sediments of the Arctic continental shelf,[34] will be released as the tundra and off-shore ice thaw more deeply with warmer Arctic summers. But, with methane itself a highly effective greenhouse gas, this may lead to yet warmer Arctic summers to follow, with even deeper thawing and even more methane released. Apart from its direct greenhouse effect, methane indirectly impacts on global warming by stratospheric chemistry which leads to more ice crystals high over the Antarctic, with further intensification of the ozone hole mechanism discussed above.

4. Warmer temperatures at high latitudes may cause a weakening of the deep ocean current leading to less supply of nutrients to phytoplankton and hence to a shift in the oceans' balance of carbon dioxide intake and output, possibly with increased levels in the atmosphere and increased greenhouse effect. On the other hand, the deep ocean current also carries carbon dioxide to the southern oceans (absorbed from the North Atlantic atmosphere centuries previously). Thus the phytoplankton (however many there may be after changed supplies of nutrients and changed levels of ultraviolet radiation) could spend less of their time absorbing ancient carbon dioxide from the depths and more of their time absorbing carbon

dioxide from the southern atmosphere, yielding a feedback that is beneficial for reducing the greenhouse effect.

5. Apart from this biochemical process, a sufficiently warm ocean will, like warm lemonade, begin to lose carbon dioxide rather than absorb it as at present. This again might lead to further trapping of solar heat, further temperature rises, and further release of the carbon dioxide dissolved in the oceans.

6. Moving into wholly disastrous climate excursions, we may make an analogy between the polar icecaps and a lump of sugar in very sweet tea. It can provide a focus for recrystallisation as the tea cools if a small part is saved from complete melting, but supersaturated solutions of sugar can be quite stable: if the polar ice caps were to melt, with a green Greenland, sea levels 200 or more feet up, and most of our cities drowned, our familiar climate regime could not be recovered by human efforts, even if there were any humans around to try.

7. And negative feedback can be too much of a good thing – if it is greater than negative two in terms of our previous numerical examples. The plunge into ice age conditions following a warming that arrests the deep ocean circulation being a case in point that would be as disastrous as the green Greenland scenario.

Whether a green Greenland could in turn lead to the ultimate disaster of a boiling ocean and, eventually, a global atmosphere akin to that of the uninhabitably hot planet Venus, nobody knows. But it is salutary to bear in mind that both Earth and Venus are condensed from essentially the same primordial material, and that Venus is not so very much closer than Earth to the heat of the sun. Rather surprisingly, scientists attribute greater significance to the content and density of the atmosphere on Venus, as regards the impact on surface temperature, than they do to the effect of distance from the sun.[35]

Detecting instability

That it has not happened in the history of the globe does not mean it cannot happen – the globe may never have previously experienced the rapid rise of carbon dioxide levels currently going on in the presence of reduced levels of ozone. Nor, it should be emphasized, is it here being argued that it will happen, or that it is likely to happen. We simply do not know enough to say one way or the other, still less do we know enough to say that what is going on cannot precipitate another ice age or, per contra, another phase of green Greenland, both of which have happened (though green Greenland much longer ago) and either of which could destroy civilization.[36*]

Unfortunately, measurement is not likely to help us much in resolving the question as to whether this assumption is safe. Meteorologists, that is people who deal with the weather as it is, per contra climatologists who theorise about how it works, have the greatest difficulty in being sure if EGE is going on or not. The steady trend is hard to measure with the degree of statistical confidence which ought to attach to such a momentous result. We have seen how volcanic eruptions can interrupt a trend, and the vulcanicity of 1991 is going to make it harder still for them to come up with a confident answer, even by the year 2010 when such an answer has been said to be likely to be ready.[37]

Sunspot variation comes into it, as does the masking effect of polar ice melt. It has recently been suggested that, between 1940 and 1970, changes in solar activity may have been reducing the impact of increasing greenhouse gases, but reinforcing it since. Over a longer timescale it is believed that variation in the earth's orbit may have affected the picture, together with changes in the quantity of interstellar material in the galaxy through which the solar system is moving and changes in the rate of energy release by the sun that take place over geological timescales.

Whatever the causes of fluctuations about a trend, the difficulty in establishing whether a trend exists makes one thing clear. This is that the possibility of measuring what we really want to know is nil. For the critical question is not whether global temperatures are rising, but whether it is an accelerating trend, and if so whether the acceleration will continue exponentially[38*] under positive feedback, or be arrested by an eventual deceleration under negative feedback and, if the latter, when.

General circulation models

So to form a judgement we may hope to rely on the modelling of climatologists. The general circulation models (GCMs) used to simulate climate patterns are, of course, immensely complex. They consist of huge numbers of mathematical equations representing the physical processes of the global weather system.[39] Because it is a circulating system the circulation has to be modelled by keeping track of what happens all over the globe.

Since computers work digitally – i.e. by having discrete numbers to represent everything that is being modelled – the continuity of real weather systems can only be approximated by a grid pattern of latitudes, longitudes and heights above sea level. Even the use of quite a coarse grid, hundreds of kilometres laterally and with only a dozen levels between sea level and outer space, results in such a multiplicity of equations that the very largest computers in the world have to run for hours to get a global climate simulation for a long time ahead.

But that is not the end of it. As we have seen, interactions with the ocean are very important. However, models of the ocean's behaviour are in their infancy and represent changes that are so slow that the atmosphere models are beyond the limit of accurate simulation by the time an oceanic variation makes itself felt. This has implications if the complex dynamics of the system are genuinely chaotic in a sense we shall describe shortly. And whatever oceanic process may be represented, its accuracy is severely limited by the paucity of information about what goes on in the deep ocean.   Another critical aspect is the process of cloud formation and the interactions of clouds at different levels, and at different times of day or night, with the potential for negative or positive feedback, and the interaction with the evaporative process in the (slowly changing) ocean. To this may be added the impact of the shifting pattern of vegetation with evolving climate and consequential changes in the proportion of sunlight reflected back into space and in the biogenic release of carbon dioxide and transpired water vapour. The upshot of all this is that model predictions are not at all reliable. For instance, whilst all GCMs predict EGE, the rate of warming they predict, given the forecast rate of build up of carbon dioxide, varies by a factor of three.

A propos of the question whether cloud feedback effects are positive or negative, it is interesting to note that, when the cloud effect equations are left out of the models, as has recently been done in an exercise to compare the various models, they all come up with closely identical results.[40] This shows that the difficulty with cloud modelling is one of the factors which makes GCMs so unreliable. Unfortunately – or fortunately from any other point of view! – the real world has in fact got clouds, and to leave them out is to put on *Hamlet* without the Prince.

The bio-dynamic and other long-term feedbacks that we have been considering are excluded from the consensus which forms the basis of the IPCC's central prediction. Thus, not only is there great uncertainty in model outcomes, there is also the problem that the models may fail to capture critical aspects of climate dynamics in the real world. In order to make the systems of equations mathematically tractable, simplifications of actual physical processes are employed to represent their behaviour in the regime of variation to which we are accustomed and for which meteorological measurements (however subject to margins of error) are available for calibrating the model.

Yet it is climate behaviour in regimes different from those to which we are accustomed, specifically with carbon dioxide and ozone concentrations far different from any experienced in the available prehistoric record, which are of concern and which we want the models to tell us about. Without a great deal of research it is not possible to answer the question whether a GCM could ever be developed into a genuine long-run global climate model which might cast light on these critical issues.   For the moment we must rely on the current generation of models and on intuitions based upon our general knowledge of the behaviour of complex nonlinear dynamic systems.

Complex system dynamics

By nonlinear, in relation to a system, is meant that a non-proportionality is involved in at least one of the equations that represent the system in a mathematical model. Proportional relationships, e.g. the relationship between cents and dollars, can be represented by linear equations such as $P=0.01pc$ where P is a price in dollars and pc is the price in cents for the same thing. The constancy of the coefficient in that equation (.01) makes it a linear relation, so called because a graphical representation comes out as a straight line. Systems of linear equations can be very easily solved using standard techniques, whereas systems of nonlinear equations (where the coefficient is not a constant, but varies in some way – say .01pc when pc is small and .02pc when pc is large, in our example above) are much harder to solve and, in principle, may be impossible to solve.

By dynamic, in relation to a system, is meant that time enters into its behaviour in an essential way. This means that what happened yesterday affects what happens today.[41*] An important feature of models that purport to be dynamic, and to give an insight into the future behaviour of a system, is therefore to start them off from an accurately specified set of initial conditions. In principle, providing it is a good model of the system being studied, it will then give useful insights into the way the system will behave over time.

It has been said that all interesting dynamics is nonlinear dynamics. A modern branch of applied mathematics, called dynamical systems analysis, is concerned with describing the overall behaviour of systems of nonlinear equations which change over time. It is different from much traditional mathematics in that, with essentially unsolvable equations, it relies upon computerised simulations of the system's behaviour and then seeks explanations for the various kinds of phenomena that the simulations throw up. The interesting behaviour of nonlinear systems is described in a weird terminology including such exotica as 'strange attractors', 'bifurcations', 'homoclinic tangles', 'horseshoe diffeomorphisms', 'wandering points' and so on.[42]

These all boil down to the likelihood of extremely complex behaviour and to the possibility – but not the inevitability – of so-called chaotic movement. In contrast with linear and well-behaved non-linear systems, such chaotic systems characteristically display aperiodic cycles, rather than the regular cycles of simpler systems, and display extreme sensitivity to the specification of initial conditions, per contra linear systems which end up at closely adjacent configurations after a given period of model (simulated) time if started off from closely adjacent initial conditions.[43]

For instance, whether the temperature in London is 12° or 15° Celsius on March 12, 2007, would constitute closely adjacent but not identical initial conditions from which a climate system might or might not move to a quite different regime by, say, December 2029. But we saw a few pages back that we cannot forecast the weather in 2007 from this present point in time, so that climate in 2029 cannot, if its behaviour is genuinely chaotic, be usefully predicted however much climatological research may be done. That is one of the reasons why this book advocates preparing a response strategy in advance of scientific certainty about global warming: such certainty may be unattainable.

Typically, with chaotic systems, if computer simulations of a very simple (one equation) chaotic motion are displayed on a television screen, the motion is approximately cyclic for a while (i.e. covers nearly the same loop on the screen) and then 'jumps' to a different approximate cycle, perhaps by way of a path that wanders all over the place for a while. More complex systems cannot be represented on a television screen, but a fundamental theorem shows that when the dimensionality (number of equations) of the system exceeds two, there is no necessity for the system to converge on a stable cycle even if one exists.

So, as the number of equations in a non-linear system rises, the potential for chaotic motion rises with it. This does not entail jumps into bizarre configurations – the laws of physics which are being modelled still apply and, if it is the climate system that is being modelled, the earth will not suddenly become incandescent like the sun. But it does mean that it is extremely hard to be sure that the system will not jump into some configuration that is possible (e.g. an ice age or green Greenland either of which, on the record, are completely possible) as a result of some shift in the values of the coefficients (or parameters, as such quasi-constant coefficients are often called) the significance of which has not been appreciated.

Certainly we have in the climate system a great many nonlinear (nonproportionate) relationships. This is true even for the current GCMs which, as mentioned, exclude many of the important long-term feedbacks. We saw that radiative interactions with dust particles and with trace gases are highly nonlinear (depending on whether the nut fits the bolt to reuse our previous analogy) so that slight global warming, which affects the typical wavelength of the earth's infra-red radiation, may have a disproportionate effect on the amount of radiation that escapes into space. The asymmetry of the heating or cooling from above of the oceans is also a nonlinearity. And the workings of water vapour in the atmosphere – its condensation into clouds, its precipitation as rain, hail or snow, and its reevaporation as circulation patterns carry it to lower altitudes – are all nonlinear phenomena, as is the turbulent circulation of the atmosphere in upward movement within the weather patterns we know of as depressions.

Dynamic systems analysis tells us that the behaviour of an enlarged system, containing more equations and more feedbacks, will be chaotic if some subsystem is chaotic – such as, for instance, that part of future more complete climate models that is already in the current GCMs. That the climate system may be chaotic, and therefore fundamentally unforecastable in the long run, will seem deeply unsurprising to anyone who has hoped to rely on a weather forecast when deciding about a fishing trip. But the system dynamic meaning of chaos is more fundamental than statistically random variation, even quite large random variation, about a well-defined mean. It means that the behaviour of the mean is subject to abrupt regime changes and that such changes of regime, or jumps, can be brought about by small and unnoticeable changes at some earlier point in time, a so-called bifurcation of the system.

An illustration

We cannot, in a non-technical presentation, do more than get an intuition of how this might come about. If we suppose all other external factors are held constant, then a chosen value for a 'forcing variable' may lead to two possible stable equilibria for an 'outcome variable' of interest. This is illustrated in figure 2.3a, with the solid lines joining possible equilibrium points. The arrows in the diagram indicate the direction of change for the outcome variable when the system is away from equilibrium because the forcing variable has been 'suddenly' (e.g. over a few decades if we are talking about climate change) shifted. Between F_1 and F_2 where there are two possible equilibria, the dotted line separates the region where movement is towards the upper equilibrium from that in which it is the other way.

Suppose, for instance, that the outcome is the size of the North Polar ice cap, and the forcing variable is the level of carbon dioxide in the atmosphere. We may have a cool equilibrium with the ice cap reflecting much of the incoming solar radiation. Or we may have a warm equilibrium, with no ice cap and increased radiation from the earth's surface balancing the incoming solar radiation. Now suppose the chosen carbon dioxide level rises: the warm equilibrium will simply be a bit warmer – and still no ice cap – while the cool equilibrium will reflect less from a smaller ice cap and with more radiation from the less cool rest of the globe. But below a certain critical size for the ice cap our feedback No.1 comes into play and the remaining ice cap disappears.

Thus in figure 3b, the dotted line divides a region in which movement is towards our familiar cool climate regime from that where movement is towards a green Greenland (seven metre sea rise) or maybe, eventually, green Antarctica (70 metre sea rise). Because of our ignorance about the connection between carbon dioxide level and temperature rise, we do not know whether the forcing caused by industrialised fossil fuel burning will, at say 500ppm, put us at 'A' on the diagram, in which case we are bound simply for a smaller North Polar ice cap (if the level can be held at 500ppm) or at 'B', in which case we are headed via path xxxx for a green Greenland.

That is unless ambitious policies succeed in moving us soon enough, say via path oooo, to reach a point like 'C', at 300 ppm, from which nature will eventually get us back to the familiar cool equilibrium.

Figure 2.3 An Adverse Climate Surprise

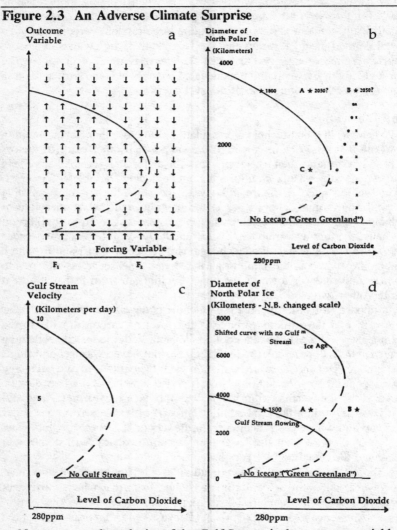

Now suppose the velocity of the Gulf Stream is the outcome variable, and that below some critical speed, polar sea ice spreads rapidly, arresting the evaporative process that causes the densification needed to drive the deep ocean convection. Above that speed, more carbon dioxide may mean more transport of fresh water towards the poles by the weather system, less dense polar waters, and a slower Gulf Stream so that we again get a diagram, Figure 3.3c, shaped like a numeral 2. What is the critical value for the carbon dioxide level? 600ppm or 400ppm? Nobody knows.

But if it is 400ppm, and the Gulf stream has lost its momentum and ceased to flow by the year 2100, our initial assumption for diagram 2.3b, that other external factors would be held constant, has been violated and we must draw a new figure 2.3d, the same as 2.3a, but maybe with a bigger ice cap for each value of the forcing variable and hence the outcome of either an ice age, with North Europe frozen over, or a green Antarctica, with only Madrid and Prague, amongst European capital cities, left above sea level. If point A is near the dotted line, movement may be slow enough to provide opportunity to repair the polar ice cap by such science fictional measures (as have been proposed) as an orbiting space shield designed to reduce the amount of incoming radiation. A stitch in time may save ninety-nine.[44*]

The moral

Thus, what can happen is that some parameter in the nonlinear equation moves through a critical value, so that what was previously an apparently stable, negative feedback system becomes unstable. The system, powered by some imbalance in the enormous energy fluxes that pass through it, then moves off under positive feedback. Maybe very slowly at first, but for an indeterminate period until some other parameter attains a value which reestablishes overall negative feedback in some new, and quite possibly very unpleasant, quasi-stable state of the system. The studies of insect fossils mentioned earlier suggests there is a strong possibility of positive feedbacks in a warming process. Wallace S. Broecker[45] has summed up the implications for climate of dynamic systems analysis as follows:

> Earth's climate does not respond to forcing in a smooth and gradual way. Rather it responds in sharp jumps which involve largescale reorganisation of Earth's system. If this reading of the natural record is correct, then we must consider the possibility that the main response of the system to our provocation of the atmosphere will come in jumps whose timing and magnitude are unpredictable. Coping with this kind of change is clearly a far more serious matter than coping with a gradual warming.

It needs an extremely good quality model of any complex dynamic system to be sure that it is secure from the risk of chaotic movement. When super computers like that at the Hadley Centre for Climate Prediction at Bracknell, England, opened in May 1990, and others like it worldwide, have been working for a few decades, in collaboration with each other, we may have sufficient information to know whether dangerous positive feedbacks will come into play at the higher carbon dioxide concentrations in prospect, or we may not, or we may know that we never can know.

For the moment we simply don't know. All that we do know is that carbon dioxide levels are way outside the range of the last 160,000 years, during which we have had no more instability than the poorly understood coming and going of a few ice ages. We also know, from the general nature of complex dynamic system analysis that, by the time the computers have worked it out, we may find out in a much more immediate and unpleasant way that positive feedbacks are, indeed, at work. To quote Stephen Schneider,[46]

> Climate models...provide only a dirty crystal ball in which a range of plausible fortunes can be glimpsed....At present we are altering our environment faster than we can understand the resulting climate changes. If the trend does not stop, we shall eventually either verify or disprove the climate models – by means of a real, global experiment whose consequences we shall not escape.

With our climate system forced into an unprecedented regime as regards carbon dioxide and ozone levels in the atmosphere, its response may be quite different from the smooth extrapolation of historic experience which is generated by the current generation of global climate models. It may be an awareness of this which led the IPCC, in its 'Policymakers' Summary' of its Scientific Assessment of Climate Change, to twice remark 'the complexity of the system means that we cannot rule out surprises' even though their main report is focused on their prediction of most likely outcomes under different policy scenarios and does not elaborate on 'surprises'.[47*]

The insights offered by dynamic systems analysis underlay the remark made earlier that it is not the rate of carbon dioxide emissions that matters, nor, probably, the level reached, nor the mean atmospheric temperature rise that it causes, but how long some high temperature or high level of carbon dioxide is sustained, with increasing probability that some regime shift will be provoked the longer the upward excursion of carbon dioxide levels persists. Most obviously, a regime shift is possible if warmer polar conditions result in decreased North Atlantic salinity which arrests the deep ocean current. But it would be an oversimplification of dynamic systems theory to suggest that regime shifts are always, or even usually, associated with some such simple phenomena. More usually is it the case that some combination of changes to the 'quasi constants' (or parameters) of the system results in some previously negative feedback becoming positive, or some suppressed positive feedback process suddenly coming to dominate the system.

Thus, as the climatologists come to grips with the problem, hopefully with models that represent the regime into which carbon dioxide and CFC emissions are forcing the climate-ocean-biosphere system, rather than the climate regime to which we are accustomed, the kind of remedy that will be required will most likely be to return to some target level of carbon dioxide by a particular date, to get the patient's blood pressure down before there is a heart attack.

In relation to a target of that nature, it is obvious that there is a last date for starting, after which its achievement would be impossible, and that close to that last date its achievement would be extremely difficult. On the other hand, an early start could make its achievement relatively easy if not almost cost free – simply the choice between two development paths which are roughly equal as regards the standard of living attainable, and different only in that the one is sustainable as regards its impact on the atmosphere whilst the other 'business as usual' path is not.

Notes

1. Unlike the rest of the book, where we will invariably be referring to EGE when we say global warming, we will in this chapter maintain the distinction, using greenhouse effect for the natural – and as we shall see far from constant – effects of naturally arising levels of greenhouse gases and EGE for anthropogenic enhancement of the greenhouse effect, i.e. the effects of human additions to their level (or concentration, usually measured in parts per million or as a percentage, with 1000 ppm = 0.1 per cent).

2. Turco et al, 1983, p.1284 and note 19, p.1290.

3. Singer, 1991.

4. Houghton, Sir J., 1990.

5. Ministerial Declaration, 1990, para 7 and FCCC Art 3.3. (INL, 1992).

6. Enquete-Kommission, 1991, Vol. 1, pp.201-15.

7. Pearce, F., 1989, Chapter 9.

8. Broecker, 1987, p.124.

9. Crowley and North, 1988, p.997.

10. Atkinson et al, 1987, point to evidence of rapid shifts of the boundary of the Arctic ice sheet from off Portugal to North of Iceland in a period of a few hundred years.

11. Pearce, F., 1989, p.95.

12. IPCC, 1992, p.71.

13. Houghton, R. A. and Woodwell, 1989, p.20.

14. These measures of carbon flow are proportional to the mass flow of carbon dioxide in the ratio of molecular weights, 44:12.

15. Enquete-Kommission, 1991, p.152.

16. Watson, 1992, p.561.

17. Tans et al, 1990, p.1438.

18. It helps close the gap of ignorance but is not a very substantial effect. Incidentally, the meaning to be attached to the 1990 work (Tans et al) has recently been reconsidered, leaving the ignorance gap much reduced, but still not closed (*Nature*, 16 April, 1992, letters by Broecker and Peng and by Sarmieto and Sundquist, with commentary by A. Watson). Norby and O'Neill, 1991, is suggestive that increasing levels of atmospheric carbon dioxide may be associated with increased carbon content in the roots of plants.

19. Beardsley, 1991, slightly misreporting Norby and O'Neill, 1991, Table 3.

20. Pearce, F., 1989, Chapter 1.

21. Indeed the huge investment in improved CFCs, the so-called HCFCs, which, as noted in Chapter 1, were intended to maintain the major chemical companies' control of the market as new entrants into the business began to compete in supplying the older CFC, may turn out to have been wasted. Vidal, 1992, reports on the growth of sales of 'Greenfreeze', manufactured in former East Germany and using a propane-butane mixture. Initial disinformation tactics against Greenfreeze have apparently been debunked and abandoned.

22. One of the aspects of industrial activity which the market system is least well adapted to handling is the possibility of delayed side effects from new processes and products which penalise (or benefit) people who do not participate in the market transactions involved with the new activity. The potential harm from putting lead in gasoline would have been obvious to a public interest protection agency, with a requirement for testing for side effects at the outset, prior to marketing. But we have had a generation of brain damaged children before the slow business has begun of unwinding the use of a technology that would never have been allowed were commercial energy materials safety-tested in the same way as commercial foodstuffs or ethical drugs.

23. Houghton, R. A. and Woodwell, 1989, pp.21-2.

24. The relative proportions of (stable) deuterium and hydrogen in polar snowfall – and the ice which is formed from it – depend upon their relative success at escaping from the ocean through evaporation and their relative likelihood of being returned to the ocean as rain. In colder times the heavier deuterium is more likely to get caught in liquid water – the ocean and raindrops – so that successive evaporation and condensation in the weather circulation distils a lower proportion of deuterium into atmospheric humidity and, consequentially, there is less heavy water in the snow which falls, and gets preserved, at the icecaps. Hence a temperature measurement. As regards age, the relative proportions of different isotopes of buried carbon depends on how long they have been buried, since the unstable radioactive isotope decays from its known proportion at time of burial. At burial, the proportion is the same as the proportion in the atmosphere, which is a maintained constant by the intensity of radioactivity coming from outer space. So measurements of the relative proportion give an estimate of the age of buried carbon, with a check provided by the sequencing of broad and narrow rings from differently sourced fossilised logs.

25. Scientists are using a doubling of the current level, to 720 ppm, as a benchmark for comparing predictions of different climate models, and by economists as a basis for estimates (largely guesstimates) of the 'damage function' to be discussed in the next chapter – until a recent realisation that, on a business as usual scenario, the level would continue to rise very much further: see Cline,

1992, for a critique and for a more realistic approach. Incidentally, it was the discovery of this stunning fact, through reading Houghton and Woodwell, 1989, that led me to become concerned about global warming and, with the realisation that the economics profession was both misinterpreting its significance and largely ignorant of the potential of sustainable biomass fuels for responding to the problem, eventually to write this book.

26. Atkinson et al, 1987, p.591.

27. Gleick, 1988.

28. Economists are familiar with negative feedback systems in terms of Keynesian macroeconomic multipliers which, subject to measurement difficulties, can be used to control the level of activity in an economy (with the response to error being discretionary, rather than automatic, as in an engineering control system). More complex systems, such as Dornbusch's open economy model, involving several markets sometimes display 'overshooting' behaviour.

29. Crowley and North, 1988, p.997.

30. IPCC, 1992, p.52.

31. Ravel and Ramanathan, 1989, p.761.

32. This work empirically refutes the suggestion of Lindzen, 1990, that the feedback may be negative. Lindzen's article provided the scientific basis for the optimistic commentary noted previously – see Kellogg, 1991, for an assessment.

33. This does not contradict our previous point about the stabilising effect of the ocean – then we were considering the relative temperature of air and ocean, here we are considering the movement of both together, and whether such joint movement is stable or unstable under the impact of the evaporative heat transfer process which keeps them linked together, at least when their joint movement is in the cooling direction.

34. Pearce, F., 1989, pp.157-60.

35. Schneider, 1987, p.77.

36. The assumption that the negative feedbacks are – despite the fact that the climate system is now in a novel regime as regards carbon dioxide and ozone levels – sufficiently robust to enable us to ignore these possibilities, is what seems to underlie the pre-1992 policy stance of the USA, with its playing down of the dangers of global warming. An appreciation that the negative feedbacks cannot be relied upon to maintain the present climatic regime (with global warming stabilised at just a few degrees, and leading to no more damaging consequences than a modest shift in climate patterns and a sea level rise over the next century of less than a meter) is what may have led to the shift in policy that saw President Bush sign the revamped FCCC. A senior American economist writing in March 1992 stated "research...should be concentrated on the extreme possibilities, not on modest improvements to median projections" (Shelling, 1992, to which we return in Chapter 9).

37. IPCC, 1992, p.84.

38. Exponential is the word used by scientists to describe a smooth and continuous growth processes similar to a periodic (annual, say) compound interest process. Both types of process get bigger in relation to how big they have already got and have a characteristic 'doubling time' which we shall meet again in Chapter 6. It has quite interesting implications when one considers waste disposal into a

dump of fixed size. Suppose the doubling time for waste production is a decade and that in 1960 we fill 1% of the dump. In 1970 it will be 2% full, in 1980 4%, in 1990 8%, etc. Sometime between 2020, when it will be 64% full, and 2030 it will overflow. It is salutary to think of the atmosphere as such a dump, with an upper limit to the safe quantity of greenhouse gases that can be dumped into it.

39. Schneider, 1987, pp.72-3.

40. Kerr, 1992a.

41. This may not seem very earthshaking, but most people are unaware that almost all economics is equilibrium economics, employing the method of comparative statics to study the effects of changes from an initial equilibrium to some later equilibrium of the economic system, with no insight into the intervening dynamics – see Chapter 6.

42. Arrowsmith and Place, 1990, index.

43. Gleick, 1988, Chapter 1, especially pp.22-3.

44. When I wrote this section originally, I thought that, although the ice cap size instability had been mathematically modelled (North and Crowley, 1985) the possible instability of the deep oceanic current had not been. The combination of two possible instabilities was (and is) highly speculative so it came to me as a surprise to learn from Dr Steve Ghan of Battelle Pacific Northwest Laboratories, to whom I am most grateful, that the oceanic circulation instability has also been modelled (Manabe, Stouffer, 1988), yielding at least two possible quasi-stable states. One of these has no deep convection and a large North Polar ice cap and the other displays a Gulf Stream-like circulation with a smaller ice cap. Of course the model is highly simplified and does not tell us whether the complex dynamics of the system under greenhouse gas forcing, starting from where we are now, will lead us, in terms of Figure 3, to 'A', 'B', or back to something we are familiar with. It does not tell us whether the phases of extremely warm climate (green Greenland, with polar ice melted and the oceans 200 feet higher) could recur or whether they depended on some configuration of the continents under continental drift which is different from the present. The investigation of such possibilities is the kind of research needed in support of the precautionary rationale advanced in the following chapter.

45. Broecker, 1987, p.123.

46. Schneider, 1987, p.80.

47. Both before and after the publication of the article on 'Global Climate Change' by R.A. Houghton and G.M. Woodwell in the April 1989 *Scientific American* which, as previously footnoted, stimulated me to work on this topic, debate had raged in the scientific journals over a great many of the questions which surround concern about global warming. A recent stocktaking article in *Science* concluded that 'many scientists are now espousing ...buying insurance ... against the possibility that ... some nasty surprise is lurking in the greenhouse. And that notion of prudence seems to be catching on at last in the White House' (R.A. Kerr, *Science*, 22 May, 1992, p.1140). This change seems to have followed the departure of John Sununu as Chief of Staff to President Bush, fortunately in time for wiser counsel to prevail prior to the Earth Summit.

3. Political Decisions in an Uncertain World

The purpose of this chapter will be firstly to see how it can have come about that world attention has been focused upon the problem of global warming for several years past without it having been appreciated that there is, in all likelihood, a relatively low-cost remedy available, as will be outlined in the following chapters. Secondly we will suggest that an approach[1] that is less well known than cost-benefit analysis (CBA, which is usually employed by economists working on environmental problems) is appropriate when addressing a problem with the special characteristics of global warming. In the second part of this chapter, this approach – using the regret concept,[2] but not the minimax criterion[3] – is exemplified using notional data and then related to the option cost concept which, as mentioned in Chapter 1, provides a framework for taking irreversible decisions sequentially. This involves some arithmetic which may be taken on trust by the busier reader.

Misguided Research

The Aristotelian tendency of scientific discipline, towards ever greater specialisation, is inappropriate to the complex system-dynamic nature of the scientific problem outlined in the last chapter. In the absence of holistic enquiry, folklore develops about the overall nature of the problem. Professional enquiry, and hence the concerns of the policy-makers who pay for it, is illuminated by the folklore and follows down pathways hedged in by narrow professional specialisms. Not only can the wood not be seen for the trees, but large parts of the wood which may be important if the climate system can undergo a shift of regime – one of Broecker's sharp jumps – remain unexplored. The folklore defines what part of the wood the professional advisors, and the research they commission, are walking in.

For instance, non-economists accept that part of the folklore which conducts policy assessment in terms of CBA even though CBA imposes infeasible informational requirements. The climatologists know that their climate change predictions are based upon incomplete global climate models of which the range of predictions may be biased by the omission of aspects such as biological and oceanic feedbacks. However, agronomists, hydrologists and other experts use the central estimate of climate change to forecast global warming effects within their area of expertise.

Then the economists come along, accepting the scientific folklore, and use these forecasted effects to estimate a damage function as a statistical entity with known variability and a well-defined expected value. By the damage function is meant the cost of the damage that will be done by the effects of global warming of different intensity. The greater or lesser avoidance of such expected damage, under a particular policy measure designed to mitigate the warming, constitutes the benefit of the policy.

Even within economics, specialisation leads to error. Traditional environmental policy, rooted in micro-economic analysis of particular markets, shows that the least cost remedy is obtained by 'getting prices right' – in the particular market where pollution is generated – by taxing the polluting activity. But with a tax on fossil fuels the global macro-economy is affected, not just energy markets, and the high costs in non-energy markets make such action needlessly costly. Thus there has been a mismatch between micro-economic selection of policies and macro-economic assessment of their impacts.[4] Of greater significance has been the economists' willingness to accept the technological status quo, with policy enquiry involving technological assessments largely disregarded in the macro-economic modelling process.

Clearly, given the basis upon which it rests, the damage function is beset with extreme uncertainty. But the context of CBA requires the statistical variability to be known, to enable the economist to estimate the expected value of damage avoided so that it can be set against the costs of implementing the policy in deciding whether a proposed policy is worthwhile. The reality is that the effects of carbon dioxide forcing on the climate cannot be predicted, the damaging effects of climate change on the biosphere and the social system dependent on it are obscure, and the expected value of such damage cannot be estimated, and that this renders the CBA meaningless. Inadequate data is misused in order to make the problem tractable to the familiar analytic framework.

Moreover, the key concern regarding the use of CBA on the global warming problem is that the essence of the CBA procedure, developed for handling a large number of small local problems where micro-economic methods are appropriate, is that the statistical probabilities average out and that repeated use of the procedure pools the risks. With 'once off' global warming, CBA is not only meaningless for lack of reliable data, but also invalid in principle – we cannot run our climate future several times and pool the risks over a number of experiences. However, CBA results are easy to understand whilst its technical procedures are sufficiently formidable to be taken on trust by non-experts.

For instance, when doing CBA, the costs and benefits of a project typically occur at different times and the method of compound interest calculation, which we will explain in Chapter 6, is used to bring all the values of market and non-market effects onto a comparable 'present value' basis. The rate of interest to be used in the compounding is, for a profit-maximising business, obviously the market rate at which it lends or borrows. When it is a public interest project, the rate of interest is usually called a discount rate and has been the subject of intense debate on the grounds that financial market rates are determined by short-term considerations at a high percentage and that the long-term public good is better served by using a lower interest rate.

An example of how the usual outcome of CBA studies of global warming can be turned around by changing the discount rate is provided in Cline, 1992,[5] a tour de force in the field of cost benefit analysis on the grand scale. It establishes a case for aggressive action against global warming – equivalent perhaps to policy option D 'ambitious reduction' in our numerical example that follows – simply by showing the costs of such action to be less than its benefits (which are, of course, the avoidance of the damage costs from the global warming to be expected under inaction, with business as usual).

To reach this result, Cline provides a very much more comprehensive account of the likely costs from global warming than have other analysts, but still leaving a large proportion of guesswork. What is most novel and important in Cline's work is his extension of the calculation into the very long term. He points out that the doubling of carbon dioxide is simply a benchmark used by the climatologists for comparing their models and has no particular significance in relation to the impact on human welfare or ecological sustainability.[6*] Settling on a timescale related to the periodicity of deep ocean mixing of about 300 years – by when, with continued greenhouse gas build up, the central estimate of temperature increase is 10 degrees Celsius, ranging to an upper extreme (barring surprises) of 18 Celsius – he estimates damages of the order of hundreds of billions of dollars annually.

These are comparable with the annual costs of an effective carbon tax, – even the high costs resulting from the high levels of taxation that would be needed were no low cost alternative energy technologies available – and thus they place 'aggressive' action in contention as a policy option in conventional CBA terms. Quite how aggressive depends upon the detailed assumptions – for instance on how much weight to place on the high end of the range of possible temperature increase for a given concentration of carbon dioxide.

However, Cline's results are controversial for two reasons. Firstly the estimates of costs due to global warming two or three hundred years ahead are so great an extrapolation from current experience as to cast doubt on their validity, carefully argued though they are. Who, in 1700, could have guessed the impact of policy then on welfare now? Strong though that argument seems, the Dutch today are not grumbling about the polders enclosed at that time, whilst we certainly would be cross with our forebears should it be proven beyond doubt that the spleen of the Dodo contained an infallible cure for aids. Thus long range costs and benefits can arise, and calculations of them cannot simply be ignored as speculative.

Secondly, in order to make such long term analysis meaningful, Cline has to employ an extremely low discount rate. His grounds for doing so are carefully argued and grounded in work of the highest economic authority[7] with which I fully concur. Unfortunately, they are unlikely to carry much weight with the conservative economists trained at the height of the 'monetarist' ascendency in economic theorising who, for some years ahead, must be expected to continue to dominate thinking in the central banks and treasuries where economic policies are determined.

We shall as far as possible sidestep that debate, since CBA is the wrong approach to the global warming problem at the more basic level mentioned previously. We mention it at this stage as an instance of a critically important technical assumption in CBA which is usually unknown or incomprehensible both to the policy decision-taker, who has to make use of the results, and to specialists in other fields, whose work feeds into the CBA – critical in the sense that the choice of different numbers for the discount rate can completely alter the balance of costs and benefits in a particular CBA exercise.[8*]

Even if a coherent procedure for achieving a globally consensual target could be agreed upon, such a target, framed within a CBA approach, would still be essentially arbitrary in the absence of a well-defined damage function against which to set the cost of following the agreed strategy. And, given the uncertainty of climate outcomes consequent upon the system dynamic nature of the problem, even a CBA that embodied a well-defined damage function (i.e. good knowledge of the economic impact of different possibilities regarding climate change) would fail to capture the essence of the decision problem. This is that we don't know now, and may not know until 'too late', what the connection is between greenhouse gas levels – including their rates of change and their duration – and the climate change, or greenhouse effect, that results. In an uncertain world we need to think about the outcomes of policies relative to whatever future state of the world, now unknowable, comes to pass.

The Regret Concept

Thus we need to adopt a framework that allows for the dimensions of uncertainty as regards the state of nature, and of uncertainty as regards the costliness of damage under different policy response to such states of nature, in order to deal with a problem of global choice – a global choice since what becomes of the atmosphere and climate affects us all. It may be a choice that is made as the outcome of a set of uncoordinated decisions taken in isolation by individually motivated decision-takers all over the world, rather than through some agreement amongst world leaders, but a choice for all that. Supposing, though, that the choice is made in some agreed manner, what rationale is appropriate for statesmen taking such a decision under uncertainty, and maybe in plain ignorance?

Firstly, we must clarify the distinction, implicit in the foregoing, between uncertainty – in which, at best, we have a subjective notion of the relative likelihood of alternative consequences from alternative decisions – and risk, when the probabilities of alternative outcomes are known with certainty so that a statistical expected value of the outcome can be calculated by weighting the values of alternative outcomes by the respective probabilities of their occurrence. Thus a horse race is uncertain, with the odds offered by the bookmakers adjusted in relation to the subjective probabilities of the punters as reflected in the bets they place, whereas the toss of a fair coin has a certain, 50 per cent, probability of coming down heads (so that, for instance, if tails is valued at \$100 and heads is valued at \$20, the expected value of tossing the coin is \$60).

Secondly, there is the phenomenon of risk aversion: faced with a choice between a certain status quo and a 50:50 chance of either trebling one's money income or having it reduced to zero, with consequential death through starvation, most (save those who are starving already) would opt for the status quo, even though the expected money value of the risky choice is 1.5 times that of the safe status quo. This choice can be taken to reflect the diminishing value to the individual of additional income in relation to the very high (infinitely high?) value placed upon the income needed for basic subsistence.

Thirdly, there is the question of irreversibility which we introduced in our mention of option costs at the beginning of Chapter 1. The precautionary policy adumbrated in these pages obviously involves the irreversible loss of consumption possibilities lost as a consequence of diverting resources into 'getting ready'. Much more significant irreversibilities may arise from the 'wait and see' option since a choice which permits a situation to develop where a positive feedback process comes into operation may be an irreversible choice. Such a positive feedback may become too vigorous for remedial action to be possible. This places an 'option value' upon choices which are not irreversible, that is to say choices which leave it open to choose again at a later date whether to go in the irreversible direction, or whether to continue to not do so.

Fourthly, and linked to the question of irreversibility, is the question of unrepresented voters from generations yet unborn. For their welfare we would expect statesmen to have the consideration which we, as mortal individuals, are unable to implement, save through the fragile mechanism of bequests. A private bequest is of no avail if an irreversible decision made by the older generation yields an environment where the bequest cannot be enjoyed by its intended beneficiaries.

Policy regret

A concept known as 'policy regret' enables us to handle uncertainty as regards the state of nature by characterising outcomes in a relativistic framework. There is not some universal scale of social well-being. To a status-seeking billionaire, the halving of income probably matters less than its trebling. For the comfortably off professional, a trebling of income would be lovely but its halving a disaster. For the peasant – subsisting on income in kind from the land available – its halving means death unless food aid is to hand.

The unknown state of nature, perhaps to be delivered by some unforeseeable jump of a climate system provoked by unprecedented forcing from greenhouse gases, may place us in the position of a billionaire. That would be if hopes for a global revival of the golden age of economic growth of the 1950s and 1960s, but shared this time by the less developed countries, are realised in a climatic environment – a benign state of nature – which makes that possible. Or we may be looking around for food aid if nature is adverse, and if we have not taken timely precautions. Unfortunately there is no interplanetary food aid, or indeed any other planet to which we can migrate.

The policy regret approach recognises the essential relativity of policy – that we can do nothing about what the state of nature is – by taking as datum the situation that would arise if we correctly guessed what the state of nature is and adjusted policy to give the best possible outcome (damage avoided net of policy implementation costs) in that circumstance. Other policies, by assumption, yield a worse outcome.

With an estimate of the costs of different policies, and, after much patient research, of the damage associated with different outcomes, we then have a 'policy regret' measure which is relative to the state of nature which has been guessed. The measure is the sum of damage costs plus policy costs for a particular policy, minus the sum of damage costs plus policy costs for the best policy in that state of nature. Clearly it is zero for the best policy, with increasing regret for policies that are inappropriate to the state of nature.

The policy which is best for one possible state of nature may, however, be not so good for another. And, we shall see, pending the outcome of patient research, it may be possible to make progress with only very poor information about damage costs. Our decision process may enable conclusions to be drawn which require only qualitative assumptions about the nature of the damage function.

An illustrative example

The idea is best grasped by an illustrative example which is constructed so as to bring out some of the other points that are being made. We suppose four possible policies: (A) business as usual, i.e. let industrialised development continue without regard to global warming; (B) a 'no regrets' policy of measures which pay for themselves through direct energy savings; (C) a possibility of slow stabilisation of emissions; and (D) ambitious emissions reduction targets (which can only realistically be reached by the adoption of something like the GREENS concept). We suppose these policies are pursued until, say, the year 2010,[9*] when news from the climatologists reveals the true state of the world and enables a target year and level of carbon dioxide (measured, as in Chapter 2, in parts per million; e.g. 0.03 per cent = 300ppm) to be specified.

And we suppose four possible states of the world: (W) benign (negative) feedbacks from projected carbon dioxide increases – say relatively more cloud in the day and global warming of 1°C per century under business as usual and a long-term carbon dioxide level of 400ppm being acceptable; (X) neutral feedbacks with global warming of 3°C per century under business as usual and a maximum acceptable long-term carbon dioxide level of 350ppm; (Y) a methane related positive feedback but other feedbacks neutral with global warming of 6°C per century under business as usual and a need to stabilize at 320ppm; (Z) all feedbacks strongly positive, with a need to return to 300ppm (still somewhat above the maximum natural level of which we have record) and the path to a catastrophic climate 'jump' irreversible by 2010 if business continues as usual.

We thus characterise these states of the world in terms of the rate of global warming under business as usual and of the tolerable long-run level of carbon dioxide (which is assumed to be lower the greater is the tendency to warming). In considering different policies, we shall suppose there is a latest date (of which the climatologists will also tell us in 2010, after their improved models have been running for a few years) by when we need to return to the acceptable carbon dioxide level. A quicker return is supposed to be needed the more is the 2010 level above the long-run acceptable level, since both the excess level and the time it persists are assumed to matter in relation to some critical factor (which might be saving the polar ice from melting away).

In Table 3.1, we show these technical aspects of each characterisation of the state of nature together with their implication under each policy. In each case, row (a) shows the carbon dioxide level reached in 2010, which depends only upon the policy followed in the meantime; row (b) the temperature rise by 2010; row (c) the date by when, it is perceived in 2010, the level of carbon dioxide needs to be brought back to the long-run acceptable level; and row (d) the downward rate of change of carbon dioxide levels, in parts per million per year, needed to achieve (c). In what follows, item (d) in this Table will be seen to be crucial. It is reached by dividing the excess level of carbon dioxide in 2010 (i.e. above the long-run acceptable level for the particular state of nature) by the time given by climatologists in 2010 for getting the level down to the safe level. For example, in the case policy (C) and state of nature (Y), the excess level is 370ppm-320ppm and the time available is 2070-2010 so that the rate of carbon dioxide reduction required is 50ppm in 60 years or 0.83ppm. per annum.

Table 3.1 Physical Characterisation of States of Nature and Related Policy Requirements

States of nature		W. Benign 400ppm	X. Neutral 350ppm	Y. Bad 320ppm	Z. Horrid 300ppm
long-term level					
Policies					
	(a)	400ppm	400ppm	400ppm	400ppm
(A)	(b)	1°C	3°C	6°C	10°C
Business	(c)	n.a.	2070	2050	2030
as usual	(d)	zero	.83ppm.p.a.	2ppm.p.a.	5ppm.p.a.
	(a)	390ppm	390ppm	390ppm	390ppm
(B)	(b)	0.8°C	2°C	4°C	7°C
No regret	(c)	n.a.	2080	2060	2040
	(d)	zero	.57ppm.p.a.	1.4ppm.p.a.	3ppm.p.a.
	(a)	370ppm	370ppm	370ppm	370ppm
(C)	(b)	0.5°C	1°C	2°C	4°C
Slow	(c)	n.a.	2090	2070	2050
stabilisation	(d)	zero	.25ppm.p.a.	.83ppm.p.a.	1.75ppm.p.a.
	(a)	350ppm	350ppm	350ppm	350ppm
(D)	(b)	zero	0.5°C	1°C	2°C
Ambitious	(c)	n.a.	n.a.	2080	2060
reduction	(d)	zero	zero	.43ppm.p.a.	1ppm.p.a.

On the basis of this characterisation of possible states of nature, we are able to proceed to an illustration of the regret calculation. Table 3.2 provides figures for (i) the cost of implementing the policy up to 2010; (ii) later costs, after 2010, of achieving the target, as announced in 2010 on the basis of the state of nature which is by then assumed to be known, and given the policy that has been pursued up till then; (iii) the cost of environmental damage, pre- and post-2010, given the policy and given the state of nature; (iv) the total cost; and (v) the 'regret', i.e. how much worse off is the global outcome for a particular policy and state of nature, compared with the best policy had we not been ignorant of the state of nature between now and 2010.

The figures are selected to illustrate the way in which regret analysis can lead to different results from CBA and to suggest how a precautionary approach can deliver useful policy conclusions even when data which is crucial to CBA remain unknown. However, it should be emphasised that none of the figures entered into these tables purport to be estimates of real world magnitudes. They are all purely notional and only for illustration of how the regret approach can be used.

Two assumptions popular with the protagonists of the 'no regret' approach are incorporated and fail to greatly affect the outcome in terms of regrets. One is the assumption that a little global warming may be a good thing. This is reflected in the damage function (iii) which shows least (zero) cost for a 1°C warming, with higher costs for both zero warming and faster warming. The other is the incorporation of quite high costs for the ambitious emissions reduction programme in row (i) of policy (D). We shall in later chapters see that these costs are in all likelihood quite low and we see later in this chapter how the use of lower numbers in row (D(i)) affects the outcome of the regret analysis.

Relatively small numbers are used for the unknown (iii) – save for case (A,Z) – in order to show that useful progress can be made on the basis of other numbers that we are better able to estimate. Relatively small as they may be, note should be taken of the unit of account, trillions of US dollars in present value terms. These are vast units. The present value of all future consumption on a global basis has been estimated, at a low social rate of discount (implying a substantial concern for future generations), to be about $1000 trillion.

So, for instance, the item (ii) cost for getting back to 300ppm by 2040 in a horrid state of nature after pursuing a 'no regret' policy until 2010, put at $300tr in box (B,Z), means that the global standard of living is reduced by 30 per cent on average over all future time. This might represent an effort to prevent the strong feedbacks which, in column (Z), horrid nature turns out to have in store for us, from getting out of control and rendering planet earth uninhabitable. The $500tr values for both environmental damage (iii) and post-2010 effort (ii), used in box (A,Z), means that, if instead of 'no regrets', the policy to 2010 had been 'business as usual', the task of getting back to 300ppm by 2030 is assumed to be impossible, with a zero consumption future reflecting mankind's doom.

Table 3.2   Economic Implications of Different Policies (trillions of dollars)

States of nature			W. Benign	X. Neutral	Y. Bad	Z. Horrid
Policies						
	(i)	Policy cost to 2010	0.00	0.00	0.00	0.00
(A)	(ii)	Later repair costs	0.00	25.00	100.00	500.00
Business	(iii)	Cost of damage	0.00	1.00	4.00	500.00
as usual	(iv)	Total cost	0.00	26.00	104.00	1000.00
	(v)	Regret from B.a.U Policy	0.00	20.00	77.75	944.75
	(i)	Policy cost to 2010	0.10	0.10	0.10	0.10
(B)	(ii)	Later repair costs	0.00	15.00	50.00	300.00
No regrets	(iii)	Cost of damage	0.04	0.25	1.00	4.00
	(iv)	Total cost	0.14	15.35	51.10	304.10
	(v)	Regret from N.R. Policy	0.14	9.35	24.85	248.85
	(i)	Policy cost to 2010	1.00	1.00	1.00	21.00
(C)	(ii)	Later repair costs	0.00	5.00	25.00	80.00
Slow	(iii)	Cost of damage	0.25	0.00	0.25	1.00
stabilisation	(iv)	Total cost	1.25	6.00	26.25	82.00
	(v)	Regret from S.S. Policy	1.25	0.00	0.00	26.75
(D)	(i)	Policy cost to 2010	25.00	25.00	25.00	25.00
Ambitious	(ii)	Later repair costs	0.00	0.00	10.00	30.00
reduction	(iii)	Cost of damage	1.00	0.64	0.00	0.25
	(iv)	Total cost	26.00	25.64	35.00	55.25
	(v)	Regret from A.R. Policy	26.00	19.64	8.75	0.00
Best policy			(A)	(C)	(C)	(D)

The 'regrets' in each column (in rows (v)) are calculated by subtracting the arrowed row (iv) cost of the best policy from the row (iv) costs of the other policies in the column under consideration. Obviously this leads to zero regret if, ante hoc, the best policy is chosen in what, post hoc, turns out to be the true state of nature.

The basis for the very large numbers for item (ii) lies in the row (d) figures in Table 3.1. They are all rates of decrease of the level of carbon dioxide in the atmosphere, and accordingly imply sequestering carbon from the atmosphere faster than it is emitted. The present rate of fossil fuel use and forest destruction, burning about eight billion tons of carbon a year, of which about four are absorbed naturally, results in an increase of 2.5ppm.p.a. in carbon dioxide levels. A zero level of net emissions would, with natural absorption, result in a decline in the carbon dioxide level of about 1ppm.p.a.

Faster rates of decrease, whilst technologically conceivable given time to reorganise social and industrial behaviour appropriately, are assumed to be very costly and, as implied by box (A,Z) of Table 3.2, infeasible on a crash basis, starting with an industrial system that had been proceeding in a business as usual direction until 2010. Thus the central perception is that carbon dioxide levels cannot be left high for ever.

With the exception of the currently unknowable damage item (iii), the costs in the Table are amenable to straightforward research. It is a technological question how much it costs to put a particular emission control policy into effect, as is the cost of possibly more strenuous measures that might be required after 2010. The difficulty presented by the damage function is circumvented by assuming that the damage function is related to the carbon dioxide excess in 2010. For in that case larger values for damage reinforce the large values for post-2010 costs. And as it is the latter which dominate the outcome, as presented in Table 3.2, only slightly different an outcome would be expected from using in (iii) the larger damage figures which may well be realistic.

Another difficulty is that comparisons are implicitly being made between costs and benefits (i.e. damage avoided) occurring at different points in time (e.g. pre-2010 and post-2010). This raises the question of the discount rate which lies with the inter-generational equity issue mentioned earlier. These questions are not central to the present discussion and are assumed to have been resolved, with all costs expressed in comparable (present value) terms.

Using the Regret Approach

Having calculated regret in this manner, the next question is what to make of it in taking decisions. Of course somewhat different results would be got from substantially different numerical inputs into the Table, but the broad 'stitch in time saves nine' result would follow from any sensible representation of the consequences of seriously adverse surprises in the jumpy climate future. Either of the more interventionist policies, (C) or (D), leads to less regret in either of the more adverse states of nature.

From regret to objection

We need to go a stage further, and think how we value outcomes, before we can proceed to making use of the regret matrix, except in a rather primitive way. Remember that one of the things we wanted to do in reaching decisions under uncertainty was to reflect the idea of risk aversion, which is tied to our greater concern about losses the less we have to lose (save for the starving who have nothing to lose but their chains – desperation breeds revolution), and to our disproportionately greater concern for big losses than for small losses. For the individual, economists reflect this idea in the concept of diminishing marginal utility of income (we care less about a $1000 raise if we are earning $50,000 already than if we are earning $20,000).

Corresponding to that, and since our regret is a measure of relative loss to the global economy, i.e. negative social benefit, we need to have a measure of increasing marginal value of regret, such that we put an infinite social value, we have infinite social objection, to a situation where future consumption is eliminated, i.e. to a situation where the globe becomes uninhabitable. Thus for any given state of nature (i.e. given by nature, not for statesmen to choose) we object infinitely to a policy choice which gives a regret equal to the entire future global well-being which is feasible in that state of nature: all minus all leaves nothing. This measure of social objection is a particular case of the general concept of a 'social welfare function' which economists hypothesize for valuing collective outcomes for groups of people, typically for valuing the level of consumption enjoyed in a particular country.

To reflect this idea, Table 3.3 gives figures for social objection related to the regrets of Table 3.2 (repeated here for convenience) on the basis

Table 3.3 Regrets and Objections

States of nature			W. Benign	X. Neutral	Y. Bad	Z. Horrid
Policies						
(A)	Business	Regret	0.00	20.00	77.75	944.75
	as usual	Objection	0.00	20.53	86.77	∞
(B)	No	Regret	0.14	9.35	24.85	248.85
	Regret	Objection	0.14	9.50	26.19	357.59
(C)	Slow	Regret	1.25	0.00	0.00	26.75
	Stabilisation	Objection	1.25	0.00	0.00	29.14
(D)	Ambitious	Regret	26.00	19.64	8.75	0.00
	Reduction	Objection	26.69	20.16	9.07	0.00
Best policy			(A)	(C)	(C)	(D)

Note: the 'regret' in each row is taken from Table 3.2 and the measure of social objection to each regret is estimated according to the formula given in the footnote.

that zero regret has zero objection whilst the objection that corresponds to zero future consumption is put at infinity.[10*] It may be seen that the substantial regrets associated with adverse states of nature and incautious policy are weighted more heavily by this measure of social objection. Any policy with non-zero risk of zero future consumption (like 'business as usual' on the figures we have been using to illustrate this discussion) is eliminated on a criterion of minimising expected objection.[11*]

What we have now done, in two stages, is to reflect two of the *desiderata* for taking decisions under uncertainty. Firstly the regret approach enables us to adopt a relativistic perspective that recognises that choices have to be made in relation to the state of nature that fate happens to dish out. Of course, this does not dispose of the 'shoot the messenger' syndrome: if nature turns out nasty, even the best, zero regret, policy will leave consumers worse off than they may be expecting from looking back at historic growth, and that may be bad news for democratically elected politicians. A horrid state of nature may make democracy impracticable.

Secondly, the objection measure imposes a uniform approach to decisions in each state of nature: in particular, we have zero objection to the best decision possible and infinite objection to the worst outcome imaginable. In relation to the four *desiderata*, we sidestep the inter-generational aspect and pass over the question of irreversibility until the end of the chapter. For the moment we focus on the implications of the risk averse precautionary principle introduced by moving from 'regret' to 'objection'.

Minimax regret: an over-simplified approach

We have still to resolve how the specific choice is to be made. Clearly, any finite, even tiny, significance given to horrid state of nature Z eliminates business as usual policy (A). But a sanguine politician may hope for benign state of nature W and aim to catch today's votes with almost painless 'no regret' policy (B). However, a risk averse and environmentally articulate democracy, expecting its government to be concerned for the long-term, will be looking for one or other of the more interventionist policies (C) or (D).

Unfortunately, one cannot pursue two policies at once, although a similar level of objection for two policies does suggest that intermediate policies might be devised and costed out – perhaps targeting for a moderate reduction in emissions, rather than an ambitious reduction. But let us suppose that Tables 3.2 and 3.3 represent the limit of policy flexibility and that we have to choose one or the other of (A) to (D). An intuitively simple approach (albeit faulty, for reasons which are discussed below) is to use what is called the minimax regret approach.

This says choose the policy for which the maximum regret is least – policy (D) in the above Table, for which the worst outcome is to find nature benign and discover that $26 trillion (or about one-fortieth of future living standards in a well-off world) had been sacrificed as insurance against the possibility that things might not have turned out so nicely. If the slow stabilisation of emissions policy (C) had been pursued, a horrid nature results in $27 trillion regret so that minimising maximum regret results in a preference for (D), the policy of ambitious emissions reductions targets. Either 'business as usual' or 'no regrets' fails badly on the minimax regret basis.

However, there is a problem with the minimax regret approach (apart from its basic conservatism, which is no bad thing where the objective is to be taking a precautionary approach). It is a very myopic approach, focusing all attention on one perhaps not very likely state of nature. The difficulty that arises from this is that the decision rule becomes very subjective and, perhaps, open to abuse by the invention of possible states of nature to suit the analyst's viewpoint.

The hostile reader may feel that state of nature (Z) has been invented to suit the theme of the book. A business-oriented analyst might invent even more benign possibilities than (W) to generate a high maximum regret for policies (C) and (D), through their failure to capture some great benefit from rapid global warming. Thus it is obviously better to find a way of incorporating the relative likelihood of the possible states of nature, even while preserving the relativism of the regret approach.

First though, it is worthwhile to compare the minimax regret outcome with that which would result from CBA. The first thing to note is that CBA cannot start unless we attribute probabilities to the different states of nature. Supposing we reflect our present ignorance by regarding each of (W) to (Z) as being equally likely to come about. This is because total ignorance means that, *ex ante*, we have no basis for regarding any of W, X, Y or Z as more or less likely than the others and should therefore regard them as equally likely. That is to say we give each a probability of 0.25 since, by assumption, (W) to (Z) exhaust the possible states of nature and one or other of them is bound to happen (by convention probability measures total to one, a probability of one being equivalent to a sure thing certainty).

On this basis the expected cost of each policy is 0.25 times the sum of the cost (iv) under each policy, e.g., for policy (B),

$$0.25(0.14 + 15.35 + 51.10 + 304.10) = 92.67.$$

The complete set of expected costs is

(A)	282.50
(B)	92.67
(C)	28.87
(D)	35.45

so that a different policy choice (from (D) selected by minimax regret) is obtained under CBA using the assumed probabilities, i.e. (C).

Perhaps not strikingly different, and many might feel more sensible, given the extremism of state of nature (Z). But to take a view of that kind – that (Z) is extremist – is to ascribe unequal probabilities to (W) (X) (Y) or to (Z). That is to make claims, about the long-run behaviour of the complex dynamic system which delivers the global climate, which we are not in a position to make. It is like betting on a horse race on the other side of the moon when there is no 'form' to go by and you are not allowed to view the runners. Such a state of ignorance is obviously costly in its potential for giving rise to expensive mistakes.

Learning as you go

It is this cost which provides the justification for spending a lot of money worldwide on climate research facilities. Some of the most valuable work that has been done by economists on policy responses to global warming has treated the problem in an insurance framework[12] and shown that such investment in knowledge is likely to be the best greenhouse insurance buy available. And, indeed, it is being argued in this book that the implementation of GREENS should, in the 1990s, take the form of 'action research' into its operational aspects, research that could be suspended or slowed if climatological research brings good news. Such 'learning by doing' is an important way of building pathways into unexplored parts of the wood, to use an earlier metaphor. Returning to the current metaphor, research establishes some 'form' as regards the various horses (W, X, Y, Z) which enables the punters (world statesmen) to better decide how to place their 'bets', i.e. policies (A), (B), (C) or (D).

The most likely prospect is that progress with research will enable us to revise our probabilities for states of nature from our current 'prior' of 25 per cent for each towards, say, 20 per cent, 30 per cent, 40 per cent, and 10 per cent by the year 2000. This updating approach, with new knowledge being used to update our probabilistic view of the world, called after an 18th century minister of religion and amateur mathematician named Bayes, can be applied to our measure of social objection.

As it turns out with the particular figures chosen, shifting to Bayesian probability weighted social objection, and using 'total ignorance' equal probabilities for each state of nature, gives the same choice as does CBA, that is to say policy (C), 'slow stabilization'. If, however, future research indicated a higher likelihood of an adverse state of nature, with probabilities shifting towards, say, 0.1, 0.1, 0.3, 0.5 for (W) to (Z) respectively, then the Bayesian approach applied to the measure of social objection would suggest a shift to the more active policy (D) earlier than would CBA. Especially if, introducing the year 2000 as a decision break point, rather than the 2010 of our tables, the learning by doing activity advocated in this book does indeed go forward, so that the groundwork for a switch to a more active policy is in place.

However, this is becoming hypothetical. The main purpose has been to show that an analytic framework is available which reflects the *desiderata* for decision taking under uncertainty which were set out earlier. Since we are working with notional data it is of no great value to follow the procedure through. It is more interesting at this stage to see what would be the impact of changing some of the assumptions which were made in constructing Table 3.2 and for that purpose we need go no further than recalculating the regret values.

Sensitivity Analysis

An investigation of the implications of changing assumptions (that were made initially in order to enable an analysis to proceed) is called a sensitivity analysis. In moving from Table 3.1 to Table 3.2, two assumptions were made at which we can now take another look. These were that a small global warming might be beneficial and that an ambitious programme of emissions reduction would be very expensive. It was said at the time that the latter assumption is pessimistic, as will be shown in later chapters, and we now see what the impact of a low-cost emissions reduction technology would be.

For this purpose we reconstruct Table 3.2 as Table 3.2a following, in which the data assumptions of Table 3.2 are retained save that the ambitious emissions reduction policy is now taken to cost $2.5tr. rather than $25tr. On a very approximate calculation this is about twice the cost (per ton of carbon emitted under business as usual) as is calculated for New Zealand in the Appendix to this book. For policies (A), (B) and (C) rows (i) to (iv) are the same. However, for policy (D), row (i) – and hence row (iv) – is different so that policy (D) has least total cost under any state of nature except benign (W). Accordingly, all the regrets are changed (with the exception of policies (A) to (C) under (W)), and the regret associated with (D) under benign (W) is greatly reduced. On these data one would need to be very sure indeed that (W) really did represent nature before adopting any policy other than one of ambitious emissions reductions. So we conclude that the previous preference for policy (C) over policy (D), in the case of the two central possibilities as regards the state of nature, arose because we assumed an unfavourable cost for policy (D) rather than because a moderate policy is a better response to such moderate states of nature.

Table 3.2a Regrets With Low-cost Emissions Reduction Technology (trillions of dollars)

States of nature			W. Benign	X. Neutral	Y. Bad	Z. Horrid
Policies						
	(i)	Policy cost to 2010	0.00	0.00	0.00	0.00
(A)	(ii)	Later repair costs	0.00	25.00	100.00	500.00
Business	(iii)	Cost of damage	0.04	0.25	1.00	4.00
as usual	(iv)	Total cost	0.00	26.00	104.00	1000.00
	(v)	Regret from B.a.U Policy	0.00	22.86	91.50	967.25
	(i)	Policy cost to 2010	0.10	0.10	0.10	0.10
(B)	(ii)	Later repair costs	0.00	15.00	50.00	300.00
No regrets	(iii)	Cost of damage	0.04	0.25	1.00	4.00
	(iv)	Total cost	0.14	15.35	51.10	304.10
	(v)	Regret from N.R. Policy	0.14	12.21	38.60	271.35
	(i)	Policy cost to 2010	1.00	1.00	1.00	21.00
(C)	(ii)	Later repair costs	0.00	5.00	25.00	80.00
Slow	(iii)	Cost of damage	0.25	0.00	0.25	1.00
Stabilisation	(iv)	Total cost	0.25	6.00	26.25	82.00
	(v)	Regret from S.S. Policy	1.25	2.86	13.75	49.25
(D)	(i)	Policy cost to 2010	2.50	2.50	2.50	2.50
Ambitious	(ii)	Later repair costs	0.00	0.00	10.00	30.00
Reduction	(iii)	Cost of damage	1.00	0.64	0.00	0.25
	(iv)	Total cost	3.50	3.14	12.50	32.75
	(v)	Regret from A.R. Policy	3.50	0.00	0.00	0.00
Best policy			(A)	(D)	(D)	(D)

To consider climate prospects closer to the mainstream of climatological opinion than the business orientation embodied in the Table 3.2 damage function – row (iii) in each policy case – we reconstruct the Table as Table 3.2b. In calculating this Table the low-cost emissions reduction technology of the previous Table is used together with numbers closer to conventional estimates of the damage function than have been used in the previous Tables.

Thus in this Table, rows (i) and (ii) are the same as Table 3.2a. However, row (iii) now shows a zero value for the case of zero temperature rise (such as results from policy (D) in the case of a benign nature). And the general level of damage costs has been increased by a factor of about four. The effect of these changes to a more mainstream view of the damage function is to show that the 'business as usual' policy (A) choice, resulting previously under benign state of nature (W), arose, in previous Tables 3.3 and 3.3a, only because of the peculiar assumption for the damage function. The penalty for adopting ambitious policy (D) in the case of (W) is trivial, under Table 3.2b assumptions and the penalty for not adopting it under other states of nature, is at least 40 times greater and generally more than 100 times. With a mainstream view of the damage function the less interventionist policies (A) and (B) fail under any easily imaginable state of nature.

Table 3.2b   Regrets With a More Conservative Damage Function

States of nature			W. Benign	X. Neutral	Y. Bad	Z. Horrid
Policies						
	(i)	Policy cost to 2010	0.00	0.00	0.00	0.00
(A)	(ii)	Later repair costs	0.00	25.00	100.00	500.00
Business	(iii)	Cost of damage	5.00	20.00	45.00	500.00
as usual	(iv)	Total cost	5.00	45.00	145.00	1000.00
	(v)	Regret from B.a.U Policy	2.75	42.30	130.70	962.50
	(i)	Policy cost to 2010	0.10	0.10	0.10	0.10
(B)	(ii)	Later repair costs	0.00	15.00	50.00	300.00
No regrets	(iii)	Cost of damage	3.20	11.25	20.00	45.00
	(iv)	Total cost	3.30	26.35	70.10	345.10
	(v)	Regret from N.R. Policy	1.05	23.65	55.80	307.60
	(i)	Policy cost to 2010	1.00	1.00	1.00	1.00
(C)	(ii)	Later repair costs	0.00	5.00	25.00	80.00
Slow	(iii)	Cost of damage	1.25	5.00	11.25	20.00
Stabilisation	(iv)	Total cost	2.25	11.00	37.25	101.00
	(v)	Regret from S.S. Policy	0.00	8.30	22.95	63.50
(D)	(i)	Policy cost to 2010	2.50	2.50	2.50	2.50
Ambitious	(ii)	Later repair costs	0.00	0.00	10.00	30.00
Reduction	(iii)	Cost of damage	0.00	0.20	1.80	5.00
	(iv)	Total cost	2.50	2.70	14.30	37.50
	(v)	Regret from A.R. Policy	0.25	0.00	0.00	0.00
Best policy			(C)	(D)	(D)	(D)

Policy Options in Real Time

Thus the regret concept, working through a social welfare function, such as we have called 'social objection', and combined with a Bayesian framework for updating the policy decision in the light of new knowledge as it becomes available, provides a suitable precautionary approach through which, with an appropriate social discount rate, the interests of future generations can, in principle, be provided for without inequitable sacrifice at present.

To say that such a thing can be done in principle, and to perform the exercise in imaginary time with simplified hypothetical data, is very far from assembling the apparatus for doing it in practice in the slowly evolving real time of future experience. Nevertheless, the informational requirements for such an exercise are more practicable than those imposed by conventional CBA. In essence a technological assessment of a specific transformation of the commercial energy system is involved. But such a transformation does not take place in a historical vacuum, and the information that will be coming forward for Bayesian updating of the probabilities – and consequential adjustments to the policy choice – will depend upon what information is sought in the research that goes forward in the years ahead. If no serious effort is made to build pathways into those parts of the woods that have so far been largely neglected as far as the global warming problem goes, then the problem is likely to continue to look as forbiddingly threatening to future generations' prospects as it has so far.

The presentation of the principles which has been adopted in this chapter, by way of illustrative numerical example, is not one that provides a suitable approach for analysing the decision problem in practice. That requires formal mathematical modelling over a series of decision points that will emerge through the political process and which will provide – or fail to provide – opportunities for taking stock of the changing situation, and of changed understanding, over the years ahead. Each decision point provides a range of policy options, each of which provides a branch of the decision tree which can branch again at the next time for decision. Implicit in such a prospect is the proliferation of Tables beyond 3a and 3b to 3c, 3d...3z, etc., yielding a problem that can only be analysed sensibly by computerised methods.

The closest quantitative approach to what is needed, albeit without setting up the formal apparatus of regret analysis in relation to different possible states of nature, comes in *Buying Greenhouse Insurance — the Economic Costs of CO_2 Emission Limits* by Alan S. Manne and Richard G. Richels,[13] which advances much of the philosophy adopted in this book – indeed, some of my terminology is derived from it. Their argument is that an appropriate response is neither to wait and see, nor to act and then learn, but rather to learn and then act. Overhasty action, such as the European Community proposal for the early imposition of a 25 per cent carbon tax, is likely to be a poor investment when compared with putting the economic benefit from refraining from such action into a decade of intensive research and other preparatory activity.[14*] *Buying Greenhouse Insurance* leads in a different direction from this book because of different technological assumptions. Thus it shows where we might need to go if the technological optimism of the present book regarding the potential of biomass proves to be ill founded. It does so on the basis of a well developed model of the world's conventional energy system linked to a long term macro-economic model.

Whether the technological optimism of the present book is justified readers will judge for themselves. In its support there are a few points to be made. Firstly, as regards noxious pollution, biomass is the raw material used in nature's underground factory for producing fossil fuels. Nature's factory is peculiarly neglectful of environmental regulations and goes so far as to mix in all sorts of unpleasant substances – mainly sulphur, but also trace quantities of other chemicals – which are very bad news in high technology applications like gas turbines. Biomass is largely free of these pollutants, which makes it easier to use. Secondly, economies of scale in energy applications are becoming less significant. With the advent of the gas turbine based technologies of Chapter 4 they do not obtain, to the extent they did, in electric power generation. And the need for large quantities of carbon in producing iron and steel, which was the original cause of the concentration of industry around coal fields, is less great with modern steel production techniques. Thus the transportation cost disadvantage of fuel-wood, which led to industrial concentration around coalfields, is less important for the growth of biomass based industry.

Thirdly, whilst the estimates of costs of biomass production – and transportation over the moderate distances needed to support viable scale industry – varies widely, most are not greatly in excess of the $2 per GJ (Giga Joule – we discuss energy units in Chapter 4) which is a rough benchmark for bulk coal costs in many analyses, including those of *Buying Greenhouse Insurance*. But, to provide a cheap response to global warming, they do not need to be less, since it is by how much greater they are, than fossil fuel costs, that we measure the cost of responding to global warming, and a precautionary approach does not require the cost to be zero before action is taken.

And fourthly, most research into agronomic productivity has been focused on food productivity or on conventional forestry productivity. A substantially funded worldwide research programme into raising biomass productivity has not been undertaken and, when it is, can be expected to make rapid advances in its initial phases as is usually the case with any study into a new area. Isolated studies of intensive production of short rotation woody crops promise well on the basis of existing cultivars – leading towards the $2 per GJ mentioned above – but little has been done to apply biotechnology and genetic engineering in this area.

As with any analytic procedure, whether computerised or not, the 'garbage in garbage out' dictum applies also to regret analysis. But one needs only to assume a finite possibility of an adverse, possibly catastrophic, climate jump, to see that plausible orders of magnitude, for emergency policies begun late, point clearly towards an active emissions reduction policy begun early (but not so impetuously as to forestall effective 'learning by doing'), especially if such precautionary policy is low-cost. Such a conclusion emerges intuitively from a concern for future generations and the main function served by the regret/objection approach is that it enables such concerns to be formalised in an operational manner. It thus yields an escape from the familiar CBA methodology which has provided the operational basis for environmental policies hitherto, but which gives poor guidance in relation to global warming policy.

That finite possibility of a climate jump may perhaps be encompassed in our 'horrid' state of nature Z. The greater or lesser damage costs that may arise if nature delivers a climate future that is free of adverse jumps, a future that is simply a calculable extension of the current climate regime (whatever that may turn out to be when the climatologists have finished their researches in 10 or 20 years time – pointing perhaps to a benign turn of events, perhaps to a neutral one, or perhaps to a forecastably bad one, or even to the conclusion that, even without climate jumps, no forecast is possible) are the concern that has mainly occupied public debate, leading to a catalogue of possible damages which we do not detail in these pages.

That omission is deliberate: reams have been written [15] on the possible impacts of climate change, characterised as a greater or lesser increase in mean global surface temperature. However, dwelling for the moment on the damage function when adverse surprise – the horrid state of nature Z – is ignored, Tables 3.2, 3.2a, and 3.2b indicate that one would, against the advice of the consensus of scientific opinion worldwide as brought together in the IPCC, have to give heavy emphasis to benign future W in order to be less precautionary than slow stabilisation policy C.

The possibility of a low-cost strategy such as is outlined in later chapters of this book shifts the balance towards the more ambitious policy D, as in Table 3.2a, while a more middle of the road view on damage costs eliminates the less active policies A and B whatever the yet to be discovered state of nature. In the absence of the computerised modelling mentioned above, these are merely hypothetical conclusions. But they do suggest that the option cost of failing to set out on the course of 'learning by doing' that is advocated in this book may be rather great even without regard to the risk of climate jumps implicit in such repeated remarks of the IPCC as 'nevertheless, the complexity of the system may give rise to surprises'. [16]

In this book we do not devote space to the damage catalogue since, serious though it is, it does not capture the essence of a precautionary concern for posterity. The problem which is of most concern in these pages is the danger of climate system instability and the danger that anthropogenic emissions of greenhouse gases, forcing carbon dioxide levels in a manner that is unprecedented on a prehistoric timescale, will result in burdens on our grandchildren (and their grandchildren, if any) which will make our present damage catalogue appear trivial. Allowing for a finite possibility of adverse surprises may raise the option cost of inactive policies A and B to infinity.

Notes

1. Elaborated from Read, 1990.
2. Eppen et al, 1987, p.622.
3. Baumol, 1977, p.463.
4. Read, 1993.
5. Cline, 1992, p.6 and Chapter 6.
6. Neither is a doubling very meaningful scientifically – as noted in the previous chapter it is used by scientists for comparing the behaviour of one model with another. But, in using it as an indicator of climatic condition, regard must be had to the normal range as well as to the average normal value. Body temperatures, indicative of metabolic condition, usually move in a range of about two degrees Celsius around the normal of 37 Celsius, and a doubling would be certainly fatal. As we saw in the previous chapter, the range for carbon dioxide concentration is only about 0.01 per cent wide, lying between 0.018 (ice age conditions) and 0.028 per cent (for most of recorded time). This is in proportionate terms on a par with the normal range of systolic blood pressure (indicative of a cardio-vascular condition, for which a doubling of an already high level would be extremely dangerous rather than certainly fatal) which is why the blood pressure analogy has been chosen.
7. Cline, 1992, Annex 6A, discussing Lind, 1982 and Bradford, 1975.
8. We have said in the Introduction that the message of this chapter gets overtaken in the rest of the book, where a rudimentary analysis of the costs of the GREENS strategy suggests it to be attractive to any decision taker with a sensibly precautionary global perspective. The decision-taking rationale advanced in this chapter provides grounds for tackling the heavier task of overcoming the political economy aspects arising from national interests, or, alternatively, for accepting the higher costs of responding effectively to global warming should the reasoned optimism of this book in the end prove unfounded – i.e. if the programme of relatively inexpensive 'getting ready' advocated for the 1990s shows that the GREENS strategy does not provide an adequate response.
9. This is for the purposes of simplifying the exposition. The reader will recollect that the precautionary policy which we advocate involves 'getting ready' in the 1990s, thus providing a decision opportunity in the year 2000 to take

advantage of the intervening learning by doing process (at the level of intensive and worldwide pilot training and demonstration schemes) by then choosing whether to implement GREENS at a faster or slower rate in the first decade of the next century. Thus it might be supposed that a decision is taken in 2000 on the basis of having learned the costs of alternative policies, but that damage function information is not forthcoming until 2010. In reality, decision points do not fall neatly at the turns of decades, but are determined by the rhythm of diplomatic and political events. However, it would be a mistake to conclude that there is infinite flexibility in the timing and sequencing of decisions – what was done or was not done at an event like the 1992 Earth Summit creates and/or forecloses options for a long time ahead.

10. A simple formula that achieves this result is (with objection = OB; regret = RG; and the minimum total cost for a given state of nature = Cmin) as follows:

OB =1000 x [{($1000tr. Cmin)($1000tr. Cmin RG)} 1].

One might employ a more sophisticated formula based upon social preferences revealed in voting behaviour, but this will do to demonstrate the idea.

11. Actually we should say 'which carries a larger than necessary risk of zero future consumption' since nothing can be done about, say, the sun's distant future as a red giant engulfing the planetary system. The alert reader will note the probabilistic connotation of 'expectation' in the context of our previous distinction between risk and uncertainty and will be concerned that we are losing sight of the objective of viewing separate states of nature separately. At some stage in the proceedings it is necessary to take a view on relative probabilities; the point is to leave it to the final stage as we do below.

12. Manne and Richels, 1992, Chapter 1.

13. Ibid, Chapter 4.

14. This of course is no reflection on President Clinton's proposal for an energy tax which, far from being over-hasty, is a long overdue alignment of US energy prices – and of US incentives for energy efficiency – with those of its competitors, and with the real costs of using fossil fuels (before taking into account the costs of responding to the threat of global warming that arises from using them).

15. Cline, 1992, Chapter 3, and works cited therein.

16. IPCC, 1992, 'Overview', p.53-4; 'Executive Summary', p.63; 'Scientific Assessment' p.79.

4. Sustainable Fuel Technology

Fuel technology is fundamental to the pattern of industrial activity. In developed countries the age of 'king coal' has given way to the age of electricity and gas as convenience fuels in factory and home, and to the dominance of oil and natural gas as raw materials. The internal combustion engine has enabled the shift from mass rail transport to the individualised automobile and, in turn, has led to the growth of the world oil trade and is the *raison d'être* for recurrent Middle East crises. The availability of cheap hydro-electricity determines the supply of aluminium and the location of that and other electricity-intensive industries. Steel and heavy industry have gone with coal as has military power (more recently with nuclear knowhow, itself an energy technology). The history of industrial change is inseparably bound up with the history of energy technology, from the harnessing of brute animal effort, through water power and the age of steam, to electricity and a current reliance on fossil fuels which is unsustainable in the long run.

Although the capacity of the oil and gas exploration business to surprise us, by finding more whenever the industry needs more, is remarkable, the amount left in the ground, waiting to be found, is finite. That, however, is not important. What matters is how hard it is to find more oil, and the number of feet of well that has to be drilled to find a barrel of oil increases, albeit unsteadily.[1] As the rising cost of oil eventually transmits into prices, so will alternative energy technologies become more attractive. A business-as-usual scenario will see increasing reliance on abundant coal and coal-to-oil technologies that have unattractive local environmental characteristics.

Thus the onset of global warming, and the incentive it provides to use non-fossil alternatives, both brings forward and changes the direction of the expected transition due to the exhaustion of the cheaper oil reserves. A renewable energy raw material, i.e. a sustainable fuel supply, is needed, powered by the solar energy that is captured in the photosynthesis involved in growing trees or other biomass. The carbon is recycled in a grow-burn-grow process corresponding to an energy capture-energy release-energy capture cycle which sees the amount of carbon in the atmosphere remain constant. But if the present scare over global warming proves to be groundless in the year 2010 (by when, it was assumed in the last chapter, the climatologists may have completed enough research to form a reliable opinion) our children will nevertheless be grateful for the stimulus it is providing towards sustainable technology.

This stimulus is needed because, as the modern, globally linked economy becomes more complex, the market provides less clear signals as to the appropriate direction of technological change. Economic theory shows that, within the oil industry, firms will optimise their exploration activity over time, to yield an approximately efficient utilisation of progressively more costly oil reserves. But there is little in the system to subvert the conservatism of oil firms as short-term commercial pressures lead them to maximise their market share and maintain a position based on the present fuel technology. Business-as-usual expectations may lead research departments to take a look at coal-to-oil, but risk-shy managements leave others to develop the technology.

There is nothing to ensure an efficient and timely transition to non-fossil fuel-based energy technologies. This can only come about through a far-reaching process of innovation that sees known alternative energy technology (made competitive by applying the polluter pays principle to fossil fuels) and inventions now emerging from the research laboratories, brought into the technological mainstream. Indeed, after the slower global growth of the last 20 years, such a shift in energy technology may trigger off a surge of innovative activity by a new generation of entrepreneurs. Schumpeterian theories of long period swings of economic activity suggest that such a 'cluster' of innovations may be just what is needed to set the global economy off on a new phase of prosperity.[2]

Clearly a changeover to a sustainable energy technology cannot be accomplished overnight. A 50 per cent reduction in emissions has been ridiculed, and rightly so if the suggestion is to do that this year, or even this decade. But, providing we are talking about net rather than gross emissions, by 2010 is not impracticable. And by 2020 not expensive, if achieved in a co-ordinated manner within a framework agreed by the international community. We leave to later chapters a discussion of the economic mechanisms needed for implementing a shift to sustainable energy in such relatively rapid time – after all, the replacement of coal by oil and gas, which has been going on for four decades, is not yet complete. Here the purpose is to see what such technologies are,[3] and what their roles might be in a global transition to a sustainable energy system.

For this we need to have some idea of the type, location and scale of demand in order to see how, when and where the different sustainable technologies can find their place. And since the transition requires global collaboration we need to look at demand worldwide and to assume some degree of success in the South in the achievement of its economic aspirations. Such success, through providing an inducement for the South's collaboration, must be an integral component of the technological transition.

Otherwise, on almost any reckoning of their economic prospects, South country increases in carbon dioxide emissions will, by a large amount, exceed the maximum conceivable reduction in the North.

Demands for Energy

Energy demands fall into three main types: bulk energy demands arising from energy-intensive industrial processing of raw materials into intermediate goods; portable energy demands from various transportation technologies; and convenience demands from the more sophisticated

Table 4.1 Global Demand and Supply of Energy in 1989
(billions tons oil equivalent*)

Fuel type: Demand type	Coal	Oil	Gas	Hydro	Nuclear	Electricity
Bulk Industrial	2.2	1.5	0.9	0.5	0.5	uses 2.8 to
Transportation		1.6				produce
Convenience			0.8			1.0

* Energy units are a nuisance to understand, partly because different kinds of energy have different properties. All can be turned into heat equivalent, as electric energy is turned to heat in an electric heater, or mechanical energy can be turned to heat by friction, or the chemical energy stored in fuels can be released as heat by combustion. At the individual level we will mostly use Gigajoules, with Petajoules (=million GJ or 22,000 tons oil) or Exajoules (=billion, i.e. thousand million GJ) at the national or global level. The technical definition of the Gigajoule is somewhat unmemorable – it is the electric energy used by running a 1kW appliance for 1 million seconds, which is nearly 12 days, or roughly the amount of chemical energy that goes into a small car's fuel tank – 1 ton of oil equals about 45 GJ. It is worth noting the technical energy storage superiority of combustion fuels: compare the cost and convenience of carrying around a tankful of petrol with the amount of electrical storage batteries needed to run a 1kW electrical appliance continuously for nearly a fortnight. That is why, despite the very low energy efficiency of conventional vehicle engines, it is very difficult to replace them with an electric battery system. Americans use Quads (Quadrillions of British Thermal Units, where a BTU is the rather tiny amount of heat needed to raise one pound of water by one degree Fahrenheit) which equal 1.055 EJ. In this table we use oil units, as do BP in their useful *Statistical Review*.

applications of light industrial, commercial and domestic users. Amongst the first are included the demands of energy industry activities that turn primary energy raw materials into marketable energy products in 'energy factories' such as electric power stations, oil refineries, gasworks,· etc.

These demands are met according to the broad pattern set out in Table 4.1 which is based, very approximately, on the *Statistical Review of World Energy for 1990* produced by BP.[4]

Growth in these demands is related to the growing level of economic activity, which may be broken down into rising standards of living, rising population levels.[5] Related to this is a shift to more convenient supplies as more advanced levels of economic development are reached, and to more efficient applications – in the sense of using less energy for achieving a given result – as the price of energy is increased. There is a wide disparity in the efficiency of energy applications between different countries at roughly the same level of development, which is usually related to historic, climatic, or traditional factors in the pattern of economic development.

Figure 4.1   Energy Consumption in Different Economies*

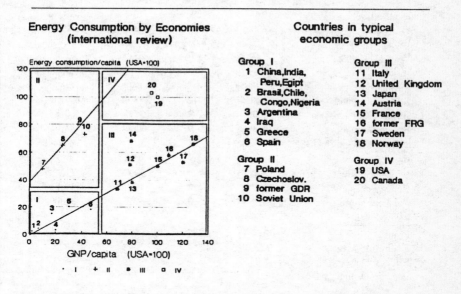

* This neat way of presenting the data is taken from a paper by H. Gaj and Z. Maciejewski of the Polish Academy of Sciences, which was given at the 1991 meeting of the International Energy Workshop held at the IIASA near Vienna.

This is illustrated in Figure 4.1 where per capita energy consumption is measured vertically and the level of development is measured horizontally, both as a percentage of the USA's. The measure of development is per capita national product, an unsatisfactory basis, but used conventionally for this purpose for want of an easily available better measure. Amongst the poorer countries, Eastern Europeans consume a lot of energy partly because the climate is quite cold, partly because energy prices were subsidised under the planning system that allocated

Table 4.2 Growth of Population, Economic Activity, and Per Capita Energy Consumption

	1990	2000	2010	2020
USA				
Population	249	262	273	282
Economic level	20740	27873	33977	41418
Energy demand	39.9	39.5	37.4	34.8
Per capita energy	58.5	55.0	50.0	45.0
Japan				
Population	124	129	132	131
Economic level	23190	34327	41844	51008
Energy demand	8.1	8.5	8.3	7.9
Per capita energy	23.9	24.0	23.0	22.0
W.Europe				
Population	431	448	460	469
Economic level	13180	17713	21592	26321
Energy demand	31.0	31.9	31.5	30.8
Per capita energy	26.3	26.0	25.0	24.0
E.Europe/former USSR				
Population	406	430	450	467
Economic level	3290	4870	5937	7237
Energy demand	39.9	41.2	40.7	39.6
Per capita energy	35.9	35.0	33.0	31.0
Rest of World				
Population	4017	4857	5651	6409
Economic level	770	1254	2043	3328
Energy Demand	4.6	73.2	108.4	149.3
Per capita energy	4.1	5.5	7.0	8.5

Population in millions; economic level as GDP (US$) per capita in 1989, projected at 5 per cent a year for Rest of World throughout, 3, 4, 3 and 4 per cent per year for the USA, Japan, W. Europe and East Europe respectively to 2000 and 2 per cent thereafter; energy demand in billions of barrels of oil equivalent a year, per capita energy in barrels of oil equivalent per capita per year. (Reproduced and elaborated, with permission, together with Figure 4.2 following, from a Shell Selected Paper, Elliot and Booth, 1990).

resources there until recently (and still does to a large extent), and partly because that same system pursued a pattern of development that emphasised energy-intensive heavy industries.

Amongst the richer countries, North America has traditionally enjoyed easy access to cheap domestic oil, gas and coal reserves, whereas Western Europe's are nearly exhausted – save for the North Sea oil and gas resource exploited since the mid-1960's and already substantially depleted – and Japan never had much worth speaking of. High prices outside North America, particularly for transportation fuels – petrol (gasoline) and diesel – are mainly due to taxes. These are imposed partly to protect declining coal industries, partly to reflect security of supply considerations, and partly for plain revenue-raising purposes. They have curbed demand and emphasised the extent to which the pattern of consumption amongst the richer countries reflects the pattern of resource availability.

It is important to appreciate the impact of demography on the emerging picture, which is illustrated in Table 4.2. This shows one possible scenario, based on a mainstream set of assumptions. It embodies demographic trends in United Nations forecasts and a plausible pattern of change in per capita energy consumption in different regions through to the year 2020. It assumes continued improvement in energy efficiency in West Europe and Japan, a more rapid improvement in energy-rich North America and former Eastern bloc countries, and improved efficiency in the rest of the world including the South and the oil-rich Middle East. In Chapter 1 we called such improvements – induced partly by rising prices and partly by a greater public awareness engendered by improved availability of information – 'economising behaviour'.

Demographic trends, short of plagues, pestilence and wars, are long-term phenomena which must become subject to global policy no less than pollution of the atmosphere if, eventually, the burden of human activity on the global environment is not to overwhelm nature's capacity to absorb. The most critical region globally, in relation to this problem, is no longer South America but the Islamic belt running from West Africa to Pakistan. The timescale for demographic change is very long term compared with most policy questions – comparable with the timescale for climate change and for change in the oceanic environment, and raising similar problems when it comes to applying consistent policy for sufficiently long to have any impact. Beyond noting that female literacy, along with economic advancement, and the institution of social security for old age to replace traditional dependence on family, appear to provide the most potent mechanisms for dealing with population growth,[6] we must in the present context take demographic trends as given.

Figure 4.2 shows that, even with the quite substantial economising behaviour assumed for the more developed nations, growth in the South should be expected to result in a near doubling of energy demands over the next three decades. So, if the North accepts the advancement of economic well-being in the South as being the *quid pro quo* for the latter's collaboration, then the prospective growth of living standards and of population globally provides the starting point from which planning for a sustainable energy future must proceed.

Although it may not be the easiest place to start from we must start from where we are, a starting place from which, clearly, control of carbon dioxide emissions is going to require the combination of both sustainable energy technology and the intensive economising behaviour mentioned in Chapter 1. In part, that energy technology transition will take the form

---

Figure 4.2　Scenario of Growing Global Demand for Energy Raw Materials

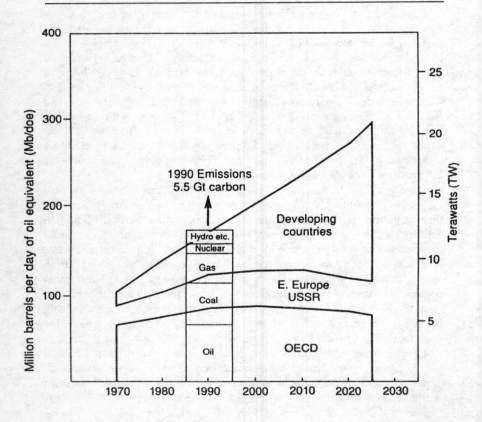

of increased use of ambient energy technologies, that is to say technologies like wind and wave power, and passive solar collection systems, which can make important local contributions where the ambient conditions are appropriate.

But to close the gap between what the climatologists may say needs to be done and what can practicably be done by a combination of economising behaviour and ambient energy systems there is a need for a sustainable fuel system. That is to say a combustible raw material, or crude fuel, derived on a sustainable basis, together with a set of applications technologies for transforming the crude fuel into the various forms required in the market.

By a sustainable fuel system is meant, of course, one that is not only free of the exhaustibility aspect of fossil fuels but also of the intensifying pollution problem presented by the accumulation in the atmosphere of the carbon dioxide waste product of fossil fuels. Clearly the likelihood of such a sustainable fuel system being able to meet demand growth is much greater, and its cost much lower, if economising behaviour and ambient energy play a substantial part. Thus the economising programme and the technological transition are both mutually reinforcing as regards outcome and interdependent as regards their potential cost effectiveness.

In relation to the pattern of demand, economising behaviour is clearly apparent in terms of the downward trend path of per capita consumption, for all countries except Rest of the World, shown in Table 4.2, and their more or less level path of total consumption shown in Figure 4.2. With developed world economic growth assumed to continue at only moderately slowing rates, this represents sharply improved economising performance compared with the last two decades.

That we do not focus on economising behaviour or on ambient energy technologies in a book which is mainly devoted to showing how the needed technological transformation of fuel supply can be brought about, is not intended to detract from the importance of these aspects for the joint endeavour. But, as is evident from the Shell scenario, vigorous economising behaviour is already accepted as part of the necessary response to global warming: what is added by the present discussion is the proposal that, on a global scale, the gap which remains can be filled by a sustainable fuel supply system.

Demand for different types of energy

Apart from addressing the rather forbidding problem presented by the growth overall of global energy demand, a programme of alternative energy technology must have regard to the different types of energy demand. Demand for bulk energy and for convenience supplies through pipes and wires can largely be considered together since electricity is extremely versatile as regards the energy raw material going into the electricity factories that we call power stations, and gas only a little less so as regards the feedstock for synthetic gas factories (or gasworks).

Thus, aside from hydro-electricity which is site specific and already exploited in developed countries to near the physical limit of supply, greenfield thermal power stations can be designed to run on coal, oil, gas or biomass with minimal difference in operations costs (excluding the cost of the fuel itself) and only modest differences in capital cost (although eliminating sulphur from flue gases can add considerably to the cost of any power station that does not use a low sulphur fuel such as biomass).

As a brief digression on a point that often confuses non-engineers, it may be noted that there is a basic difference between heat energy and the mechanical energy that can be used directly for turning machinery, and that the latter is more valuable than the former. Thus, all production of electricity (which is a form of mechanical energy since it can be used to turn an electric motor and hence drive machinery – of course it is even more valuable because of its electronic uses) from traditional thermal power stations involves the loss of from 60 to 80 per cent of the heat energy content of the fuel used to fire the boiler, how much depending on how modern and well designed the power-station is. Modern combined cycle gas turbine plant does better (45 to 50 per cent lost).

If any fuel other than electricity is used for driving machinery rather than heating purposes, precisely the same kind of energy loss occurs as at a thermal-power station (for instance, motor vehicles typically lose about 80 per cent of the energy in the fuel either through the radiator or down the exhaust pipe). Thus electrical energy is sometimes quoted in terms of its 'heat value', i.e. the heat energy required at the power station in order to generate the electricity, as well as the directly available electrical energy, the first being about three times the second (2.8 on average, globally, from Table 4.1).

Gas production from anything other than natural gas is more or less equally costly, except for feedstock costs, and involves technical inefficiency (i.e. the energy content of the produced gas is less than the energy content of the feedstock). Natural gas is the convenience fuel from amongst the fossil fuels and also, from the point of view of carbon dioxide emissions, is preferred since its carbon content per unit of heat produced is less than for coal and oil (Table 4.3 below). Indeed, one of the major ways that has been proposed for reducing carbon dioxide emissions in the short term is to use natural gas to fuel thermal power stations in place of coal (even though, to a traditional energy technologist, that seems a terrible misuse of a high-quality 'premium' fuel).[7]

Transportation fuels

Transportation fuel represents a different and less tractable problem. Vehicle engines are designed to run on highly specific types of fuels, be it gasoline, diesel engine fuel, avtur for jet planes or whatever. Most transportation is a risky business and risks of engine failure and consequential accident are minimised by strict specification of fuel quality and requirements on vehicle manufacturers to produce engines that run reliably. Substitution of alternative fuels is fraught with difficulties of a regulatory nature, with the need to set up an infrastructure of supply points, and with the start-up problem of establishing a sufficiently large vehicle fleet using the alternative fuel sufficiently quickly for the economic viability of the operation.

Nevertheless, alternative transport fuels have been introduced – for instance gas-driven cars with tanks of compressed natural gas (CNG) or liquid petroleum gas (LPG – mainly propane and butane) and alcohol fuels such as Brazil's 'gasohol' scheme. However, the specificity of vehicle engine requirements means that considerable trouble is involved, and sometimes considerable energy losses, in deriving a satisfactory fuel from non-petroleum raw materials. The consequence is that it is very much easier, in a programme to replace fossil fuels, to work initially on the 75 per cent which is used in furnaces for heating homes and commercial premises, and for industrial process heat, rather than on the 25 per cent which is used for transportation.

Pollution Due to Different Fuels

Different fuels are more or less serious offenders in terms of the carbon dioxide greenhouse gas emitted in relation to their energy content, as set out in Table 4.3 below.[8] Clearly a considerable reduction in emissions

Table 4.3 Carbon Dioxide Emissions and Energy Content of Fuels

Fuel	Energy Content Gigajoules per ton(GJ/t)	Carbon content Tons carbon per ton fuel	Carbon/energy ratio Tons carbon per Gigajoule
Coal	30	0.75	0.025
Oil	43	0.85	0.020
Gas	54	0.75	0.014
Wood	20	0.52	0.026

These are typical values for hard (bituminous) coal, crude oil, natural gas and oven-dried wood. All of these fuels, particularly coal, show a great deal of variability in their natural state. It is, of course, not customary to measure natural gas by weight and it is done here for purposes of comparison. One cubic metre of natural gas at standard temperature and pressure weighs 0.7Kg and has an energy content of 0.038GJ.

can be achieved simply by using natural gas in preference to coal and oil, as mentioned above in relation to the fuel used in power stations.

The table makes clear that it is no better to burn biomass fuels than it is to burn fossil fuels if burning the fuel is the end of the story. Indeed, it is slightly worse. The point about renewable biomass fuels is that it is not the end of the story. As part of a process that recycles carbon to and from the atmosphere, biomass fuel is a story that has no end or beginning. Which is why biomass, along with wind-power, wave-power and solar energy, are loosely referred to as renewable sources of energy, though we have distinguished the first as a sustainable fuel and the others as ambient energy technologies.

Apart from carbon dioxide emissions, it is worth drawing attention to other aspects of pollution due to fossil fuels. Natural gas is by far the least offensive, as the harm done when there is a leakage (providing, that is, that nobody lights a match) is no more than a minor addition to greenhouse gases. However, both coal and oil cause environmental problems, apart from either greenhouse effects or accident risks.

Coal got from underground has scarred the landscape with its spoil tips and polluting run-off since the dawn of the industrial revolution. Land subsidence occurs as a result of underground coal mining, while death and injury in minor and largely unpublicised accidents are common, in addition to which there is the occasional newsworthy disaster. Opencast mining leaves the landscape scarred and, even with restoration work in more environmentally sensitive parts of the world, lost for a generation, if not for longer.

Along with carbon dioxide emissions, the burning of coal releases other pollutants into the atmosphere, most obviously sulphur which gives rise to acid rain. This has damaged Central and North European forests and forests in parts of North America and is also responsible for the loss of river fish and recreational fishing in some areas. Some coal is low-sulphur, but no coal is no-sulphur.

Although biodegradable in the long run, crude oil is also very messy and the quality that has given it its technological dominance, its easy transportability, leads to the most pervasive pollution, that is to say the quantity of the stuff that is floating around the oceans due to casual leaks and to escapes from shipping and tankers that fail to follow good practices in cleaning down fuel tanks. Nowadays oil tankers use 'load on top' procedures and are required to clean tanks in harbour in many countries, disposing of the filth in proper shore facilities, but that still leaves the more spectacular kind of pollution, resulting from shipping accidents. In the 1970s the Amoco Cadiz fouled up the Brittany coast for a decade, and more recently the Exxon Valdez has more notoriously, if less heavily, done the same for Prince William Sound.

Apart from the oceanic pollution attributable to the bulk transport of crude oil, there is the localised pollution attributable to the operation of refineries and the more dispersed acid rain pollution due to the burning of sulphur-rich heavy fuel oils in power stations and other large industrial installations. And the practice of adding 'lead' to petrol (gasoline) to improve its octane rating, plus the emission of nitrous oxides from road vehicles, creates a health hazard for anyone within range of heavy traffic.

Although by no means free of environmental hazards, biomass fuel is virtually sulphur free and, in its road vehicle fuel products, is characteristically cleaner-burning than petroleum-derived fuels. The chemically unmixed nature of alcohols derived from biomass (compared with the mixtures that go to make up petroleum-derived transport fuels) makes them more suitable for use in clean technologies, such as fuel cell technology, which are now on the horizon. It is certainly true that inefficient burning of biomass at low temperature, yielding the copious smoke of garden bonfires and old-fashioned domestic open fires, is also highly polluting, with the smoke containing dangerous carcinogens as well as forming corrosive and unsightly deposits. However, such inefficient and old-fashioned burning takes no place in the scenario which we envisage in this book for industrialised reliance on biomass fuel as the basis for controlling carbon dioxide levels in the atmosphere.

Biomass Production and Disposal

It is obvious from the central role played by energy in the conduct of economic activity that effective control of the atmospheric carbon dioxide concentration is not to be achieved simply by cutting back on emissions. Even if the South were to stay less developed and if the former East bloc and North America were to achieve the energy efficiency foreseen in Figure 4.2 for Japan and West Europe, emissions would remain at around 70 per cent of current rates and the level of carbon dioxide would continue to rise. Even to stabilise the carbon dioxide level, still the more if we are to try to control the level downwards, the impact on material living standards of doing so by cutting emissions even further would be unacceptable.

Thus we need to think about how to get carbon dioxide out of the atmosphere and address global warming concerns in terms of net emissions rather than gross emissions. Given what we learned about the natural carbon cycle in Chapter 2, the obvious thing to do is grow a lot of biomass. And not just grow it as an emissions 'offset', but find some way of disposing of it in order to make room on the ground for growing more and thus set up a sustainable process rather than just a 'once off' respite from the rising level of carbon dioxide in the atmosphere.

Making coal?

One possibility, and we shall see that it is not so absurd as it sounds, is to set about making coal. Since the greenhouse gas problem arises from our burning of fossil fuels got from underground, a logical response would seem to be to imitate the process by which nature put it there in the first place, some several hundred million years ago in the case of hard coal and more recently for lignite. Coal-making is a slow business and we shan't be around to see the product. But, to get the amount of carbon dioxide in the atmosphere back towards the level we want, all that is needed is to start the process off, through burying biomass or 'pickling trees'. So long as the required fraction of the global carbon inventory that is underground is trending back to where it was a century ago it is immaterial whether it has completed the process of becoming coal, or only just begun it.

The advantage of using this approach is that it doesn't require much transportation: the biomass – trees most probably – can simply be buried at or near where it is grown. Furthermore it enables existing energy technology infrastructure to continue to be used, save for the extent that paying for the biomass to be grown and buried raises prices, reduces demand, and perhaps gives rise to redundancy (despite continued underlying growth, especially in the South). However, the price increase required to achieve a given reduction in carbon dioxide emissions this way is far less than is required to get the same result wholly by inducing economising behaviour.[9]

The disadvantages are two-fold. Firstly it seems wasteful to grow biomass simply to bury it. But that may not necessarily be true since the activity is essentially a pollution clean-up service. The buried biomass is embodied rubbish. It is no more wasteful to bury unwanted carbon dioxide in this way than it is to bury any other rubbish at the municipal tip. However, that may not be a wholly satisfactory rationalisation given the extent to which the concomitant programme of economising behaviour depends upon public consciousness-raising. If the object is to make unambiguous signals about the importance of a conservative and sustainable approach to nature, it may be counter-productive to engage in seemingly wasteful coal-making, however rationally.

The second reason is less presentational. To simply bury biomass under a handy shovelful of dirt may result in a perverse outcome, as it does at the municipal tip. (Methane emission from garbage disposed of as land-fill is a significant component of anthropogenic greenhouse gas emissions).[10] This is because buried biomass is liable to rot down to compost plus methane, and the methane (natural gas) may escape upwards into the atmosphere where it is a far more powerful, if shorter lived, greenhouse gas than the carbon dioxide which has been sequestered by burying biomass.[11] Thus it would be necessary, in making coal, to do it quite carefully. Maybe to bury the biomass under a layer of tough plastic to trap the methane and maybe to pipe it off to displace fossil fuel that would otherwise be used.

That however is all trouble and trouble means expense. It seems to make more sense to collect the biomass and use it – all of it, or what is left over after some fraction has been used in traditional ways, say as pulp for paper making – as replacement for fossil fuels. Apart from the presentational aspect, however, it is simply a matter of costs whether it is better to set about making coal, and to continue to raise fossil fuels, or to set about substituting biomass for fossil fuel with a view to slowing – and maybe eventually completely ending – the use of fossil fuel.

Given the advantage of oil products as a portable fuel for transportation purposes, there could well be a long period, while reserves of cheap oil last, in which we may see coal-making carried out in some parts of the world to compensate for the continued use of oil in other places where biomass production is difficult. That could especially be the case if hoped for economic growth in the South failed to materialise so that there was little energy demand to provide a local market for the newly available sustainable fuel supply that may arise there.

Biomass as a fuel raw material

As replacement for fossil fuels, biomass requires no new technology when we are thinking of the 75 per cent of global fossil fuel supply that goes into furnaces to fire boilers and/or provide process heat. Focusing our attention on woody biomass, we may note that wood firing preceded fossil fuel firing in every technology that is more than 200 years old: ceramics, pottery, metal smelting, etc. were all conducted with wood, and its derivative charcoal, at that time. This does not imply that wood can only be used in technologically out-dated equipment.

On the contrary, wood is a satisfactory fuel for modern technology boilers and can be used in substitution for fossil fuels anywhere where fuel is needed for burning as a source of heat energy. Indeed, being sulphur free, it can compete with somewhat cheaper fossil fuel when flue gases need to be de-sulphurised to meet local environmental requirements. The problem with tars emitted in low temperature combustion with excess air supply, and an environmental hazard with garden bonfires, etc. is resolved with proper furnace design.

To the question 'why, if our ancestors abandoned wood-burning two centuries ago, can it be economic to revert to it now?' one answer is that there is nothing inherently regressive in moving from one fuel to another, as the business-as-usual prospect of renewed reliance on coal when oil gets more expensive demonstrates. Progress – or, less emotively, technical change – consists of choosing the best technology in the light of changing circumstances. With the advent of the factory system, and demands for large quantities of fuel in one place, our ancestors abandoned wood because transport was very costly – to shift a ton 20 miles was a day's work for horse, cart, and driver – so that it was 'progressive' to concentrate industry and industrial habitations in cities located on coalfields. Nowadays a truck and driver can shift 50 tons 400 miles in a day, a thousand-fold productivity increase. Transport costs are still important with biomass, leading to the eventual prospect of a less concentrated pattern of habitation, but no longer a dominant factor in relation to fuel requirements for industrial-scale furnaces. When the new consideration is greenhouse gas emissions, a reversion to a previously used raw material, but different from coal, is the best choice because coal, like oil, in non-renewable. The net cost of reducing greenhouse gas emissions is then quite small since the saved costs of fossil fuels can be deducted from the costs of biomass fuels.

Any furnace has, as one of its fundamental components, equipment for handling whatever kind of fuel is being used. In large boilers this can be very elaborate, especially with coal which is hard to handle. Machinery for passing the coal steadily through the furnace on a moving chain has given way to equipment which pulverises the coal to dust and blows it into the furnace in much the same way as oil is squirted in through nozzles into oil-fired boilers. More recently the idea is a 'fluidised bed' in which finely divided solid fuel together with inert material to dilute the intensity of heat release (and possibly to absorb pollutants such as sulphur) is supported in a rising stream of combustion air, with the hot products of combustion passing over the boiler tubes or other surfaces for receiving the heat.

Handling fluid fuels like oil and gas is obviously much easier. That is but one of the many reasons why the use of coal in advanced economies has become increasingly restricted to large-scale installations where its relative cheapness in bulk supply makes it worthwhile installing the elaborate fuel-handling and pollution-control equipment that is needed.

In a greenfield site, or other new installation, equipment that can handle coal can be replaced by equipment to handle fuel-wood, with savings due to its minimal pollution impact. Where a compact fire chamber is required the wood can, at some cost, be gasified outside the boiler and be as easy to handle as natural gas, an option which may also be attractive where it is desired to 'retrofit' wood-burning to an existing installation. That is not to imply gasification to a gas that provides a technical substitute for natural gas in reticulated supply to domestic, commercial and industrial consumers in cities and towns. But it is cheap to gasify wood to a low-grade producer gas, which is perfectly satisfactory for burning in boilers and other furnaces. This immediate availability of wood-fired boiler technology is emphasised because, as argued in the previous chapter, the 'stitch in time' nature of the global warming problem means that reliance on technologies that are coming off the drawing board, or which are expected to become economic at oil prices forecast for two decades hence, may not provide an adequately timely response. If a 'horrid' state of nature becomes apparent, in which it is urgent to achieve a rapid stabilisation or even reduction of the carbon dioxide in the atmosphere, resulting in a huge quantity of biomass being produced, then its disposal, other than by burying it and 'making coal', can be achieved quite simply, if somewhat expensively.

What would be needed is a large-scale programme of converting existing furnaces to wood-burning. However, a much lower cost option is to concentrate on new plant, and on replacement old plant as it comes to the end of its useful life, equipping new furnaces with fuel-handling equipment designed to burn fuel-wood. Here the hopes for economic growth, and the prospect of rapidly increasing energy demands in South countries, fits in nicely with political pressures for the response to global warming to assist rather than hinder their development process.

And, it may be noted, a programme of fossil fuel displacement in furnaces may be all that is needed. This is because it is only necessary to sequester 75 per cent of emissions in order to stabilise carbon dioxide levels (bearing in mind that we are assuming, from Chapter 2, that the proportion of current emissions dealt with by natural absorption is 25 per cent). Unless, that is, the objective eventually turns out to be a return to some carbon dioxide level lower than the 380 to 400ppm that is inevitable by 2010.[12]

Indeed, as there is the very wide margin of error in the estimates of natural absorption discussed in Chapter 2, it may well be that stabilisation of carbon dioxide levels can be achieved with a lower percentage of sequestration. On the other hand, a need to compensate for rising levels of other greenhouse gases, which cannot so easily be absorbed as carbon dioxide, may work the other way. Whatever the percentage may be, the main point is that it can be achieved in a programme starting this decade, without the need to await the results of any further research on new energy technologies.

Of course, to start now is not the same thing as to reach the target, say 75 per cent, level of sequestration this decade. A long, drawn out industrial dynamic is involved, with lead times in the production of seedlings, in their growing to the stage of fuel-wood cropping, in the reallocation of land from existing use or disuse, in the progressive conversion of the existing stock of furnaces and its replacement by more modern equipment – biomass-fired of course – as it becomes worn out or obsolete. The New Zealand example described in the Appendix involves a 20-year transition.

The process would involve the build-up of an infrastructure – of specialist equipment manufacture, new fuel transport systems, mass production consumer equipment manufacture, etc. – for all the multitudinous changes that would be entailed in a two to three decade energy technology revolution. Given that the new technology is cost-effective in its intended purpose (i.e. supplying a renewable fuel that resolves the greenhouse gas problem at a cost not too far out of line with conventional supplies) such a long, drawn out dynamic would impose no unacceptable cost burden. Such would not be the case for a crash programme, begun late, even if it employed such tried and tested technology as the wood-firing of furnaces.

Intensive tree growing

If the burning of wood in furnaces is such a simple and well-understood technology, why, it may be asked, has it not been recognised earlier that the answer to global warming is simply to grow more trees and burn them in lieu of fossil fuels? For to do so, and then to use the land that was cleared when the trees were felled to grow more trees, would seem to provide the basis of a sustainable energy technology.

The answer to that question is that tree-growing is a slow business and takes up a great deal of space, leading to the apprehension that there is not enough land in the world to do the trick. However, that is probably an incorrect answer as has been shown by research in the last decade in New Zealand, the USA, Scandinavia and elsewhere.[13] This research has investigated quantitatively what is, in fact, a very ancient silvicultural technology called coppicing.

A coppice is an area of trees that are cropped for small stems on a regular cycle. Traditionally only a few stems are taken each year from each rootstock located in small coppice plots, or coppices, using hand tool technique, in order to get long, thin and supple young growth for the fencing and hurdles (mobile fencing) needed for traditional shepherding methods. The technique was not used traditionally for firewood production since the latter was obtained by gathering fallen wood and 'by hook or by crook' – i.e. by pulling deadwood down from large trees – in established forests that were often otherwise reserved for hunting by the nobility.

The coppicing process, like the allied pollarding technique where branches are cropped off tree stumps at head height (resulting in the knobbly winter treescapes of the early Van Gogh), results in very rapid growth as new shoots are forced by the large rootstock in the ground. It was this feature that led to parallel research in several places (co-ordinated for New Zealand by Massey University's Agronomy Department) begun in the early 1980s as a response to rising oil prices and as part of the search for cheaper sources of energy.

In mild temperate regions like New Zealand and the south-central states of the USA, growth rates of 20 dry tons per hectare per year are regularly obtainable using selected cultivars of eucalypt and poplar species, *inter alia*. This may be compared with the range of 4 to 10 tons for conventional forestry, and reduces the land requirement for meeting a given demand for energy by fuel-wood by a factor of around three.

Much higher growth rates may be possible,[14*] subject to questions of soil quality sustainability discussed in Chapter 9, by using genetic engineering and/or traditional selective breeding to develop ultra-rapid growth rate cultivars. Most such research in relation to agriculture has, in the past, focused on maximising the output of starchy food biomass and the potential for maximising the output of cellulosic and woody biomass for fuel purposes is relatively unexplored. Given the rapid rotation time with coppicing, shorter periods for cultivar development are practicable than with other silviculture.

Clearly, the greater the growth rate per hectare, the less are the land requirements for a given achievement in reducing net carbon dioxide emissions. And, to the extent that some part of the trees grown for fuel-wood cropping may have a conventional commercial outlet, the rapid rotation reduces the risks inherent in the very long lead times of conventional forestry. However, greater economy in the use of land does not necessarily mean market viability and an ambitious policy aimed at controlling atmospheric carbon dioxide levels would require economic incentives, as discussed in Chapter 7.[15*]

In the event, with the fall in oil and other energy prices brought about by a loss of discipline amongst OPEC members, intensive fuel-wood cropping has not proved viable as a low-cost fuel in the market. But it is not far off being competitive in areas where cheap coal is not available and the penalty from using it when the objective is to reduce net carbon dioxide emissions is correspondingly small. Coal in the USA typically costs less than 1.5$ per GJ (projected rise to around $1.8): in Europe rather higher figures obtain – $2.5 to $3.[16] The figures are for middling to large industrial users – penny packets of specially prepared coal for domestic use cost far more.

The cost of collectable and producible biomass in the US ranges between $1 and $4 per GJ, with produced fuel-wood costing up to $3 per GJ delivered, dried and chipped.[17] These relate to production in the Northern Plains for which data is available and lower costs are likely in the warmer South and East where most of the available land has been identified.[18] Also, for the bio-technological conversion technologies mentioned later in this chapter, the wood does not need to be oven dried whilst the "BIGSTIG" electricity generation technology can make positive use of moisture in the wood. Moreover, land rents are an important component of these costs, and such rents are boosted by agricultural support policies, so that the true economic cost should be put somewhat lower. In New Zealand timber wastes are a costly nuisance and a figure of US$2.2 per GJ seems attainable with large-scale fuel-wood production.[19] Lower figures can be attained in tropical and sub-tropical climates.

Such figures provide the basis for the claim of this book that the cost of reducing carbon dioxide emissions (on a net emissions basis) is very much lower than the economic estimates based on the assumption that emissions need to be reduced on a gross basis, which can only be done by reducing energy use drastically, with consequent need for severe economic adjustment. Depending on the location and the application – we will come to application technologies later – biomass is only a little more costly than coal, sometimes a little less. Providing it is introduced gradually, either in replacement plant, as older fossil fuel plant becomes due for retirement, or in plant installed to meet demand growth (mainly in South countries) the transformation to a sustainable fuel system can be quite cheap.

Biomass and Land

Some very simple arithmetic is all that is required to demonstrate the prima facie plausibility of the fuel-wood scenario. Table 4.3 shows that, allowing for natural absorption of 25 per cent of carbon dioxide emissions, it requires the growing of about 1.5 tons of wood, containing 0.75 tons of carbon, to offset the remaining 75 per cent of the carbon dioxide emitted by burning a ton of carbon in any fuel. Thus the use of one hectare for the intensive coppicing of trees sequesters enough carbon from the atmosphere to stabilise the carbon dioxide level from the impact of burning 13.3 tons of carbon every year. The 20 tons of trees yielded each year contains 10 tons of carbon which is 75 per cent of 13.3 tons of carbon, such as would be contained in about 17.5 tons of coal, 15.5 tons of oil or 17.5 'tons' of gas.

In fact 3.1 billion tons of oil, 2.2 of coal and 1.7 of gas, containing 5.6 billion tons of carbon, were burned in 1989,[20] giving a need for 430 million hectares of coppice. This yields sufficient fuel-wood to offset all fossil fuel-related carbon dioxide emissions, net of 25 per cent natural absorption, if energy demand were held constant at the 1989 level, and if it were as easy to substitute for the transportation uses of fossil fuels as it is for their use in furnaces. However, it is not, and allowing for the inefficiencies of producing vehicle fuel from biomass could raise the land requirement to around 580 million hectares were it not for the availability of substantial amounts of currently dumped industrial biomass process residues. These are equivalent to 2.8 billion tons of wood annually, that would otherwise need 140 million hectares.

Allowing for some continued waste of residues, we will use a ballpark figure of 500 million hectares, or, more convenient to think of, five million square kilometres i.e. an area roughly 1000 miles by 2000. This is just under 55 per cent of the area of the USA or perhaps rather more than the area lost from tropical forest since World War Two (the rate of loss averaged 9 million hectares a year over the 15 year period 1972 to 1987, on a rising trend).

This sounds like a lot of land but it is most probably available. To be certain, however, would require detailed research into land capability and availability on a global scale. Satellite survey is inadequate for this purpose and a laborious process of 'ground truthing' such surveys is needed.

In reality the data base, even as regards changes in the actual use of land, is not very consistent.[21] For instance, in South America, land lost from tropical forest is categorised as various kinds of farmland, albeit largely degraded through inappropriate ranching, whereas in other parts of the world it is called 'other' land, i.e. unproductive. Of course, such an area could not be given over to intensive coppicing overnight but a staged programme seems, *prima facie*, to be practicable. The programme outlined in Chapter 7 envisages a build up towards 75 per cent absorption over a period of two to three decades, with surplus temperate land being used to start with. As mentioned in Chapter 1, the reasons for starting in temperate areas are because these are where the more developed countries are located, and where furnace fuel applications of fuel-wood raw materials can most easily be found, and because a considerably longer lead time is involved in starting up an intensive fuel-wood programme in less developed regions than is needed in developed countries.

During those two to three decades demand will of course have increased, more or less in line with Table 4.2, and other technologies, apart from the ambient energy technologies and economising behaviour that have already been mentioned, will be needed to supplement biomass unless the uncertainties about land capability and availability turn out more favourably than is assumed below. However, there is good reason to suppose that other technologies, for instance direct photovoltaic conversion of sunlight, will in fact begin to be preferred for electricity generation by about 2010.

The second decade of the next millennium could see a shift in the use of biomass, away from furnace fuel and towards transportation uses, and/or for 'making coal' to compensate for continued oil production. Ultimately biomass production could find its place as the source of carbon with which hydrogen (obtained by the hydrolysis of water using photovoltaic power) would be combined in the synthesis of future transportation fuels.

And if the greenhouse gas fear has by then gone away, the coppices can simply be allowed to grow to natural maturity or, with a certain amount of thinning out, to commercial timber. However, before going on to those aspects, let us take a look at present land use. What grounds are there for thinking it likely that such a huge area of land might be available for fuel-wood cropping?

Temperate regions

The US pays farmers not to grow crops (as does the EEC) and fuel-wood production on such land, together with the use of municipal wastes (not included in the industrial process wastes mentioned above) could displace a quarter of US energy raw material needs.[22] Bearing in mind the contribution from US industrial wastes, and that only 75 per cent of emissions need to be absorbed to achieve the carbon dioxide stabilisation under consideration, the USA could deal with most of its emissions by using biomass originating within its borders. Some of the biomass is reckoned to be a bit more expensive than existing coal, gas and oil supplies, and some less, but the costs are not dramatically out of line.[23]

In West Europe it is not so easy although 15 million hectares of agricultural land will become surplus if subsidies under the Common Agricultural Policy are brought under control. Even in crowded England it is claimed that six million hectares could become available for coppicing by 2010,[24] enough to supply over half the UK's electricity needs. In addition, a substantial proportion of Europe's 120 million hectares of forest are severely affected by acid rain and could be reclaimed for intensive fuel-wood production of suitably resistant species. It is the evergreen species that appear most affected, while coppicing in Europe has traditionally been done with deciduous species.

But in less densely populated and more severely polluted East Europe and Russia, with new-found market incentives to raise agricultural productivity and release land, and/or the clearing of a proportion of the 900 million hectares of boreal forest for fuel-wood production, much greater possibilities exist. The idea of clearing existing forest for fuel-wood production is a bit antipathetic. But we are considering a gradual rather than a sudden process, with some forest cleared on a regular basis for commercial purposes that can be replanted in suitable species for fuel-wood production rather than being left to slowly regenerate its present flora.

In the Southern hemisphere vast areas in western New South Wales need to be restored to tree cover to reverse the process of rising salination that has followed the nineteenth century clearances. The natural process of transpiration and evaporation from the original tree cover meant that much rainfall that now goes into the ground was formerly returned to the atmosphere in short time. Now it causes a rising water table and, having mixed with underground salt, leads to the salination problem.[25] In Australia, as in New Zealand and temperate South America, agricultural production is frustrated by trade barriers in former traditional markets. As described in the Appendix, New Zealand can satisfy its domestic demands for energy by using only a few per cent of its pastoral land for fuel-wood production.

Of course, a successful conclusion of the GATT Uruguay round would see a shift of agricultural production to currently excluded Southern producers and the release of more Northern land for fuel-wood cropping, nearer the main centres of energy demand. If such a desirable rationalisation comes about, more of the fuel-wood would actually get into furnaces; if it doesn't, a larger proportion would go to transportation fuel at an earlier stage, or simply to 'making coal'.

Tropical regions

As mentioned, the FAO data suggest that tropical forest has been lost at a rate of about nine million hectares a year for the last two decades, with considerable media apprehension of speed-up in recent years. Casting back to the 1950s, when the post-war phase of environmentally aggressive growth took off, suggests that total lost tropical forest since World War Two is of the order of 300 to 400 million hectares.

It would obviously be facile to assume that all such land is available for reafforestation. Some has become urbanised, some is in active use, and some may have become so derelict as to be incapable of sustaining regrowth, leave alone intensive fuel-wood cropping. (Of course the same may apply to acid rain-affected land in temperate regions, mentioned above.) And it would be a mistake to attribute the loss of tropical forest to the notorious fuel-wood shortage in some South countries. Studies show that the principal reason for tropical forest loss is the land hunger of an expanding peasant population, engaged on subsistence agriculture that moves on when the initial fertility of the newly cleared forest soil begins to decline. So most of this land is now used for low productivity subsistence farming, inefficient tropical cattle ranching or has simply become wasteland.[26*]

Apart from the contribution to anthropogenic carbon dioxide emissions, the loss of tropical forest has other environmental impacts. The loss of forest cover in upland watersheds causes enhanced run-off, flood damage downstream and loss of soil out to sea. It has been estimated that 160 million hectares come into this category so that its reversion to tree cover, albeit fuel-wood cropping rather than original native forest, provides benefits beyond the energy market.[27] However, much of this upland would be too steep for regular cropping and more suited to long-term reafforestation with sustainably managed conventional forestry.

Additionally, 100 million hectares of grassland pasture in Africa, Latin America and South East Asia are said to be degraded to the point of worthlessness by over-grazing.[28] The interaction between fuel-wood cash cropping and the development of sustainable agricultural systems for such lands, and the preservation of a diversity of ecological niches for wildlife species, is discussed briefly in Chapter 9, but deserves another book.

In the present context we merely raise the question whether such land could, in part, be made available for an energy biomass programme and note that African, South American and South Asian grasslands and savannas total around 1500 million hectares.[29] A system designed to rescue the most degraded grasslands could presumably be extended to cover a proportion of these lands with a more diverse pattern of land use than currently obtains. Sometimes it requires only the erection and maintenance of effective fencing for diversification to become possible. On the other hand it may be more effective to simply crop grass or other non-tree crops as a biomass fuel source.

As this question is central as regards the practicability of GREENS it seems worthwhile to refer to a study done for the US Department of Energy that relates specifically to it.[30] This concludes that 'it is physically possible to remove 5 billion tons of carbon per year from the atmosphere either in new forests, in intensively managed forests on existing forest land, or in some combination'. Citing earlier work[31] Marland comments that a perceived incompatibility between reforestation to limit atmospheric CO_2 and increases in wood production is true enough 'unless we are prepared to either use or store wood in such a way that the carbon is not oxidised' (i.e. this book's 'making coal') 'or unless we can replace fossil fuel consumption with wood consumption' (the core proposal in the GREENS concept).

Summing up on land availability, the claim that, *prima facie*, sufficient is likely to be available to grow the biomass needed to meet current rates of carbon dioxide emissions seems plausible. Or at least sufficiently plausible to warrant a serious effort to improve the information base on the lines suggested above and discussed in Chapter 9, and to warrant setting out on this sustainable energy technology path, even if experience over the decades ahead points some new directions along the way.

Applications Technology

In order to establish a credible scenario for a biomass energy future it is necessary to go beyond simply demonstrating that it is practicable to provide a sustainable fuel supply at reasonably competitive cost. The bulk of energy is delivered to final consumers in refined or convenience form, as was shown in Table 4.1. In meeting the demands currently met by oil refinery outputs biomass is at a technical disadvantage as is also the case, to a lesser degree, in meeting demands for reticulated gas supplies – which is a relatively low priority given the smaller environmental impact of natural gas compared with other fossil fuels (Table 4.3 above). With electricity, however, biomass is at an advantage in relation to greenfield sites for meeting expanding demands.

But even for supplying bulk heat energy to industrial furnaces, the cheapness of biomass will not necessarily result in the 'backing out' of fuel oil (by which is meant substitution of biomass for oil fuel in that market). This is because to do so implies the need also to supply transportation fuel from biomass. This is on account of refinery balance considerations. To see this we need to take a brief look at the way the oil industry works.[32]

Oil refineries are essentially 'unmixing factories' in which the mixed bag of crude oil constituents that comes out of the ground – and of course crude oil from different places can contain very different mixtures – is separated out. Simple refineries do this just by 'fractional distillation', but more modern plants use so-called 'hydro-crackers' and other sophisticated equipment to break up the heavier and less valuable constituents and reform them into more desirable products. By using different combinations of crudes, and by varying the working conditions (temperatures and pressures) at various points in the processing, the product mix can to some extent be adjusted to suit demand. And blending with the products of other refineries provides further flexibility in meeting market demand for such products as heavy, medium and light fuel oils, diesel oil and gasoline, kerosene, the liquid petroleum gases (butane and propane), etc.

Ingenuity, and investment in yet more sophisticated plant, has its limits which are reflected in the discounted price at which the less desirable products are sold. This is why the availability of cheap biomass does not necessarily mean that it will be used as fuel in lieu of fuel oil – although the same consideration does not of course apply when it comes to backing out coal. Unless the more valuable refinery products are also backed out, the oil companies will simply discount their heavy fuel oils further and load their costs onto the more desirable products, at least in the short term, until new investment enables the balance of refinery output to be structurally changed.

Indeed, that is essentially what brought about the rapid decline of the European coal industry in the 1950s and 1960s, when petrol (gasoline) demand expanded rapidly in the post-war automobile sales boom.[33] With the rather unsophisticated refineries of the day, a huge volume of fuel oil was co-produced with the gasoline. It was essentially a by-product which was sold on the bulk fuel market at prices that undercut coal sufficiently for the oil to find a sale. Of course, in those pre-OPEC days, crude oil was cheap (as it is again today) and the price of heavy fuel oil needed to be cheaper still in order to dissuade consumers from simply buying the more easily handled crude oil as a fuel oil substitute, leaving the heavy fractions unsold and piling up at the refineries.

Such an oil industry response, in the face of competition from biomass, would see more 'coal making' as the end use for the fuel-wood produced, which may be desirable or may not. Essentially the outcome depends upon the relative cost of biomass and of crude oil at the point of delivery and the balance of product mix from the biomass and fossil sources. Given the large stake in the biomass market that would be taken by the oil companies, facilitated by the TAO mechanism to be discussed in Chapter 7 and motivated to protect their long-term corporate interests, their choice, with biomass more suited to furnace applications and with oil still providing most of the transport fuel, would be between investing in still more sophisticated refineries or undergrounding carbon, either 'making coal' with their biomass, or reinjecting their heavy fuel oil into older wells (perhaps as part of a 'tertiary recovery' programme).

On the other hand, in many parts of the world, where imports of crude oil present an economic or strategic concern, diversification into biomass for meeting some or all of transportation demands could become a government-preferred option, as it was in Brazil in the 1980s, with potential for tension between commercial operators and political objectives.

Brazil's ethanol from biomass experience

Brazil has been using ethanol – a variety of alcohol – produced from biomass as a vehicle fuel, for a decade. Its sugar cane to ethanol programme saw 62 per cent of the country's vehicle fuel (i.e. 72 million barrels) produced from sugar cane in 1988.[34] This is basically the process for making rum, with the distillation of the fermented brew carried to a stage of near pure alcohol, instead of stopping at the palatable stage. Difficulties encountered – exaggerated by opponents of the scheme – include unforeseen environmental problems with disposing of the lees and a rising price of sugar which makes the process seem uneconomic.

This is because, at the margin, it would seem to be a better bet to process the cane for the sugar market. Maybe a small proportion of the sugar could profitably be diverted to the food market, but if all Brazil's production were to be unloaded in that way the oversupply would drive its price down to a level that would ruin other producers. So to value all Brazil's sugar cane at a price derived from the food market and then to say that the process is uneconomic is pretty silly.

This is not to deny that Brazil's ethanol programme is heavily subsidised – no doubt that makes a great deal of sense in a country that is notoriously burdened with foreign debt. Particularly since, with very little indigenous oil, and if it uses more gasoline for its vehicles, Brazil must either import the expensive refined product or import more crude for refining in Brazil, with the oil fuel by-product sold in competition with its locally based energy industries.

Recent advances with ethanol technology

A programme of research at the Solar Energy Research Institute (SERI) at Golden, just outside Denver Colorado,[35] has in the last decade been directed at evolving technology for converting cellulosic biomass to ethanol, aiming at a product competitive with gasoline from oil at $25 a barrel. This programme was undertaken in response to the US strategic exposure to rising oil prices and, remarkably, survived the cutbacks in expenditure on alternative energy resources under the Reagan presidency. Its present significance is in relation to the global warming problem, though it may well be that forecasts for an oil price of $25 a barrel by the year 2000 will bring a coincidence with its original purpose at about the time when it becomes important to the scenario being elaborated here.

Cellulosic biomass is of interest because the number of places where sugar can be produced is limited by the specific agronomic requirements of sugar cane and sugar beet. Furthermore sugar is only about 30 per cent by weight of such crops whereas cellulose is the main constituent of all plants. Woody feedstock is the focus of SERI's work because trees of one kind or another can be grown almost anywhere that anything will grow, so that prospective competition with food production is minimised.

Wood in fact contains three main constituents, lignin and hemi-cellulose in addition to cellulose. Work at SERI has developed micro-organisms that can convert both of the cellulosic components to sugar, with the lignin prospectively relegated to the role of boiler fuel for the energy requirements of the final process of distilling the ethanol from the watery medium in which the fermentation process is conducted. SERI has also developed pre-treatment processes for the cellulosic components that facilitate more complete conversion to ethanol.

At the current stage of research SERI has laboratory confirmation of their entire process yielding 'base case' design study estimates for a 58 million gallon a year plant selling ethanol at $1.27 per US gallon with wood chip feedstock charged in at $42 a ton and covering annual capital charges set at 20 per cent of the estimated investment of $150 million.[36] Their intention is to proceed with a pilot scale proving plant in the next few years. Their expectation is that further laboratory progress with their process, optimisation of the plant size to about 250 million gallons annually (requiring a radius of about 13 miles for woody feedstock production) and a reduction in feedstock costs to the $38 target of the Oak Ridge National Laboratory programme,[37] mentioned above, will see the selling price halved by the end of the century. This seems not unreasonable given that the price was estimated at $3.60 in 1980 and that work in New Zealand, *inter alia*, confirms an expectation of commercial scale fuel-wood production costs of about NZ$50 (equal to about US$32) per ton.

A production cost of around $65 a US gallon for ethanol makes it competitive with gasoline from oil at $25 a barrel, which is fine for SERI's objective and also fine for dealing with global warming. It will not entirely dispose of the current disadvantage of biomass for transportation since the whole problem of supply infrastructure and vehicle fleet conversion needs to be addressed. And to the engineer, rather than the accountant, biomass-to-ethanol carries a basic thermodynamic inefficiency. This partly takes the form of its poor carbon conservation (some of the carbon in the biomass is given off as carbon dioxide in the process of fermentation – which is why bread rises, champagne bubbles, etc.) and partly the large energy requirement of the final distillation stage. (This inefficiency is why the land requirement was increased, a few pages back, to allow for a proportion of ethanol production.)

Nevertheless, a combination of ethanol for transport and fuel-wood for burning in furnaces provides a pair of backstop technologies that enable biomass to be seen as an alternative to the currently dominant fossil fuel raw material, that is to say oil and gas. By a backstop technology is meant a technology that has a large enough supply capability to be relied on as a last resort if hopes for better renewable technologies are disappointed.

Other renewable fuel technologies

However, the basic advantage of oil in terms of flexibility in meeting a variety of user requirements by ringing the changes in refinery output, remains and presents second order cost penalties for reliance on biomass energy. For instance, in compression ignition (diesel) engines, so-called cetane improvers, possibly expensive, may be required to initiate combustion of biomass derived fuel.[38]

That having been said, it should be re-emphasised that the backstop technology concept does not represent the range of renewable energy technologies available. This concept represents what can be done if nothing better presents itself.

As far as electricity generation goes, there is a range of proven and near proven technologies available, some doubtless better in particular locations. These go from nuclear power (suffering a bad image post-Chernobyl and, in terms of economic viability, from a technological impasse when it comes to de-commissioning at the end of their safe working life) through wind power, tide power, wave power, photovoltaic power, and geothermal power to biomass-based developments to which we shall shortly come.

For other end uses currently met by oil products, fermentation is not the only method for treating biomass. We have already mentioned gasification to a low-grade product – so-called 'producer gas' – in the context of retrofitting existing furnaces to use biomass fuel. A wood-fuelled producer gas unit, trailed around behind a petrol or diesel vehicle, was a common sight in war-time Europe. With cheap biomass supplies, such producer gas can provide a convenient way to fuel stationary internal combustion engines with non-fossil fuel, although experience in less developed countries has not been good, with poorly trained operators failing to prevent the build-up of tar deposits on critical engine components.[39] Biomass gasification to producer gas is, then, a well-established technology with commercial designs on the market.

Two other technologies are significant. Anaerobic digestion – basically what goes on in the stomachs of ruminant cattle, etc. – involves a cocktail of micro-organisms working on biomass in a warm, dark and oxygen-free environment. This process can be industrialised and yields a 'biogas' comprising carbon dioxide and methane. Methane is the main constituent of natural gas and the biogas can be purified and compressed into the natural gas transmission system.

The last biomass conversion technology to be mentioned is pyrolysis, which means stewing the biomass in an oxygen-free environment to drive off a variety of gases, some of which condense to liquids and tars at room temperature. The residual is charcoal which can provide a suitable smokeless solid fuel for barbecues, domestic open fires and closed grates, etc. A variety of organic chemicals is produced, so that pyrolysis could provide the basis of a biochemical industry if a contraction of petroleum extraction saw the petrochemicals industry short of feedstock.

Biomass for electricity generation

The conventional technology for electricity generation has – when the scope for local hydro-electric generation has been exhausted – until recently been large-scale thermal (steam turbine) plant fuelled either by coal or by nuclear reactor. As mentioned above, the near future sees the possibility that coal will increasingly be replaced by natural gas as carbon dioxide emissions targets come to be implemented. However, that can only be a medium-term response if the objective is to control emissions rather than just mitigate them. For natural gas has a carbon to energy ratio 60 per cent that of coal (Table 4.3) and a target of zero net emissions cannot be achieved that way (still less negative net emissions if that turns out to be necessary). And natural gas is, in any case, believed by most authorities to be an exhaustible resource (although there is an unsubstantiated conjecture that it is emanating continuously from the earth's mantle).[40]

Biomass fuelling of large-scale conventional stations runs into trouble because their very large size means that the fuel has to be transported long distances. For instance, a 1000 MW station running on base load, i.e. in operation for about 6000 hours a year, requires to be supplied by three million tons of fuel-wood, needing, with 20 tons per hectare per year, plantations covering 1500 square kilometres. Whilst a greenfield development could be located in the middle of a forest 40 km in diameter, the likelihood of finding such an area near a power station that had been located with different considerations in mind – e.g. near a coalfield – is small, so that costly haulage is involved. But this does not make fuel-wood for power generation prohibitively costly since the bulk of fuel-wood supplies would not go to such stations.

This is because a new generation of smaller-scale power stations, typically of 100 MW capacity, which may be dispersed in locations close to their 150 sq km (say 14 km diameter) fuel-wood supplies, is coming to maturity. On grounds of lower running costs, these can be expected to take over the base load from the present generation of mega-power stations (which are designed to squeeze the most out of the economies of scale to be achieved with very large steam boilers). The new stations will be based on gas turbine technology developed for aero engines.

In relation to coal, fuel-wood has a particular advantage for this kind of advanced technology generator since its sulphur-free make-up means its higher technical efficiency can be achieved with no need to incur expense preventing corrosive sulphur getting at the gas turbines. Furthermore, since the producer gas input to the turbine can be hot, tar does not get deposited as with the producer gas/internal combustion engine units mentioned above. And the biomass does not need to be pre-dried since steam released in an integral pressurised drier can be injected into the gas turbine, with improved performance.[41]

This BIGSTIG concept, biomass gasifier/steam injected gas turbine generator, may be particularly suited in South countries, with the high technology gas turbine component in modular form that can be removed as a whole and taken to the aero-engine servicing facilities that already exist to service the international airlines. Like the less advanced combined cycle gas turbine mentioned previously, where the gas turbine exhaust heats a steam boiler for a second (steam) turbine, these design concepts are aimed at increasing thermal efficiency and reducing the amount of heat that is wasted.

A study reported in the Shell Selected Paper mentioned previously[42] envisages using a Rolls Royce RB211 gas turbine as the primary power unit in a conventional combined-cycle design. This design gives electricity costs on a par with the most efficient conventional coal plants, without taking account of burdening the latter with a carbon dioxide emission penalty. The study concludes, rather conservatively, that 'unlike many renewable biomass options, combining a biomass gasifier with a gas turbine power station system appears to be capable of producing commercial energy at a cost not substantially higher than conventional technologies.' Thus, imposing a carbon dioxide emissions burden on fossil fuels would certainly see biomass as the preferred feedstock for such new capacity and also see the new plant preferred for base-load operation. Then the older (i.e. current generation) power stations, perhaps fired by natural gas to eke out their economic life in the face of the emissions burden, would shift down the generating 'merit order' and be used only for meeting peak demand during the winter months.

An Adaptable Scenario for a Biomass-Based Energy Future

This book is not the place for presenting detailed quantified scenarios of the future for biomass energy.[43] Much research of the kind this book calls for must precede such quantification. The pattern of development will be affected both by the changing appreciation of climate change and by technological advances in biomass and other more advanced alternative fuel and energy supply systems. So here we merely sketch out a qualitative description of the way these technologies could play a major role in an ambitious policy – say policy option D of Chapter 3 – designed to have control of carbon dioxide levels in the atmosphere by 2020.

To provide perspective, we reproduce as Table 4.4 a summary of the technologies that have been mentioned, drawn from a report prepared for the Office of Technology Assessment of the U.S. Congress (Larson, 1991) where it is stated:

> Biomass has attractive attributes ...particularly by comparison to coal. Sustainable biomass use releases no net CO_2 to the atmosphere. Also biomass contains much less fixed carbon, ash, sulfur and nitrogen than coal and much more oxygen. Biomass is thus much more readily converted than coal to gases, liquids, or electricity....On the other hand variability in physical and chemical composition...complicates the use of biomass,...the need to tailor-make conversion technologies to specific biofuels. Also...low bulk density limits the extent to which economies of scale...can be captured.[44]

However we have seen that such scale economies are less significant with gas turbine technology.

With the necessary research on land capability completed in a timely manner, the year 2000 could see choices made regarding the more or less rapid penetration of biomass technology. Modifications of policy would ensue as the climatological evidence of later years alters our Chapter 3 Bayesian style probabilities of the future and as our perceptions of the option costs of different policies follow suit. So the timing of change needs to be appreciated. Even starting in 1994 with an ambitious policy, no biomass would be produced until 1997 because that is how long it takes to get to the first coppice crop from even the shortest coppicing cycle. On the assumption that implementation would be a progressive business, starting off from small beginnings to move up some sort of learning curve, not much impact on the energy supply side could occur this century.

However, that is not to say that little impact could be made on emissions before 2000. Quite the contrary, since fuel-wood coppices will be absorbing carbon dioxide from the moment they are planted and, under an ambitious programme similar to that described for New Zealand in the

---

Table 4.4   Biomass Applications Technologies (based on Larson, 1991)

Comparative summary of estimated costs and technological status for energy products from biomass raw material. (E) indicates the results are based on operating experiences; (CR) on commercially-ready, but not commercially implemented technologies; (NC) on technologies that are near commercialisation; and (Y2) technologies which could become available by the year 2000 with a concerted R & D effort. All costs are in 1990 US dollars.[a] (Comparative data for fossil fuels are derived from Manne and Richels, 1992, October 1991 draft – but comparisons should be treated with extreme caution owing to variations in time, place and technical assumptions.)

		Stage of technical development	Production capacity	Installed capital costs	Total production costs[b]
			10^3 GJ/yr or kW	\$/GJ/yr or \$/kW	\$/GJ or \$/kWh
Gases	(cf natural gas \$2.75/GJ (1990) rising to \$6.25/GJ)				
Biogas	(Domestic)	(E)	0.016-1.2	30-12	11-5
	(Industrial)	(E)	3.6-167	13-2.5	1.4-2.5
Producer Gas[c]	(Small)	(E)	1-12	2-0.7	5-3
	(Medium)	(E)	20-200	6-3	ne
	(Large)	(E)	1420-2840	ne	ne
Electricity	(cf new coal fired steam turbine with desulphurisation – *\$0.05/kWh*)				
Steam-turbine		(E)	*5-50000*	*1900*	*0.07*
Biogas-diesel engine		(E)	*5*	*1200*	*0.10*
Producer gas-diesel engine	(E)		*5-100*	*680-420*	*0.24-0.15*
Producer gas-gas turbine	(NC)		*50000*	*1150*	*0.05*
Producer gas-gas turbine	(Y2)		*100000*	*890*	*0.04[d]*
Liquids	(cf gasoline costs \$5/GJ for oil at 20\$/bbl rising to \$10.1 with oil at \$40/bbl)				
Methanol		(CR)	10000	30-50	10-13
		(Y2)	10000-40000	30-12	5-9
Ethanol from cane		(E)	1000	10	10
		(Y2)	2000	9	8.5[e]
Ethanol acid hydrolysis	(CR)		1000-2000	80-60	19-21
acid hydrolysis		(Y2)	2000	50	15
enzymatic		(NC)	5500-27000	18-27	9-11
enzymatic		(Y2)	6500-12700	11-15	6-6.5

(a) All figures are approximate for purposes of cross-fuel comparisons. Total production costs assume a 7 per cent discount of \$2/GJ for biomass, and capacity utilitisation rates as discussed in appropriate sections of the report. 'ne' indicates that no estimate was made in this study.

(b) Units are $/kWh where the product is electricity and $/GJ otherwise (1GJ = 278kWh).
(c) Wood fuel (not charcoal).
(d) Stand-alone electric power generation – 20 per cent lower with waste heat utilisation (e.g. district heating schemes).
(e) Assumes use of biomass-gasifier/gas turbine cogeneration, with export of excess electricity, the revenues from which are credited against the cost of ethanol production.

Appendix, quite a lot will have been planted this decade even though only a small proportion will have reached the cropping stage. The main impact on the energy system could come in the first decade of the next century, with the changeover nearly complete by 2015 if scientific opinion continued to favour urgent action.

Apart from timing we need to consider the geographical pattern, with a shift towards the developing South in the consumption of energy and the location of fuel-wood production activity. Initially the action will mainly be in developed countries, with the available temperate land, or some of it, providing the venue for the development of machinery and equipment for large-scale coppicing activity. At the same time, the major survey of land capability will be in progress and, as available temperate land sufficiently near to centres of demand to provide the venue for power generation and other bulk energy processing activities runs out, the focus would shift to more distant venues. These might be located in temperate regions of Asia and in the southern hemisphere, or they might be in tropical countries, depending on the extent to which such business is welcomed politically and efficient economically.

As South countries find they can finance their development by providing a venue for atmospheric pollution clean-up services to developed countries – an invisible export like the traditional invisible exports of developed countries – market forces reflecting the comparative advantage of tropical regions in the production of biomass would see growing activity there. The upshot would be expected to be the production of energy crops in South countries that would enable them to fuel modern power generation plant on a scale more suited to their natural development path than has characterised the current technology of mega-hydro schemes (which have often served to inundate fertile land and to power the processing and export of natural mineral resources in a way that has made little contribution to the natural path of indigenous development).[45]

To the extent that a surplus arose over requirements of power station and other furnaces, biomass crops could be expected to go into portable fuel manufacture, either to satisfy local transportation demands, or simply to turn the product into a form that can conveniently be exported. To the extent it was more efficient for other countries' transportation demands to be met from traditional oil refining activity, such surpluses would otherwise be buried in discharge of the pollution clean up service and thus constitute 'making coal'. Either way round there would be income to the host country in relation to its provision of pollution clean-up services to fuel burners in temperate developed countries, where fuel-wood coppicing had either become relatively expensive or simply been unable to find enough land available.

Other countries, perhaps those more constrained by debt burdens, might seek to enter the pollution clean-up business in order to provide the raw material to 'do a Brazil' and to avoid increasingly expensive oil imports. Thus they might adopt the biomass-to-ethanol route as the cost effective solution to meeting their transport fuel needs, or the biomass-gas turbine route for meeting expanding power needs economically.

How far this exclusively biomass-based direction could go would depend on how soon problems of competition with other uses of land lead to cost increases, and how soon technological developments in non-biomass sustainable technologies begin to render the direct biomass approach obsolete. The former is simply unknowable in the present, but is an uncertainty which is perhaps more easily resolvable, by research on the ground, than the uncertainties that surround the climate system.

Obsolescence for biomass would probably arrive soonest in power generation, where photovoltaic cells, which fundamentally capture solar radiation far more efficiently than does nature's photosynthesis, are expected to follow closely the advanced gas turbine concepts discussed above.[46] And, like all ambient energy systems for generating electricity, it faces the storage problem (which we mentioned in relation to the advantage of liquid fuels for transportation) of matching the pattern of demand over time to the availability of the supply.

The pattern that can be expected, then, under an ambitious emissions-reduction programme, is for biomass to take an early role in furnace applications for space heating, bulk industrial heat and in power generation, first in temperate areas and later in the development path taken in tropical regions. With the move of biomass production away from regions of high energy demand, and with an expanding volume of biomass production, the emphasis would shift towards the production of portable fuels (ethanol on the basis of the backstop technology outlined above, but possibly others) with power generation shifting to photovoltaic and other non-biomass based sustainable technologies.

Eventually, massive power generating photovoltaic facilities, located in the world's arid and sunny deserts, might serve as the basis for electricity-intensive industry. Hydrogen produced by hydrolysis would be pipelined to centres of population, and maybe the eventual shift to a hydrogen-based transportation system, as envisaged by many knowledgeable commentators, would be seen in the latter part of next century – possibly combined with biomass-based carbon for easily portable liquid fuels.

The key point to emerge from this chapter is that the technology to begin a low-cost transition to a biomass-based energy system that would give global control over the level of carbon dioxide in the atmosphere already exists. We know how to produce biomass cheaply on the massive scale required and there is certainly enough land to go very far down that route, although maybe not enough to avoid some painful choices later on if the global warming outlook gets worse. And we know how to use the biomass produced, at least as furnace fuel, with ethanol for transportation, biomass-fuelled gas turbine electricity generation, and biodigester based gas supply technologies within easy reach.

Putting these known technologies into effect in an orderly and planned manner is a not very difficult matter of choice facing the global community. Thus the more painful choices which, it was argued in the previous chapter, should be prepared for on a precautionary basis, even at considerable expense if that were the only way to protect posterity, turn out to have a low-cost alternative. As regards the technical options, 'what to do about global warming' is obvious and hardly painful at all.

Notes

1. UK Department of Energy, Annually (a), Appendices 2 and 3 for exploration success; BP, 1992, p.2 for reserves ratios.

2. Dosi, 1984, p.83.

3. Johansson et al, 1993a.

4. BP, 1990, pp. 10, 22, 29, 30, 32.

5. Manne and Richels, 1992, Chapter 1, Section 5 and Chapter 2, Section 3.

6. World Bank, 1992, p.22.

7. Manne and Richels, 1992, Chapter 1, Section 6.

8. Based on UK Department of Energy, Annually (a), Conversion Factors, etc., back pages.

9. Read, 1993.

10. IPCC, 1992, p.30.

11. Ibid, pp.16, 71.

12. Ibid, pp.69-70.

13. Sims, 1990; Wright and Ehrenshaft, 1990; Willebrand and Verwijst, 1992.

14. For both coppicing and conventional forestry, two- or three-fold increases have been reported in experimental situations (Maclaren, 1993; Sims, 1993). How far largely experimental experience with coppicing is comparable with commercial experience of conventional forestry is debatable.

15. On whether the land constraint is acute there are conflicting views (Hall, 1990, p.12; Myers, 1989, p.76). On the most optimistic view, sequestration into

standing timber is possible until advanced sustainable energy technologies become available. But for commercial forestry, the choice between conventional longer rotations (mostly resulting in carbon absorption) and short-term rotation (mostly for fuel production and hence carbon recycling) depends upon the proportion of conventional forest product that can be sold and will change over time as the market for fuel-wood expands, and as the relative cost of land rises, under the impact of increasing incentives for absorption and possible variation in their temporal impact (i.e. how quickly absorption needs to take place to count as a valid offset against a firm's carbon tax burden or towards its discharge of an absorption obligation). Ecological benefits in relation to the preservation of existing forests and bio-diversity habitats may point to a pattern of longer term incentives that yields a higher proportion of conventional forest products. The need for extensive 'learning by doing' in this area, (inter alia, the object of this book's advocacy of 'getting ready') is manifest.

16. IEA, 1989, 4th Quarter, pp.286-7; Williams and Larson, 1993, p.748; Manne and Richels, 1992, Appendix C.

17. Hall et al, 1990 and 1991, Table 4; Williams and Larson, 1993, p.748.

18. Moulton and Richards, 1990, Table 12.

19. Sims et al, 1991, p.61 (here converted from original NZ$ data).

20. Table 4.1 and Table 4.3 above; also Hall, 1990, p.17.

21. FAO, any year, Table 1.

22. Hall et al, 1990 and 1991, Table 4; BP, 1990, p.33.

23. Hall et al, ibid; IEA, 1989, p.73; UK Department of Energy, p.67.

24. Hall et al, 1993, p.638; Tasker, 1992, p.4.

25. Common, 1991.

26. But in parts of South East Asia population pressures are very great and clearance is for high productivity permanent settlement rather than slash and burn. As we have noted, there is some limit to the population that Earth can support.

27. Myers, 1989, p.76.

28. Ibid.

29. FAO, any year, Table 1.

30. Marland, 1988, p.56.

31. Trabalka et al, 1985, p.266.

32. Leffler, 1985, for technology; Skeet, 1988 and Odell, 1974, for political economy.

33. Odell, 1974, p.104.

34. Goldemberg et al, 1992, p.841.

35. Texeira and Goodman, 1991.

36. Ibid, pp.27-35.

37. Wright and Ehrenshaft, 1990, Table 2.

38. Waring, 1992.

39. Larson, 1991, p.15.

40. Anon., 1992, p.158.

41. Williams and Larson, 1993, p.760.

42. Elliott and Booth, 1990, p.10.

43. Johansson et al, 1993b.

44. Larson, 1991, p.3.

45. Goodland et al, 1992, pp.509-10.
46. Hamakawa, 1987, p.82; Anderson and Bird, 1992, p.11.

5. Economic Theory and the Environment

In this chapter we will briefly sketch the optimising framework that underlies the mainstream (neo-classical) economist's mental set. We will explain some difficulties with that approach that arise in practical market situations and the contrasting remedies that economists adopt when analysing energy sector problems and environmental problems. We then discuss one approach to environmental problems which suggests that, with suitable institutional arrangements, they can be left to the market. The reader who is economically trained can safely skim read this and most of the next chapter.

The Invisible Hand

Consideration starts from the proposition that there is some best or desirable level for any economic activity, including the activity of cleaning up mess. This arises from the existence of constraints on the overall level of all activities taken together. We cannot enjoy an infinite standard of living at zero cost – live like lords without the need to go to work – because all that is consumed has to be produced, either by nature or by people working with nature. And the quantity of resources available for production is limited, either by nature's bounty in the case of natural resources, by human fecundity in the case of labour resources, or by past investment decisions in the case of the produced means of production which we refer to as capital, be it the physical capital of plant, equipment, buildings and infrastructure or the inalienable capital of human knowledge, skill and experience.

Among these factors of production, labour is of course double-edged in the sense that it adds both to supply and to demand. Corresponding to the concept of standard of living (usually measured as production per head of population, but conceptually closer to consumption per head of population), there are measures like capital/labour ratio and resource/labour ratio which enable comparisons of economic development to be made between countries of different populations.

Given the limited supply of productive forces, output of one desirable good (where 'goods' encompass all kinds of goods and services contributing to material well-being) is at the expense of another. That is subject to an efficiency assumption that productive forces are not being wasted.

It is the central claim of neo-classical economists that the market system, working through prices which signal the use of productive resources embodied in any marketed good, results in a socially desirable bundle of goods being bought and sold, and accordingly in a desirable allocation of productive resources.

If the good produced did not yield so much satisfaction to the people who buy it, demand would fall, and with it the price and the profit to be gained from production, so that producers would reallocate resources to the production of something else. Similarly, if the production of some service involves a resource that becomes scarcer, the cost of employing that resource would rise and be reflected in the selling price of the service, so that consumers would be signalled to switch their demand to something else.

This property of yielding maximum satisfaction at minimum cost, claimed of the market system, was likened to the working of an 'invisible hand' by Adam Smith, the (or at least a) founder of modern economic thought. Magically, everyone – profit-maximising producers and satisfaction-maximising consumers – acting self-interestedly in response to a pattern of prices resulting from the impersonal workings of market forces, results in the best of possible allocations of resources and the highest possible level of consumer satisfaction through the production of what is most wanted at least possible cost.

Before we get to look at some of the problems of invisible hand economics, and to seeing how it can be applied in practice, e.g. in relation to greenhouse gas pollution of the environment, we will look at the theory a bit more closely. This will help us understand something of how economists think about such problems, to see why they often have to make do with rather crude approximations, and to learn a little more of their language.

Convexity

An important condition for the theoretical invisible hand to work properly is that consumer preferences and production possibilities are such that their representation in the formal analysis can be done by mathematical expressions which meet the requirement of 'good behaviour'. Such well-behaved mathematics can be represented graphically by smooth curves that do not 'bend back'. Depending on which side you look at them from, they appear to be either continuously convex or continuously concave. We will summarise all that by the single word 'convexity' and not burden these pages with the mathematicians' convention for distinguishing one from another – when we use 'concave' it will be to emphasise that one curve is continuously and smoothly bending in the opposite direction from another.

Convexity is equivalent to the notion of diminishing marginal outcomes for a given marginal input where, by 'marginal', economists mean a small change from the status quo. Such 'marginal thinking' is basic to an elementary introduction to invisible hand analysis. In consumption theory the convexity requirement means that additional satisfaction gained from a bit more of some good is less than the loss of satisfaction from a bit less of it.

This diminishing marginal satisfaction follows from the supposition that consumers are rational, that they satisfy their most urgent wants before their less urgent wants, and that the urgency of a previously unsatisfied want can be equated to a measure of satisfaction. Since it is a logical consequence of the assumptions, the satisfaction measure, or utility as economists usually call it, cannot in fact be measured and is empirically vacuous.

It follows from diminishing marginal satisfaction from each good that, if you have a lot of something, say food, you would be easily persuaded to give some of it up for a bit of something else of which you may be lacking, say liquor to drink with it. If on the other hand you have little food, and are going hungry, you would be less willing to substitute other goods for food. Economists call this diminishing marginal substitution in consumption. This is in principle observable and is normally observed in practice, with sensibly categorised groups of consumption goods.

On the supply side of the market, convexity requires that the additional resource cost of producing a bit more of some good is greater than the resource cost saved by producing a bit less. It may be intuitively obvious – or otherwise will hopefully either be taken on trust by the reader or become apparent from the geometric illustration following – that, by a process of reallocating productive resources from one activity to another, the effect of such diminishing marginal returns to scale in the output of each good is that production substitution possibilities change depending on how much of each good is produced.

Thus, if a tremendous lot of food is being produced, it is very hard to produce more and a lot of other goods have to be forgone to get more food. If, however, only a little food is being produced, not much effort is required to produce a bit more, and only a little of other goods need be forgone to get more food. Thus we also have diminishing marginal substitution in production along a convex production possibility frontier.

Unlike the empirical vacuity of consumers' diminishing marginal satisfaction, it is a technical question whether production activities do in fact display diminishing returns to scale. In practice many do not, which leads to 'non-convexity' in the mathematics. This means that a general equilibrium, represented by a set of prices that yields equilibrium in all markets – including markets for the services of factors of production, as well as markets for consumer goods and services and for the goods and services that are intermediate in the inter-firm production process – may not be unique, and therefore cannot be relied upon to be optimal since some other general equilibrium may be better. The invisible hand may guide the economy to the wrong destination.

Indeed, the fitting of increasing returns in the production of some goods into the logical structure of general competitive equilibrium presents the theoreticians with some knotty problems. However, that is but one of many problems with the invisible hand in the real world, some of which we will come to shortly. For the present, note that the main lesson to be learned from the convexity discussion is the fairly general existence of diminishing marginal substitution in production and the economist's universal assumption of diminishing marginal substitution in consumption.

A diagramatic illustration

For those with a geometric turn of mind, general equilibrium with convexity is illustrated in Figures 5.1a, b, c and d, in which the economy has only

Figure 5.1a Tastes

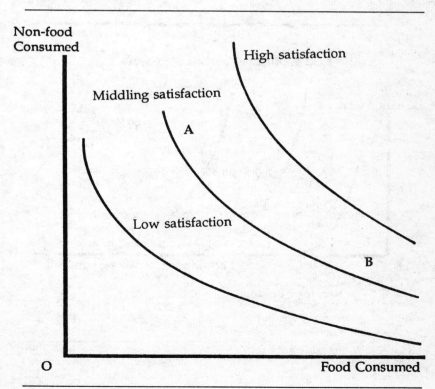

two kinds of productive forces, labour and capital, and only two kinds of good, food and non-food.[1*] 'Convexity' refers to the shape of the curves in Figures 5.1a and 5.1b, labelled 'tastes' and 'technology' respectively, which are convex shapes when viewed from the origin 'O'.

Figure 5.1b   Technology

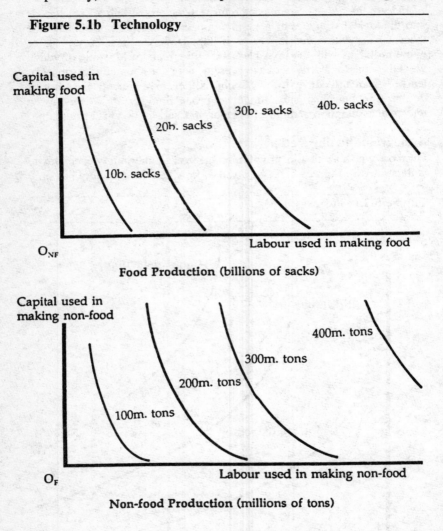

Food Production (billions of sacks)

Non-food Production (millions of tons)

The convexity of the family of curves representing different levels of social satisfaction can, with a bit of thought, be seen to imply diminishing marginal substitution in consumption. Thus, at point A on the middling satisfaction curve, society is willing to give up a lot of the non-food of which it has relatively plenty, in order to get a bit more food, whereas the converse is true at point B. Here 'is willing to' means 'would be no worse or better off if it were to' since movement along the curve of middling satisfaction means, precisely, that the level of satisfaction is unchanged.

The additional requirement of diminishing returns to scale in production must also be represented. This is done by drawing the output curves in the technology diagrams further apart at higher levels of output, implying

Figure 5.1c A Box Diagram of Constrained Production

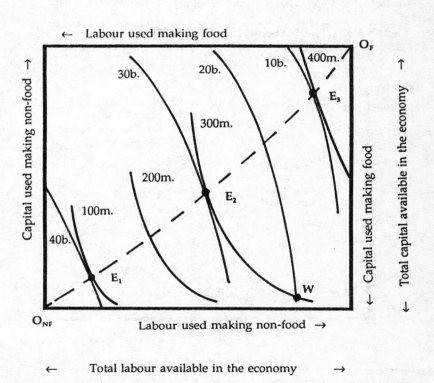

more than twice as much input to get twice as much output.

The food and non-food technologies are reproduced – with food upside down and left to right – in the box diagram, Figure 5.1c, that shows how production is constrained by the availability of productive forces, since the lengths of the sides of the box are drawn to represent total labour and total capital available. Pairs of efficient outputs are represented by points E – they are efficient in the sense that, for each output of one good, say food, no higher output of the other good, non-food, is possible than at points 'E'. This is in contrast with wasteful production at a point like W where only 20 billion sacks of food are being produced for 300 million tons of non-food even though it is possible to produce 30 billion sacks and 300 million tons.

Efficient pairs of outputs are plotted in the production possibility frontiers of Figure 5.1d. Convex technologies, and diminishing returns to scale for both food and non-food, lead to a concave 'production possibility frontier' under society's constrained supply of labour and capital.

Figure 5.1d The Invisible Hand Succeeds

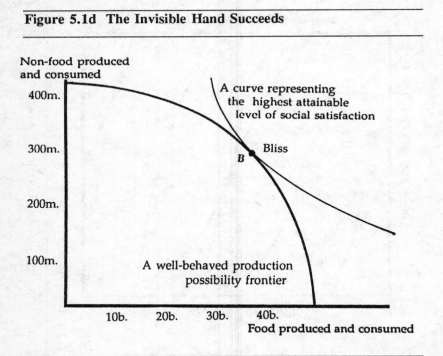

Diminishing marginal substitution in production is represented by the concavity (as seen from the origin of the diagram) of this production possibility frontier whereas the presence of increasing returns to scale over some range of production of one or other good can result in a portion of the production possibility frontier being convex, as in Figure 5.1e.

Superimposing this concave production possibility frontier on 'tastes', the family of convex curves representing different levels of social satisfaction, results in there being a unique optimum allocation of resources yielding a maximum of social satisfaction at the so-called 'bliss point' B. The relative price of food and non-food – how much of one must be given up to get more of the other – is given by the slope of the two curves where they touch at B.

Working back through the analysis, it can be shown that the price of labour relative to the price of capital (wages to profits) is given by the slope of the technology curves at the selected point of efficient production of each good, this slope being the same for both technologies when resources are efficiently allocated as at points like E.

An 'all income is spent' assumption gives the relativity between goods' prices and the prices of productive forces. The complete set of prices signals the information needed to cause millions of buyers of food and non-food (who are also sellers of labour and capital), and hundreds of thousands of buyers of labour and capital (who are also sellers of food and non-food), to do just what is required to get to B, which is best for everyone. Magic.[2*]

Figure 5.1e   The Invisible Hand Fumbles

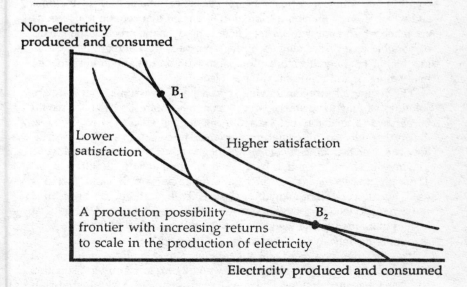

Two-dimensional paper limits geometric illustration to a two-dimensional economy. With hundreds of different types of productive force, and thousands of different types of goods, advanced mathematics is required to demonstrate all this formally. However, it is quite straightforward providing the multi-dimensional equivalent of well-behaved convexity is assumed throughout the analysis. Also much philosophy is needed to support the procedure of aggregating individual tastes into social tastes. But if the reader will take that on trust, the essential ideas in the theorising that goes to support invisible hand style economics is contained in these diagrams.

Also illustrated in Figure 5.1e, is the kind of problem that can be caused by increasing returns to scale in production. The arrows indicate the direction of movement of the system locally, towards locally stable equilibria B_1 and B_2. Unfortunately there is no mechanism to ensure the system gets to preferred local optimum B_1 rather than inferior local optimum B_2, in the case where the production possibility frontier is not 'well behaved'.

Comparative statics

It is the ingrained force of the invisible hand theorem, reiterated with increasing sophistication at all levels of their training, which leads economists to approach problems with the mind-set which was outlined in our introductory chapter. The underlying perspective is one of optimal equilibrium, with a set of equilibrium prices that obtain most of the time and which convey enough information to ensure that economic decisions are made which eliminate waste. There is no dynamic process: the effects of possible change are studied by the apparatus of 'comparative statics' in which a final equilibrium is compared with an initial equilibrium, the intervening period represented by a 'black box'.

The engineer's problem-solving approach which assumes that there are solutions waiting to be worked out (which in economist's language would be phrased as available but unused technological advances) is of course deeply disruptive to this equilibrium-oriented mind-set. In a rational world, how can it be that all available technological advances are not employed? The invisible hand theorem is based on the assumption of full information. There are no secrets, so that the best technology is available to all and is used by all producers. Anything less is both wasteful of productive resources and inconsistent with the profit maximising axiom. Without that assumption the outcome is indeterminate and sophisticated invisible hand theorising inapplicable – it becomes 'mere theory'.

The fact that one can walk up the high street and see modern and obsolete vehicles driving along side by side is explained by a distinction between long-run decisions, which relate to investments in durable capital, and short-run decisions, which take the stock of capital as fixed. Yet no satisfactory description of the transition from the short to the long run – an essentially dynamic process driven precisely by the application of available but previously unused technological advance – exists in conventional economic reasoning, or can exist given the reliance placed upon comparative statics.

Problems with the Invisible Hand

However, let us focus upon what can usefully be learned from invisible hand-style analysis. To do that we first need to understand some of the difficulties. Of course, there are many critiques from within the economics discipline, of which the most well known is Marx's. This is concerned with the consequences of concentrated ownership of physical capital and its implications for control of the system, and for the enjoyment of life, by different classes of society categorised by the type of productive factor which they supply – natural resources by rentiers, labour by workers, etc.

It is interesting to note that Marx was essentially writing about the social dynamics of capitalism, a concern which can only be sidestepped by neo-classical rationalisations which start from comparative static analyses. However, we are not in this book concerned with that critique (except in so far as it underpins some of the political dimensions of applying the GREENS concept through its influence on theories of neo-colonialism). Mainstream economists respond to questions of distribution of ownership by arguing that such questions are for decision by the political process and that, when it has been decided, the invisible hand is available to ensure that the best allocation of resources, and the greatest possible benefit to consumers, ensues through perfect competition in a market framework.

But there is a collection of difficulties for the invisible hand which are recognised by neo-classical economists under the general notion of market failure. Failure that is to deliver quite that optimal bundle of butter, guns, environmental pleasure, etc., that theory claims it should, which is not by any means to say that markets do no good at all. Such titles as 'the palsied invisible hand' and 'the invisible foot' decorate the economic literature, bearing witness to professional concern with difficulties which cause some markets to be distorted and others to be simply missing. Following is an incomplete list of such difficulties, with brief explanations.

Risk aversion: many economic decisions have probabilistic outcomes. Most importantly, investment decisions are risky as regards outcome, which can then be calculated only as an expected value. It is rational for the individual to be risk averse since she has satisfied her most urgent needs first and loses far more by having all her income taken away than she gains by having it trebled. So she will not take that risk (supposing the outcomes are equally likely, decided by the tossing of a coin) even though its expected value is a 50 per cent increase in income.[3*]

Uncertainty: the outcome of the horse race, in Chapter 3, was described as uncertain – no statistical basis existed for predicting the winner, with punters placing their bets on subjective grounds. With no statistics, insurance against uncertain outcomes is not to be got, and rationally risk-averse decision-takers will fail to undertake potentially desirable but in some way uncertain projects.

Transactions costs: are a kind of pervasive friction that impedes the smooth working of markets. For instance, it is simply too much bother to completely optimise your weekly shopping; you don't have the time to traipse around every supermarket in town and buy what's cheapest in each, but form shopping habits suited to your pocket and based on experience.

Asymmetric information: you don't know whether or not this secondhand car I am selling is a 'lemon', so I have to discount its price below its value in order to compensate you for the risk you take in buying it. This may mean that I decide not to sell, since the discounted price may be less than the car is worth to me. Thus the opportunity for mutually beneficial trade is frustrated. With insurance against failure of educational investment there would be 'adverse selection' – able people would not need to insure themselves so the insurers (ignorant of their clients' educational potential) would have an adversely biased group of clients. And also 'moral hazard' – unpleasantly clever people would insure themselves heavily and then deliberately flunk out, living off the insurance company for the rest of their lives.

Awareness of the importance of informational asymmetries and transaction costs is spreading amongst economists and much very interesting modern research is concerned with investigating just how palsied the invisible hand is on these accounts – maybe to the extent that many possible and desirable markets have to be categorised simply as 'missing markets'.

Principal-agent theory provides a particularly important application of asymmetric information theory for much of public policy, including pollution policy. Any agent lower in a hierarchy has knowledge of his own capabilities which are unknown to his superior principal. How can the principal know whether actual performance is all it might be? When British industry went onto a three-day week in the miners' strike in 1974, far less output was lost than might have been expected. Worried about their pay packets, many workers worked as hard as possible for three days, rather than as hard as normal for five.

A concern is that managements will run firms for their own benefit (so-called management slack) rather than in the profit maximising way wanted by their shareholders. The discipline of share prices and threat of takeover is similar to using a sledgehammer to crack a nut. The designers of any policy for pollution must have regard to the likelihood that those who will respond to it – in many cases the managements of firms – will have different motivations from the motivations of the policy makers or the profit-maximising motivations which underlie invisible hand thinking.[4*] Indeed, so must electors be wary of policy makers whose motives may be different from what they appear to be when they present themselves for election or selection.

Returns to scale we have already considered and illustrated in Figure 5.1e. Three further sources of market failure require more elaboration in the context of our focus on energy economics and atmospheric pollution. The first is related to returns to scale since increasing returns result in decreasing average costs so that the largest firm, with lowest costs, can undercut its competitors and dominate, if not monopolise, the market. This enables it to set the price in the market by controlling the supply – it becomes a price maker. Market power, sometimes in the extreme form known as natural monopoly where competition is technically impossible (as with the distribution of electricity from street to a customer) is pervasive in the energy sector.

Price-making behaviour and the Schumpeterian vision

It is important to distinguish two meanings of the notion of competition. Firstly there is the static notion, bound up in the model of perfect competition implicit in the invisible hand theorem, where all the many agents, households and firms, respond to price signals that arise from the play of market forces. Technological information is freely available and there are no barriers to entry into any market. So the existence of profit in any market instantly attracts new entrants and prices are held down at the level where all producers must produce at minimum possible cost in order to survive the competition, and the 'all powerful' consumer is supplied at the lowest price possible.

Such 'price takers' are in contrast to 'price makers' that have power in a particular market. In the extreme, price makers can be single sellers, monopolists, or single buyers, monopsonists (e.g. trades unions selling labour in a 'closed shop' situation or mine owners buying labour in an isolated mining village, to take two contentious labour market situations).

Perfect competition is compared favourably by mainstream economists with various types of imperfect competition. The contrast shows a state of wasteless efficiency delivered by perfect competition in an environment of freely available information such that all production is by the most efficient technique available and economic bliss is delivered as per B in Figure 5.1d.

Secondly there is the dynamic notion of competition, often linked to the name of Joseph Schumpeter in whose writings there has in recent years sprung up renewed interest. Schumpeterian competition is red in tooth and claw; entrepreneurs, anxious to secure and expand their market share, exploit innovations to get a step ahead and are in turn brought down by others with newer ideas. This process of 'creative destruction' is beneficial to society as a whole because it provides the engine for change, innovation and progress.[5*]

The role of information is starkly different, with success dependent upon maintaining secrecy long enough to reap the profit from an idea before others can emulate it. Thus, at any point in time, a snapshot to freeze the situation would reveal a picture of highly imperfect static competition yielding an inefficient allocation of resources and of wasted opportunities to improve standards of living.

The Schumpeterian entrepreneur-hero is inherently anti-social in the imperfectly competitive present, despite his role as catalyst for future progress. Accordingly it is part and parcel of Schumpeter's message that such competition is open to abuse and can proceed benignly only in the institutional context of an appropriate legal and regulatory framework designed to liberate initiative whilst protecting the consumer (who is very far from 'all powerful').

Public goods and the need for government

What makes pollution different from butter, and to some extent different from guns, is that people buy butter in the market with their income in order to satisfy their private appetite. The employment of some productive resources in producing butter is reflected in the use of other resources in producing other goods, sufficient to yield the income needed to buy both the butter and the other goods. Equilibrium in the markets for productive factors ensures that the two sets of productive forces are equivalent at the margin in production. Equilibrium in the goods markets ensures that the butter and other goods are equivalent at the margin in consumption. Some people have a private appetite also for guns in order to go hunting or robbing banks, but most people's appetite for weaponry is satisfied by state purchases of such things and their deployment to secure law and order and the safety of the realm. Such goods as law, order, safety and a clean environment, are called public goods by economists since it is not possible for them to be supplied to one person without them being supplied to the public at large. Their consumption is 'non-rival', per contra private goods which provide benefits to the consumer from which the public at large is excluded by the act of the individual's consumption (if I eat this butter you can't, whereas if the law protects my property it protects yours also).

For that reason the purchase of public goods cannot be left to the decision of a single individual. I might be willing to buy $500 of public safety if it gave me the security I want. But in reality precious little security can be got for anyone for that sum of money. The New Zealand police cost more like $500 million than $500 and, furthermore, what little public safety could be got for me would also benefit all the people that hadn't paid $500. Thus the need to provide public goods (including the public good provided by the existence of institutions that enable markets to operate freely) constitutes one of the economic justifications for the existence of the state.

The state provides public goods and, through taxation, ensures that the cost burden that results is shared around without 'free riding' – i.e. the enjoyment of the benefit by people who haven't paid their fair share, as with using public transport without paying the fare. The state – however organised and sustained, be it monarchy, dictatorship, democracy or whatever – provides for the diversion of productive resources from making private goods into making public goods.

But the fact that a clean environment is a public good does not necessarily mean that the state can most efficiently deliver that good by accepting a responsibility to clean up pollution to a particular standard. This is because nature provides us with a clean environment to start with (or, more accurately perhaps, because the evolutionary process has produced ecologies of life forms, including homo sapiens, that are well adapted to the particular environment we have got). Thus pollution – the placing in the environment of material that is unnatural to its pristine state – is the result of human activities, in general market-related activities, which impose external costs on others.

Externalities and environmental pollution

Such human activities include both consumption and production. Nature is unable to tell whether the carbon dioxide and other pollutants coming from a particular vehicle are incidental to a family trip to the beach or to the delivery of ice-cream to a vendor on the beach. When the vehicle was filled up at the filling station, whether to go on a productive trip or to be used for consumption activities, a commercial transaction took place that, inevitably, would lead to the production of pollution, which is a public bad.

Goods or bads like these, produced incidentally to a commercial transaction, are called externalities by economists. They can be public goods or bads, as with the public bad caused to the atmosphere by emitting pollutants from a vehicle exhaust, or private goods or bads, as when my neighbour's decision to keep bees results in my fruit orchard becoming more productive through better pollination.

And, as with the production of marketed goods, their production can be increased or reduced by greater or lesser employment of productive resources. I might erect nets to keep my neighbours' bees off, my vehicle might be fitted with pollution-reducing gear such as is required in parts of the world where vehicle smog is a severe problem. But nets and exhaust gear don't grow on trees and have to be produced, displacing production of alternative goods.

However, the invisible hand is of no help in deciding how many productive resources should be devoted to increasing the production of externality goods or to decreasing the production of externality bads. As the good or bad resulting from vehicle emissions is experienced by people not engaged in the filling station transaction, their dissatisfactions are not reflected in demand, any more than does the cost of supplying fuel reflect peoples' deployment of productive resources in combating the pollution – e.g. in stitching up old clothes to be used as smog masks. This is per contra normal, internalised, production costs which reflect the resources directly employed by manufacturers in the various stages of the productive process, and are passed on to the consumer in the price he pays.

Responding to Market Failure: the Second Best

The implications of all these forms of market failure for the invisible hand are more serious than may at first sight appear. Surely it should be possible to devise a general rule that would result in our working towards where the invisible hand should put us? Sadly this is not the case: the theorem of the 'second best' shows that there is no general 'more market' remedy which guarantees improvement from introducing more competition into a distorted system.

If there is market power and price-making behaviour in the supply of beer and of wine, then more competition in the business of wine supply could worsen rather than improve resource allocation, and more competition for both could also worsen allocation given that, say, agricultural prices influencing the use of land for vineyards and barley production, are distorted more generally. One can only be sure that an improvement results from a given policy shift by working out all the costs and benefits of a proposed change.

The response of mainstream economists to the second best problem is quite different in the two areas of applied economics which are of most interest in this book, that is to say energy economics and environmental economics. We deal with the first before continuing the main business of this chapter.

Theoretical solutions – the indicative planning approach

Theoretical answers to problems of market failure have been laboriously addressed by economists, engineers and mathematicians under the label of 'second best theory', using cost-benefit analysis and planning theory in the context of elaborate computer models and detailed quantitative analysis of engineering and market information. Such work can be put to use to resolve the problems of co-ordination inherent in tooth and claw competition.

The results are likely to be more successful in relation to a well-defined economic sector, such as land use, transport or energy, than in relation to larger aggregates, such as the economy as a whole, or manufacturing in general. Economy-wide planning models suffer from informational difficulties and from judgemental problems as to what is important and what should be omitted (given the need to simplify in order to keep the model computable).

However, a particular sector, sometimes known as a natural economic unit, is described as a collection of industries having a high degree of interdependence and weaker links with the rest of the economy. The more successful economies, Japan, Germany, France and the emergent Pacific rim economies, all have arrangements that, with varying degrees of success, resolve co-ordination problems within such natural economic units.

The term indicative planning has been coined to distinguish such work from the command and control apparatus of direct government intervention conjured up by memories of the centrally planned economies of the former Eastern bloc. Rather is it in the nature of co-ordinating the plans of separate but interdependent decision takers, a co-ordination based on collecting the information needed for understanding the joint effect of their intentions and analysing it in a complex 'second best' model of the behaviour of the natural economic unit as a whole.

Clearly information is the key to good decision taking. Commercial secrecy in the context of 'tooth and claw' competition arises because there is no way of ensuring that one firm's disclosure will be matched by another's, though all would benefit if all were revealed. Obviously disclosure by one firm alone would place it at a commercial disadvantage. Thus all firms that operate in the real world of Schumpeterian dynamic competition conduct their activities under a socially costly cloak of commercial secrecy that is taken for granted in business life (and is far removed from the full information assumption that is made in the formal analysis of perfect competition and the invisible hand).

One of the important benefits of successful indicative planning is, through the creation of discrete communication networks, a reduction of the costs of misinformed decision taking, thus enabling the benefits of Schumpeterian competition to be achieved in a less wasteful manner. The object is to ensure that each firm's plans are compatible with each others [6*] and jointly with policy objectives.

This mutually beneficial two-way process provides forward information which market prices cannot, and enables firms to plan for themselves with less uncertainty. And it helps governments to devise policy incentives with better understanding of their effects and better prospects of getting acceptance from firms (and their consumers) for public interest policy objectives such as sustainability.

Energy is pre-eminent amongst the economic sectors that need to be treated as a natural economic unit. Not only can all energy goods (electricity for gas, etc.) be substituted for each other in most applications with a bit of ingenuity, but many of them can be – and in fact are, as we saw in Chapter 4 – converted into each other in the supply industries. Accordingly, planning the management of a particular energy resource without regard to the plans that may exist for other energy resources is futile.

Furthermore, the typical energy firm is large, operating with substantial market power and using technologies that display considerable returns to scale – sometimes to the extent of natural monopoly. Its internal planners need to make guesses about rivals' intentions in a strategic interplay which can lead to wasteful outcomes. This is prone to be particularly wasteful since many energy technologies have very long lead times – power stations can take a decade to build, oilfields can take as long to bring into production, coal mines can take as long to sink.

So there is plenty of time for misconceived projects to get well advanced before information becomes available to stop them, by when it may be too late. Thus most energy economists would favour some form of indicative planning process to provide the basis for economic prescription in the energy sector. To repeat, finding out what is economically desirable in this way should not imply forceful control of the actions of independent economic agents, but the discovery of what needs to be done, by way of incentives and constraints, to ensure that the market outcome is socially desirable.

Pollution economics in theory

Pollution is at the opposite pole from the energy sector as regards the application of second-best planning methods. Nothing could be less like a natural economic unit than the diffuse way in which pollution enters the cost structure of any economic activity one cares to think of. And convexity arguments suggest this might be a good *locus operandi* for the invisible hand.

As regards technology, to return to Figure 5.1b, the technology of abatement (i.e. emission prevention and/or clean-up) generally exhibits diminishing returns. Perfect cleanliness requires infinite pains, but we can get a floor vacuumed fairly easily, with more care get a kitchen hygienic for cooking, at considerable trouble prepare a theatre for surgery, and so on. Lower toxic emissions from vehicles can be engineered at some expense, zero emissions are infeasible.

As regards tastes, recalling Figure 5.1a, nature provides us with a large supply of the public good of pristine environment, so that a little pollution, which means giving up a bit of nature's generous supply, does not hurt us much. After a lot of pollution, however, we have not much of the pristine good left, and the damage represented by losing what little we have is very great. For example, in relation to so standard an environmental pollution problem as the water quality of a river, bathing parties won't notice minor pollution but will object to obvious filth.

The increasing marginal dissatisfaction from increasing pollution is one element of the harm done by pollution which we referred to in Chapter 3

Figure 5.2 Optimal Pollution

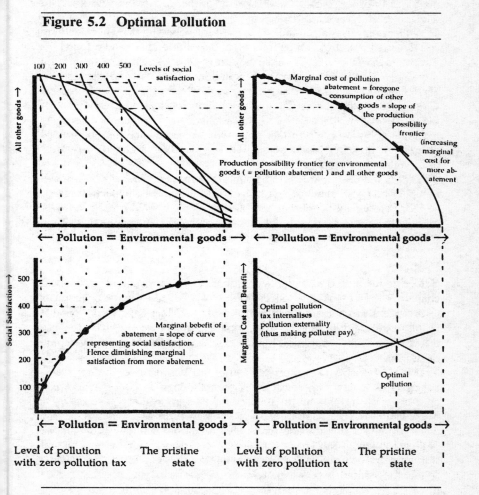

as the damage function. Although seemingly somewhat intangible, we may note that economists have developed techniques which put a cash value on such marginal dissatisfactions.

But another damage also arises, apart from lost enjoyment by consumers of the public good of a pristine environment. The other damage is the practical impact of the dirty river on the production of other goods – be it water supply, which now has to use extra purification or even come from a less accessible source, commercial fishing lost, corrosion of structures in the river, or whatever.[7*] In relation to conventional pollution problems, this second kind of damage usually also displays increasing marginal impacts so that the convexity properties of the two kinds of damage reinforce each other.

A theoretical basis can thus be argued for believing that, in relation to conventional pollution, an optimal level of pollution tax can be found, as illustrated in Figure 5.2. We have the damage cost increasing at the margin more and more, as the level of pollution increases, and the cost of abatement increasing more and more, as the level of pollution decreases. Clearly, then, there must be some pollution level at which the cost of marginal abatement is equal to the aesthetic dissatisfaction caused by marginal pollution (with further pollution clean-up which may be needed as an input for other production activities properly charged to consumers of the other products).

That is the desirable level of pollution. More abatement would result in higher marginal abatement cost than the marginal dissatisfaction saved, so more abatement is not worth it. Less abatement would result in lower marginal abatement cost saved than the marginal dissatisfaction that would result, so that less abatement is a false economy.

Property rights
Before going on to deal with interventionist policy instruments in the next chapter, we first look at a concept which is believed by some economists to provide a mechanism which enables the invisible hand to do its stuff despite externality problems. It is of interest in its own right and because it lies behind one of the more practical policy proposals which we come to shortly.

If the externality is of a private nature, as with the bees and the trees, negotiations can be undertaken between the parties concerned. I can encourage my neighbours to keep bees by offering them payments. Or beekeepers can go around offering to put their beehives in my orchard or other people's orchards, and find which orchardist will pay most for the pollination benefit received. Of course, orchardists may wise up a bit and start charging beekeepers for the nectar that the bees get from their orchard. In fact the symbiosis between orchardists and apiarists is the classic case in which negotiations between the parties results in commercialisation of what would otherwise be an externality effect.[8] A market in the placing of beehives gets established which results in an efficient – or at least reasonably sensible – allocation of beehives around the available orchard areas. In that case the externality gets internalised into the market system. Note that negotiations are conducted between well-defined groups of people and that one group, the orchardists, starts off with well-defined legal rights in the land. The placing of the beehive is, ultimately, by permission of the orchardist.

This example has led many supporters of invisible hand-style economics to propound the idea that all externalities are open to similar treatment. That the misallocations that result, for instance, from emissions of dirty smoke from factories can be reduced to the desirable level by appropriate market internalisation. The level would be undesirable if, for instance, the cost of cleaning up the factory process were less than the injury to health plus the cost to many households of having to do the weekly washing over again when it comes in dirty off the clothes line.

A theorem named after economist Ronald Coase[9] propounds that, so long as property rights are well-defined, the market provides a basis for the efficient allocation of resources in the presence of such externality effects. Under threat of legal action from people with a defined property right to clean air, the smoke emitter either pays for the second wash (and the excess health bills) or installs smoke abatement equipment, whichever is cheapest.

Or, if he has a clear right to emit, then the injured parties can either pay for his smoke abatement equipment, or continue to suffer the injury, again whichever is cheapest. The Coase theorem thus suggests that externality inefficiencies arise because of the lack of certainty in legal process, that if all property rights were clearly defined externality problems would go away.

However, the property rights approach is fraught with practical difficulties, as is obvious when one remembers that legal redress for tort – be it injury to health, or to one's washing put out to air – is already available to John Citizen by civil action through the courts. Property rights do in fact exist, are open to enforcement, and yet fail to do the trick.

Taking legal action is expensive. The damage to each citizen is small. The difficulties of organizing and sustaining group action may be great. The identity of the polluter may be in doubt (which factory's smoke dirtied whose laundry). The burden of proof may be insurmountable (think of the ludicrous pseudo-scientific nonsense put out by the tobacco companies in their decades-old campaign to delude the public regarding the carcinogenic properties of their product). Information is hard to come by (for instance as to the technical possibilities for smoke abatement, or regarding the possibility that the financial burden of smoke abatement, or of compensation for non-abatement, might close down what may be an important local employer). And so on. Certainty of property rights is not certainty of outcome from legal process, save for certainty regarding the fees of lawyers and of economists called in as expert witnesses.

Notes

1. And, in the original version (Bator, 1957, reproduced in a great many intermediate economics texts) with only two consumers. The economically literate reader will notice that I pass over the business of trades between individual consumers, and the aggregation of individual satisfactions into a social satisfaction frontier ('grand utility possibility frontier') of doubtful convexity, to be set against a social welfare function. Not much is lost thereby.

2. Providing we are satisfied with the distribution of spending power – we get a different B for each possible pattern of social tastes derived from aggregating the individual choices of the millions of owners of labour and capital, some more lucky than others as regards their share.

3. This has important implications for educational policy, where the benefit from the expense incurred might be related to a statistical distribution of ability. Education is sometimes analysed as an investment in 'human capital'. The rationally risk averse individual will, at her own expense, undereducate herself since, for reasons we come to in a moment, she cannot gain insurance against failure. Thus the state should provide education, thereby pooling the risks involved, setting the winners off against the losers and, indeed, recovering the expense from the winners through their subsequently higher tax payments.

4. Thus unsophisticated policy makers, informed with only a smattering of economics such as comes from certain generalist courses, may quite misjudge the effect of zealously marketist policies in relation to environmental policy and to much else. A multi-disciplinary approach is not an undisciplined one.

5. Indeed, Schumpeterians hold that it is the clustering of innovative activity, triggered by a shift to some new technological 'paradigm' which stimulates long-term phases of economic prosperity. The reader may recollect the suggestion in Chapter 1 that the technology of sustainable energy might provide the paradigm shift that could trigger a sorely needed resurgence of global economic activity.

6. For instance, in the British energy planning procedure with which I was at one time involved, it was invariably the case that the individual industry's demand forecasts, when added up, totalled more than the forecast growth of energy demand as a whole. The provision of excess capacity, based on such optimistic forecasts, is precisely what economic theory would predict as the outcome of a struggle for market share in an imperfectly competitive market. Of course, if such wasteful competition is not negotiated away through a planning process, the cost is carried by the consumer.

7. For the production of these other goods, environmental cleanup is an intermediate input in the chain of production. When pollution is at the desirable level, such cleanup (if still needed at the, presumably lower, desirable level) is properly part of the cost of the other goods. But the additional cost due to excess

of pollution over the desirable level is part of the damage function associated with excess pollution.

8. Cheung, 1973.
9. Coase, 1960.

6. The Economics of Pollution Policy

In this chapter we find that much invisible hand theorising is of little help in relation to practical policy for the environment. The 'least cost theorem' is, however, of use although it does not pretend to achieve even a 'second best' outcome. Various possible policy instruments are described and reviewed in the context of the global warming problem, which is characterised as a stock pollutant. As such it is the rate of emission net of absorption that matters, and the problem is seen as essentially dynamic and time dependent. Some essential tools for thinking about economics over time are introduced and the special features of sequential, as opposed to 'once-for-all' policy are discussed.

The Unattainable Second Best

We have seen that, in theory, there is likely to be an optimal level of pollution which policy should aim for. However, the second-best theorem confronts the theoretician again, and this time it presents insurmountable difficulties. The generation of wastes is pervasive to every kind of commercial activity and to many consumption activities. This is the case both in markets that are close to the perfectly competitive model, such as vegetable markets, and in those like energy markets which comprise a natural economic unit that is far removed from that model.

And if there is market failure somewhere in the system then the second best theorem spreads virus-like through the whole. To build a model to take account of all the interactions of pollution and of all possible environmental protection measures, as would be necessary for the application of planning methods to the choice of pollution-control policy, would involve a detailed model of the entire economy, and that has so far eluded policy analysts (though the continued rapid advance of computing technology may be bringing that day closer).

So, in the real world of imperfect competition, and removed from the esoterica of planning models, practical people must make do with rough and ready answers. And it remains a rough and ready truism, roughly reflecting the invisible hand, that more of one good means less of another. This is because, while the economic system as a whole may be wasteful, individual agents in their local situation are fairly well able to perceive the waste of whatever resources they themselves have control over and eliminate such waste in order to better themselves. Thus if they turn their resources to producing something else, they produce less of whatever they were producing before.

An exception of course is where people are denied the opportunity to deploy their resources, as in the case of involuntary unemployment. People can be regarded as involuntarily unemployed if they would take their old job back at the wage rates now being paid for similar work.[1] And that includes quite a lot of people under the doctrines that nowadays obsess the makers of budgets and the directors of central banks.

However, if we take those doctrines as given, which we do in this exposition of neo-classical economics, it is reasonable to believe that more butter means less guns. And, since pollution is a bad that requires the employment of productive resources for its removal, less pollution means less guns and/or less butter. To the extent the economy is away from the point of optimal pollution, optimally priced through an efficient pollution tax (at which point its input and output at intermediate stages of the production process of other goods would be properly internalised into the costs of those other goods) pollution is a joint product with those other goods in technologies that have evolved without regard to the cost of pollution, so that less of it may involve sharply less guns or butter. We may simply not know how to produce butter without producing pollution also, never previously having had an incentive to pay engineers to solve the problem.

Coarse economics

How much more butter and/or guns for less pollution depends upon the prices that obtain in the imperfect world that manifests market failures such as those discussed in Chapter 5. Because of non-optimality, with the invisible hand palsied, these prices will be wrong prices which only roughly reflect resource costs. So the costs and benefits of alternative policies – and the regrets and objections of Chapter 3 if a decision process for a major 'one-off' choice is being followed – will be known only approximately.

The essence of the invisible hand is that the prices of goods and of productive forces are actually paid by consumers buying goods and firms buying productive forces, so that the choices of technologies used by firms and of purchases made by consumers are motivated by an actual loss of opportunity to choose something else. Sufficient information is available, in the market prices which exist, for selfishly motivated consumers and producers to make decisions which invisible hand reasoning shows to be efficient.[2*] We have seen that, once determined by the market, these prices guide consumers and firms to decisions which, in the absence of market failure, yield the best possible allocation of resources.

However, the going prices of Schumpeterian competition enable potential trade-offs to be estimated, but provide no clear basis for knowing which would be socially desirable and which harmful. And insuperable obstacles stand in the way of closing the information gap in the way that we saw it may, with luck, be closed in a sectoral planning process. The limited number of economic agents within the natural economic unit may have joint interest in getting reliable information from the indicative plan and in maintaining a reputation for providing reliable information. Such common interest cannot be generated across the pollution-affected economy as a whole.

For instance, although techniques are available to establish the value put upon a public good amenity that actually exists (by investigating material choices related to the use of the amenity, for example how much opportunity for other enjoyment do people forgo to get to a national park), it cannot value amenities that do not exist. And policy towards pollution is directed towards restoring an amenity that has been damaged by the pollution and which does not attract people to come and enjoy it (in the way it would if it actually existed in its restored state) and the forgone alternatives of which enjoyment can therefore not be measured.

Simply asking people what a reduction in pollution is worth to them cannot be expected to yield a truthful answer since they will have no interest in their reputation in relation to the impersonal workings of the economy-wide market. Their motivation is to exaggerate their dissatisfaction with the pollution on the grounds that somebody else will pay most of the cost. Similarly, polluters will have an incentive to exaggerate the cost of abating pollution, in the belief they are most likely to bear such costs, if imposed by policy, and that truthfulness on their own part would bring them no reputational rewards within the impersonal workings of the economy-wide productive sector.

Thus what would to the economist be the natural approach – to direct policy at achieving an efficient level of emissions as per Figure 5.2, in which the marginal cost of added pollution is just equal to the marginal cost of abating pollution – is not available. The margins we are at are not the margins we need to be at in order to be able to measure, from market prices, what we need to measure for determining the efficient level of pollution and for the achievement of an optimal policy. We are, in fact, in an area of thoroughly coarse economics, very far removed from the beauty of the invisible hand's magical cunning.

Abatement targets and the least-cost abatement of pollution

With economics able, at best, to give only a rough guess at the desirable level of pollution, and often not even that (as, in relation to greenhouse gas emissions, with our ignorance of the damage function discussed in Chapter 3), resort may be had to what economists call arbitrary policy targets. It would be arbitrary in the sense of being determined otherwise than by economic reasoning. Typically it involves asking experts – medical people, scientists, engineers and so on – what they regard as safe or satisfactory or feasible levels of pollution abatement, and then adopting such opinions, or some compromise of the opinions of several experts, as the policy objective.

Arbitrary as it may be, even in the pursuit of such targets, and far removed from the workings of the invisible hand, the economist is not without something to say about how to deal with pollution efficiently. For emissions are, in general, not from a single source – certainly not in the case of greenhouse gas emissions or the carbon dioxide emissions which, we have seen from Chapter 4, are the key to controlling global warming.

What economics does say is, providing that marginal income for each agent has the same social value (i.e. providing the distribution of income question mentioned earlier has been satisfactorily resolved) then the burden of pollution abatement should be imposed in such a way that the marginal cost of abatement per unit of emissions should be the same for all emitters.[3] This 'least cost theorem' shows that the social burden of achieving some non-optimal – i.e. economically arbitrary – target for emissions reduction is least when that marginalist proposition is followed. The argument is simple, starting from the contradictory proposition.

Suppose there are only two firms, and (contrary to our proposition) that the least costly reduction of emission has been achieved with a marginal cost of abatement of $2 per ton of carbon for A and a marginal cost of abatement of $1 per ton for B. Then if A emits one ton more it saves $2 and if B emits one ton less it costs only $1, so 'society', comprising A and B, has achieved the same abatement at a saving of $1 in production costs. So the contradictory proposition is false and the proposition originally claimed – i.e. the least cost theorem – is proved.

Practical Pollution Policy Instruments

Now we are ready to review the economic efficiency of various established policy instruments for controlling traditional pollution problems before going on to consider the special problems raised by greenhouse gases. Before taking other approaches in historic order we may recollect that the most recent, the property rights approach, falls down (but for a few specialised instances) in the face of what we earlier called transactions costs. Applications of the Coase theorem are limited to rather a few instances in North America, where there is money to burn on lawyers (and where lawyers can make the running with 'no win, no pay' arrangements with prospective clients). Elsewhere, environmental concerns are reflected in more direct economic remedies. Nevertheless, as we have said and shall see, the theorem lies behind an important proposal for dealing with carbon dioxide emissions.

Regulation

A venerable approach to externality 'bads' is to prevent them by force of law. Typically, an area may be declared a smoke-free zone. Then laundry can safely be aired outdoors because the factory owner faces not a poorly organised group of disgruntled launderers but the force of law. Infringements are reported to the inspectorate who take a look for themselves and prosecute the offender if the evidence of infringement is sufficient.

A traditional area for regulation is in the area of public health and safety. Motor vehicles that are not able to stop quickly present a danger to the owner and to other people. Many libertarians would hold that the first danger is her own business, and that may well be properly so – providing she is also fully responsible for her own medical bills or has adequately insured herself, having informed her insurers that her vehicle has bad brakes.

The second danger is an externality of the owner's transaction in buying the car and buying the petrol. Of course, the act of driving even a well-equipped vehicle is in itself a danger to other people which, in New Zealand, is reflected in the price of petrol, part of which goes towards financing New Zealand's splendid Accident Compensation Scheme, which keeps so many lawyers out of work.

However, the driving of a vehicle with bad brakes presents an additional element of public bad externality – 'public' because, if one person is at risk from this driver, so is everyone he happens to drive near. In most countries that kind of public bad externality is simply regulated away. Vehicles have to come up to certain standards of construction before the manufacturer is allowed to sell them for use on the public roads. It is the obvious place to put the onus because the manufacturer may be expected to have knowledge of how to install safe braking and also, in practical terms, because it is more efficient (i.e. less demanding of productive resources which could otherwise be employed making something else) to do the job in the factory when the car is being made. So the purchaser pays the cost of preventing that public bad as part of the price paid for the vehicle.

Similar measures to protect the public are to be found in the laws relating to the sale of food and medicines. Cleanliness in the preparation of food, and particular care with products prone to high toxicity deterioration such as pre-cooked meats, are normal requirements in advanced countries. A particularly interesting example of the benefits of such regulation is to be found in the case of pharmaceuticals in the USA.

There the Federal Food and Drug Administration requirements on safety testing have resulted in a reduction of the numbers of new drugs coming onto the market for purely product differentiating reasons. The days when an aspirin with a new flavour was peddled to the unfortunate medical practitioner every time the door bell rang are in the past. Instead there has been a concentration of research onto the new 'science-based (sic) drugs' which represent a sufficient advance for the prospective profit to be worth the immense expense of the testing procedures required by the FDA.[4] An example of the benefits to be gained from Schumpeterian competition when it is subjected to an appropriate regulatory framework.

Pollution taxes

Taxes are the traditional remedy of economists to the problem of public bad externalities. The argument is quite simple: since the problem arises because some commercial activity results in a public good being consumed without charge (or, equivalently, because a public bad is produced without charge) the selling price does not represent the full cost of the activity, and too much of it will be going on since demand will be greater at the too low price.

Pollution reduction comes about as a result of three possible mechanisms. Firstly, the tax makes the activity of which the pollution is an externality more expensive, so that the price of the good produced is raised and demand in the market falls, with a reduced production rate for the activity concerned and consequentially less pollution.

Secondly, the producer will try to continue the activity in a less pollution-intensive way, maybe to the extent of installing pollution collection and disposal equipment, in order to minimise the tax burden and sustain his activity profitably. Thirdly, the government may spend its tax revenue to clean up the emissions after they have been released. These latter two are, respectively, working on two aspects of abatement costs. It is an efficiency question whether, for a particular pollutant, it is better to emit the pollution and then clean it up, or better to collect it prior to emission and to dispose of it harmlessly.

We may note the possibility of a slip twixt cup and lip: treasuries and budget departments have a penchant for seizing tax revenues from whatever source and simply adding them to the general flow of government funding. To raise a tax with a view to spending it on a particular purpose may be called dedicating a tax. In the context of carbon dioxide emissions and their clean up, we will refer to a tax-funded clean-up scheme as a Dedicated Carbon Tax.

Despite the New Zealand example in relation to motor vehicle taxes and the Accident Compensation Scheme mentioned above, tax dedication is anathema to treasuries because it reduces their discretionary power to shape the pattern of government spending. And most treasuries are very jealous of that power, the exercise of which provides their *raison d'être*. The British Treasury have a label for it, calling it the 'hypothecation' of taxation, and will advance all manner of specious objections to it.

For in reality people are often very much more willing to pay a tax if they can perceive what particular public good they are paying for with the tax in question. And willingness to pay in a free market (nobody is forced to buy or sell anything) provides the ideological justification for the system. Thus an oversized (but technically efficient) health service funded by tobacco and alcohol taxes that people are accordingly more willing to pay, may be preferable to an efficiently sized service funded out of resented general taxation.

Too high a pollution tax results in too much pollution reduction or too much clean up – the consumer is forced to forgo too many other delights which might have been produced by the productive forces being devoted to maintaining the environment. And conversely for too low a level of tax. But that does not answer the question of at what level the tax should be set. If there is knowledge both of abatement costs and of the damage function (and we have pointed out that this is often not the case because of informational difficulties) then the tax should be set at the level at which the marginal damage from additional pollution equals the marginal cost of abating it.

Given rising marginal costs for each, this prescription can easily be demonstrated to yield a 'coarsely efficient' answer (for instance by way of the 'proof by contradiction' approach used above for the least cost theorem). Coarsely in the sense that no attempt can be made to adjust for market failure. This is the kind of *faute de mieux* result for which economists, in the absence of a healthy invisible hand, instinctively aim, with the tax resulting in a coarsely desirable version of the ideal level of pollution of Figure 5.2.

With poor knowledge of the damage function, resort is to 'arbitrary' abatement targets for emissions reduction. But in achieving the target, should the tax be set at the cost of public clean-up, or at the cost of private prevention? Obviously the tax needs to be set at only slightly above the lesser of the costs of doing one or the other. If it is cheaper to prevent emission, then the polluter will pay the costs of doing that in order to avoid the tax. If it is cheaper to emit and then clean up, the emitter will pay the tax and leave the state to clean up the emission, or to pay a contractor to do the job.

But it is the exception rather than the rule for these costs to be constant (flat) costs. Our recent reference to convexity suggested that abatements cost would normally rise, in line with economists' customary marginal thinking. With rising marginal costs for both clean-up and prevention, it may be the case that both will be used simultaneously, or that one is sufficiently cheaper for the target to be achieved without the other being needed. Here we are measuring costs as costs per unit of emission, and taxing at a rate per unit of emission, so that every emitter, in maximising profit (if a producer) or minimising loss of satisfaction (if a consumer) emits at the rate where the marginal cost of emissions is equal to the tax level and therefore the same for everyone, satisfying the least-cost theorem.

Emissions permits

Emissions permits are a modern development[5] inspired by the Coase theorem in response to problems with regulation and taxation. The problem with regulation is that it contravenes the least-cost theorem. For instance, it may be very easy to substitute low sulphur fuel oil at a power station built on the coast, near a refinery in an oil-importing country: the electricity firm just pays the oil refinery to import low sulphur crude for part of the refinery's throughput. On the other hand an inland power station built near a high sulphur coal field has either to close down or to install expensive sulphur removal equipment to clean up the flue gases.

So if a 10 per cent reduction in emissions is regulated, the marginal cost to the coastal power station is small but to the inland station it could be very substantial. The same reduction in emissions could be achieved at much lower cost if the inland station continued as before and paid the coastal power station to reduce its emissions not by 10 per cent but by 20 per cent.

And the problem with taxation is uncertainty as regards its effect. As we saw, ignorance regarding the private prevention costs of abatement could lead to an excessive degree of abatement in relation to the abatement target that has been set. (Of course, uncertainty is even greater if the objective is to achieve the 'coarsely efficient' level of taxation since that involves knowledge of the damage function also. That problem does not arise with regulation since it is already plainly inefficient in its contravention of the least-cost theorem, without regard to the question of whether the marginal costs of more abatement equate to the marginal saving in damage.)

An economically effective response to these difficulties is implicit in the idea of one power station paying another to do its abatement for it. Essentially there is a trade in abatement performance, with the power station that can more easily do the job being paid to do it by the one that finds it more difficult.

That kind of response is formalised in the idea of tradeable emissions permits. Emissions are simply banned unless in accordance with a permit, with the total quantity permitted fixed in line with the target, and with permits tradeable. Trade can be between existing emitters and with potential emitters or with environmentalist groups – the latter can leave such permits unused if they believe that the arbitrary target is insufficiently ambitious. Trading with potential emitters deals with a previously unmentioned problem with regulation. If all emitters are required to reduce by 10 per cent, how do you start up a new business for which some emission is necessary? 10 per cent, less than nothing last year is nothing this year, and new business is frustrated by a 'barrier' to entry.

But with tradeable permits, new businesses simply increase the demand for permits, forcing up the price and causing some emitters – say the coastal power station – to find it profitable to reduce emissions further and sell some of their permits. Questions of considerable interest are how the permits are allocated in the first place, whether they are permanent as regards the quantity permitted to be emitted each year (or week, say) or variable, or are reissued each year and whether they need to be paid for.

Such questions find correspondence in relation to pollution taxes – are they constant from year to year, do they discriminate between classes of emitters, say as regards traditional emissions and incremental emissions, their location, the nature of their business, etc. Another field of interest is the business of monitoring and administration of any scheme – information requirements, emission measurement techniques, penalties for non-compliance, etc. – be the scheme regulation, taxation or tradeable permits.

Fascinating as it may be to analyse them in detail, their general study is for a more specialist text.[6] Their merits in relation to the Tradeable Absorption Obligation that we advocate in these pages, will be discussed in the next chapter. Here we have simply described the basic idea of a tradeable emissions permit and seen that either taxes or permits can be related to the tonnage of pollutant emitted and thus meet the requirements of the least-cost theorem, while regulation cannot.

In relation to the difficulties with regulation and taxation, the total issue of permits enables the degree of abatement to be accurately achieved. And their tradeability ensures (subject to the existence of a sufficient number of buyers and sellers in the market to establish healthy competition) compliance with the least-cost theorem. Referring back to our discussion of property rights, we can see that the Coase theorem is implicit. The creation of explicit permits to emit confers a right to the holders which, by virtue of tradeability, makes the right equivalent to property.[7]* It is of interest to note that a system of tradeable emissions permits has been introduced in the USA under the 1990 Clean Air Act in relation to the problem of sulphur and nitrogenous emissions from power stations.[8]

However, these benefits are not unalloyed. The problem with emission permits is that the cost they impose is uncertain and may be very great if expert opinion as to the degree of abatement to be achieved is unrealistic. Fundamentally the same information gap besets both permits and taxation: the private marginal cost of emissions prevention, at different levels of abatement, is not accurately known to policy makers. A tax fixes the marginal cost of abatement but leaves the quantity of abatement open to doubt. A permit system fixes the amount of emissions but leaves the cost in doubt. Their problems are but opposite sides of the same coin.[9]

The Nature of Carbon Dioxide Pollution: Gross and Net Emissions

Before proceeding to a discussion of the novel economic instrument which is advanced in the next chapter, we first review the economic characteristics of carbon dioxide emissions and see why the types of policy instruments that have been outlined so far are unsatisfactory for dealing with the global warming problem.

As we have noted, three types of costs or benefits arise. Firstly, the direct public good cost of reduced aesthetic environmental quality. Second, the private and public costs of suffering or adapting to the indirect effects of pollution – properly intermediate costs of production if pollution were, by chance, at the optimal level. And, thirdly, the cost of abating the pollution, either privately as prevention of the emission, or as a public service afterwards, by cleaning up the polluted environment.

In relation to carbon dioxide emissions, the first of these can be ignored: the pollution is odourless, invisible and presents no known health hazard. It is, indeed, as we have seen, a normal component of the atmosphere so that its presence in greater than usual concentration does not impact directly on our enjoyment of life and our level of satisfaction with it. And the second type of cost, as we have pointed out in Chapter 3, cannot be measured in our present state of understanding.

Accordingly, we are involved with the coarse economics of target achievement for which the third type of cost – abatement costs – is what matters. Indeed, it provides the focus of this book. In particular, our central claim is that the very high costs of reducing emissions on a gross basis (relating to what we have called the private cost of pollution prevention) can be avoided by working on the alternative public good activity of clean-up, which involves focusing on net rather than gross emissions.

Before continuing we may note that there is no reason of logic or of science and technology which dictates that the second kind of cost, the one that matters in relation to the damage catalogue for carbon dioxide pollution, should have well-behaved convexity properties. From experience, convexity is usually assumed in relation to riverine and local airborne flow pollution, the two cases which constitute the bulk of practice with applying coarse invisible hand theorising to environmental problems.

This second kind of damage, in the case of global warming from carbon dioxide pollution – such effects as rising sea levels, increased climatic freakiness, faster desertification, risks to the food supply chain, loss of species diversity, etc – may be related to foreseeable extrapolation from conventional climatic experience or it may be related to unforeseeable regime jumps, precaution against which, it has been suggested in Chapter 2, should be the real concern regarding greenhouse gas emissions. Neither what is known of the damage function nor such jumpiness is very like the smooth convexity of invisible hand theory.

Problems with conventional instruments for abating net emissions

It is obvious that any combination of tax on emissions, subsidy on absorption, tradeable permits on emissions and tradeable offsets against permits or taxes (giving four possible combinations of fiscal and permissory measure) is qualitatively equivalent. This is in the sense of each being capable of generating a scheme that would secure a least-cost reduction of net emissions in line with some economically 'arbitrary' target. Both in reducing emissions and in increasing absorption there is a price-quantity relationship and, providing both aspects of the net emission target are acted on by either a quantity or price instrument of appropriate magnitude, and with scope for arbitrage (trade-offs) between individual emitters, market forces will result in the target being achieved at least cost (in the coarsely efficient sense discussed above).

For instance, one scheme could be to tax emissions, save to the extent that the taxed emitter had offset its emissions with some quantity of absorption, with such offsets tradeable in the sense that the emitter could sub-contract the offset to another energy firm, or indeed more likely, to a specialist fuel-wood producer. The least-cost equivalence of such schemes means that, in the comparative statics of 'coarse' economic equilibria each of them will, in however long a run it may take to reach equilibrium, eventually do the job. There is no comparative statics reason for preferring one to another.

We do not propose to weary the reader by analyzing the full variety of such possibilities but will focus in the next chapter on the particular one that seems most advantageous, what we have called the Tradeable Absorption Obligation (TAO). Its advantages will arise not only from its static properties but from its administrative convenience in relation to the technological realities of global warming and to the dynamics of energy industries and to the geo-political situation to which it is addressed.

With carbon dioxide a stock pollutant, and its emission flow closely tied to a core activity of industrial and commercial activity, that is to say energy conversion, its absorption is very much less costly than trying to reduce emissions – save to the extent that the economising behaviour and ambient energy technologies of Chapter 1 are concomitantly induced. Cleaning up carbon dioxide from the atmosphere is a global-scale public good – it does not matter where in the globe it is done since we all share one atmosphere which mixes up pretty fast in relation to the timescale of global warming.

The need for absorption arises, then, as an externality of private market actions, principally the burning of fuels for commercial and domestic purposes, and of forests to provide room for human settlements and agriculture. The scale of the prospective absorption activity is vast: six billion tons of carbon requiring nine billion tons of trees to be grown (allowing for 25 per cent natural absorption) at around $30 per ton leads to a figure of, say, $300 billion a year. That it is a vast figure is not surprising since it is proposed eventually to largely displace existing fossil fuel extraction and, if the cost were very much less, such displacement would take place under market forces.

The addition of such a vast figure to the costs of fossil fuel extraction would, accordingly, lead to the kind of doubling of raw fuel prices that has been reported in the context of the 100 per cent carbon tax designed to achieve a reduction in gross emissions solely by means of inducing economising behaviour. If the cost were simply added on (as would be the case with the 'coal making' alternative discussed in Chapter 4) it would nevertheless be greatly more effective than the carbon tax in that it would achieve not a 20 per cent reduction of net emissions by 2020, but around 75 per cent, i.e. all that is needed to stabilise the level of carbon dioxide in the atmosphere, allowing for 25 per cent natural absorption.

If the reported 20 per cent reduction in emissions brought about by economising behaviour induced by such a 100 per cent tax is correctly calculated, then the cost of 'coal making' would likewise induce such economising behaviour and, with 95 per cent reduction of net emissions and 25 per cent natural absorption, we might be well on the way back to the natural range of carbon dioxide concentrations below about 280 parts per million. However, that would be to forget increased emissions from growth in less developed countries.

Whilst such a 'coal making' approach is obviously about three times as good as a simple carbon tax, the net cost of the whole business is reduced by the extent to which the biomass (fuel-wood) produced is used in lieu of fossil fuels and accordingly enables the costs of fossil fuel extraction to be avoided. Whether the additional cost, compared with fossil fuel extraction, is 10 or 20 per cent, or nil, or negative, is not a question that can be argued in the absence of the detailed 'ground truthing' study that is called for in this book. Nor can it in the absence of an assessment of likely technological advances in the production of fuel-wood, in terms of silviculture, species selection and improvement, and harvesting and transportation technique which would be induced by the 'learning by doing' approach which is advocated in this book.

We will not speculate about what are essentially empirical questions but simply note the key point. This is clear: the net emissions concept, linked to the use of the biomass product as fossil fuel substitute, is likely to be two substantial orders of magnitude cheaper than the use of economic instruments that are designed simply to induce economising behaviour. Nevertheless, the scale of prospective business is 10 times the total annual global aid bill, and this alone is sufficient to rule out the idea of a globally organised Dedicated Carbon Tax (DCT).

In the USA, and possibly elsewhere, such an approach also comes up against very strong ideological resistance to new taxes, as captured in President Bush's 'read my lips' electoral slogan of 1988, and to the arguments against big government generally. To shift the main business of energy raw material production out of the field of commerce, where the coarse invisible hand imposes some discipline on behaviour, and into the graft-laden framework of bureaucratically controlled public spending, is, even without the complications introduced by the international dimension of the problem, surely a recipe for disaster.

That is not to say that a carbon tax additional to the TAO, but in replacement of existing taxes – i.e. going into general tax revenue and not to subsidise biomass production – may not play a useful role in some countries for fine tuning the local impact of a globally operating TAO. Alternatively, a small DCT to fund administrative, research and other incidental aspects of implementing GREENS might well be a desirable and commensurate application of dedicated taxation. Indeed it could well be applied to researching a more wide-ranging approach to sustainability issues, and/or to ameliorating the social costs of progressively reorienting land use and human skills to a new direction of development.

But to use a DCT to finance fuel-wood production means either that the scale of the activity would be far too small to do the job or that the flow of public funds would be far too great to be acceptable. Similar arguments apply to a tradeable emission permit system from which the revenue is used to subsidise biomass fuel production.

We should, however, remind the reader of a point made in Chapter 1. This was that it is incorrect to regard the whole revenue from such a tax (i.e. from an undedicated emissions tax working in the way that economic policy analyses of the greenhouse gas problem have conventionally envisaged) as a burden, since such revenue would be used, at least in part, as an offset against other possibly distorting taxes. Indeed, it is wrong to regard a tax that is imposed to correct an externality effect as a distortion on the market, rather the market failure that is being corrected should be seen as the distortion. However, alternative means for internalising the externality may be preferable as, we will argue in the next chapter, is the case with global warming arising from the (free) disposal of greenhouse gases.

Pollution dynamics and economic dynamics

There is a more fundamental difference than the distinction between gross and net emissions that separates the global warming problem from the familiar experience of pollution economics. Carbon dioxide in the atmosphere is a stock pollution problem in the technical sense that the damage comes from the level, quantity or stock of carbon dioxide in the atmosphere, rather than the net rate of flow of carbon dioxide into the atmosphere. The flow, net of additional natural dispersion, represents the rate of change of the stock.

More precisely, it may be not the stock but the stock times, the length of time for which it persists, that matters, as was suggested in the context of the 'stitch in time' precautionary policy advanced in Chapter 3.[10*]

The reason for this difference is that local riverine pollution or airborne smog is the emptying of waste into a disposal resource which is flowing by and, therefore, constantly being renewed. In such cases an obnoxious concentration of pollutant requires a regular flow of the pollutant into the river or air stream – say a one ton flow of pollutant per hour into a one million tons per hour river stream resulting in a one part per million concentration, which may or may not be obnoxious, depending on the nature of the pollution.

However, the atmosphere – and the oceans for that matter – are sinks from which pollutants are not carried away but in which they must reside until chemical breakdown or other natural process renders them harmless. It is not the flow of carbon dioxide and other pollutants into the atmosphere, at a rate of a few per cent of the natural flows, that rouses concern over global warming, but the uninterrupted cumulation of those net flows since the industrial revolution and particularly in the last few decades.

What are the implications of a stock pollutant in relation to a set of economic instruments that have developed as responses to flow pollutants?

Firstly, most importantly, and as has been explicit in much of our discussion, it means that it is just as good to take the pollutant out of the stock as it is to reduce emissions into it. It is cumulative net emissions that matter, not the rate of gross emissions, which have been the focus of public attention and of much analysis by economists. If taking pollution out of the environment is easier than not putting it in, then that is the thing to do. That this is the case is, to reiterate the point, obviously a main message of this book.

Secondly, it turns the problem into one to which economics is not well adapted, that is to say an essentially dynamic problem about which the comparative static approach has nothing to say. If climatological research eventually confirms that the risks of persisting with carbon dioxide levels above the natural range of 180 to 280 parts per million are too great to be taken, then the global economy will – if the international community can get its act together – be involved in a long transitionary process for many decades ahead. This may follow initially, i.e. for the next two or three decades, the kind of path sketched out in the scenario at the end of the last chapter.

Whatever path is followed, it will be fundamentally out of equilibrium throughout the process, with one generation of technology following another, diffusing through the global economy, and leading to possibly quite substantial relocations of energy and agricultural activities. Furthermore, the path of aggregate economic growth can, in the context of equitable development, be expected to be slower in developed areas than in less developed, and maybe to decelerate overall in response to sustainability concerns and as developed standards of living become more widely shared.

The mainstream economic approach to the obvious reality of economic change is to idealise it as a process of steady state growth in which equilibrium is maintained but with production and other economic indicators growing at a constant compounding rate (as with compound interest at, for example, 10 per cent, turning $100 into $110, $121, $133.10, $146.41, etc. in successive years). Such steady state growth displays none of the characteristic turmoil of Schumpeterian-style competition and is indistinguishable from perpetual equilibrium, from one period to the next, apart from overall expansion. Relative scarcity, and the prices that reflect it, remain constant (save for the price of exhaustible resources which increases at the same rate as the rate of growth).

Within that approach, comparative dynamics consists of comparing different steady state growth paths and choosing the 'turnpike' path of optimal growth towards which policy makers, or in-built stable feedback processes in the economic system, guide progress.[11] If the initial or final state of the economy is inconsistent with optimal growth, turnpike theorems are about spending as much of the time as possible in between on the optimal growth path (just as you may drive quite a long extra distance between A and B in order to go most of the way on a fast motorway or turnpike – there are no time-wasting traffic jams on the turnpike of optimal growth theory!).

Time, Opportunity Cost, Present Value, and the Discount Rate

In Chapter 3 we sidestepped discussion of how to make comparisons between costs and benefits that arise at different points in time, and the question of inter-generational equity which is implicit in the process. But, with carbon dioxide a stock pollutant, and therefore a dynamic problem with time entering essentially into the nature of its analysis, we must now look briefly at some of the tools economists use when dealing with problems that involve time. In the process we shall also introduce the notion of opportunity cost which will come in useful (and will be seen to be akin to the option cost concept introduced at the start of the book, save for the latter's connotation in the context of sequential decision taking).

In choosing to spend our money in one way, or to employ productive resources in a particular activity, we forgo the opportunity to spend it on an alternative, next-best purchase or the opportunity to employ the resources on the next-best activity. Next best, since if it were better it would, under the economist's fundamental assumption of behavioural rationality, be the choice that we would actually take, and since the next-but-one best is, by the same token, irrelevant to the choice. The value of the next-best opportunity forgone is called the opportunity cost of the choice that is actually made.

When it comes to taking decisions involving cash flows at different points in time (typically investment decisions and decisions about the depletion of exhaustible resources but, in the present case, decisions about whether to add to the stock of polluting carbon dioxide in the atmosphere now or later) the existence of a capital market provides an alternative opportunity which is in principle generally available.

A perfect capital market implies that it is possible for anyone to shift their pattern of consumption backwards and forwards, in their lifetime pattern of earnings and expenditure, by borrowing money at a rate of interest that is the same for borrowers and lenders and is without limit as regards the amount borrowed and lent, subject to the individual's rational judgement of what is best for himself or herself.

With the assumption of a perfect capital market, the market rate of interest presents the opportunity cost of investment. Thus, if a project could earn more than the market rate it would be undertaken. And no project that could so earn would fail to be undertaken, since such failure would be an irrational loss of opportunity for profit (however much money is needed can be borrowed without hindrance and the borrowing repaid out of earnings from the project, with something over as profit). Similarly, no project that earns less than the market rate would be undertaken.

But real economic projects over time – whether investment, depletion or pollution – do not perform in the steady manner in which taking the universally available capital market opportunity, i.e. putting money in the bank, yields a steady flow of interest payments. To compare the lumpy cash flows of such projects with the capital market opportunity, economists employ the concept of present value, that is to say they convert all the cash flows concerned back to the present time (although any fixed date will do in principle) by means of compound interest calculations. Thus, with an interest rate of 10 per cent, $100 today is the same as $110 next year, $121 the year after, etc. If the interest rate is one per cent, the figures are $100, $101, and $102.01, etc.[12]*

Clearly the rate of interest that is used in present value calculations is crucial when long time intervals are involved. Any discount rate has a halving period – for instance, with a 10 per cent rate, $100 in seven years time is approximately $50 in present value terms ($51.32 to be more exact). At two per cent, the halving period is about 35 years, with 25 per cent it is about three years. The 'rule of 70' yields these approximate results, with the per cent rate of interest times the halving period equal to roughly 70 (the mathematically sophisticated reader will perceive that approximate exponential growth is involved, with the natural log of 0.5 equal to - 69.3 per cent).

The social rate of discount

Thus high rates of interest – say 12 per cent, such as may be typical of money markets, with a halving every six years, that is to say down to less than one-tenth in 20 years – mean that the future is heavily discounted. Given that the margin of accuracy for future cash flows (when engaged in, say, a choice of investments) is likely to be worse than 10 per cent, events more than a generation away are simply ignored. This is what economists mean when they say that market decisions tend to be short-sighted and prejudicial to the interests of future generations which are not represented in the market.

High interest rates naturally discourage investment projects because they raise the opportunity cost of investment generally. But, apart from the extent that the investor is persuaded simply to keep his money in the bank and to draw interest, they also introduce bias against long-term investments and in favour of short-term projects.

An important special case is a zero rate of interest, which yields an infinite halving period, and means that costs and benefits are no more or less important if they occur today or in a thousand years' time. In principle, a negative interest rate is conceivable, resulting in today's costs and benefits counting for less than the next generations.

Two ethical considerations apply, inter-generational equity and the democratic principle (based on social research that suggests that electorates expect governments to take responsibility for long-run decisions that are beyond the power of the individual to influence).[13] These, together with the practical reality that money markets are influenced by a variety of factors apart from investors' concerns to provide for their own future (and, by invisible hand reasoning, everybody's future), have led economists to search for a social rate of discount to be used in present value calculations related to long-run choices made in the public interest.[14]

In general such social rates of discount are set much lower than market rates of interest, typically between one and four per cent, depending on the expected rate of growth of per capita economic activity. This is on the grounds that a high rate of growth will leave our children better off than ourselves, and in that case, why should we give up more present consumption for their benefit than we would choose to do in order to provide for our own old age? For that is what is involved in long-run investments, devoting productive resources today to the production of capital assets that will yield more benefits in the distant future and less in the shorter run.

The social rate of discount is put higher when the expected growth rate is high, and lower if the future is stagnant. If a 'horrid' nature imposes a declining standard of living, a negative social rate of discount may be appropriate, to encourage a huge diversion of effort away from current consumption and into preserving a future for the next generation. Of course, the impact of such a discount rate, if transmitted into the money market, would destroy equilibrium. It would simultaneously discourage the saving needed to finance investment and encourage a significant surge of private sector investments (some of which might be wholly inimical to the interests of future generations). But there is no suggestion that such transmission should occur. The social discount rate is for deciding what should be done in the long-term public interest. The question of how the necessary savings should be induced is a separate matter, involving tax policy and government interventions in the financial system which might well drive up market rates of interest.[15]*

Discounting and the depletion of exhaustible resources
Idealising an exhaustible resource as a cake waiting to be eaten costlessly, on the lines originally proposed by economist Harold Hotelling in the 1930s,[16] its price and consumption pattern is influenced by the discount rate (or rate of interest in relation to decisions taken by a private resource owner in his own profit-maximising interest). The day before it is finished, its value will be the cost of the backstop technology that will replace it in satisfying consumer demand on the following day; say the cost of ethanol from fuel-wood on the day before stocks of petroleum are exhausted.

That value will be less a year earlier, on account of money market appreciation of the price over the interval, and less again the year before. In fact 'Hotelling's rule' states that the difference between price and cost (with cost equal to zero in the idealised case of 'cake eating') will rise at the rate of interest (discount rate for public interest analyses) until it reaches the backstop technology cost just when the resource is fully depleted.

Given that the quantity demanded is less at higher prices, the rate of depletion thus diminishes as the point of exhaustion is reached, until it matches demand at the price determined by the backstop technology and at the point in time when, with the exhaustible resource exhausted, the backstop technology has to take over. Prices today are thus lower at high (market-related) interest rates and higher at low social rates of discount.

Thus, as with encouraging investment for the long-run future, a low, socially-related, rate of discount for resource depletion decisions protects the interests of future generations in having a share in their use. It raises present prices and reduces present demand. In subsequent time periods it

Figure 6.1 The Discount Rate and the Price of an Exhaustible Resource

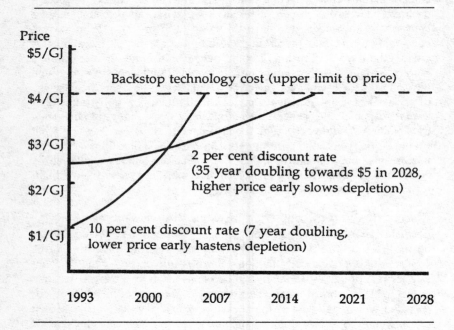

results in the price rising more slowly, till finally it reaches the backstop technology price later than the price profile corresponding to a high rate of interest. As illustrated in Figure 6.1, the two price profiles cross over. Thus a depletion path based on a low social rate of discount results in an earlier period in which prices are higher, reducing the amount consumed in the earlier period, and a later period when prices are lower, when the more that has been left over for the future is eventually consumed.

It does not follow that social decisions based upon a low social rate of discount result in low market rates of interest. Quite the contrary is the case, with the funding requirements of resource conserving investment squeezing financial markets and leading to high rates of interest and lower investment to meet growth of resource using consumption.

For instance, the slowly rising price profile of Figure 6.1 is not the price profile that would be charged by a private owner of the resource. Responding to money market rates of interest, he or she would price according to the more quickly rising price profile. The difference represents a royalty imposed by the government, which siphons funds out of the private sector, to be available for resource conserving investments. The idea that a low social rate of discount encourages growth and the exhaustion of resources to the disadvantage of future generations is thus fallacious:[17] a low rate of discount is a response to an expected low rate of growth, not a mechanism for securing a high rate of growth.

Policy Over Time

From a theoretical point of view, the essentially dynamic stock pollution nature of the global warming problem presents formidable difficulties. This is because the informational problems that have been discussed do not go away with a transition to dynamics. For the foreseeable future, and in relation to greenhouse gas emissions, we are saddled with ignorance regarding the damage function – and maybe for ever if long-run climate models turn out to be essentially chaotic. Fortunately we do not need to worry too much about that beyond taking a highly sceptical view of prescriptions based upon heavily theoretical optimal growth models.

Accordingly, the appropriate style of economics is the coarse economics of abatement targets, and their approximately efficient achievement in the context of the set of 'false prices' thrown up by the real world markets which actually exist, now and in the future. And in that context there are some quite benign aspects of a stock pollutant compared with a flow pollutant.

For instance, getting the tax wrong in relation to a flow pollutant results in irrecoverable damage in the time period concerned – too much abatement this year yields too great a loss of consumption goods otherwise producible, too little next year will recover the consumption goods but with above the recommended safe level of pollution and at lower marginal satisfaction (since produced additionally to the 'right' amount – we would rather have a car all the time than no cars this year and two the next). With flow pollutants, two wrongs don't make a right.

However, with a stock pollutant, slow progress towards a target can be made up later, possibly more efficiently as a consequence of 'learning by doing' in the meantime. Essentially a trial and error approach can be adopted towards achieving a target and, indeed, in the spirit of the Bayesian approach to uncertainty mentioned in Chapter 3, a trial and error approach towards deciding what the target should be can also be adopted. Of course, such an approach is not costless if the adjustments are made very late and need to be very sharp. One of the main points being made in this book is that the balance of probabilities is that the global system (climate-technology-development-demography-ecology) is well off-course and that prudence requires a stitch in time alteration of direction.

Policy consistency

In such an approach, the credibility of the procedure is critical. Very large and very long-term investment decisions will be made in response to the signals which emanate from it – decisions such as the motive power technology for the next generation of transportation, the role of electronic communication, the location of habitation, its dispersal in small-scale settlements or its concentration in further megalopolies, the global allocation of land use, etc., in addition to the decisions on the next generation of energy technology (and on research for the generation following) which are the focus of this book.

If economic agents do not believe in the announced policy direction, they will ignore the policy and private decisions will continue to be inconsistent with public objectives. For instance, the Amazon rain-forest will continue to be destroyed by fire and unsustainable agricultural processes unless the people involved are provided with incentives – both stick and carrot – to do otherwise, and believe that those incentives will be maintained over the time horizon appropriate to the decisions they are taking.

This problem of time inconsistency has been of great interest to economists in the context of pursuing credible macro-economic policies to secure acceptable levels of employment and inflation in a democratic political system.[18] It arises equally for developing countries seeking to attract inward investment with attractive tax packages which successor governments may fail to honour – the so-called 'sovereign risk' problem when looked at from the perspective of investors.

In the present context, this credibility problem can only be resolved at the international level by the application of sufficient economic power by a sufficiently large partial consensus of concerned nations, as suggested in Chapter 1. That, of course, is a necessary but not sufficient condition. The targets agreed and adopted by such a consensus must also, at the least, be arrived at – and adjusted in a Bayesian spirit – in a rational and transparent process so that a maximum of information is available to economic agents in making their long-run decisions.

Even so, credibility will not attach to a policy that is constantly being jiggled about in the light of the latest snippet of research into, say, the performance of blue algae in the Sargasso Sea. Nor to one that is so firmly nailed to the mast at a particular level or, in a dynamic context, a programme of levels for the years ahead, as to be unresponsive to changes of the prudent and considered view of the future.

Economists would call a policy 'perfect' which was announced in such a way that agents would expect its dynamic response to new information to be what it actually is, and what it actually is to be the best response possible in terms of an appropriate framework for decision-taking under uncertainty.[19] Private agents would then both believe in the policy and be guided by it to take their decisions, in the markets for investments and other long-term matters, in a way that is consistent with the announced policy.

Clearly policy perfection in the field of climate change and greenhouse gas emissions can only be achieved at the very general level of a reliable and consistent process of Bayesian adaptation. With the state of nature seen through a glass darkly, some degree of regret about past decisions is inevitable. However, the avoidance of mistakes, in the co-ordination of responses to the state of nature as it is perceived, can be aimed for with a credible policy openly arrived at.

Policies for controlling net emissions over time
The property rights approach is not much use in relation to carbon dioxide emissions: supposing a group of concerned citizens where I am writing in Palmerston North, New Zealand, want to stop carbon dioxide emissions by the South African Sasol plant that turns coal into vehicle fuel. The damage is causing concern here but the dirty deed is being done two continents away. We would have no standing in a South African court and Sasol would not appear in Palmerston North's District Court. Only governments can bring actions at the Hague International Court.

We have considered three possible instruments: regulation, taxes and permits which might be used for the trial and error dynamic achievement of long-run stock targets. Such a target might be 'getting back to the 1950 level by 2060', for instance. Having regard to the net emissions dimension implied by such a stock target, each instrument can be linked to carbon dioxide absorption activity. In a regulatory vein, a duty to use some proportion of renewable energy input might be imposed (as is being done with UK electricity suppliers). In a fiscal vein, absorption might be subsidised. In a permissory vein absorption offsets might be allowed.

The first of these would, again, contravene the least-cost theorem. There is no reason to suppose, for instance, that it is easy to locate the production of renewable (biomass) energy close to the coastal power station of our previous example. Being near an oil-refinery, it might well be in a heavily populated region where land is extremely valuable and cannot easily be spared for growing fuel-wood.

The high-sulphur coal-field which decided the location of the inland power station might, on the other hand, be found in a remote part of the country where land could easily be spared for fuel-wood crops and the necessary labour force available through retraining mine workers who otherwise could find no alternative employment in such an isolated community. Thus a regulation that each power station had to use, say, 20 per cent biomass fuel-wood would be very costly for the coastal power station, and therefore impose higher than necessary costs on consumers.

The second and third of the three possible regulatory instruments both face a possibly not very well-known price-quantity relationship, in the same way that taxes and permits face the private cost of different levels of abatement. Thus if absorption is subsidised, the quantity absorbed may be difficult to predict. And offsets may be uncertain as regards their impact on costs. An effective instrument will be designed both to make maximum use of market forces and to keep uncertainty to this necessary minimum. The TAO to be discussed in the next chapter avoids additional uncertainties arising from the agent-principal relationship that is involved.

System Effects in the Global Economy

Before moving on, to consider the application of economic theory to the problem of controlling the level of greenhouse gases in the atmosphere, we must briefly describe the kind of economics, different from that we have been discussing, which is employed when considering the behaviour of an economy as a whole.

The kind of economics discussed so far was stated to be 'the optimising framework which underlies the mainstream (neo-classical) economist's mental set'. While that type of economics is largely unquestioned as regards the analysis of what is called microeconomic behaviour – that is to say the behaviour of individual decision takers in a market situation – its validity in relation to the behaviour of the economic system as a whole, what is called macro-economics, is much more questioned. And its aggregation into heavily theoretical optimal growth models was indeed questioned above in relation to policy formation in a dynamic context.

The static 'snapshot' model of general competitive equilibrium provides a description of a 'blissful' outcome from the interactions between the millions of goods-consuming and productive factor-owning households and the hundreds of thousands of goods-producing and productive factor-using firms to which we referred earlier. Steady state growth then consists of the progressive (compound interest) enlargement of the general competitive snapshot, to yield a moving picture.

That snapshot is the flower of decades of intense intellectual effort to extend the mathematical rigour and logical consistency of the neo-classical analysis of the behaviour of individual agents into an all-embracing economy-wide system. It is a flower that has withered, as regards empirical plausibility, in the face of the variety of add-on assumptions that are required in order to handle the complexities of real world market failure discussed in Chapter 5, and the over-simplifications of human psychology that are introduced in order to render the model tractable to mathematical manipulation.[20*]   In the terminology of Lakatos[21] it has ceased to be a progressive research programme.

The neo-classical doctrine is questioned, in relation to macro-economics, on account of its failure to account either for the fluctuations of economic activity, with accompanying bouts of unemployment or inflation, which provide the newspaper headlines – sometimes unemployment and inflation – or for the variations in performance between nations, despite the common knowledge base available to all.

A milestone in modern thinking about these macro-economic phenomena was the 1936 publication of J.M. Keynes' *General Theory of Employment Interest and Money*. It was a milestone because it characterised the interacting behaviour of the markets for products, for labour services and for money in terms of systemic aggregate behaviour rather than as the behaviour of individual agents writ large. Moving away from the smooth convexities of our Chapter 5, where involuntary unemployment is inexplicable, the non-linear features of aggregate behaviour opened up a complex feedback system with more than one possible equilibrium and with scope for policy interventions to shift the outcome towards more desirable states.

The dynamics of Keynes' system have never been adequately absorbed by a profession conditioned to the comparative static mode of analysis. Controversies have raged over the theoretical basis – whether or not grounded in rational optimising behaviour – of the quasi-equilibria which his system can, subject to stabilizing policy interventions, maintain. Real world behaviour, featuring slow change in the institutional structures which constitute some of the parameters of this complex dynamic system, and shifts in the analytic perceptions, may eventually flip it into a different regime in (analogous fashion to Broecker's sharp jumps of the climate system which we quoted in Chapter 3).

One such shift of perceptions was the 1970's move away from the full employment management of overall economic activity, based upon the so-called IS/LM analysis of Keynes' system, which had fostered the 'golden age' of economic growth and prosperity post World War 2. Focusing on some loose ends of the IS/LM analysis, and feeding upon concern about inflation allegedly caused by the accumulated impact of government interventions (but in reality due more to the knock-on effects of the OPEC oil price increases), the monetarist analysis heralded both a reduction of full employment oriented interventionism and a slowing of economic growth amongst those countries which took the analysis most to heart.

Although it has seemed important to provide insight into the neo-classical economist's way of thinking, founded in the comparative statics of general competitive equilibrium, this book does not need to review the macro-economic story also. That is not needed since the root of the misperceptions that have arisen about the economics of global warming are to be found in neoclassical modes of micro-economic thinking. Even the much more limited story of the various attempts, some neo-classically inspired some not,[22] to model the system impact of measures to handle the global warming problem, would require whole chapters of explanation of macro-economics.

Such modelling includes sectoral models (of which the Appendix to this book describes a rather crude example related to the New Zealand energy sector) where the 'natural economic unit' assumption is that the side effects in the rest of the economy, from changes in the sector under consideration, are sufficiently small to be ignored. Where they cannot be ignored, macro-economic models are needed which fall into two broad groups.

Firstly there are econometric models which bring past statistical information to bear on the problem in a more extensive, rigorous, and efficient manner than any other. In doing so they are as firmly related to reality as can be and they make explicit the difficulties faced – be it the paucity of data appropriate to the consideration of so long term a problem as global warming, or the absence of experience of the workings of an economy changed by an effective response, for instance as in the GREENS scenario of technological transformation in the energy sector.

More useful in long-run studies are simulation models of the macro-economy which can be in the neo-classical optimising mould or follow the Keynesian tradition of characterising aggregate behaviour. The latter, modernised to examine the aggregate implications of market failure in a choice theoretic framework, can be designed to follow dynamic response in the economy, but they suffer from unreliability in their description of the longer term. It should also be mentioned that neither these nor any other economic model has been developed which provides reliable predictions of the behaviour of the global set of interacting markets and countries when policy coordination between governments is ineffective.

Despite that shortcoming, high level economic analysis of the global warming problem has been largely based upon looking at the system impact of carbon emissions taxes. Such a 'top down' approach is in principle to be preferred in terms of theoretical consistency and completeness of coverage. Unfortunately computational limitations impose a compromise between complexity of formulation in the global macro-models (in which policy coordination is, implausibly, implicit) and detail in the modelling of the energy and other greenhouse gas emitting sectors like transportation and agriculture.[23*] Additionally, the selection for these models of a carbon tax, as the assumed instrument of response, is based upon the least cost theorem which, we have seen, derives from one-market partial equilibrium analysis in the neo-classical tradition.

Thus there has, as was noted in Chapter 3, been a mismatch between the analysis used for the selection of instrument and that used for measuring its impact. In the presence of system effects, lower overall costs result if the alternative technologies are subsidised or forced by an appropriate policy instrument (e.g. a carbon tax dedicated to recycling activity, or the TAO to be described in the following chapter). Without such forcing there is an additional element of overestimation in the costs of response, although by no means so significant as that which results from technological myopia. An efficient instrument may knock a worthwhile fraction off the estimated cost of response, compared with a simple carbon tax, whereas an inappropriate technological choice may raise it by an order of magnitude.

Keynes wrote of the difficulty he had in breaking free from traditional modes of economic thinking, and the habit of invisible hand thinking may perhaps account for the misperceptions that have arisen from these high level economic analyses. For 'getting the prices right' – e.g. by taxing the externality – is, to the neo-classical economist, sufficient to yield an efficient outcome. Appropriate technologies, it would be thought, will be brought into play by such prices and the idea that unused technologies, unrepresented in models of the existing system, may have a crucial role that will be overlooked if such models are used for policy analysis, does not come easily. Still less the idea that, in order to minimise macro-economic system costs, such technologies may need to be forced by subsidy or the TAO, rather than induced by tax incentives.

Notes

1. Blinder, 1988.
2. I.e. Non-wasteful of opportunities to make anyone better off without making someone else worse off, given the particular distribution of spending power – as derived from ownership of the means of production, labour, capital, natural resources and entrepreneurial ability – that exists. Invisible hand theorising takes the question of the distribution of ownership of productive resources, and of the spending power that goes with it, as separable from the question of how those resources are allocated to most efficiently meet market demands. The distribution question is, of course, linked to the philosophical question, referred to in a previous note, of how to aggregate individual satisfactions into a social welfare function such as our social objection measure in Chapter 3. For practical purposes, the philosophical difficulties meet with political necessity as the mother of administrative invention. Such 'political'

decisions (deciding which of the possible 'bliss' points of the previous chapter – one for each possible distribution of spending power – is most socially desirable) provide a second rationale for the existence of government in a market economy, one which hopefully can be resolved by 'redistributive taxation' adequate to pay for the provision of the efficient supply of public goods.

3. Baumol and Oates, 1971.

4. Grabowski, 1990.

5. Tietenberg, 1988, Chapters 14-16.

6. Grubb, 1989, Chapter 5; Pearce, D. 1991.

7. The transactions costs problem of the property rights approach is, however, not wholly overcome. Certainly trades between potential emitters can be efficiently organised. But the problem of disseminated nuisance to, say, a large number of launderers partly remains. Group organisation is difficult to sustain and there is the temptation for individuals to 'free-ride' the efforts of others. On the other hand the burden of proof is eased – if they think that factory A is doing the dirty deed – as far as their own laundry is concerned; they can buy out that factory's emission right if the nuisance they experience is sufficient to overcome the factory's reluctance to sell. Of course they might be wrong, with the pollution coming from somewhere else. And they will be negotiating with a particular seller, not buying the permit on the open permit market, so the deal would involve the seller's agreement not to go out and buy another permit the next day. This could involve a very different price from the open market permit price and require protracted and expensive negotiations.

8. Lamarre, 1991.

9. Hoel, 1991.

10. Mathematically trained readers will recognise this as the second integral of the flow variable, with the stock being the first integral.

11. Jones, 1975, pp.214-24.

12. Obviously there is a mathematical formula for this sort of thing. If r is the rate of interest, assumed constant from period to period, a cash flow of amount C occurring t periods ahead has a value today, a present value of

$$PV = C/(1+r)^t.$$

Thus the present value of a cash flow of 100 dollars next year, 200 two years later and 250 a year after that is, with interest at 5 per cent:

$$100/(1.05) + 200/(1.05)^3 \ 250/(1.05)^4 = 62.33 \text{ approximately.}$$

13. Pearce, D. et al, 1989, p.149; Cline, 1992, pp.238-45.

14. Lind, 1982.

15. Optimal growth theory will have none of this – more investment means more growth with more national product from which more can be saved to fund more investment and yet more growth. The process is constrained only by private rational choices, mediated through a perfect capital market, regarding consumption now or consumption later. But that path, apart from its unreality, ignores problems of sustainability brought about by environmental damage. (Though, on the assumption that no exhaustible resource is essential – i.e. that there is a backstop technology for everything, and it's certainly bad news if the assumption is false! – it can handle the exhaustion of resources like oil, as we see below).

16. Hotelling, 1931.
17. Pearce, D. et al, 1989, p.150.
18. Holtham and Hughes Hallett, 1987, pp.130-2.
19. Ingham and Ulph, 1990, p.15.
20. Particularly the non-existence of so-called 'missing markets' that are required to handle time realistically, when account is taken of (calculable) risk, asymmetric information and the strategic behaviour of firms in imperfect competition. The existence of incalculable uncertainty, and plain ignorance, such as lies at the core of the global warming problem, and for which we developed a framework for rational decision taking in Chapter 3, is incompatible with the general competitive equilibrium approach, as is the continuous disequilibrium of technological innovation and sectoral transformation in energy markets which provides the basis for the response to global warming we have described in this book.
21. Lakatos, 1970.
22. Boero et al, 1991, pp.S7-S9.
23. As the modellers are often more familiar with the macro-economic theories that underlie the models than they are with detailed sectoral technology, the result is that logical consistency is pursued at the cost of relevant technological detail. But it is high level economics that has the ear of governments, so that policy making – such as that lying behind negotiations towards the FCCC – has been informed by misperceptions about the cost of response. For instance the global macro-models generally fail to incorporate carbon absorption technologies or carbon recycling sustainable fuel technologies, which this book shows can probably provide a low cost response.

7. The Economics of Controlling Greenhouse Gas Levels

We first describe the Tradeable Absorption Obligation (TAO) and discuss the dynamic time path for the assimilation of biomass into the commercial energy system which results from its progressive application and also what is meant by a net target in a dynamic context. Then we extend the TAO to a Tradeable Net Absorption Obligation, an extension which would be desirable if the TAO is applied at different levels in different countries. Finally we look at the way in which the costs of this response to the threat of global warming can be assessed in a partial equilibrium, neo-classical, framework and conclude the chapter with a discussion of the ways in which the picture might be altered by consideration of global macro-economic system effects.

The Tradeable Absorption Obligation (TAO)

It will be remembered from Chapter 1 that, as far as global warming goes, what is to be absorbed is greenhouse gases, and in particular carbon dioxide. Since there is *prima facie* likelihood that the supply elasticity of fuel-wood at acceptable costs is large,[1] the obvious place to look for a response to the global warming problem is in a market-oriented arrangement that is designed to induce the adoption of fuel-wood and biomass technology with minimal uncertainty of effect. This is precisely what the TAO is aimed at doing: forcing the uptake of these technologies at a rate prescribed by policy targets, with least cost secured through the tradeability of obligations.

The possible uncertainty is two-fold. There is the unavoidable market uncertainty of the technical relationships between fuel-wood production and cost at different levels of activity on a global scale, and between energy prices related to this backstop technology cost and the amount of economising behaviour and ambient energy technology implementation which is induced by such prices.

And there is the agent-principal problem (which applies equally to taxes on net emissions and to permits with absorption offsets) regarding the response of firms in the energy industries to the incentives provided. Although it is possible, on a best estimate of the technical relationship, for the policy makers, as principals, to set up a net tax scheme, or a permit with offsets regime, in order to encourage absorption, it does not follow that energy firms, as agents, will respond to those incentives in the way expected. For the kind of market to which the TAO is oriented is the dynamic Schumpeterian market of imperfect competition and strategic manoeuvring found in the energy sector of the real world, rather than the perfectly competitive model which provides the intellectual backdrop to many market-oriented prescriptions. Energy firms are involved in strategic relationships with each other, with their shareholders and other sources of capital, and with individual governments on an international basis in so far as they are multinational energy firms, which many are.

Accordingly, their response to incentives will be variable and, from a policy making perspective, opaque. In all likelihood it will also be muddled – it is a mistake to assume that managements are all-seeing and all-calculating in their decision-taking process. Given the stock-pollutant nature of the problem, inaccurate fulfilment of policy may not be very serious, since there can be adjustments in a later time-period, providing the adjustments are sufficiently well considered to avoid hurting the credibility of the control regime.

However, such uncertainties, to the extent they may be perceptibly unnecessary, are damaging to the credibility of any scheme through their potential for causing the policy path to be time-inconsistent in the sense described in the last chapter. Accordingly, an effective instrument will be designed not only to make maximum use of market forces but also to by-pass needless uncertainty.

What specifically is involved in the Tradeable Absorption Obligation (TAO) is that energy sellers, at the wholesale level, are required to absorb some proportion of the carbon that is emitted when their product is used by the purchaser, or to contract with other firms to carry out this obligation. The tradeability of the obligation, i.e. that it can be discharged by third party contractors or their sub-contractors in exchange for money payment (the direction of money flow depending upon who owns the biomass product and its value relative to the cost of production), means that the cost per ton of carbon emitted is the same for all emitters, thus achieving economic efficiency in terms of the least-cost theorem.[2*]

This obligation is imposed as a regulatory requirement and thereby avoids the agent-principal uncertainties of response to price signals – whether brought about by taxes or by tradeable permits. The justification for such a requirement is a traditional justification for government intervention in markets, that is the preservation of public safety. Energy firms may be required to sell a safe product in the same way as motor manufacturers have to sell cars that can be safely braked and pharmaceutical firms must safety test their products.

The danger against which protection is sought is global warming. It is not certainly happening, but neither is it certain that an unsafe car will kill anyone. Initially the level of absorption required would be quite low for practical reasons which we will come to. As regards the protection of the public aspect, the initial low level can be regarded as a low-premium insurance, appropriate to a possibly not great risk.

It is a premium that can be reduced if and when evidence is forthcoming that the risk is, in reality, not very great. In the more probable outcome that the risk is substantial – and maybe even very great – TAO premium can be stepped up until the scheme effectively becomes no longer an insurance against global warming. Instead it would become an on-going arrangement to control the level of carbon dioxide in the atmosphere (maybe to be extended to the control of other greenhouse gases, if ways could be found, as does not at present seem scientifically very likely). Otherwise it can be stepped up further so as to reduce – rather than simply stabilise – carbon dioxide levels, and compensate for rising levels of other greenhouse gases.

Impacts on energy firms' operations

The reason why this form of regulation does not contravene the least-cost theorem is that the regulation makes no direct impact on the actual operations of the energy firm concerned. The coastal power station of our previous discussion can burn low-sulphur fuel oil or high-sulphur fuel oil as it sees fit, under whatever scheme obtains for handling sulphur emissions. The inland power station can burn all the coal it needs to. The cost of the TAO per ton of carbon emitted is the same for each and the TAO therefore meets the requirements of the least-cost theorem. This cost, for each, is the least cost of growing additional fuel-wood somewhere in the world (i.e. the economist's marginal cost) in line with their TAO.

Of course their actual costs may be different because of bad management, and that difference will be passed on to their electricity consumers along with the cost or benefits of all their other bad or good management decisions. Thus the power of competition to operate on behalf of the customer, seriously palsied though the invisible hand may be in the energy sector, is undiminished by the impact of the TAO. Indeed it may be strengthened in so far as fossil fuel extraction is significantly subject to imperfections of competition, whilst barriers to entry in the fuel-wood production business can hardly be as great.

While an electric power supply utility would be regarded as the wholesaler, and therefore carry prime responsibility for discharge of the TAO in relation to electricity supplied, it would be open to its existing suppliers of fossil fuels to offer a product (either fuel-wood or fossil fuel certificated as being supplied on a TAO-discharged basis) which relieved the utility of its duty. The power of the utility to choose to provide and burn its own fuel-wood (or to contract with forestry firms somewhere round the world for the discharge of its TAO, should it choose to burn non-TAO-discharged fossil fuel) would provide additional elements of flexibility and competition within the energy sector.

The inwardness of the TAO mechanism is that the obligation to grow fuel-wood is incurred at the time the precursor fuel was burned (technically, when it was sold at the wholesale level, but inventory hold-up with fossil fuels is brief at the retail and consumer level). Accordingly the costs incurred in producing the fuel-wood are unavoidable from the perspective of the energy firm which is obliged to produce it. Consequently, as far as the energy firm is concerned, the fuel-wood, when it has been grown, is a free good in the economist's sense of zero opportunity cost. By zero opportunity cost is meant that no alternative productive opportunity was forgone in producing the fuel-wood since the resources so employed had to be employed in that way in order to discharge the firm's TAO, which was incurred when fuel was sold at an earlier time.

However, the production of fossil fuels does incur opportunity costs in terms of the actual men and machines employed to hew coal or drill for petroleum, and of the lost opportunity to consume the fossil fuels at a later time (bearing in mind that, with an exhaustible resource like oil, and unlike a renewable resource like biomass, what is consumed today must be taken away from what can be consumed later). Accordingly, given a choice between selling zero opportunity cost fuel-wood or positive opportunity cost fossil fuel, energy firms will sell the fuel-wood in order to minimise avoidable costs.

Of course, where fuel-wood is produced in very remote locations, chosen maybe because land is very cheap there, or because of environmental considerations, say the protection of steep hillsides from erosion, then its utilisation may involve substantial, and avoidable, transport costs. Then the in situ coal-making option may be selected, with energy firms continuing to supply more easily transported fossil fuels from low-cost resources like Middle East oil and Siberian natural gas.

And to say that the fuel-wood has zero opportunity cost does not mean that it costs nothing to use it, since doing so incurs a further TAO (to grow more fuel-wood to absorb the carbon dioxide emitted when the first lot of fuel-wood is burned). But burning fossil fuel involves both the cost of the TAO and the avoidable resource cost of getting the fossil fuel out of the ground.

Despite the additional degree of flexibility and competition mentioned above, the inside position of existing fossil fuel extracting firms, in the downstream processing and distribution of energy products, would leave them powerful players in the era of sustainable energy, with the ability to transfer their operations, and their sources of fuel-wood and/or traditional fuels, in a way that would not be available to new entrants into the business – say specialist forestry firms. The progressive pattern of biomass penetration into the energy market that is envisaged below leaves them with plenty of time to taper off existing commitments and to diversify into the new technologies. Given that their product has emerged as potentially dangerous, they can hardly expect a smoother ride.

The detailed working out of this pattern over time, and by geographical region, is the proper subject of an energy sector model such as might underlie an indicative planning framework for the globally coordinated implementation of GREENS and can certainly not to be undertaken in this book.[3*] Information sharing for such work is a commitment under the FCCC which has been accepted by North and South countries alike. This book is limited to seeing how such a model for New Zealand, albeit rather informal as described in the Appendix, works out dynamically, that is to say the pattern of changing fuel-wood availability over time. Multiplying by 1000, since New Zealand's carbon dioxide emissions are about one-thousandth of global emissions, gives a rough idea of the global impact.

The Dynamics of Net Emissions Targets

The notion of a net target immediately raises dynamic questions since biomass (i.e. plant life) takes time to grow, quite a long time in the case of some tree species under natural conditions. The GREENS concept involves the intensive growing of biomass and the calculations of its effect which have so far been worked out are based upon a known (backstop) technology for coppicing eucalypt species, as follows.

Consider a duty to absorb 100 per cent of 100 tons of carbon emitted in a particular year, as per Figure 7.1a. Using the figure of 52 per cent carbon per ton of wood (Table 4.3) this requires the growing of 192 dry tons of trees on 1.05 hectares at the rate of 21.33 tons per year, absorbing 11.11 tons for each of the following nine years, and yielding three 64-ton crops in years 3, 6 and 9 after year 0, the particular year in which the fuel is burned (Figure 7.1a). In the following discussion, implementation at some percentage rate in a particular year will be taken to imply a process proportionate to the above, commencing with the establishment of seedlings in the year in question (year 0).

It may be that further crops from a coppice can be taken at subsequent three-year intervals, with a saving due to spreading the costs of establishing the seedlings, but New Zealand experience with eucalypt coppicing does not extend further back than 1982. If it is necessary, after say 9, 12 or 15 years, new seedlings may be re-established upon the same ground. Or some long-period rotation of crops may be beneficial, with food crops or pastoral activity benefiting from the nutrients brought nearer to the surface by the deep-rooted trees.

Figure 7.1a 100 per cent Policy for One Year

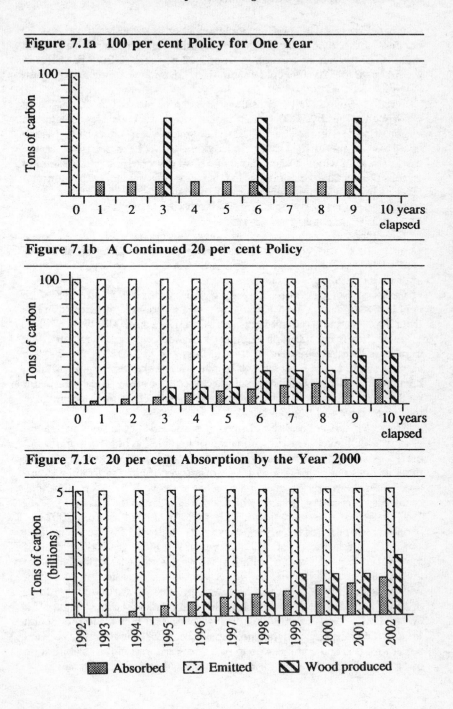

Figure 7.1b A Continued 20 per cent Policy

Figure 7.1c 20 per cent Absorption by the Year 2000

▨ Absorbed   ▨ Emitted   ◨ Wood produced

Next, Figure 7.1b, consider implementation at a constant level, say 20 per cent, rather than 100 per cent for just one year. This implies a gradual build-up of the rate of absorption from 2.22 per cent (=20/9 per cent) in the first year to 20 per cent per annum from the ninth year onwards (Figure 7.1b).

Finally, Figure 7.1c, consider the achievement of a 20 per cent absorption target by 2000 (which happens to have been New Zealand's target prior to signing the FCCC), i.e. seven years after 1993 (which could, when the analysis was undertaken,[4] have been regarded as the earliest year in which it was practicable to start such a policy). Assuming 20 tons per hectare per annum as in Chapter 4, this entails, with a constant level of implementation, planting approximately

0.2 x 192 tons per year x (1/7) / 20 tons per year per hectare
= 0.27Ha annually from in 1993.

Given the mismatch between the nine-year coppice cycle and the seven years to 2000, this would lead to overshoot with stabilisation at 20 per cent x 9/7 = 27.4 per cent absorption by 2002 if the policy is continued after the target date is reached.

Crops of fuel wood of 16.2 tons arise in 1996, 1997 and 1998, with double that amount in the following three years and three times the tonnage from 2002 on. Land requirements reach 2.43Ha from 2001 (Figure 7.1c).

Scaled up from 100 tons to global emissions of six billion tons, this implies a land requirement of 146 million Ha in 2001, or around the amount suggested in Chapter 4 to be available in the temperate Northern hemisphere, without displacing sub-Arctic conifer areas. Hence the claim made in the Chapter 4 scenario that the initial action need not involve intrusive activity in tropical areas.

However, it is not realistic to envisage a sudden start to implementation at such a high level. The dissemination of knowledge of how to carry out the intensive coppicing of eucalypts or other species on such a scale requires time, as does the propagation of seedlings (even if cloning techniques are used). Furthermore the question of what to do with the 97 million tons of low-grade eucalypt biomass which would appear on the market in 1996, 1997, 1998, double quantities in 1999 to 2001 and treble from 2002 on, is one which requires a learning curve to be followed for the answer.

For these reasons, practical policy requires a more gradual build-up of the level of implementation, with likely overshoot of any particular target level in the years following the target year. Such overshoot is consistent with an assumption that targets represent progress towards a higher level of achievement as regards reducing carbon dioxide emissions. Figure 7.2 graphs policy level, carbon dioxide absorption and fuel-wood production for a particular policy which approximately passes through the 20 per cent target for 2000 and continues on to two thirds absorption (i.e. stabilisation of net emissions, allowing for one-third natural absorption) by 2015.

The data for Figure 7.2 are in Table 7.1, which in turn is a thousand-fold replication of the data for policy 5 from the New Zealand Appendix (since, as mentioned, NZ emissions, are about 0.1 per cent of global carbon dioxide emissions). It may be noted that, with expected increases in the price of oil, the cost of this policy, in New Zealand, works out at an average increase in relevant fuel costs of around 10 per cent, peaking around 17 per cent in 2005.

Taking account of the macro-economic impacts would alter the cost a little, but not sufficient to upset the general picture.

Figure 7.2   Stabilising the Level of Carbon Dioxide in the Atmosphere by the year 2020

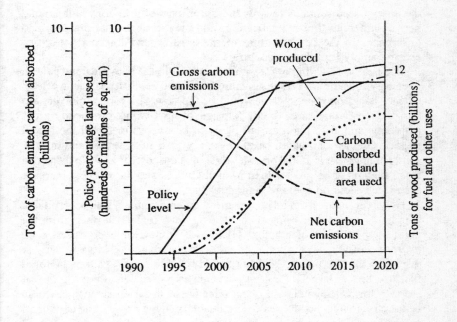

However, this can only be a very approximate representation of the global impact of implementing GREENS since there are dimensions of national variation to be expected in calculating the effects in different places. These arise both from differences in growing conditions, from differences in what may be the best way to dispose of the woody biomass produced (both as regards the use of most of it in different ways within

Table 7.1 Policy Level, Carbon Dioxide Absorbed and Wood-fuel Produced

	Policy level per cent	Carbon dioxide emission billion tons	Carbon dioxide absorption billion tons	Land area million km^2	Fuel-wood produced billion tons
1995	10	6.3	0.1	10	0.0
2000	35	6.3	1.0	100	0.8
2005	60	7.0	2.7	270	3.9
2010	75	7.5	4.6	460	7.7
2015	75	8.1	5.7	570	10.6
2020	75	8.4	6.1	610	11.9

the energy sector and as regards the use of part of it in conventional and new commercial timber applications and maybe some coal making) and differences in the cost structure of the existing and forecast pattern of energy supply in different countries.

The heavy weighting of transportation fuels in the New Zealand pattern of energy consumption results in more fuel-wood being used in the wasteful ethanol backstop process than would be the case on average globally, so that the cost, land area used, tonnage of fuel-wood produced, gross emissions and absorption are all likely to be overestimates of the global impact. On the other hand, baseline energy costs in New Zealand may be a little high *vis-à-vis* global price levels so that the cost offset from displaced fossil fuels may be greater than in many places and the net cost increase accordingly less on average than globally.

However, apart from its benign growing environment (but less suitable than hotter and wetter tropical countries), New Zealand suffers (from the point of view of implementing GREENS) from a high dependence on hydro-electricity, a resource of natural gas that has already largely displaced the use of coal and, as already mentioned, a pattern of fossil fuel use that is largely for transportation purposes (entailing the use of biomass for inefficient liquid fuel production at an earlier stage than would be the case in many countries). These factors suggest that some countries, particularly those which are more heavily dependent upon imported oil for their general energy needs, would find it even cheaper than New Zealand to convert their energy sector economies to substantial dependence on biomass raw material over the next few decades.

It should also be mentioned that an assumption was made, for the New Zealand calculations reported in the Appendix, that economising behaviour and ambient energy technologies will jointly stabilise effective demand for fuel products (whether derived from fossil fuels or from the biomass fuels that displace them). While this may be reasonable for slow-growth New Zealand, it may be more difficult to achieve globally without a very active process of energy technology transfer to the expanding and developing South economies.

Variation in application between countries

If more than a token impact is to be made upon the level of carbon dioxide concentration in the atmosphere, the supply of low-quality woody biomass would be large in relation to the annual global demand for conventional forest products. For instance, the yield by 2020 would be 12 billion tons compared with current forest product demand around one billion tons.[5] No use for such a volume of woody material can be envisaged save as an energy raw material input to the industrial system, which is why the focus of Chapter 4 was on energy technologies that can make use of biomass inputs.

Nevertheless, some proportion of the woody crop could find higher value application, as pulp for paper making, and in the manufacture of various composition boards and other timber substitutes in the construction and furnishing industries. In doing so, GREENS would not only be remedying the global warming problem but also providing a substitute for the depletion of natural forest which is also, of course, a major global environmental concern.[6*]

The extent to which this would occur would vary with the local situation, the state of development of the forestry industry and of industry based on forest products, and the extent to which local demands are met from overseas. However, it may be noted that conventional forestry supplies are often highly wasteful in terms of fractions left behind as logging residues which rot down partially to methane, a worse greenhouse gas than carbon dioxide. (On the other hand, in conventional timber applications, the period of time for which carbon is sequestered is greater, in some cases very much greater, than is the case for use as fuel wood).

Thus, apart from helping to meet concerns about dwindling stocks of virgin forest globally, and the particular concern about wildlife habitat destruction, the partial displacement of conventional forestry by joint production of fuel-wood and timber substitute would have an extra beneficial impact on global warming through the reduction of wasteful conventional forestry practices. Not commercially wasteful, it should perhaps be said, but the consequence of cost-effective production (with environmental externalities left out of account) in the often rugged terrain in which conventional forestry is conducted, where it is usually profitable to extract only the most valuable logs.

A further element of local variation results from different patterns of fuel demand. Some countries are well endowed with hydro-electricity, others have a heavy dependence on industry, others again depend upon fossil fuel imports and can, perhaps, easily switch to lower carbon content inputs such as natural gas (Table 4.3) whilst some, like New Zealand, use fossil fuels mostly for transportation.

The opportunity to switch to natural gas is particularly important in Europe, where a large shift in the pattern of primary fuel consumption would result if outdated Cold War restrictions on the pipelining of natural gas from Siberia were to be lifted. The obsolescent European coal industry can be scaled down very rapidly, if the will to do so exists, with elimination of the acid rain problem. Furthermore, in the post-Communist period, it is better to establish sensible commercial relationships with former Soviet Union countries than to get into a pattern of food charity.

Each such variation in national energy system has an impact upon how easy it is to make use of fuel-wood in the domestic system and upon the incentive to discharge the TAO at a distance with resulting fossil fuel displacement in other countries than that in which the duty is incurred. In principle market forces can be expected to ensure that the international trade in TAOs, and in energy products, will result in a low-cost outcome globally. In practice the outcome may be less satisfactory for one or other of the many possible reasons for market failure. In responding to this problem, global arrangements under the FCCC, for co-ordinating indicative energy planning at the national level, can obviously play an important role.

However, an appreciation of these complications further explains why this book must be restricted to portraying the global effect as New Zealand's writ large. The global process of indicative energy planning that may develop under the FCCC will need to take account not only of these between-country variations but also of the different behaviours of different energy firms. The costings that have been worked out for New Zealand are based on an informal model of biomass technology diffusion, driven by the TAO, and have not been optimised to minimise costs. It represents no more than a first approximation of how GREENS could work out in practice in that country, and is a marker for the planning needed worldwide.

The Meaning to be Attached to a Target

We may now clear up some ambiguity in the definition of a net target, that is to say in what it means to claim that, for instance, a 20 per cent reduction in net emissions has been achieved in the year 2000.

Since woody biomass, as a raw material, has a different energy/carbon ratio than other energy raw materials, its use as an energy raw material affects the level of carbon dioxide emissions for a given level of final energy demand and a given structure of technological conversion (from crude heat energy released by the energy raw materials, whether renewable or exhaustible in origin, through to retail energy products – gas by pipe, electricity by wire, petrol by pump, etc.) As we saw in Table 4.3, woody biomass has a carbon energy ratio of 0.026 t./GJ, compared with 0.014, 0.020 and 0.025 t./GJ for gas, oil and coal respectively, so that the use of woody biomass as an energy raw material raises the level of gross carbon dioxide emissions, particularly to the extent it displaces natural gas.

Moreover, with the conversion of woody biomass into a portable fuel, a much less efficient process than the refining of crude oil, additional emissions of carbon dioxide result for a given final demand. On the other hand, the use of some proportion of the fuel wood crop in substitution for conventional timber means that extra carbon dioxide has been absorbed for a given displacement of fossil fuel.

In the light of these complications we note there are (at least) four candidate ways of defining a net target, viz:

1. The policy level in the year of the target which, although likely to be quite different from what is achieved in that year, depending on how long the policy level has been in operation, does represent the proportion of that year's emissions that will eventually be absorbed as a result of that year's policy.

2. The proportion of actual gross emissions in the year that is in fact absorbed in that year – if gross emissions have been substantially increased because of the use of fuel wood (particularly in lieu of natural gas and/or as a portable fuel) this could mean that net emissions have hardly been reduced at all, or even that they may have increased.

3. The reduction in net emissions, i.e. gross emissions net of absorption, as a proportion of predicted emissions based on a forecast of business as usual energy development, i.e. assuming no GREENS and no TAO (or other policy measures).

4. The reduction in net emissions relative to emissions in some initial year, say 1990 – either net or gross, since they are the same thing prior to the introduction of GREENS.

In relation to Figure 7.2 and the data in Table 7.1, and considering the year 2005 in relation to 1990 as a base year (when emissions, net and gross are taken to have been 6.3 billion tons), the four measures are:

(1) 60 per cent,
(2) 2.7/7.0 = 39 per cent,
(3) taking 8b.tons for predicted 2005 B.a.U. emissions,
      $(8 - (7 - 2.7))/8 = 46$ per cent,
(4) $(6.3 - (7 - 2.7))/6.3 = 32$ per cent

Of the four, the last is preferable on grounds of greater ease of verification and reduced scope for manipulating forecasts of levels of emission for political purposes. However, given the expectation of continuing economic growth, particularly in South countries, it will be recognised to be the most severe definition, leading to less numerically impressive targets. Furthermore, given the variation of circumstances between countries, both as regards the energy sector and conventional forestry, not to mention climatically, a given target may be harder to achieve in some countries than others. Comparisons of net targets thus need to be done carefully, having regard to the manner of definition, *inter alia*.

Efficient Emissions Reduction

At this stage we turn to a problem that arises when there are different targets for different countries. We have mentioned that the FCCC commits developed countries of the North to more, by way of controlling net emissions, than is required of the South, and in the next chapter we will discuss an elaboration of this differentiation. But whatever its merits, it flies in the face of the least-cost theorem, whether or not adjusted to allow for macro-economic system effects. For instance, it is likely to be greatly more cost effective for already highly energy-efficient Japan to spend its money on reducing emissions in energy-inefficient China than to take highly sophisticated measures to improve its own system further.[7*]

The focus of this book has been on net targets and, in particular – rather than reducing gross emissions – on increasing absorption through applying an economic instrument, the TAO, which achieves least-cost absorption. It has been argued that the curbing of fossil fuel consumption would be induced by rising energy prices and by effective exhortation based upon the breakdown of institutional and informational barriers which currently inhibit economising behaviour. And it was suggested that the public's response would take impetus from the effectiveness of parallel absorption activity on the supply side of the energy market. However, net targets can involve reduced emissions as well as increased absorption, and nothing has yet been said about the non-least-cost inefficiency on the emissions side, of the China-Japan variety just mentioned.

Indeed, under the FCCC as signed at Rio, such inefficiency would be pervasive given that the developed countries, committed to limiting emissions to 1990 rates, are already rather highly energy efficient whilst energy technology that is inefficient (and often seriously damaging in its local pollution impact) is often employed in other parts of the world. Thus, under emissions targets that are likely to be acceptable in the South, a great deal of rather costly reduction in fuel consumption – and hence reduction of emissions – may go on in the North, with very little in the South, where it would be quite cheap.

Under the arrangement for implementing GREENS by way of the TAO that has so far been discussed, a considerably better, but still unsatisfactory, result would emerge. There would be developed countries engaging in reducing fuel consumption and hence gross emissions by raising efficiency in use up to the point where the cost is no longer lower than the cost of increased absorption. At that point, determined by the world price at which TAOs are exchanged in the market for TAOs, they would meet the rest of their target by absorption, initially in temperate regions in the North but later in a world market.

At the same time, South countries with no more than a best endeavours commitment may rest content upon modest improvements to their energy efficiency, and with reducing the rate of growth of their emissions, at costs which never reach the threshold of the world absorption cost. (Economically trained readers will recognise that these costs are to be taken in the sense of marginal costs per unit of carbon dioxide emitted or absorbed.) Thus it would remain the case that opportunities for low-cost emissions reduction would be wasted in any country where the cost of emissions reduction remains lower than the world price for absorption.

Consider again the case of China and Japan. In all likelihood, in view of the low costs of coal production in China (and therefore locally high opportunity cost of using fuel-wood), China's rather lenient commitment would be achieved by somewhat less inefficient fossil fuel utilisation, with the cost of biomass substitution not nearly reached. Japan might then find it more economic to meet its own target by paying for a further raising of the efficiency of fossil fuel use in China, before it began to think about intensive fuel-wood production either in Japan, China or anywhere else.

This however raises the mechanism by which the TAOs incurred by Japanese firms could be discharged other than by absorbing carbon dioxide. For, while we have been discussing what China or Japan might be doing, this is inconsistent with the market-oriented nature of the TAO mechanism. It is for firms located in China and Japan to achieve these results as the outcome of the incentive provided by the TAO. The two governments merely set the policy level for the TAO in their own country, in accordance with their commitments under the FCCC.

Tradeable net absorption obligations

An appreciation of this point, however, makes it immediately clear how market forces can achieve the efficient result. A Japanese firm with a TAO to discharge, and finding the cheapest way available to it for reducing net emissions to be the reduction of emissions in a Chinese factory (rather than increased absorption at the world price for TAOs or attempting further efficiency increases in its own factory) could apply for permission for its TAO to be discharged in that way. Indeed, the TAO could, as its normal mode of operation, treat emissions reductions as tradeable *pari passu* with increased absorption and thus ensure that the least-cost theorem applied evenly as regards emissions and absorptions on a global basis.

TAOs would simply become Tradeable Net Absorption Obligations (TNAOs – but we shall use TAO, leaving the 'N' to be understood).

This would ensure there were no isolated places where low-cost opportunities for emissions reduction were being neglected because the local target for net emissions reduction happened to be so undemanding that the threshold of absorption costs had not been reached. Thus a Japanese firm could contract to supply a new, high-efficiency power station to the Chinese system, with demonstrable reductions in the overall use of fossil fuel by the Chinese economy. The question as to whether a new fossil fuel-efficient power station in China, supplied by Japanese firms, counts towards China's target or towards Japan's, then simply turns upon how it is paid for.

If it is paid for by the Chinese electric power company, under whatever finance is available to it – either within the financial mechanism set up under the FCCC, Article 11, or otherwise – then it counts towards China's target and is reflected in China's electricity price. If it is paid for by a Japanese firm in discharge of a TAO incurred as a consequence of its activity in Japan, then it counts towards Japan's target and puts up energy prices in Japan.

To complete the picture, if it is paid for by a Japanese firm in discharge of a TAO incurred by that firm's Australian subsidiary (or subcontracted from an Australian coal firm in which the Japanese firm might or might not have a shareholding) then it counts towards Australia's target (and, ultimately, it would be Australian consumers of energy that face the higher price in that case – unless it was Australian coal to be exported to Taiwan, when it would be Taiwanese consumers that paid and the target that was counted towards would be Taiwan's). We mention these possible complications to illustrate what will be taken up later – that accountability and monitoring are complicated and substantial tasks. The upshot of these arrangements would be that market forces would eventually exhaust all the opportunities for low-cost emissions reduction. South countries would first finance the achievement of their own not very onerous commitment, on whatever funding basis is available to them, and then benefit from having their energy system up-graded at the expense of consumers in some other country. Eventually the opportunities for low-cost emissions reduction would become exhausted. In the process the South country would have benefited from the technology transfer which was so much a concern of South governments at the Earth Summit.

Then the decision as to whether to reduce emissions or increase absorption, which would face all firms with the TAO operating globally, would be decided on the basis of the backstop cost of biomass absorption activity. The potential of economising behaviour and of ambient energy technology for low-cost reductions in emissions would be taken up wherever opportunity arises, with fuel-wood or other biomass production activity then expanding into whichever location worldwide is the cheapest remaining available.

As the cost of absorption rises in the long term, with increased demand for land, so would the incentive for reducing gross emissions, and for the introduction of advanced renewable energy technologies, also increase. With the TAO inducing firms to seek out the most effective place worldwide for the discharge of their obligation, such advanced technologies would be spread globally by the most innovative firms, rather than spreading only by the slower mechanisms of market-induced technological diffusion.

The 'Cost' of Energy Environment Sustainability

Although we have argued that GREENS provides a low-cost response to global warming, we have not claimed it to be a no-cost response and we must consider how the costs arise before going on, in the next chapter, to consider the political economy aspects, which largely revolve around the question of who pays. For some it may not be a cost at all. In many countries with small reserves of fossil fuels and facing the prospect of rising oil import bills later this decade, the production of biomass energy raw material can provide escape from a mounting burden on their future economic prosperity. For others, facing rising extraction costs, with secondary and tertiary recovery techniques needed to eke out supplies from older oil fields, biomass will become economically competitive within the timespan of our 30-year scenario.

However, with the impact of increasing quantities of biomass upon the market for oil, the price of oil will not rise as fast as it otherwise might be expected to, and there may thus appear to be more of a cost than there is in reality, compared with an alternative business as usual scenario with continued reliance on fossil fuels. Essentially, with a major shift in energy trading patterns, prices at the margin would not be a good guide to intra-marginal costs.[8*]

Measuring the burden
The nature of the calculation involved in quantifying the burden can be seen from consideration of Figure 7.3 which illustrates the computations for the New Zealand results reported in the Appendix. The upper panel shows quantities of fossil fuels, with the upper line representing what would be extracted in order to meet demand that rises in line with business-as-usual economic growth, in the absence of global warming worries and in the absence of alternative technologies. The middle line represents what would be extracted on a business-as-usual basis given the natural pace of development of alternative energy technologies, and the

lower line what would be extracted under an ambitious net emissions reduction programme, implemented efficiently, e.g. through the TAO. Although vast reserves of fossil fuels, mainly coal, have been proved – perhaps at the behest of enthusiastic governments, unmindful of the possibility of technological obsolescence – it is the difference between the middle and lower line that represents TAO-induced substitution of fossil fuels by biomass, and which is relevant to the computations.

Figure 7.3 The Cost of Doing Without Coal

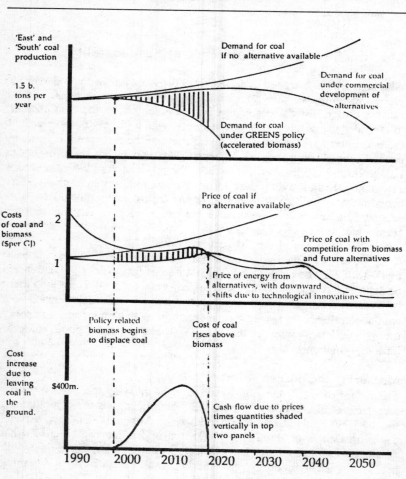

In the centre panel one curve shows the per unit cost of extracting fossil fuels. The essential difference between countries where what in Chapter 1 we called 'the burden of history' arises and other countries, where the burden is negligible, lies in the starting point for this curve, which may be at $2 per GJ, $1.5 per GJ or even $1 per GJ ($60 down to $30 per ton of coal). West Europe, where coal reserves are substantially depleted, and the bulk of South countries which have no commercial fossil fuel, may be regarded as having a starting point above $2 per GJ – oil at $150 per ton is about $3.5 per GJ, but leading to lower prices for heavy fuel oils as explained in Chapter 4. In the absence of alternative technologies, the fossil fuels cost rises, in line with the usual assumption that a profit-maximising industry will extract the more easily got and therefore cheaper reserves first, delaying expenditure on more costly reserves until it becomes necessary. In terms of our outline of Hotelling's resource depletion theory towards the end of Chapter 6, successively more costly resources constitute the backstop for earlier exploited resources, with the price rising in a series of interest rate related steps. But in practice many different reserves are being exploited at the same time and the over-lapping steps get averaged out into a rising trend.

A second curve shows the per unit cost of renewable sources of energy. This cost first falls to represent technological advances by innovative entrepreneurs discovering the possibilities of the newly available sustainable energy system described in Chapter 4, and then rises slowly, to represent the rising opportunity cost of land for fuel-wood production (i.e. the effect of competition for land from food production and from recreational uses). In later decades it drops in steps to represent technological advances in non-biomass renewable energy sources such as photovoltaic cells. Again the starting point is variable, depending upon growing conditions, and low costs depend upon plant for the various biomass fuelled applications technologies being located close to the growing area.

The third cost line represents the cost of fossil fuels given the existence of alternative sustainable technology. Reserves are exploited more slowly and only the more easily extracted portions of reserves are economic to produce. The cost of extraction is constrained by the competing supply to a margin which represents the users' cost savings in sticking with the existing technology and thereby avoiding the costs of re-equipment.

There is an element of history dependency in this curve in that global warming provides a stimulus to the early development of renewable energy technology, without which some currently uneconomic fossil fuel reserves might have become economic to exploit before long-run cost competition from renewable energy technology led to the ending of fossil fuel extraction. Also, the cost curves are open to policy intervention, in terms of the direction of research expenditures for instance. A completely horrid state of nature could see huge resources diverted to avoiding catastrophe – *inter alia* by pushing the advanced alternative technologies.

If science and the future show the current global warming concerns to have been well founded, the delayed development of the renewable technology would be a mistake, and it can hardly be appropriate to measure costs in relation to reserves that could have been used only by mistake. If science comes up with a more optimistic prognosis, precautionary expenditures on accelerating the take-up of biomass fuels would constitute the option cost of the 'be prepared' approach advocated in this book. However, the reader will recollect from Figure 7.2 that the level of activity in the 'learning by doing' phase of the 1990s is relatively low, with the expenditures that represent this 'option cost' correspondingly small.

The bottom panel shows the cash flow stream represented by the difference in resource costs, up to the point in time when fossil fuels become more costly than renewable fuels (shaded in the middle panel) multiplied by the loss of sales volume (shaded in the lower panel). This represents the pattern of costs imposed by progressively abandoning the use of fossil fuels in favour of sustainable technology. Clearly it is a burden which passes through a peak and may be expected eventually to tend to zero.

These diagrams only convey the principle of the calculation. Fossil fuels have different values in different places, depending on the purposes to which they are put. Fossil fuels production also is open to technological advance. And fossil fuels production resources, particularly labour resources, can be redeployed more easily in some places than others, thus affecting the fossil fuel's opportunity cost.

More importantly, the successful development of South countries will see the wage costs of fossil fuel technologies, e.g. mining wages, rise along with the rural wages relevant to biomass production. On the other hand, alternative technologies can be more easily deployed in some places than others. And there are some applications where the special characteristics of high grade fossil fuels are particularly valuable and where it may be more sensible to continue to use fossil fuels and to grow the fuel-wood elsewhere for coal making, rather than to try to substitute entirely for fossil fuels in all applications.

The Global Macro-economics of GREENS

We noted at the end of the previous chapter that theoretical consistency and completeness of coverage require the impact of GREENS to be considered in the context of a macro-economic system analysis, rather than the single fuel market context (partial analysis in economists' jargon) that has been used in the previous section. As we implied, when remarking in the previous chapter that they implausibly assume policy coordination between nations, the models of the global macroeconomy that have so far been constructed do not take account of political economy. In the absence of a model of the partially coordinated macro-economic muddle of the real world, any discussion of the system effects of GREENS can only be couched in the most general terms.

In that spirit we now employ a broadly Keynesian perspective to re-examine the assumption made in passing in Chapter 6, that we would take the level of involuntary unemployment – and the macro-economic policies from which it results – as given. We will discuss the impact upon employment and inflation, both in the North and the South, of a linked long term programme of global redevelopment, connected with a shift towards reliance on biomass as the basic energy raw material

As we shall see below, there is reason to suppose that the implementation of GREENS would provide a stimulus to the global economy. A renewal of economic prosperity on these lines must clearly be in a different direction from that of traditional economic development. Our new understanding of the ecological relationship between human society and its environment imposes the constraint of sustainability and lends urgency to the notion of redevelopment – i.e. development which cleans up the mess of the past rather than forever developing new greenfield sites. While it may be an exaggeration to say there are no open spaces left, they have become a scarce resource.[9*]

Without going into the sophisticated choice theoretic approach of modern Keynesians, the principal insight introduced by Keynes is summed up in the aphorism that, in an underemployed economy, 'demand creates its own supply'. Thus, in the circular flow between households and firms (households buying goods from firms with income got from selling factors of production to firms) the injection of additional demand – for instance by the government paying more people to teach in the schools – has a multiplier effect. After paying taxes and putting a bit by for a rainy day, the teachers spend most of their new-found income on consumption goods. But such spending becomes revenue to the various firms selling goods to the teachers, which pay their workers (and newly hired workers) for making the goods, who then go out and spend the money again, or most of it, thus providing yet more income to firms, and so on. Providing that not all marginal income is spent, the circular process stabilizes with the level of employment and global income and expenditure higher than previously by some multiple of the original government injection.

This leads on to the idea of a balanced budget multiplier, with increases in government spending, even when fully offset by additional taxation, having the effect of increasing total activity in a country. This is because government spending directly increases demand for goods and services whereas increases in taxation are partly offset by reductions in saving –

what was previously a voluntarily saved diversion of spending power in part becomes a diversion that is forced by taxation.

If the world economy were one, the impact of GREENS, imposed as a once-for-all measure could be summarised as that of a tax-financed public works programme combined with a redistributive shift of personal income from the rich North to generally less well off wage earners in the South. In an initial situation of under-employment, its comparative statics impact could be analysed as a balanced budget multiplier process, with a broadly stimulating effect, to which could be added some additional stimulation from the higher spending propensity of the less well off. And, in terms of normative distribution theory (which seeks to take account of the diminishing marginal value of income) a gain in welfare on account of the redistribution of income.

However, the world economy is an interacting set of national economies, most of which have individual currencies, and each of which would be differently affected by GREENS. Rich countries in temperature zones burn most of the fossil fuels whereas the hot wet climate, best suited to rapid rotation fuel-wood cropping, is mostly located in poor and populous regions. For convenience we shall for the moment assume that GREENS is implemented by way of a Dedicated Carbon Tax (DCT), rather than by way of the TAO or net TAO that have been described.[10*] The macro-economic impact is not greatly different and this simplification casts GREENS into the conventional macro-economic policy categories of taxation and government expenditure, thus making it easier to consider the impacts on activity that would result from its adoption.

We can usefully consider the orders of magnitude involved. The cost of growing enough wood to absorb present carbon dioxide emissions, of about five billion tons carbon annually, would be about $400 billion a year. (As we shall see in the next Chapter, such a scale of operations confers a second, and overwhelming, advantage to the TAO, *vis-à-vis* the DCT – or auctioned tradeable permits with dedicated revenues – in addition to the avoidance of agent-principal uncertainties that has been mentioned). How much would actually go to the country where it is grown is open to debate. The wood would have value, so how much needs to be paid depends upon who owns the wood when it is grown.

Nevertheless, starting with this broad order of magnitude, assume that much new growing capacity would, in the long run, be in tropical countries such as Brazil, India, Indonesia, Nigeria and other countries where former tropical forest land is now going to waste or being used inefficiently. To a lesser extent, but earlier on in a global transition to biomass as outlined in the Chapter 4 scenario, other large but less climatically suitable countries such as the USA, Canada, the Russian Federation and Australia would play a part, depending on the timing, intensity and cost-effectiveness of tropical countries' involvement. How this tree growing activity would be shared between particular countries is obviously to be determined by market forces. But suppose that one tenth of the activity fell to each of Brazil, Indonesia and Nigeria, all of which have lost large areas of tropical forest and presumably have suitable land available. This would imply payments, essentially from the industrialised countries, to each of those countries of about $40 billion each year. That would compare with the present levels of exports of goods and services annually from those countries of respectively $40 billion for Brazil, $20 billion for Indonesia, and $3 billion for Nigeria.[11]

Obviously this represents the resolution of the debt repayment problem in so far as it affects the first two countries. As regards Nigeria, which we think of as one of the largest African economies, it serves to illustrate the disparity between that continent's poverty and improving standards of living in developing countries in Asia and Latin America. The whole of Africa between South Africa and the Sahara has a GDP of less than $150 billion and trades less than $30 billion a year. Something more than debt relief is needed in Africa and to many people one of the principal attractions of GREENS could be the prospect of providing that economically devastated continent with the means to earn a living for itself by invisible exports of pollution clean-up services.

It is also interesting to compare this figure of $400 billion, which would substantially become a component of international trade, with some indicators of present world trade. The single most valuable commodity traded in the world is oil, with total annual trade, including refined products, around $300 billion when crude oil is at $18 per barrel. World trade overall totals around $4,000 billion.[12] These trade flows are, of course, largely mediated through commercial firms, with governments and financial authorities involved through the process of currency conversion needed to provide traders with legal tender in the different countries where they deal.

The GREENS concept would thus imply a financial flow on the same scale as the current oil trade, but ultimately going to millions of workers growing trees. This is in contrast with the flow of cash following the OPEC oil price increases of the 1970s, when the extra cash (in excess of normal oil trade cash flows) went mainly to the owners of land where oil was lifted. Such landowners tend to spend this income unproductively (*inter alia* pushing up the price of real estate in the North). No such problem arises with tree growing, which gives income to impoverished peasants to buy the food they need for cash. One of the reasons the Uruguay round of GATT negotiations made such slow progress is because of problems with global food surpluses. How much more satisfactory a way to resolve that problem it would be to feed the hungry – indirectly, with their spending of the money the North pays them to absorb carbon dioxide and which the South additionally earns from producing sustainable fuel – than to pay US and European farmers to produce less.

How much a globally balanced budget DCT – taxation of energy users in one country and spending on tree growing in another – would increase total world activity is difficult to say. Economic theory finds it more difficult to determine the impact on total demand of changes in fiscal activity in a country that interacts with others. Even in a single country, modern analysis of a balanced budget policy is complex. Much depends on related changes in monetary policy, and also on how interest rates are affected and how people shift their portfolio of assets between financial assets, real assets, and currencies. With many countries involved, and with shifts in their overseas trade position, one country's policy change causes changes in another's which in turn influences the out-turn in the first country. As mentioned above, no global model exists which does not assume policy coordination as the norm.[13*]

But South countries development ambitions are in many cases held back by a shortage of foreign exchange. Thus having extra foreign exchange available would be likely to enable them to expand more rapidly, buying imports from North countries. There would certainly seem to be a good chance that this policy would accelerate the growth of some industrialising countries and thus act both towards stimulating the economy globally and equalising incomes between South and North. In so far as some of the tree growing countries are ones now badly affected by indebtedness, the extra receipts, say $40 billion a year for Brazil, would be extremely welcome in the North as well as the South, by helping such heavily indebted countries once more to become able to use the world's financial markets, where lack of confidence due to Third World bad debts would be correspondingly reduced – we will look in the next chapter at the benefits to be gained from some systematic connection between the Third World debt problem and GREENS.

Thus the fossil fuel price rise implied by GREENS is quite different in its impact on the world's financial system from the OPEC price rises. Many of the oil producing countries had (and have) small populations and extremely limited ability to absorb their new found wealth domestically. The results for the world's financial system we will come to in the next chapter. With intensive tree growing an on-going and labour intensive activity, the spending has to trickle down to labourers and subsistence farmers so that the cash flow cannot so easily be diverted towards palaces in the Riviera.

For the spending to be absorbed in the Third World, it is of course necessary for unemployed resources to be there waiting to be mobilised – as noted above, Keynesian multipliers are related to an under-employed economy. That this is the case in prospective tree growing areas can hardly be doubted, since it is hunger, and the absence of income generating rural employment, which drives peasants to the mushrooming barios and shanty town slums which surround the cities of the Third World.

And in the North, even after the initial phase of GREENS, in which we have envisaged that fuel-wood production would mainly be in temperate regions, environmental values (beyond the fixing of carbon dioxide) and other multi-purpose aspects of increased areas of woodland can, together with GREENS related funding, continue to provide a positive return even where tree growth is less rapid than in the tropics. Despite the economistic casuistry that seeks to describe the unemployment of the 1980s as voluntary,[14*] there are long-term unemployed groups in the North that could also become employed in tree growing. The employment of such otherwise unemployable groups on tree growing, outside the mainstream of conventional economic activity, would not generate the inflationary pressures in the more sensitive areas of the labour market which have made traditional Keynesian, full employment, fiscal policies less accepted since the 1960s.

Indeed, in its impact on North countries, GREENS is disinflationary, with a net burden on the economy, on the polluter pays principle, going to pay for the South's new invisible export of atmospheric pollution clean-up services. It would be for individual countries to decide how far this disinflationary effect[15*] would need to be countered by appropriate domestic monetary and fiscal measures. Whatever policies might be decided on, one thing is clear. This is that the GREENS package of transfer-type fiscal stimulation does not (as far as North countries go, where concern about increasing prices is greatest) have the inflationary impact that is normally associated with fiscal stimulation. The inflationary impact falls in South countries, where labour market conditions are different and which can be insulated, through exchange rates movements, from transmitting their price increases, if any, back to the developed countries.

With the passage of time, and the reduction or elimination of excessive debt, South countries would no longer be so subject to a binding balance of payments constraint. They may then be expected to show a high propensity to import consumer goods out of their growing income, stimulated by receipts for their invisible export (and, eventually, for their physical exports of fuel-wood products or of liquid fuels derived from woody biomass). Their imports of consumer goods, reflecting the comparative advantage of North countries, can eventually provide a stimulus for export led growth in the North and, with it, employment for skilled workers currently and prospectively laid off as a consequence of reduced military procurement in the decades ahead. How long it might take for this to come about – for the multiplier process to spread back to developed countries so that all countries, rich and poor, benefit materially from GREENS, in addition to its intended impact on global warming – is a matter for research.

What is clear, however, is that the conclusion that has been reached by many economists, using global macro-economic models to analyse the impact of uniform carbon taxes in models which lack an adequate specification of alternative energy technologies, i.e. that the economic impact of dealing with global warming is likely to be hugely expensive to the global economy, is pessimistic. The cost estimates come down significantly when allowance is made, as in more recent models, for the reduction in other taxation that is made possible by the carbon tax.[16] But such budget neutral models still require far higher tax levels in the energy sector – and consequently far higher macro-economic costs – to achieve a particular target reduction in net emissions than is the case if the tax revenues are dedicated to absorption.

Notes

1. Hall et al., 1993, Tables 11 and 12; Moulton and Richards, 1990, Figures 3 and 4.

2. Coarse efficiency, of course, as described in Chapter 6. The need to take account of macro-economic system impacts, as discussed above, does not alter the desirability of tradeability to ensure that the carbon absorption is done as efficiently as may be. What this need does lead to is an assessment of the benefit from the greater or lesser forcing of the overall level of absorption and recycling activities, relative to what would result from the incentive effect of the signal given by a simple net emissions tax or tradeable permit scheme.

3. Rather is it the case that this book was undertaken as a preliminary to developing such a model. Johansson et al, 1993b, provides a far more detailed renewables intensive scenario, but without the policy forcing of renewable fuel technology that drives the GREENS scenario.

4. Read, 1991.

5. FAO, Annually(a), Table 1; Sutton, 1992.

6. But the mechanism may be less by way of reduced logging and more by way of providing stable waged employment and the energy infrastructure for a dispersed pattern of industrial development. Logging, and traditional fuel-wood gathering, are a minor cause of tropical forest destruction compared with slash and burn subsistence agriculture and other demands for land caused by expanding population (Leach and Mearns, 1988, pp.12, 197).

7. In relation to the very modest commitments agreed in the FCCC, this kind of approach is becoming spoken of as 'joint implementation', that is two or more countries combining to meet their joint commitment at lower cost than working separately. A recognition is beginning to emerge of the complication that more substantial commitments will have to be met by the actions of firms registered in the countries which undertake such commitments, with the potential for an agent-principal problem.

8. The economists' concepts of consumer and producer surplus are involved. They require consideration of the value and cost of each increment of changed demand and supply in terms of the prices that consumers would be willing to pay and producers willing to accept for that particular increment. Mathematicians would recognise them as the integrals under the demand and supply curves.

9. Should it seem contradictory to write a book based upon the supposition that there is plenty of room to grow ten billion tons of fuel-wood a year and yet that open space is in short supply, the view being taken is that, when the empirical question has been answered by painstaking 'ground truthing' work, it will become apparent that much current use of land is inefficient or even wasteful, and that the solution to many problems facing the world today can come about by much more careful husbandry of the gift of nature.

10. For the avoidance of doubt, not a conventional carbon tax with the revenue going to general government purposes, with the reallocation of resources into absorption and recycling of carbon that results from agents' responses in the market to altered price signals, but the forcing of recycling and absorption technologies that results from dedicating the tax revenue to these technologies.

11. World Bank, 1990, Tables 9 and 2

12. Ibid; BP, 1992, p.16.

13. However, experiments can be done with them to simulate imposed patterns of non-coordination – but that is a different matter from a model in which non-coordination is inherent.

14. 'Ask the following simple question of job losers: "would you willingly take your previous job back on the terms now available on the market?" If the answer is "yes" the person is involuntarily unemployed'. Blinder, 1988.

15. This fiscal impact would be reinforced by the effect of a reduction in their monetary base as North countries collectively went into current account deficit, or reduced surplus, to pay for their invisible imports.

16. Dean, 1992; Hoeller et al, 1992.

8. National Interests

In this chapter we address what was, in the opening pages of this book, foreseen to be the most intractable aspect of the global warming problem.[1*] The technological basis exists, and the economic mechanisms have been described, for a low-cost response that can, subject to the caveats regarding land capability, achieve the reduction in net emissions needed to stabilise the *level* of carbon dioxide in the atmosphere. But the mechanisms will leave some countries winning and other countries losing from putting GREENS into operation, a reality which brings the need for a political resolution of these conflicts of national economic interests.

After some preliminary remarks on the nature of political economy which acknowledge my intellectual debt to Thomas Schelling's essay 'Some Economics of Global Warming'[2] we provide some background data, and discuss some advantages of the TAO in this global setting. There follows a discussion of the Third World debt problem and of the political-economic advantages of linking GREENS to its substantial restructuring. The next section discusses a refinement of the equity principle, beyond what is already embodied in the FCCC which would make it more appropriate to the long-term dynamic context. The chapter concludes by revisiting our Chapter 4 scenario with this political-economic structure added to the former technological basis, and with some reference to particular countries or groups of countries.

Political economy
The nature of political-economic questions leaves them to some extent beyond the reach of analysis. What is claimed to be fair by some parties may seem to others to be unfair. Or others may claim it to be unfair in order to increase their bargaining strength. Or in order to respond to what they perceive, in another's original claim, to have been likewise strategically motivated. Such a climate of shared distrust – the stuff of modern game theory – makes for sterility even in essentially bilateral diplomatic exchange, as witnessed in the Byzantine complexities of the interlocking rounds of disarmament negotiations of recent decades. With multiple objectives and multilateral participation, as in the post-Earth Summit process, it is ruinous.[3*]

In this book we suggest that the cost to the North is likely to be much lower than has been widely represented, and the cost to the South to be not a cost at all, but the springboard for a new developmental opportunity.

In this chapter we discuss the fairness and unfairness of different arrangements. Nonetheless we cannot expect to come to a positive analytic conclusion as to what the outcome should be. The outcome must contain an element of horse trading. All we can hope for from analysis is to alter perceptions of what the costs are and thus to help it to be understood that the obstacles are not as great as they have been perceived to be. To bring the horse traders to water does not force them to drink.

A global resolution thus requires political vision which this book may call for but cannot supply. However, with the South impelled by a developmental imperative and the North by a perception of the unsustainability of its traditional pattern of growth, the motivation for such vision may exist. If it is lacking, it may be provided through the work of non-governmental environmentalist organisations and their allies in the media. Whether it is sufficient motivation to overcome the obstacles depends upon perceptions of how great the obstacles are, as well as upon how great they actually are.

The underlying reality of Figure 4.2, and related Table 4.2, is that whatever measures are taken by developed countries, they cannot, on their own, deal with the global warming problem which they have largely caused – both North and South must be involved. The collaboration of South countries that is needed has two aspects, giving rise to problems A and B of Chapter 1. Firstly, the majority of them which are not well endowed with large commercially proven reserves of fossil fuels need to be persuaded to adopt a development path that uses renewable energy technologies rather than following along the lines pursued historically by now developed countries.

Secondly, those which are well endowed and – as is implied by the word 'commercial' – already embarked along traditional lines of energy development, need special consideration. The most significant reserves lie in the Middle and Far East. Diverting these countries' energy sector development so that their resources of cheap fossil fuel, particularly coal, remain in the ground (or, if extracted, balanced by 'making coal' elsewhere in the world) imposes a cost which we called the burden of history.

Some Economics of Global Warming is a sceptical essay that draws attention to some of the simplifications of thinking that have attended the climate change debate and, unusually for an economist, displays an awareness of the risk of climate system surprises, advocating that 'climate research should focus more on the extreme possibilities rather than on improving the median projections'. Schelling's judgement is that 'no greenhouse taxing agency is going to collect a trillion dollars a year in revenue...Reduce the tax by an order of magnitude and it becomes imaginable, but then it becomes trivial as greenhouse policy'. And he is equally disparaging of the prospect of an effective tradable emissions policy. He also regards it as 'altogether improbable that developing countries ... will incur any significant sacrifice in the interest of reduced carbon (nor would I advise them to do so).' His advice would be based upon a judgement that 'their best defense against climate change may be their own continued development' and 'In a hundred years, adverse changes in climate ... would be far more tragic for [those countries]... with populations then totalling 12 billion than if they totalled 9 billion'. Concluding that 'there is a mismatch between those who may be vulnerable to climate change and those who can afford to do anything about it' (barring catastrophic surprises that will affect everyone) Schelling states the moral argument that 'developing countries are vulnerable and we care'. But, if we want to give them more money, it would be better spent on economic development rather than carbon abatement.

Given his information base, one cannot disagree with these judgements. However, they are based upon the conventional economic wisdom regarding energy technology possibilities, without knowledge of the potential of the alternative technologies discussed in Chapter 4. Thus his remarks do not apply to GREENS, which imposes burdens on rich nations that fall into the imaginable rather than the unimaginable and which provides a response that helps rather than hinders development in the 'South'. Furthermore none of the cash flows through governmental hands or through supra-national agencies (save for low level taxes to cover the administrative and research costs of monitoring, etc.). Nor does GREENS run counter to Schelling's 'we know that carbon fuels are not going to be discontinued' for carbon fuels do continue under GREENS, but the carbon does not come from underground. With only modest additional cost, the carbon can come from biomass, enlisting transnational industry to achieve the sustainable energy technology transfer that will contribute to developing countries' economic growth, not diminish it.

Furthermore, like the Climate Change Convention, and unlike the conventional wisdom that is embodied in the cost estimates so far forthcoming from 'top down' macro-economic modelling, this essay recognises the importance of increased absorption, as well as reduced emissions (but, unsurprisingly given the technological assumptions) fails to close the circle as regards sustainable fuel technology. Indeed, stopping or slowing deforestation is seen as more important than reforestation. And esoteric technologies for scrubbing carbon dioxide from smokestacks or even screening the earth with orbiting sunshields are entertained – albeit with the scepticism they deserve.

As far as this book goes the most significant contribution of this essay – apart from the intellectual appeal of the concerned common sense which it displays – comes from its commentary on the modus operandi of any collaboration amongst nations that may come about in responding to global warming. It is a perspective that is reflected in – and may well have contributed to – the last-minute revisions to the FCCC, which saw it contain not a set of legally binding obligations, but a political commitment to work collaboratively towards an agreed target with specific provisions for sharing information and reviewing progress. And it is a perspective which has proved to be very helpful in making sense of the difficult problems of political economy discussed in the latter part of this book.

Schelling cannot foresee negotiated national quotas subject to serious enforcement, with financial penalties, etc. He looks instead to examples of previous collaboration amongst developed nations (given that it will be developed nations that carry the burden) for his model of a viable way to mediate significant resource transfers, referring to negotiations on the allocation of Marshall Plan dollars amongst potential recipients, and on the burden sharing of the costs of NATO. It is a model which suggests that 'participating countries in a greenhouse-abatement regime would submit for each other's scrutiny and cross examination plans for reducing carbon emissions. ... any commitments undertaken would be to policies, not to emissions. ... policies like taxes, regulations and subsidies, and would specify programmes (like research and development), accompanied by very uncertain estimates of their likely effects ...'

'This will require ... developed countries to find a way to mobilize their populations in support of national greenhouse policies'. To that I say 'Hear hear', adding that the sharply reduced costs envisaged under GREENS, the greater promise of effective remedy, and the low level of operational involvement of governments and of supranational agencies under the workings of the TAO, make the prospect of success from such a negotiating process the greater.

Data and background

In order to point up our discussion it is helpful to have some notion of the quantities involved. Table 8.1 sets out the proven fossil fuel reserves of selected countries as reported in 1988, their rate of local consumption and export volume together with relevant economic indicators such as total indebtedness, population and per capita income. The basis for inclusion is somewhat subjective, the possession of substantial commercially proven reserves of fossil fuels or other significance in relation to the political economy of global energy being the main guide.

Omitted from the table are about 130 other members of the United Nations, many of which have locally significant reserves of fossil fuel. World figures halfway down the table indicate what is omitted, i.e. about 10 per cent of consumption and of oil reserves, about 20 per cent of gas reserves and a somewhat indeterminate proportion of solid fuel reserves, the difficulty being the unavailability of consistent data on commercially proved reserves of coal and lignite.[4*]

Table 8.1 Economic Development, Debt and Fossil Fuel Data for Selected Countries

	Per Capita Income	Pop- ula- tion	For- eign Debt	Gross Dom. Product	Oil+ Nat. Gas Reserves	Coal+ Lignite Reserves	Fossil Fuel Used	Fossil Fuel Ex- ported
	$US	m.	$USb.	$USb.	b.tons+ tr.cu.m.	b.tons +b.tons	m.tons p.a.	m.tons p.a.(net)
Low income economies								
Bangladesh	180	111	10.7	20	0+0.4	0+1	7.3	-3.0
Nigeria	250	114	32.8	28	2.2+2.4	0.2+0	17.0	85.4
India	340	833	62.5	235	0.7+0.5	1.9+(129)	235.5	-35.6
China	350	1114	44.9	418	2.5+0.9	(120+651)	820.1	48.7
Pakistan	370	110	18.6	36	0+0.6	0.1+0	30.2	-11.5
Indonesia	500	178	53.1	94	1.1+2.1	-	51.3	81.7
Lower middle income economies								
Egypt	640	51	48.8	32	0.6+0.3	-	34.2	30.4
USSR §	288				8.1+41.1	137+104	1953.9	390.8
Turkey	1370	55	41.6	72	-	5.9+0.2	50.3	-33.1
Poland	1790	38	43.3	68	-	11.7+28.7	179.8	-6.1
Mexico	2010	85	95.6	201	7.7+2.1	0.6+1.2	140.2	97.4
Argentina	2160	32	64.7	53	0.3+0.7	0+0.1	62.2	-3.8
WORLD	3838	5206	-	19981	123+106	403+396	10013.2	nil
Upper middle income economies								
Venezuela	2450	19	33.1	44	7.8+3.5	0+0.4	57.6	109.5
Rep. S. Africa	2470	35	+?	80	-	0+55.3	108.0	20.3
Brazil	2540	147	111.3	319	0.3+0.1	1.2+0	112.5	- 52.7
Yugoslavia	2920	24	19.7	72	-	16.5+0	59.0	- 26.9
Iran	3200	53	?		13.0+13.9	0+0.2	69.5	103.3
Czechoslovakia	3450	16	?	50	-	(7.2)+2.7	96.3	- 35.4
Korea*	4400-	63	+?	212+	-	(0.3)+0.5	144.8	- 85.1
Iraq	?				13.6+0.7	-	13.0	171.0
High income economies								
Saudi Arabia	6020	14	++?	81	22.7+4.1	-	81.4	300.5
Australia	14360	17	-?	282	0.3+1.3	45.6+45.3	113.6	80.8
UK	14610	57	+?	718	0.7+0.6	(1)+3.3	282.0	30.0
Italy	15120	58	+?	866	0+0.3	-	207.6	-162.9
Kuwait	16150	2	+?	24	12.7+1.2	-	15.6	88.0
France	17820	56	+?	956	-	0+0.2	204.6	-148.4
Canada	19030	26	-?	489	1.0+2.7	3.1+3.8	275.0	92.2
Germany*	20440	79	++?	1189+	0+0.4	56.1+23.9	468.6	-234.0
USA	20910	249	--?	5156	4.4+5.6	102+113	2457.9	-429.1
Japan	23810	123	++?	2818	-	0+0.8	480.1	-450.3

§Dollar figures for USSR are based on a conversion of the greatly devalued rouble at time of writing.

*Korea North and South, Germany East and West for energy data, but not for economic data which are hard to get, as also for then USSR and the foreign asset/debt position of OECD, OPEC and some other countries. Iraq economic data is for 1988, otherwise data is mainly for 1989 as reported in the World Bank's *World Development Report* for 1991 (OUP, 1991). Energy data is mainly 1985 to 1987 as reported in United Nations *Energy Statistics Yearbook* for 1988 (UN, New York, 1990) with 'recoverable reserves' quoted, where available (which excludes China from the World Total) in the case of coal and lignite, otherwise in (). Fossil fuel use is in coal equivalent with net imports indicated as negative net exports (coal exports sometimes offset oil imports in energy equivalent volume, but in cash terms a ton of oil is from three to ten times more than a ton of coal).

It should, perhaps, be mentioned that the proving of commercial reserves of coal and lignite, being mainly the consequence of effective local or regional demand, leaves enormous quantities of estimated reserves, particularly in areas where commercial activity has not previously justified the expense of detailed proving. Development in currently less developed countries would, without the alternatives in renewable energy technology, bring much of these estimated reserves into the proven category. However, the sustainability rationale means that reserves currently unproved must remain largely unproved. Nevertheless, the potential of fringe supplies, small on a world scale but quite sufficient if depleted rapidly to upset the global carbon balance, is a factor which requires a specific safeguard to which we will shortly come.

It is also worth noting from the table that, although historically North countries may have been mainly responsible for getting the level of carbon dioxide in the atmosphere to where it is today (in addition to their cumulative fossil fuel consumption from the eighteenth century on, the temperate forests were cleared for agriculture before World War Two, mostly long before), their current consumption is not greatly in excess of South countries' (led by Middle Eastern and Asian countries). Thus fossil fuel used in the 10 largest high income countries cited in Table 8.1 is less than half the world total and forest clearance is now mainly in the latter regions. However the North's population is only about one-tenth of the world figure so, on a per capita basis, they are around 10 times as responsible for current carbon dioxide pollution as the rest of the world (although less than 10 times so when other greenhouse gases are considered, owing to methane emissions from rice paddies etc. in the rest of the world).[5]

The Political Economy of the TAO

For convenience we discussed the macro-economics of GREENS, in the previous chapter, in terms of a DCT, a mechanism that is only slightly less implausible in relation to cash flows of $400 billion than in relation to the $1 trillion annually for a carbon tax-financed aid programme which, we noted above, is seen as 'unimaginable' (Schelling, 1992). The difference in these figures arises partly because Schelling is considering the very large levels of carbon tax needed to achieve even quite modest reductions in gross emissions. Such taxes amount to more than doubling the price at which fossil fuels would be sold, so it may seem surprising that the DCT cash flow, which we have said may add 10 or 20 per cent to fuel costs, is as much as 40 per cent of Schelling's $1 trillion.

The answer there is that the DCT finances the supply of renewable fuel and yields savings in fossil fuel costs whereas the $1 trillion is added on top of the cost of fossil fuel supply. Thus, although the net cost of biomass substitution   may be low compared with the costs of simple carbon emissions taxes, it is the gross cash flow that would be collected by governments and spent on renewable fuel production. To quote Schelling – and it is hard to disagree – 'No greenhouse taxing agency is going to collect a trillion dollars per year in revenue...' And the same is true for $400 billion. Such sums are an order of magnitude wrong *vis-à-vis* aid flows, and, however much it may be felt that aid should be more generous, it is a mistake to build a response to global warming on an assumption of reformed behaviour. Equally it is undesirable that the North's willingness to give should be taken up in dealing with what is essentially an externality to the commercial activity of the fuel industry.

Furthermore, with the application of the DCT to renewable fuel supply, the involvement of governments becomes even less imaginable. Firstly, it involves the 'hypothecation' of taxes to which, as noted in Chapter 6, treasury officials tend to be inveterately opposed. More seriously, it would involve governments as agents in the energy business – on a very large scale if the tax level (and biomass fuel produced) are raised to the levels implied by Figure 7.2. Apart from ideological objections to 'big government' it is questionable whether such a vast monopoly, placed in the middle of the energy business (or of the forestry business) of particular countries, is desirable whoever may own it. The monopolist would need to decide whether (or in what proportions) to give the biomass produced to the forestry industry (to compensate the latter for lost business from traditional timber production) or whether to give it to energy firms (in order to ensure displacement of fossil fuels by presenting the firms with a zero opportunity cost substitute).   Of course, the firms (or their customers) will have paid for the biomass, through the DCT during the growing phase, but those are sunk costs at the time the biomass fuel raw material becomes available.

With the globalisation of GREENS that is needed for it to be effective, government involvement becomes even more objectionable. In the context of transnational pollution, a DCT system would involve governments in undesirably commercial relationships with each other, with potential confusion of sovereignty and efficiency issues. The problems with the DCT become even greater seen in the light of the fact that, while consumers in the North have the ability to pay, it is in the South that carbon emissions are forecast to grow more quickly. It would leave the effectiveness of response permanently hostage to the possibility that taxpayers in the North would grow tired of paying, or that politicians would, country by country, cheat on their obligation, 'free riding' on the better behaviour of others.

The Tradeable Absorption Obligation, as described in Chapter 7, avoids these difficulties by internalising such transactions into the conduct of business by energy and forestry firms. Under, say, a 10 per cent TAO, an energy firm might pay a forestry firm to grow timber for conventional markets, the payment reflecting the difference between the discounted cost of plantation timber production and the cost of timber production by traditional exploitation (sometimes destruction) of natural forest.

Under a 60 per cent TAO, the main market for produced biomass would be as an energy raw material so that energy firms, in order to maintain their market position, would most likely retain ownership of the product, with forestry firms acting as contractors. Possibilities for optimising joint production of conventional forest products and of biomass fuel would occur as with traditional forestry (timber waste arisings forming an important energy input into the paper industry, for example). Vertical integration of biomass production into downstream energy sector activity could occur, or horizontal integration between energy firms and forestry firms. We do not need to go into the industrial organisation ramifications to see that the role of governments, and of supranational organisations in a global context, becomes supervisory rather than commercial.

And the payments which, on a government to government basis are 'unimaginable', become perfectly imaginable when internalised into the energy business. Indeed, as we have seen, they are of the same order of magnitude as those to which we are accustomed as a consequence of the oil industry's international activities. However, they would go largely as wage payments to the biomass industry workforce, rather than to oilfield rentiers, with the same potential for beneficial multiplier effects and beneficial impacts on the balance of trade for debt constrained South economies that have been discussed in the context of a DCT.

The TAO may be thought of as embodying the subsidiarity principle,[6*] with government governing, divorced from commercial activity, and with business operating commercially within a legal framework which aligns the profit motive with the public interest. A natural function of the superior level of government is to protect the most subsidiary level, the consumer, from dangers that may arise from operations at the intermediate level of the firm. Protection of the public from the actions of traders is, indeed, an ancient function of government, from the establishment of legal tender and of statutory weights and measures down to modern consumer protection legislation. Some of this imposes substantial burdens upon industry in securing the safety of the public from dangers, such as dangers from inadequately tested pharmaceutical products.

It does not seem 'unimaginable' that, within the framework agreed at the Earth Summit, nations can negotiate to operate policies that impose such burdens on the energy industry, and on the largely transnational firms of which it is comprised. Perhaps the equitable basis to be discussed later in this chapter would provide a starting point. Thus, were the world to comprise only the UK and India, with roughly equal greenhouse gas emissions, but a 50:1 per capita measured income difference, a TAO of 100 per cent in the UK and two per cent in India would secure a 51 per cent reduction in emissions. Negotiations could ensue over the relative importance of the informal sector and of differences in climatic and other circumstances, leading perhaps to agreement on 98 and four per cent TAOs.

But the governments would then collaborate, under guidelines provided by a protocol of the FCCC, and with the support of monitoring and technical field extension services provided under the FCCC, to ensure that energy firms – often transnational energy firms – properly discharged their TAOs, wherever incurred. The incentive to South countries, and 'East' countries such as India, to participate (at the minimal levels indicated – but rising with hoped for improvements in the standard of living) would be the penalty of exclusion, under the FCCC Protocol, from the potential benefits of hosting energy firm spending on biomass production on their own soil, and of technology transfer to modernise their energy systems.

Third World Debt

Debt restructuring and GREENS

Foreign debt is included in Table 8.1 for two reasons. Firstly, since we start from Figure 4.2, and from the necessity of including the South in an effective response, we cannot ignore this primary cause of the feelings of injustice in the South that were so clearly articulated in the Malaysian prime minister's remarks quoted in Chapter 1.

No debt figures are quoted for higher income (OECD) countries since, although it is known that several members of this 'rich countries' club are in debt (outstandingly, the USA), their financial affairs are not exposed to the glare of publication in any conveniently available form.[7]* This in itself may seem to South countries to be inequitable, but their major concern is that the pattern of events in the last two decades has led to a situation in which, during the 1980s, South countries were making net payments to North countries, rather than the other way round, as may be seen from Table 8.2. That this net outflow has been largely corrected in the last few years is no great consolation since the correction has largely taken the form of even greater indebtedness from renewed lending to the South.

Table 8.2 The Third World Debt Problem in the 1980s (US $b)

	1980	1982	1984	1986	1988
End year debt	572	819	855	1047	1156
1. New borrowing	112	108	97	103	108
2. Debt repayments	46	46	50	76	88
3. Debt increase	66	62	47	27	20
4. Interest payments	47	65	69	65	72
5. Cash flow to South					
(1 - 2 - 4 = 5)	+19	-2	-22	-38	-52
Average interest rate	8.2%	7.9%	8.1%	6.2%	6.2%

Adapted from J.MacNeill et al, *Beyond Interdependence*, OUP, New York, 1991, and based on the World Bank's *World Debt Tables*, 1989-90, Vol 1, p. 78, World Bank, Washington DC.

The second reason has to do with limiting the 'burden of history' represented by problem B of Chapter 1, with the calculation of which – or at least a description of how the calculation might be done – we concluded the last chapter. It was noted that the entry of biomass resources into the market could increase the apparent size of this burden by depressing the expected rate of increase in the price of oil. However, payment of part of this burden to owners of oil reserves, including some of the richest countries in the world, is hardly a political reality.

Furthermore, oil is hard to substitute for and, save for the Middle East, most countries' proven reserves would be exhausted profitably in a regime of rising prices over the few decades of transition envisaged in our Chapter 4 scenario. In the case of natural gas, its use will be accelerated since substitution for coal is likely to be an important tactic in reducing net carbon dioxide emissions, along the way to full reliance on renewable technology.

Middle East oil could take longer to exhaust and find a continuing high value niche in a global fuel market that, after 2020, could be dominated by biomass-sourced carbon and by more advanced renewable technologies. But, in the absence of unforeseen technological advance, biomass-based liquid fuels are going to provide a profitable target for any oil that can be extracted for less than the $25 per barrel with which such renewable substitutes are expected to be competitive by 2000.

That certainly includes most proven reserves of oil for which exploration costs have already been incurred, and in all likelihood there is plenty waiting to be found. It is hard to imagine international oil companies, in competition with each other, voluntarily foregoing such profitable opportunities. So a mechanism is needed for ensuring that such oil exploration is brought to an end, and that future generations are not faced with the alternative of an ineffectual global warming response strategy or the need to pay continuing compensation, or bribes, to prevent 'new' oil being used. The *reductio ad absurdum* would be continued exploration in order to attract such bribes, rather than with any intent to extract – or, indeed fake – exploration with pretend reserves and fraudulent compensation claims.

Thus the role of debt restructuring in GREENS is as the *quid pro quo* for a moratorium on fossil fuel exploration in participating countries, motivated also by potential benefits from other aspects of GREENS. The double effect of such a moratorium would be (a) to neutralise resistance to GREENS from owners of proven oil and (b) to diminish the future's, then apparent, 'burden of history'. This is because restricting proven oil reserves to what has already been found will create future scarcity, thus ensuring that oil prices do indeed increase, in a manner similar to what can be expected (with costs of extraction rising due to continued, business-as-usual exploitation) in the absence of a GREENS transition to biomass.

The background to the Third World debt problem
For it to be sensible for the North to employ the debts it is owed by the South in this way it is necessary to consider whether what would be given away is in any way as essential to the North as the assurance of effectiveness in responding to the threat of global warming – should science confirm that a precautionary response is needed – that is sought in exchange. A detailed discussion of international debts, and of how the Table 8.2 situation has come about is beyond the scope of this book. Here we provide no more than a broad outline.

The successive oil price increases of the 1970s saw very large sums of money flow to the oil-producing countries. These were in excess of what could be absorbed in their domestic economies through investment in productive assets, military security, infrastructure and human capital, and through conspicuous consumption. The excess was invested in the world's financial markets at a time of economic recession and slow growth. Of course bankers have to make a living, which they do by lending out the money which they borrow, charging more interest than they pay their depositors. However, the recession, induced in part by OPEC's pricing policies, made it difficult to lend profitably in North countries and the OPEC deposits eventually found their way as commercial lending to South countries. This was different from the government to government lending (official lending) which had constituted the bulk of aid to developing countries in the 1950s and 1960s.

The inflationary spiral in North countries, set up by the successive oil price increases, coincided with a shift in economic orthodoxy which ascribed inflation to expansionary policies. It led to tight money and high interest rates, the effects of which were made worse for South countries by Reagan's 'high dollar' policy of the early 1980s (since most Third World debt is denominated in US dollars). This exacerbated the intensity of the recession and led to a double impact on the South. Firstly, the interest rates on their borrowing increased, out of line with expectations at the time of commitment and, secondly, the markets for their exports dried up, with sharp reductions (again, in relation to expectations of both lenders and borrowers at the time of commitment) in the income available for paying off the loans.

The after-effects have been a succession of repayments crises in various countries (mainly, but not exclusively, in Latin America) which have led to loan renegotiations, reschedulings and restructurings. These may be regarded as euphemisms for different forms of non-enforcement, i.e. for letting the debtor country off part or all of its obligation to repay its loans, either by direct cancellation or by delayed repayment (which we saw, in Chapter 6, amounts to the same thing, given that the applicable procedures of compound interest discounting mean that money is worth less the further away it is into the future). In many cases the loans came to be traded in a market in secondary loans, where the original commercial lenders accepted a repayments shortfall in return for reduced risk.

Thus the pain has not all been one-sided. But for the debtors the pain has been greater, with South countries forced to undertake harsh and sometimes humiliating steps to run their economic affairs in accordance with the requirements of their creditors.[8*] While the North has continued to prosper, albeit not so rapidly as in the immediate post-World War Two decades, the South's inability to attract further investment and achieve the growth required to catch up with the North has in many cases seen its poverty worsen rather than diminish, sometimes leading to the destabilisation of decently democratic governments.

The nature of debt relief

It is this situation, the rich getting richer while the poor get poorer (most in relative terms, many in absolute terms, on a per capita basis),[9] that is unacceptable to the South. Failure to address this, in the context of future Conferences of the Parties under Article 7 of the FCCC, or in some forum outside the Climate Convention, may result in the South's involvement continuing at its present low-key level, thus leaving the FCCC ineffectual as a starting point for effective action against climate change. So, in looking at a global pattern in which the creditor nations of Europe, Japan and the USA[10*] would relinquish further substantial portions of their claims upon the debtor nations in return for the exploration moratorium, we must consider what is implied by debt relief and debt restructuring operations.

An important distinction must be drawn between the 'official' debts of debtor countries to creditor governments (essentially government to government debts) and the debts of individuals, firms and governments in debtor nations to overseas private sector creditors, generally speaking to the North's commercial banking system. Commercial banks live on confidence, that is to say they relend a large proportion of the money deposited with them so that, at any one time, only a small proportion of deposits can be repaid. Any doubt about the reliability of a bank may cause a 'run' in which depositors try to get their own money out while they can (which may not be for very long if a lot of the bank's lending is long term, for instance on development projects). So debt default in relation to a commercial loan, however foolishly undertaken by the bank in question, can hurt a lot of people in addition to the responsible managers in the bank.

In contrast, official debt has no direct impact on agents in the market, either financial markets or the markets for real goods and services. The discharge, or failure, of such debts affects nobody's individual fortune and nobody goes broke on account of default on official debt. Equally, nobody is personally affected by the relief of such debts. Of course the granting of official loans, and their repayment on schedule, or the failure to do so, affects the economic climate of both lending and borrowing countries. So the payments and repayments of official debt are more than simple book-keeping exercises between governments. But they are a lot less than default on loans between individuals or between individuals and banks and other financial institutions. Nobody loses their shirt, and the stability of the commercial banking system is not at risk.

Indeed, given that debtor country's internal currency is generally not viable as an international medium of exchange, and that such a country's need for relief is symptomatic of a foreign exchange constraint on its trading behaviour, relief of official debt is usually good for the commercial creditor community as well as for the debtor country. Firstly, the risk of default on remaining, or unrestructured commercial loans, is reduced since it is more possible for the debtor countries to service the smaller overall debt burden. Secondly, the debt burdened economies are able to use more of their constrained overseas currency spending power on imports of real goods from creditor countries, thus boosting effective demand in the developed countries – indeed it can be regarded as a basis for stimulating benign, export-led growth in the developed world.

The changed pattern of cash flows affects the payments balance and asset position of the countries involved, but in ways that can be compensated by suitable adjustments to monetary policies. Thus the relief of official debt need have no direct impact upon the economic position of developed countries save for the beneficial impact of more business coming from the formerly debt-constrained countries. And, indirectly, the substitution of low-risk official debt for high-risk commercial debt, and the consequential lowering of interest rates generally, must have a stimulating effect, much needed in the state of chronic under-employment that has emerged in the last 20 years.

An obvious question to ask, if international debts can be cancelled beneficially and apparently painlessly, is why doesn't the international community simply do this. Why wait for the need for a redirection of global development in a more sustainable direction to come along before restructuring global debt? For instance, why not engineer a takeover by North countries of outstanding commercial loans to the South, with the creditor banks receiving payment from, say, the Japanese or British governments, and those governments becoming the South's creditors, maybe at lower rates of interest or with part of the debt simply written off?

The answer here is that, although the benefits that would flow from a global round of debt restructuring are widely recognised, a reputational question is involved. If such debt reduction is essentially a recognition of mistaken decisions in the past, what is the incentive effect of relieving lenders and borrowers of the consequences of their folly? The fear is of another round of unwise commercial lending and Third World spending and of financial irresponsibility on the part of borrowers (whose information about their own intentions and prospects is better than that of prospective lenders) if it appears that such behaviour, in the end, carries no penalty.

But, whilst it is the case that mistakes were certainly made by the debtor nations, much of their debt burden arises from no fault of their own, as we have seen. Furthermore, allocation of blame is backwards looking and unhelpful once the advent of the global warming concern, as an area in which developed countries need collaboration from less developed countries, shifts the balance of debt market negotiating strength. Of course, that does not mean that North countries are 'over a barrel', any more than indebtedness has brought South countries to collapse – though bad economic management, of which excessive debt is symptom rather than cause – has come close to doing so in some cases. It is more the case that a shift of circumstances creates a new balance in the competitive market for development loans, and that the market can operate better in the new situation if the shift is taken as the occasion to write off the overhang of past mistakes.

In the new situation, debt restructuring can cease to be a reluctant renegotiation motivated by development guilt, and become a mutually beneficial deal in capital assets – i.e. potential fossil fuel reserves against debt liabilities – that reflects a corresponding mutual benefit in the current accounts – i.e. the transfer of sustainable technology in exchange for environmental collaboration. Whilst the longer term objective would be to ensure increasing scarcity of oil, the main impact would be in relation to coal and lignite, of which there are vast estimated but unproven reserves that would remain forever unproven under this aspect of GREENS. Of course, for that to be practicable, there would have to be a continuing commitment to meet energy development needs by technology transfer in the area of low-cost renewable systems, but that continuing commitment would be matched by continuing observance of the moratorium on exploration.

International Equity in Emissions Targets

We saw in Chapter 7 that the implementation of the TAO, in a programme of rising policy levels, can be an effective and economically efficient mechanism for mediating the needed technological transformation in a particular country, New Zealand, and, by extension, on average globally. However, beyond noting the distinction that exists in the FCCC between developed countries (with a commitment to limit net emissions in 2000 to their level in 1990) and the rest (with no such commitment), nothing has so far been said about what targets, for achievement through the TAO or otherwise, should be acceptable in, and set by, different countries. The existing distinction arises simply as an expression of the political reality that North countries were willing or able to make such a commitment and South countries were not.

Such willingness or unwillingness at a point in time when considerable misperceptions existed about the nature of the problem, and of possible responses to it, is clearly not a satisfactory basis for permanently differentiating between countries as regards the effort they are called on to make. The world changes, and a satisfactory long-term arrangement within GREENS must incorporate some basis for the way in which the distribution of the burden of history should change with it. What might seem now to be a fair burden on Japan, compared with, say, Switzerland, would not have seemed fair 30 years ago, and may be no less relatively unfair in 30 years. Also, the willingness of South countries to be involved, as they must be bearing Figure 4.2 in mind, may change as their perception of what's in it for them changes.

So the question arises, if targets are to be different in different countries, and to change over time, on what basis can they be assessed? We saw in the last chapter that different carbon dioxide net emissions targets for different countries need to be compared carefully, having regard to the manner of definition. Furthermore, given the variation of circumstances between countries, both as regards the energy sector and conventional forestry, not to mention climatically, a given target may be harder to achieve in some countries than others. And higher growth rates make a given target (under preferred definition 4) harder to achieve.

This last aspect introduces a general presumption that the South, forecast to grow more rapidly than the North (Table 4.2), should be set lower targets. However, there are much stronger grounds for setting lower targets, and therefore imposing lower costs, in the South. Such grounds have been advanced by the distinguished Japanese economist Hirofumi Uzawa.[11] His basis for setting carbon dioxide emissions reductions targets is to relate them directly to each country's per capita income. (And, indeed, effectively on a net rather than gross basis, since he also favours – alone, so far, amongst senior economists – a linked carbon tax and subsidy for afforestation).

The rationale for Uzawa's proposal which, for a given global target set by the scientists, would see North countries making a larger contribution than South countries, is distributive justice. Recollect from Chapter 6 that, in discussing the least-cost theorem which provides the rationale for the TAO, it was subject to the proviso that the distribution of income question had been satisfactorily resolved. That may, with some willingness to suspend disbelief, be true within individual countries where redistributive taxation and social spending, backed by sovereign power, are available to achieve such a result. And even if it were not true, the question of social and distributive justice within a sovereign country is, for practical purposes, regarded by the international community as an internal matter for each country to settle in its own way.

But no supranational mechanism for international redistribution exists beyond the rather small contribution from official aid and assistance programmes, far outweighed by the adverse impact of the debt position as discussed above. Indeed, the lack of international justice in economic rewards is precisely what gives rise to the conflictual perspectives on the North/South problem discussed in Chapter 1. And it is the reason for the relative willingness and unwillingness of North and South countries respectively to make the existing FCCC commitment to stabilise net emissions at the 1990 rate, inadequate though it is, since it will see the level of greenhouse gases continue to increase.

Given that the principle of redistribution has, of political necessity, entered into the FCCC from the outset, Uzawa's proposal provides a basis both for only a minor modification of the initial differentiation and for preventing the initial differentiation becoming an obstacle to change. For, as in the UK-India example cited earlier in the chapter, the burden on low-income countries is low, and would remain so until such time as their hoped for development increases their ability to carry part of the cost. As the advantages of inclusion in the scheme (in terms of effective technology transfer through firms seeking to discharge their TAOs by raising the efficiency of South countries' existing use of fuels, and in terms of balance of payments gains through firms alternatively discharging their TAOs by producing biomass in South countries) became apparent, so could come about a willingness on the part of South countries to incur the low burdens involved.

But the differences between developed countries are not to be ignored. What may seem to be a fair burden on environmentally conscious Switzerland (per capita income $32,680) may seem less so to Greece ($5,990). Obviously more fuel, per capita, is consumed in Switzerland than Greece, but the difference (3.9 to 2.1 tons of oil equivalent)[12] is far less than the difference in standards of living. Given that our burden of history arises as a consequence of accumulated net emissions over the history of industrialisation, those who have inherited most from that history inherit not only the ability to pay but the responsibility. The incorporation of Uzawa's equity proposal into the FCCC would impose a substantial negotiating task upon the present North signatories, redistributing the commitment which they have already jointly made, for which the incentive would be the earlier involvement of South countries in active participation and hence the prospect of an FCCC that is potentially effective in relation to greenhouse gas levels.

Continuing with the Swiss example, they may claim that their heavy dependence on hydro-electricity makes them less responsible than most. But the steel for their gas turbine industry (to mention one that would prosper under GREENS) is smelted elsewhere, and their tourists burn fuel to get there. To attempt a historical re-construction of each nation's contribution to, and responsibility for, the accumulation of greenhouse gases would be to open a Pandora's box filled with red herrings. Uzawa's proposal combines rough justice, as regards past responsibility, with political practicability in the present and for the future. For, with wide disparities between the North and the South, his proposal makes very little short-term difference to what the North as a whole has committed itself to, or to what the South has not committed itself to. And it provides a basis for continuing adjustment as the ability to pay changes with hoped for development in the South.

The Practical Politics of Negotiating the Burden

The redistributive impact of Uzawa's equity proposal provides for the burden of history to be paid by those most able to pay it, with TAO percentages in the richest countries possibly exceeding even 100, eventually, when the global average has risen in line with Figure 7.2. Then would North consumers be paying for the absorption of the South's emissions. To suppose, however, that sovereign states will accede to their different targets being set by an international bureaucracy according to an automatic formula based on published statistics is unrealistic. *A fortiori* if penalties for under-achievement, raising sovereignty issues, are proposed. Even amongst developed country signatories of the FCCC, the Swiss-Greek example suggests that the parties involved will want to have a say in the factors to be taken into consideration and in what account should be taken of them.

It helps that the commitment is to net rather than gross emissions limitation and that the overall burden can, through renewable fuel technologies, most probably be kept to a fraction of what has been perceived. And it helps that the most energy-dependent of the rich countries are, in North America, endowed with large areas of land available for intensive fuel-wood production. Even the prospect of global macro-economic stimulation under GREENS may help generate a positive negotiating atmosphere if global macro-economic modelling can be advanced sufficiently to demonstrate its likelihood.

But as Schelling remarks,[13] a greenhouse regime that takes the form of Universalist commitments to specified reductions of emissions might be 'an indication of insincerity'. So how might the model he finds plausible, the negotiation of the share-out of Marshall Plan dollars in post-war Europe, be adapted to the GREENS scenario? If commitments are out, then targets become just that – targets for policy – and it is the policies that become the stuff of negotiations. The debate, in the context of Uzawa's equity basis, is not 'are you, New Zealand, treated unfairly by a legally binding commitment to reduce net emissions by 30 per cent by 2005, compared with Fiji's commitment of 10 per cent?' but, rather, 'is New Zealand doing enough, towards a global target of a 20 per cent reduction, by imposing a 25 per cent TAO when Fiji's is 15 per cent?'

One way in which negotiators would have to do better than in the past is that there is no longer a big daddy around to sort out the squabbles that can arise. In relation to the Marshall Aid experience, Schelling writes:

> The United States insisted that the recipients argue out and agree on shares. In the end they did not quite make it, the US having to make the final allocation. But all the submission of data and open argument led, if not to consensus, to a reasonable appreciation of each nation's

needs. The negotiations were professional; they were assisted by a proficient secretariat...Good relations were observed throughout; and proficiency in debate, acceptance of criteria, and negotiating etiquette steadily improved.

However, we need not rest hopes that the negotiators might do better simply on the wish that resort to big daddy occurred only because big daddy was there. For the Marshall Aid negotiations were about government to government transfers where 'the resources involved for most recipient countries were immensely important'. With GREENS we are talking about costs of the order of one per cent of gross world product, that is a six-month delay in world growth. And, with the TAO, we are talking about cash flows that do not form part of the revenue and expenditure of governments but of commercial firms – many of them transnational firms.

The negotiations would be over regulations on fuel wholesalers which result in the burden of history being transmitted, under polluter pays principles, to the consumers whose demands require the burden of history to be carried (if we no longer wanted to consume greenhouse gas emitting fuels, the fact that previous generations had used up nature's capacity to absorb them would not matter). Providing the games theoreticians can be prevented from snarling the whole process up with too sharp a characterisation of particular countries' interests, and that the process is driven by a statesmanlike concern for posterity, there may be some hope that the constructive experience of Schelling's precedents can point the way to negotiating an effective response to global warming through the process to become available under the FCCC.

The impact on coal
When discussing the role of debt restructuring it was implied that existing proven reserves of oil and gas would be used, gas more quickly and oil more slowly than under the business-as-usual outlook (and with the debt bargain preventing further exploration). Thus it is on the prospects for coal that GREENS must have its major impact. Because solid fuels, coal and lignite (which we will usually refer to as just 'coal'), comprise far and away the largest reserve of fossil fuel (around 80 per cent of total commercially recoverable reserves of fossil fuels, perhaps 98 per cent of total estimated reserves) that impact is hopefully all that is needed. Unless, that is, the climatologists come up, in the next decade or so, with even more substantial concerns regarding adverse climate surprises than they have hitherto, or unless studies of the impacts of middle of the road predictions of climate change prove nature to be more horrid than we yet know. Nonetheless, except on the most benign state of nature, most of the coal will have to stay in the ground.

The process of industrialisation has seen the substantial depletion of coal resources located in the longest developed regions of the globe. Thus, although the USA,[10*] Australia and Germany still have large reserves, 'leaving coal in the ground' means the devaluing of resources in countries located mainly outside the developed North. These countries are by no means uniformly under-developed. There are major coal reserves in Eastern Europe and the former Soviet Union, China, India and South Africa, *inter alia*.

Although they include some amongst the lowest per capita income countries in the world, they contain substantial and, by North standards, often very energy-inefficient industrial sectors. Thus reductions in their net emissions may go a long way before the question of using sustainable biomass technologies arises, simply by the transfer of energy-efficient technology under the influence of the net TAO in the way that has been described. Negotiations to involve China, say, in a minimal level of TAO in exchange for the modernisation of its existing energy system, at the expense of high TAO North consumers, could be pushing at an open door.

The increased fuel efficiency resulting from this process, while it reduces the amount of fossil fuel consumed, has the ironic impact of postponing the day when biomass technology is competitive in places where coal is very cheap. Given the high population density in many of the coal-rich countries of the south, fuel-wood competition with food crops may set in at an early stage after that, so that biomass costs would rise faster than elsewhere in the South, thus limiting the rate of market penetration of biomass technology.

This aspect may prove important in densely populated parts of China where it may be expected, given the advanced development of China's nuclear programme, that nuclear power (hopefully non-emitting unlike Chernobyl) will play a substantial role, despite the high costs and technical risks of decommissioning. It may also be expected that, with a modern energy system and increasing economic interdependence with other countries, and with an already advancing programme of economic betterment, China should before long be willing and able to carry a higher proportion of the cost of meeting the, by then, higher global target.

Thus those low-income countries with large commercial reserves of coal would pass through successive stages in which their net emissions were first reduced by rising efficiency in their use of fossil fuels, then by absorption on their own soil, to a greater or lesser extent depending on land availability,[14*] and finally by absorption elsewhere in the South. How the balance of paying for this would, in time, shift from mainly North energy consumers to a shared burden for these two groups of South countries and North consumers, would be related to their relative economic progress. There would be plenty for the negotiators to discuss, hopefully in the civilised and constructive manner of the Marshall Plan negotiations.

The GREENS scenario revisited

In seeing how these ideas work out in relation to the scenario we have in mind from Chapter 4 we must relate them to the sequence of change that was proposed. With per capita income approximately 10 times greater than in the South and fossil fuel consumption about half the global total, the cost of the programme of 'learning by doing' in the 1990s (rather small – see Table 7.1) is carried almost entirely by the developed countries. Of these, the USA and Canada, with around twice the general per capita energy consumption of developed countries, pay most. On the other hand, as noted above, these countries are richly endowed with resources of land which can, with notorious oversupply of cereal crops, be turned over to biomass production.

In the following decade of take-off for biomass energy, it is mainly an internal reallocation of resources, away from coal and into biomass production, for these North American countries, possibly with some need for adjustment cost support to the mining communities. Other developed countries, in Western Europe and the Far East, less well-endowed with land, face the prospect of continuing import bills for their fuel supplies (which could begin to take the form of imported ethanol to meet transportation demands as increasingly scarce oil rises in price). For them it represents a gradual shift of expenditure on energy imports from (mostly) OPEC countries to those South countries which are best placed to grow biomass surplus to their domestic needs. Whether it would also lead to some reallocation of land in developed countries towards bulky energy crops, leaving more easily transported food products to be imported rather than the ethanol just mentioned, is an interesting question, which involves the outcome of the Uruguay (and later) rounds of GATT negotiations, and which is beyond the scope of this book.[15*]

In the decade to 2020 however, with per capita income hopefully rising, population growth tapering off only slowly, and energy efficiency also improving as an offset, the South's energy demand rises to almost as much as the entire rest of the world's (Table 4.2) with the South carrying a modest but significant share of the (by then larger) overall cost of controlling global carbon dioxide net emissions. But at that stage many South countries are also benefiting from their natural advantage as the preferred site for biomass production, as the initial phase of production in temperate areas reaches maturity and tops out. Thus, by the time that the South is making more than a token contribution to the cost of dealing with the global warming problem, it is also beginning to benefit substantially from the operation of GREENS.

Impacts in Particular Countries

There are four regions where a turning away from future use of coal and lignite has a major impact. Firstly China, pre-eminently amongst a group of Eastern Asia countries; secondly the former Soviet Union and Poland, pre-eminently amongst Eastern European countries; thirdly the Republic of South Africa (RSA), amongst a Southern Africa group; and fourthly India in a Southern Asia group. Another area with less at stake from a fossil fuel exploration moratorium, but with a different cost arising in taking a sustainable future energy path, is Latin America, with Brazil pre-eminent amongst forest burners.

Each of these areas, with the possible exception of Latin America, has been the focus of some of the major political concerns of the post-World War Two era, with Eastern Europe emerging from the shadow of the Cold War, South East Asia the scene of some of its hotter encounters, a continuing concern over human rights in Eastern Asia, and Southern Africa hoping to bury the conflicts generated by apartheid policies in the RSA.

It is not reasonable to suppose that political conditionality can be successfully laid on the back of a response to the global warming problem and pressure to do so could be interpreted as covertly directed at sabotaging the prospect of effective action on climate change. Rather is it reasonable to hope that, through the economic benefits that would flow from debt relief, from sustainable energy technology transfer, and from exports of sustainable energy products, will come further progress towards politically less conflictual relationships than those of the last 40 years. Such hopes may perhaps enlighten the negotiating process.

For instance, perhaps through a bilateral relationship with Japan, or perhaps through a more general settlement, the redirection of China's energy technological base along a sustainable route would see the introduction of higher efficiency in the use of energy and the deployment of advanced sustainable energy technologies. The consequential cultural inter-penetration may, with the passage of time and personalities, do more to alter the oppressiveness of the Beijing regime than any amount of rebarbative rhetoric from Western politicians, more concerned with their domestic image than the welfare of the Chinese.

In Southern Africa the availability of local work in the biomass industry can reduce the traditional dependence of the RSA's neighbours upon income from migrant workers in the RSA's mines. Within the RSA, more work on the land in fuel-wood production and processing could serve to arrest the migration of the black population to the townships, thereby alleviating internal tensions. The needs of densely populated Britain and Netherlands to discharge their TAOs, or net TAOs, overseas could lead to a bilateral relationship with a Southern Africa freed of its post-colonial bush wars.

In Eastern Europe the debt overhangs – and the pressing need to find an effective route to economic viability, even prosperity, in the vacuum left by the collapse of central planning – points to an obvious bilateral relationship, tied to sustainable development, with the environmentally conscious EEC. The potential for increased movements of Siberian natural gas to Europe, both Western and Eastern, is clearly a major factor. Given Russia's vast resource of gas, its rapid depletion is likely to provide an important component of that country's emergence as a viable market economy as well as ameliorating Central Europe's acid rain and carbon dioxide emissions problems.

In all of these possible bilateral relationships, a partnership rather than dependency style of interaction is appropriate to a situation in which the developed countries need the collaboration of the South and East to deal with a problem that has arisen from the past nature of their own development. Rather than an exploitative use of advanced renewable technology, a joint venturing approach is appropriate. Not the collective fuel-wood farm or the fuel-wood plantation run by expatriate masters, but the fuel-wood co-operative of smallholders and richer peasants, with, perhaps, a nucleus plantation providing training, advice and the capital infrastructure for efficient collection and processing based on the development of extension field services that relate sensitively to the cultural and family scale economic realities of traditional societies.[16] The fostering of such arrangements would be a vital task for the international agencies to be set up under the FCCC, as will be discussed in Chapter 9.

Progress towards global co-ordination may take the form of information exchange and policy convergence across bilateral relationships and regional schemes, within guidelines embodied in a Framework Convention on Climate Change, or in a more directly binding agreement amongst those involved. Quite how such progress can be made is not to be detailed in advance. There are too many unknowns and too many players for any blueprint to carry conviction. But the importance of local actions and national initiatives as the stimulus to collaboration and co-ordination on a broader scale, and eventually globally, cannot be underestimated. Indeed, one purpose of this book is to enable local initiators to be confident that economically viable technological solutions are available, which do not require politically daunting choices to be made, and which are being pursued elsewhere.

OPEC and the Middle East

Unmentioned above is, of course, the most worrying political problem left after the Cold War – indeed the problem which many commentators felt was more likely than any to have turned it into a hot war. No early prospect of substituting completely for oil has been proposed in transport fuel product markets – and indeed, the moratorium on exploration secures continuing OPEC dominance of the oil market, albeit a market of declining importance. However, the application of the TAO means the early displacement of oil from heating fuel markets, with a need for increasing development of high tech 'refineries' designed to process the whole barrel to transport fuels, with the growth of biomass fuels reducing the Middle East's power in the market.

Thus the prospect is of a decreasing market role for oil and a sharply diminished strategic significance for the Middle East. Dominating the world's major remaining reserves of cheap oil, their expectation, in the absence of carbon dioxide emissions concern, has been to reap huge profits in competition with expensive secondary and tertiary recovery from elsewhere. Even though the volume of oil they export is unlikely to fall appreciably this century, the GREENS scenario faces them with a price ceiling imposed by the increasing availability of renewable products at costs competitive with oil at $25 a barrel (or lower if the SERI process, taken as the backstop technology in Chapter 4, is improved on further or superseded by other developments).

Relative to that ceiling, the cost of production in Arabia would still leave a substantial margin to provide finance for continuing development in the region. Oil companies, relieved of the need to finance ever more difficult exploration, and North governments, relieved of the prospect of everlasting dependence on their reserves, could leave Arabian oil producers to control their depletion in the interests of their own economic development, that is to say at the rate needed to finance the absorptive capacity of their developing productive sectors.

Happier though such an outcome might be in the longer run for the people of those countries than a continued pattern of conspicuous spending on military hardware and extravagant lifestyles for the ruling elite, it is hard to believe these rulers would not see their countries as the main losers from GREENS. However, given their fortune in recent decades, and their extreme affluence relative to other South countries (and, in some cases, relative to many North countries also), these countries can – especially with memories of the oil price hikes of the 1970s still sharp – hardly expect much sympathy.

The Middle Eastern oil exporters can be divided into the sparsely populated, semi-feudal and hugely rich lands to the south of the Persian Gulf, politically dependent on the US, and the populous and poorer countries to the North. The latter, harbouring deep-seated antagonisms between the Sunni and Shi'ite branches of the Islamic faith, and between clerical Iran and secular Iraq, devastated by a decade of war, is an obvious area of concern.

The political dependence of the southern group, and its heavy investment in the capital markets of the North, suggests that the greater risk of such undermining of GREENS does not lie there. While Iraq remains politically isolated in the aftermath of Saddam Hussein's Kuwait adventure, a change in regime there may call for a magnanimous approach. Iran, with reducing prospects from oil, may need support from outside the scope of the GREENS framework for its continued development, whether or not in the context of a central Asian economic union. One needs only to mention these issues to reinforce the importance, as regards responding effectively to global warming is concerned, of avoiding conditionality and decoupling the concerns of the Earth Summit from other political issues.

However, with environmental pressures spurring the emergence of alternative biomass technologies, OPEC's bargaining power becomes much weaker and making the best of their wasting asset (albeit with its market value sustained by the exploration moratorium) would be their prudent policy. Nevertheless, the possibility cannot be discounted that needs for cash, maybe to support adventurism against Israel, would lead some or other of these countries to offload oil so cheaply as to undercut the selling price of a renewable fuel industry in neighbouring emergent economies. To counter this would need firm policy, by a core group of countries, working together towards achieving sustainability, maybe involving the application of collateral pressures outside the GREENS framework to achieve the common good objective of responding to global warming.

The special position of the USA

The USA is unique amongst the major North countries, obviously, as a military superpower, but also as heavily indebted, and as the owner of large commercial reserves of cheap coal. Indeed it is easy for some in the sustainability debate to pick out the USA as the bad boy in the class, not only because of its reluctant posture in the FCCC negotiating process, but because of its disproportionate per capita contribution to current and past greenhouse gas emissions, and because of its past role, through misguided energy policies of the 1980s, in fostering global dependence upon politically unstable Middle East oil (imposing costs on other oil-importing countries as well as on itself). However, such posturing is as sterile a direction to take as it would be to exert economic pressure on China in pursuit of ulterior political objectives.

Rightly or wrongly, the USA regards itself, in collaboration with the United Nations, as the saviour of the Middle East from Saddam Hussein's adventurism, possibly from his regional hegemony.[17*] And it congratulates itself on the success of decades of pressure upon totalitarian communism in turning Eastern Europe in a different direction, hopefully prosperous and only temporarily chaotic. Its debts it regards as honourably contracted in its role as military protector of democracy.

The turning of US policy on global warming must depend upon understanding its position rather than enviously belabouring the wickedness of its ways which, to the majority of Americans, do not seem to be wicked at all. Of course, this does not mean that the USA should not fulfil its role, along with other developed countries, in negotiating a commitment for relatively burdensome policies, e.g. a high TAO on US carbon fuel sales, to reflect the income redistributive aspect which is needed to secure the involvement of the South. However, unlike most other OECD countries, the USA has very large reserves of cheap coal, and unlike any other OECD country, the USA has carried the burden of Cold War confrontation and is, perhaps consequentially, deeply in debt.

With US banks taking a leading role in the build-up of the Third World debt problem, especially as regards heavily indebted Latin America, the American commercial banking system remains exposed to the risk of further default. Thus, in addition to consideration of the official US debt, there are grounds for concern that whatever deal is struck should safeguard, rather than further expose, the US commercial banking system.

Accordingly, the debt deal suggested previously, involving the restructuring of unsound Third World debt in exchange for a moratorium on exploration for fossil fuels, could involve the takeover of the written down debts by those North countries that have built up large reserves in the last decade, rather than further extending the US position. Such an arrangement could also reduce US indebtedness to Europe and Japan and, perhaps, reflect a retrospective consideration for the US role in bringing about the reduction in military tensions since 1991.

Nevertheless, the North American burden from GREENS is more substantial than for any other North country. The cheapness of its coal causes the opportunity cost of substitution by biomass to be greater than for other North countries, and the coal lobby in the USA is strong. However, many parts of the USA have no coal and stand to gain from an internal reallocation of resources towards growing fuel rather than digging for it. So the turning of national policy may follow a period of change led by local initiatives, with state legislatures taking the lead towards protecting, say, environment-conscious Californians and New Englanders from the dangers of fossil fuels.

And maybe Southern states would see a way, based upon their better climate, both to promote their environmental image to sun-seeking migrants and to create local jobs in fuel-wood production and technology, maybe finding alternatives to their current dependence on military spending. However such domestic politics may go, the importance of Schelling's negotiating process as a forum where the particular needs of individual FCCC participants can be addressed, is obvious *per contra* the alternative model of a centralised bureaucracy operating legally binding commitments.

Global Mutual Advantage

Thus the implementation of a global (or initially regional or bilateral) phase of debt relief could not only be a one-off recognition of past errors in the relationship between North and South, linked constructively to a moratorium on exploring for fossil fuels, but also a closing of the book on the Cold War era, with both fittingly linked to – and occasioned by – the initiation of a movement towards more sustainable development.

The errors were not necessarily foreseeable, but with the passage of time appear as errors brought about by ignorance rather than folly. In terms of Chapter 3, we are regretting decisions taken in ignorance of what the state of nature would turn out to be – in the event slower growth and mounting environmental problems.

The North's error has been the pursuit of a development path that has been neglectful of the sustainability of nature's inputs and which, in particular, has been overly dependent upon fossil fuels to a point that puts posterity at risk from their continued use. The South's error has been in accepting a subordinate role in relation to that development path, which has left it environmentally despoiled and vulnerable to market fluctuations, rather than taking the slower path of development related to the South's indigenous needs and capabilities. The South has accepted, or been subjected to, dependency on the North's technology, rather than demanding aid based on appropriate technology and developing self-reliance on it.

Whatever the errors of the past, the global nature of the problem created by the fragility of its one atmosphere requires a solution based upon globally sustainable energy technology (which, we have seen, is more appropriate to the development of South countries than was the previous technology, based on minerals which many do not have). The argument of this chapter is thus that the linking of debt relief and sustainable technology provides a response to political concerns in both North and South. The North concerns are over the environment, and global warming in particular, and the South concerns are over the constraints which undeserved debt and obsolete technology place upon their economic progress.

Debt relief that is broadly conditional upon progress in the direction of sustainable energy technologies – and collaboration with GREENS that is broadly conditional upon debt relief – provide the basis for a mutually advantageous accommodation. Jointly they provide both the pretext needed to escape the bind of the reputational problem concerning the financial discipline of indebted nations (and hence to liberate the world's financial system to underpin a new and more equitable prosperity) and, through the TAO, a mechanism that can give momentum to Global Redevelopment with Energy Environment Sustainability.

A miraculous 'born again' conversion of national economic behaviours is, of course, improbable. But debt relief need not be instantaneous even if it is one-off in nature. Indeed, a process of staged debt relief or suspension, conditional upon progress towards sustainability, and upon demonstrated effectiveness of the exploration moratorium, would be more appropriate. Equally, as envisaged in our Chapter 4 scenario, progress towards sustainability should be a process of deliberate and collaborative haste rather than precipitate unplanned confusion.

Nor is the solution proposed for the general problem facing all countries of how to meet energy demands arising from the development process – that is to say the GREENS concept implemented through TAOs negotiated on a country-by-country basis – dependent in its initial stages upon a solution to the specific problem of how to compensate those South countries that are already basing their developments on their own cheap fossil fuel resources. That must come about through much higher commitments being negotiated for North countries and through energy firms finding that the cheapest way to discharge them is to go into these latter countries and transform their energy systems, initially at the expense of their North customers but less so as the South generally comes to enjoy a higher per capita income.

In the meantime, individual countries like New Zealand that have within their borders sufficient land relative to their population to grow biomass as the cheapest way to meet their own policy commitments to emissions reduction can simply get on with it. And other countries, that are deeply concerned about global warming but which do not have the land available, can get on with it in partnership with another country that does have the land, and which welcomes the income, in some kind of bilateral arrangement. With the passage of time, even the most reluctant amongst North countries will find themselves persuaded by the increasing weight of scientific evidence – as they have been with the cautionary experience of CFCs – or, alternatively, the more concerned countries will, with scientific evidence pointing in the other direction, move towards a less active policy.

Were the world to be run by a world government, the technological and economic problems of managing this, and dealing effectively with global warming under the GREENS concept, would seem not very great. The evidence now available would lead any prudent world government to undertake the rather low precautionary expenditures in the 1990s which are implicit in Figure 7.2. As was said at the outset, the aspect of the problem which entails precautionary effort, beyond the rationale of cost-benefit analysis, lies in the field of political economy.

The difficulties arise because of the divisions between nations, because of the difficulty of facing up to the transfers to coal-rich countries like India and China, because of the conservatism of bankers when it comes to thinking of debt from an economic rather than a legalistic perspective, because of the reluctance of successive American administrations to face their voters with the true costs of gasoline, because of the power of wealth in the hands of OPEC and the major energy firms, and so on.

The prospect is daunting indeed. But we must hope for statesmanlike recognition that these resistances must be overcome. It may not come from the North, for it is a mistake to suppose that South countries are unmindful of the future just because they demand prior attention to the injustices of the present. So far, debt difficulties have arisen on a country-by-country basis which has left the South country concerned in a weak bargaining position. It is quite possible that a failure by the North to address the South's debt grievances in the context of the Earth Summit and its subsequent processes could lead to collective debt default by the South in order to induce a world order less unfair to them and to future generations. Especially may this be the case as South countries become aware that an effective response to the global warming problem could embody a more equitable world trading order, beneficial to them rather than inhibiting their growth and, in particular, providing the technology transfers needed to secure their future energy needs on a sustainable and economic basis.

However long it may take for a global settlement to come about, at either the North's instance or the South's, it seems unlikely that the North will this century be taking any very costly steps. Providing that the relatively low-cost programmes of precautionary research, training and institution-building are undertaken in a timely manner, take-off for GREENS can occur next century, as and when the weight of scientific evidence begins to move the political process. Political economy need not be an obstacle to 'getting ready'. Being ready may in due course make the political economics easier.

Notes

1. An earlier essay on this aspect is in Read, 1992a.
2. Schelling, 1992.
3. The economists' model of rational selfish individualism, which is the starting point for non-cooperative game theory, can hardly be less conducive to the realisation of a shared global benefit. In its modern extensions this rationality is projected into strategic behaviour of superrationality. The complexity of such models is matched only by their lack of operational relevance, their multiplicity of possible outcomes, their implausibility of assumptions as regards the amount of common knowledge per contra the lack of common purpose, and their generally bleak perspective on human nature. No scheme to achieve a shared global benefit can be designed watertight against the ingenuity of bureaucratic leak detectors informed by this dispiriting outlook. Certainly the great common good for both

donor and recipients of post World War II Marshall Aid, conceived at the apogee of J.M. Keynes' benign intellectual influence on the 'dismal science' of economics, would not be realised by the collective wisdom of the modern profession. At an international conference on economic policies for the environment, it was noted with surprise that the Montreal Convention on ozone-destroying CFCs was quickly agreed by politicians without any economists of note being present and without much support from career officials and diplomats. But it may have been precisely because of these absences that politicians were able to reach agreement at all – *per contra* the long drawn out saga of the Uruguay Round of GATT negotiations. An effective response to global warming depends on politicians being motivated to impose such an outcome upon bureaucratic doubting Thomases – in which they may take heart from Holtham and Hughes Hallett, 1987, who note, in relation to the political dealing prior to the Bonn Summit of 1978,' that the possibility of reneging was never perceived as an obstacle to agreement' and, referring to the importance of reputation in continuing negotiations, comment that, 'Economists have perhaps focussed on moral hazard problems because of their interesting logical character rather than because of their empirical importance'.

4. The interpretation of measurements of mineral reserves must be based upon an appreciation of the motivations of enterprises to find and define such reserves, which is a costly activity. When commercial concern about continuity of oil supply arises, then renewed effort is put into exploration. It is not by chance that new reserves of oil have so far always been found, albeit with increasing difficulty and on the back of advances in exploration technology, as existing reserves fall below about ten years of current usage. The inference of reserves existing from traditional, noncommercial recovery activities or from casual knowledge of surface traces, seepages or outcrops is a different matter from proven reserves of given underground delineation and proven economic exploitability using known extraction technology and taking account of the market conditions that exist locally.

5. Simonis, 1992, Table 2.

6. This jurisprudential doctrine, fashionable in the context of the role of EC national governments in relation to the Brussels bureaucracy, has been claimed to underlie the Social Economy approach evolved clandestinely in Nazi Germany by those who subsequently formed the post-war government and, in the context of Marshall Aid, achieved Germany's 'economic miracle'. It aims systematically to devolve responsibility for action in a hierarchy (individual, family, firm, local government, central government) to the lowest level that can cope with it (Lachmann, 1992).

7. Indeed it is extremely difficult to establish the debt position of North countries, with different countries publishing data on different bases in different places. The meaning to be attached to the concept of foreign debt is also somewhat elusive when huge flows of currency reflecting the day-to-day transactions of foreign exchange brokers are mixed up with flows related to commercial transactions of a short, medium and long term nature in off-shore money markets. Financial liabilities of governments are often matched by assets of their citizens and the financial and/or illiquid assets of companies registered in their country, possibly partly or wholly owned from abroad. Disentangling all this in order to

establish whether the asset position of a country, and/or its citizens and corporations, is in overall debt reveals rather little since indebtedness does not act as a constraint on transactions – lines of credit are extended as necessary between central banks of countries that are in good standing, with macro-economic management resulting in shifts of exchange rates and interest rates that hopefully maintain a long term balance.

8. It has even led to the idea (Payer, 1991) that loan assistance is necessarily damaging to the South since repayments of interest plus principal necessarily exceed the original loan. However (unless collateral economic and trade policies are pursued which inhibit growth in the South, as has substantially been the case in the 1980s) the normal expectation is that the repayment of interest would be less than the growth of output attributable to the loan so that the South would be a net beneficiary, and both lender and borrower would be the better for the transaction, as is normally the case when money is borrowed to finance a project for which there is a favourable judgement of the prospects.

9. World Bank, 1992 and 1989, Table 1; Enquete-Kommission, 1990, p.367.

10. The USA is a net debtor but a major creditor as far as the Third World is concerned since much of the OPEC sourced money was channelled through the USA on its way to the Third World, especially South America.

11. Uzawa, 1990.

12. World Bank, 1992, Table 5.

13. Schelling, 1992, p.13.

14. Maybe the 'making coal' option would be cheaper than transporting biomass to China, particularly if the bulk of demand there continues to be for industrial purposes (requiring cheap furnace fuel, e.g. wood chips) rather than for motor vehicles (requiring more easily transported ethanol) and if the nuclear option appears unattractive on a full cost basis. In effect, this would be to say it is easier to lift coal in China, and 'make' it in Australia, than to shift several hundred millions of Chinese to live in Australia.

15. It is a question not without interest to New Zealand and Australia where a liberal outcome from the Uruguay Round would result in renewed exports of food products to traditional markets, whereas continued high protection for Northern temperate farmers could see the development of substantial invisible exports of pollution clean-up services, together with visible ethanol exports, from the antipodes. For New Zealand it is mainly a bread and butter issue, although there are substantial local environmental spin-offs. But for Australia, with much of its traditional agriculture becoming unsustainable due to rising salination, a replacement of a substantial proportion of its ancient tree cover should be an urgent priority.

16. Leach and Mearns, 1988, pp.172-5.

17. To those who believe the Cold War to have been an unnecessary historical excursion, that the nightmare experience of the last 45 years could have been avoided if the bombing of Hiroshima had never happened, and that Eastern Europe would now be a better place if Marshall Aid had not been conditional upon conformity with Western-style democratic government, any positive recognition of the benefits of Pax Americana would be anathema. Such people may

console themselves by hoping that the kind of global settlement that is being conjectured could leave US military power with a less dominant role in future.

9. The Road from Rio

The FCCC that was signed at the Earth Summit in June 1992 makes the writing of this chapter remarkably simpler than it might have been had earlier versions, focusing on gross emissions of carbon dioxide rather than net emissions of greenhouse gases generally, gone forward for signature at Rio. For the objective of the Convention is, as this book has emphasised it should be, 'to achieve ... stabilisation of greenhouse gas *concentrations* in the atmosphere at a *level* that would prevent dangerous anthropogenic interference with the climate system' [italics added].

Thus the task of explaining why it is the wrong sort of FCCC, and of describing the changes needed before it can provide the basis for effective action in pursuit of its own objective, does not present itself. Still less do we need to explain why the targets that have been agreed on are overly ambitious or why the carbon tax that has been agreed on is premature and burdensome. For the target is modest – maybe overly modest but easily changed within the negotiating framework provided – and carbon taxes (the need for which has been the main theme of economists' advice, save to the extent it has been directed against taking any action at all)[1] are nowhere in sight.

The modesty of the target for net emissions reductions, embodied in the Article 4 commitments, and upon which press interest contentiously focused during the negotiating process, is far less important than what makes it the right sort of FCCC. Pre-eminently this is that it can provide an effective forum within which developing ideas as to what needs to be done about the threat of climate change can be integrated into a process of global policy formation. Given continuing political will, the institutional structures are in place to enable the option costs of alternative courses of action to provide the basis for rational policy choice, along the lines advocated in Chapters 1 and 3. This requires the costs to be regularly reassessed, with Bayesian updating of beliefs about an unknown state of nature and of the technological possibilities, with those beliefs and possibilities expanded purposefully by appropriate choices of research directions. After the Stockholm conference of 1972, and Rio in 1992, we do not need to wait until 2012 for the next move.

In this chapter we accordingly first describe the main features of the FCCC and then discuss the way in which it can be made to work in putting into operation over the next few decades the sequence of activities which comprise the long-term strategy of this book – what I have called the

GREENS concept. The 1990s are a period for getting ready and learning by doing on a pilot scale and at low levels of policy (low TAO percentages). This is essentially a programme of research, in the broadest sense of the word, and we next look in more detail at two research areas of particular concern. We will discuss the problems of measurement introduced by the biomass carbon recycling process that provides GREENS' scientific basis and, more briefly, by the net TAO technology transfer mechanism (net absorption), and by the fossil fuel exploration moratorium. We will review some of the sustainability issues raised by enhanced biomass production through intensive forestry, together with the intensive programme of action research, on the ground, and in the community, that is involved in getting ready by the end of the decade for whatever needs to be done at that time.

The United Nations Framework Convention on Climate Change

Signatories of the FCCC agree to be bound by it after it comes into force subsequent to ratification by at least 50 countries. They are referred to as Parties to the Convention which comprises some 25 Articles. Of these, the last 12 deal with the formalities of procedures for settling disputes, amending the Convention, adding protocols to it, signing and ratifying it, its entry into force and prior interim arrangements, etc., and the first provides some obviously needed definitions including, crucially, one for greenhouse gas 'sinks' as well as one for 'sources'.

The meat of the Convention is in Articles 2 to 13, of which the first states the 'ultimate objective' mentioned above and Article 3 sets out five Principles which indicate that the North should take the lead on grounds of responsibility and ability to pay; that the needs of South countries should be fully considered, particularly those most vulnerable to climate change; that precautionary steps should be taken ahead of full scientific certainty of their need; that the Parties should have a right to sustainable development; and that they should promote an open international economic system supportive of sustainable economic growth, with measures to combat climate change not acting as a restriction on trade.

Authority under the Convention runs from the Conference of the Parties (CoP) which is constituted as the FCCC's Supreme Body under Article 7. Of course national sovereignty remains with the Parties, but to remain in good standing they must fulfil their obligations, as developed by the CoP. Obviously the CoP's authority will depend upon its effective discharge of its duties, which include periodically examining the commitments of the Parties in the light of experience of implementation and of the evolution of knowledge (i.e. Bayesian updating), and helping Parties to co-ordinate their implementation policies (e.g. by facilitating

Schelling's negotiating process, which may be regarded as institutionalised in Article 13, requiring the establishment of a multilateral consultative process to resolve questions arising from the implementation of the convention).

The CoP is also charged with developing measures of the Parties' performance, assessing such performance, publishing reports on progress, and making recommendations as regards implementation. In pursuit of this the CoP is to set its own rules of procedure and financial control at its first meeting (by consensus, which could prove a stumbling block); to mobilise the financial provisions of the Convention; to establish the necessary organisation; to work with other international organisations; and, generally, do what it needs to do in pursuit of the Objective (Article 2). The necessary organisation is to include, specifically, Article 8, a Secretariat and two subsidiary organisations, one, Article 9, Scientific and Technical (taking over the work of the IPCC?) and the other, Article 10, for Implementation, which apparently will be some kind of ginger group intended to keep the CoP on its toes.

Money makes the world go round and the FCCC is waste paper unless adequate finance is available and controlled in a manner consistent with the objective and guiding principles. Article 11, the Financial Mechanism, provides for the control of available funds to be under the guidance of the CoP, thus giving the South a say in how cash provided by the North is spent. Although operational responsibility lies with an existing international entity, the Global Environment Facility (GEF) formerly controlled by the World Bank, in turn controlled by its paymasters in the North, is to be restructured to enable it to operate under North-South control as an interim arrangement. This is prior to the first session of the CoP, which cannot take place until the FCCC comes into force (having been signed and ratified by 50 countries, as previously mentioned when a transparent system of governance with an 'equitable and balanced representation of all Parties' is to be implemented.

This is a quite radical departure for a United Nations institution, where control of the purse strings has traditionally been retained by the providers of cash. Of course, control of spending is not the same thing as power to levy contributions, and where the money comes from is dealt with elsewhere. But Article 11 is a marker for the shift in North/South relationships which follows from the North's need of the South's collaboration in dealing with global environmental issues.

Where the money comes from is committed under Article 4, which not only covers the much publicised targets discussed previously. It also commits North and South alike to collect and communicate information about sources and sinks of greenhouse gases (save CFCs, covered by the Montreal Protocol); to prepare programmes of response measures; and to promote net emissions-reducing technology, sustainable management, adaptation strategies, impact-minimising planning procedures, scientific and technological research and data collection, information exchange, and public awareness programmes including participation by non-governmental organisations.

The money for this, and for the costs of complying with requirements for implementation information (Article 12), and for expenditures under the Financial Mechanism (Article 11), all comes from developed country Parties, i.e. the North, under a commitment requiring adequacy and predictability in the flow of funds with 'appropriate' burden sharing among North Parties (an area for negotiation, assisted by a proficient secretariat). Additionally, the costs of assisting vulnerable countries also fall on the North. And, alongside all this, bilateral and regional arrangements that are directed at the ultimate objective are acceptable in fulfilment or part fulfilment of commitments under the Convention.

That leaves Articles 5 and 6 which provide more specification of the commitments on scientific research and data gathering, and on education, training and public awareness, mentioned under Article 4. So it is Articles 4 (Commitments), 7 (Conference of the Parties), and 11 (Financial Mechanism) which constitute the effective core of the Convention. In so far as it provides a framework in which the Parties can, with goodwill and the support of a proficient secretariat, negotiate their financial contributions and policy responses to the commitments entered into, it is, with its Articles 2 and 3 Objective and Principles, well adapted to the implementation of the GREENS strategy set out in previous chapters. If the sovereign horses cannot be made to drink, there is at least a trough for them to drink from. We now turn to considering some of the problems that arise if they do, indeed, take the medicine.

In considering what needs to be done to make GREENS operational under the FCCC we will be thinking about the work of the Article 8 Secretariat, the work of the Research and Implementation Subsidiary Bodies (Articles 9 and 10) as well as the work of the CoP itself. Given that the other bodies work under the guidance and authority of the CoP, we will for convenience talk about what the CoP does, bearing in mind that it will largely do these things through its guidance of the various agencies.

Using the FCCC to Achieve GREENS

In the sequenced GREENS scenario outlined in the last chapter and in Chapter 4, the balance of activity changes, with a major focus on research in the 1990s, the period of 'getting ready' and of 'learning by doing'. A shift begins towards the end of the decade, with increasing emphasis on facilitating implementation as the average global TAO percentage is raised in the following few decades, at a rate decided on by the CoP in the light of continuing input from climatological science. And with changes in the global average will come changes in the commitments of individual countries which will emerge from horse trading between the Parties, brokered by the CoP in the context of Uzawa's equity principle. With the passage of time, the initial emphasis on temperate regions as the location for absorption activity shifts to South countries, at a rate depending on their perceptions of the advantages of participation.

Unless the next 30 years sees the South as a whole raise its economic performance, relative to the North, at the rate achieved by Japan in the last 40 years, the GREENS transformation of commercial energy technology will be complete before economic parity between North and South has been achieved. Thus it can be assumed that the completion of the transformation will be such that, on balance, TAOs are incurred more in the developed North and discharged more in the still developing South. That is the best that can be hoped for by 2020, even if the FCCC is used effectively and the optimistic prospect for Global Redevelopment is successfully attached to the achievement of Energy Environment Sustainability, as envisaged when we introduced our acronymic GREENS concept in Chapter 1.

However, we have also argued that, to start with, such a South-oriented activity for the operation of GREENS is not needed and should not dominate its initial implementation. The impact of a sudden and ill-organised scramble to discharge the bulk of developed world TAOs in unprepared tropical countries would be disruptive and discredit the work of the CoP, possibly to an extent that would prejudice the continued viability of the FCCC. (On the other hand, such arguments do not apply against the early implementation of technology transfer in the context of 'net absorption', particularly to East countries.)

Thus a component of the TAO system must be the development of sustainability guidelines in relation to the way in which absorption activity is actually conducted in particular field situations. Such guidelines would emerge from, and be progressively updated through, the programme of sustainability research to which we will shortly come. One task, the mechanics of which are discussed below, would be to monitor the discharge of the TAOs by the firms which incur them, including the observance of the sustainability guidelines, and to report back to the country of origin of the TAO, where observance of the guidelines would be written into the TAO, and non-observance be subject to penalty.

However, in relation to the initial phase of absorption activity, there is plenty of land available in temperate latitudes for the initial low levels of TAO (e.g. beginning at only a few per cent absorption in the mid 1990s) to be discharged within the borders of emitting countries in the North. Relatively sophisticated environment protection systems already exist in these countries, thus providing the competence for a critique of the CoP's initial work as input to the learning by doing process.

The subsequent TAO levels in the late 1990s – then slightly higher – can also be discharged mainly by operations restricted to temperate latitudes, albeit not always with absorption occurring in the initiating country of the TAO. Thus 1998 or 1999 might see quite substantial discharge in Eastern Europe of EEC-initiated TAOs, or in the former Soviet Union or South Africa, with Japanese-initiated TAOs discharged in China or Australasia. Land-rich North America would still be able to handle its target absorption mostly within its own territory. These developments would provide the CoP with a field trial for the transnational aspects of its monitoring activity and an opportunity to refine its practices.

Quite early in the process some of the more go-ahead South countries – say Malaysia, given the statements of its Prime Minister – would be seeking to further their development through full participation in the (equitably adjusted) commitments of the FCCC. There would be a demonstration effect and, as the opening decade of the 21st century progresses, an increasing number of South countries would be seeing the advantages of full commitment (in addition to technology transfer aspects). Thus the direction of trade – both in biomass-based energy products and in pollution clean-up services, i.e. the discharge of TAOs – that is eventually needed, if the South is to benefit fully from the GREENS concept, would begin to be established.

But initially the work of the CoP will largely be research, both formal scientific research – in the climatological field, obviously, but also in relation to sustainability issues we shall come to – and informal research in which the CoP learns how to do what needs to be done, creating its own corps of workers in a process of action research, building institutions and training people worldwide. For in order to bring about, with all deliberate speed, the prospect of global mutual advantage under GREENS, outlined at the end of the previous chapter, a collaborative process comprising not simply a research exercise, but a training exercise as well, is needed. First the trainers have to be trained and, by them, the extension fieldworkers. If technology transfer to South countries is to be a reality, these workers must be carriers to the grassroots of developing societies of the knowledge that needs to be there.

At the same time, they will be collecting and maintaining the detailed data base about land capability – and updating it, since technical advance whilst 'learning by doing' makes land capability a dynamic rather than a static concept. It is the aggregation of such detailed field data which will guide statesmen regarding the costs and practicalities of implementing a carbon absorption policy and a related renewable biomass-based energy system or, if the news is bad, lead them to consider alternative and harder choices for dealing with global warming (if indeed positive action continues to appear to be the prudent policy).

Evolving naturally from this continuing activity are the businesses of monitoring the performance of firms in the discharge of their TAOs and of providing the accountability needed in relation to country commitments under Article 4 of the FCCC.[2*] Thus a basic activity of the CoP, given the tradeability of absorption duties, is to act as the recipient of data relating to the countries of origin of TAOs, from the firms wholesaling fuel and which have primary ownership of the obligation (and against which the government in the country of origin can proceed in the event of failure to discharge), and from the successor firms which contract and transnational for the discharge of the TAO. And, of course, to register such transactions and keep track of the TAOs until they are finally discharged.

This function of monitoring and accountancy for discharge of the TAO is one which evolves naturally from the research and training function mentioned above. That function would see the development, on an international basis, of a cadre of extension workers who are technically equipped to facilitate the discharge of the TAO wherever that may be done, motivated to see that it is done by their initial commitment to such a career choice, and by a concern for sustainability fostered through their training, and maintained in their international loyalty to the CoP by the collection of carrot and stick influences which constitute the reality of the employer-employee relationship.

The political dimension of the CoP's work

As the representatives of the CoP in the field, and on the territory of the individual Parties as hosts, the long-term viability of the FCCC depends upon a continuing welcome for the CoP's extension workers. This in turn will reflect their ability – beyond the occasional personality clash and other contretemps which can make any diplomatic representative persona non grata in the country where she or he may be accredited – to provide an extension service to the host country, in terms of technical transfer, economic competitiveness and rural development, which outweighs the cost to the host country of informational transparency.

Apprehensions that the operations of the CoP as a monitor of firms' behaviour would be seen by ex-colonial countries as back-door intrusion into their internal affairs could flourish in the aftermath of the ill feeling that arose during the run up to the Earth Summit. It is thus a further advantage of the phased introduction of GREENS, with trade in TAOs concentrated initially in temperate regions, that such concerns would be alleviated by the demonstration that such monitoring activity had been initiated in the North and been made acceptable to sovereign countries of the highest status.

In the longer run, it is but one reason amongst several for the importance of using an economic instrument that follows the subsidiarity principle, with agent-principal relationships that are congruent with political and jurisdictional realities. For the least-cost theorem implies that the absorption aspect of one country's national performance, in relation to target, may be conducted in another country's territory, i.e. 'joint implementation' as noted in Chapter 7, Note 7. However, the agent-principle relationship embedded in the TAO means that it is not a government but a firm, and a firm subject to local national law, which conducts operations in host countries.[3*]

The sanction against misbehaviour by firms in relation to their TAOs is exemplary penalties against delinquent fuel wholesalers in the country where the TAO is incurred (together with the normal legal recourse of contract enforcement between firms involved in subcontracted TAOs). Any pressures on governments would be of a last resort nature (perhaps against one that was flouting its FCCC commitments – maybe by way of a temporary suspension of good standing under the FCCC, or partial withdrawal of some of its advantages) in the same way that (extremely rare) trade sanctions under the GATT do not trespass upon the internal functioning of member states.

On a more positive note, the process of detailed global housekeeping, in the field of sustainable energy technology and carbon accountancy, can form the prototype for a transition to global sustainability in a more general sense. It can mark the beginnings of a recognition that the future relationship between humanity and nature must properly reflect the value of nature's inputs and the cost of anthropogenic insults upon nature. Consistent with that would be the provision by the research community of guidelines as regards species diversity, soil fertility maintenance, disease resistance, water utilisation, intercropping practices and other aspects of sustainability which raise concern when the notion of intensive fuel-wood cropping is advanced.

Commercial complexity

With upwards of 150 nations hopefully becoming signatories to the FCCC, and with thousands of energy firms burdened with TAOs to discharge, a complex web of obligations and performances will develop. South countries will enter into full participation and commitment when they see fit, accepting an equitably low net absorption commitment in exchange for the benefits of hosting absorption activity, and foregoing potential benefits from licensing exploration for fossil fuels in exchange for some degree of restructuring of debt. As these better venues for absorption activity become available, energy firms will be queuing up at the doors of the Rural Development and Planning Ministries of favourable South countries, seeking licences to contract with the landowners to develop fuel-wood plantations. No doubt there will be some internal politics to ensure that these licences are sold dear enough to cover development and infrastructure costs that the fuel-wood operation imposes.

Probably treasury departments in South countries will be concerned to see that the licenses are not sold so high that the business goes to other countries. And the Energy and Industry Ministries will be concerned as to whether the fuel-wood product is to be used for a gas turbine-based electricity plant – and if so whether some other TAO will be discharged as 'net absorption', underwriting the necessary technology transfer – or for an export-oriented ethanol plant owned by the firm – and if so whether the firm will guarantee an export price. Maybe, in the meantime, another firm may see long-run opportunities in the conventional timber market that will lead it to discharge its TAO by afforestation with selected timber species in some other country, which may have special amenity areas where fuel-wood plantations would be inappropriate.

Many of these initiatives will make sense to the energy companies in ways which are mysterious to the outsider, and which represent the different companies' differing perceptions of their future role in the energy market, and indeed perhaps, through diversification, into other markets. What is 'least cost' to an energy firm may be far from what would be perceived by the CoP's global energy modellers as a sensible line of development. It is of the essence of reliance on market mechanisms that these many small mistakes and misperceptions do not impose excessive cost and that they avoid the greater danger, inherent in centralised approaches to allocation, of misperceptions in the planning department driving the whole system expensively off course.

It makes for a complex and busy picture of interaction in which national absorption commitments and development plans may become tangled up with the commercial objectives of energy firms. South countries, including notably China and India, will not want their territory to be used for the discharge of a TAO incurred in the North unless there is something to be got out of it for them. That such will be the case follows as a matter of course from their ability to control – and profit from – the operations within their territory of overseas-based energy firms that have a TAO to discharge, possibly by auctioning licenses to carry out absorption activity.

However, competition in the market for pollution clean-up services will act as a check upon excessive profiteering. Essentially the profit that can be extracted will derive from comparative advantage in the absorption process, with zero profit going to the marginal absorber. Falling profit from absorption activity (conventional afforestation) or recycling activity (fuel wood production and/or 'making coal') would, after the early years of the next century, most probably occur in the temperate regions that first get into the business. There the growing demand for food in a hopefully more prosperous world could see a revival of cereal production in the

North and rising land values there. Thus rising costs, and increasing competition from the lower cost South, could see the beginnings of a scaling down of the temperate region absorption activity that would peak, perhaps, sometime around 2010.

Monitoring and enforcement

Given the nature of the TAO as a bad to be lost, rather than a good to be kept securely, there would be an incentive for firms to find ways to 'double count' absorption in host countries (either in the North, earlier on, or in the South later), both for the discharge of a TAO incurred elsewhere and towards the local target. This would be matched by a temptation on the part of governments of host countries to connive in such double counting and extract profit on absorption activities related to their own commitments for which such governments are themselves responsible.

Such opportunities for illegal profit from the workings of the scheme would, of course, exist during the initial phase of activity when the trade in TAOs is conducted mainly in temperate and developed countries. They are examples of the problems involved in trading in bads rather than goods which mean that firms cannot be relied upon not to 'lose' the bad unless effective accountability procedures are in place. They are the kind of avoidance problem that arises in any pollution-control measure and which requires the setting up of appropriate monitoring and accountancy procedures.

Since the design of the TAO is directed at ensuring that the carbon is absorbed wherever in the world it is most efficient to do so, the avoidance problem is compounded by sovereignty issues and the familiar problems of regulating transnational business. Under the GREENS scenario, the institutions set up by the FCCC will be operating in the later 1990s period with low levels of the TAO, having as their purpose a learning by doing process both for the CoP and for the Parties individually, not to mention energy firms operating in their territories.

A complication of the TAO as a mechanism for the achievement of a national net emissions target by a particular date is that it has so far only been specified as a percentage absorption related to the specific pattern of the standardised coppicing cycle illustrated in Figure 7.1a. But it has been suggested, in Chapter 4, that a variety of medium and long-term growing patterns could be chosen by energy firms. Slower cycles having the same lifetime absorption make less contribution to target achievement by a particular date. So firms which, for their own commercial reasons, choose such slower growth would expect to have a higher eventual absorption imposed in their particular TAO by the government in the country where it is incurred (the initiating government).

One country may offer energy firms a choice as regards the TAO it undertakes, say between 80 per cent absorption within 10 years or 120 per cent over 20 years – quite apart from the flexibility offered to firms by the 'net absorption' option, i.e. to achieve the desired result in part or in whole by technology transfer. Thus the registration of a TAO with the CoP would specify both the quantity of carbon dioxide to be absorbed and the pattern over time by which it is proposed to be done. Subsequently commercial considerations may lead the energy firm to wish to vary the growth pattern with consequent increases or decreases in its obligations to be negotiated with the initiating government.

The CoP would accordingly have a continuing need to monitor the actual absorption performance of particular firms' specific, and possibly changing, obligations to particular initiating governments, and to report and publish the outcome on a regular basis – possibly in aggregated form to preserve commercial confidentiality, if such questions arise. This provides the initiating government with the data needed to enable it both to check that the TAOs it issued had been properly discharged, and to establish that its own net emissions reduction commitment had been achieved.

Insurance

The CoP's main check would doubtless be computerised scanning of regular coverage by satellite surveillance, with a randomised spot check on the ground and detailed review where these procedures reveal significant departure from expectation. Such departure need not be indicative of foul play but may quite easily arise from natural variation (within the average performance established in the data base developed from experience gained during the earlier research and development phase). Or it may arise from natural hazard such as storm and fire damage or pests and plant disease.

A response to such variation, given the penalties for under-performance which may be exercised by the initiating government, may well be an insurance scheme, possibly run by the CoP. Indeed, such insurance may be made a compulsory component of the TAO, with income to pay for the CoP's activities arising from the profits of the insurance business. Such insurance could take the form of a direct CoP-managed absorption activity, thus providing the CoP with an ongoing field activity for expanding absorption research, training new extension workers and otherwise maintaining 'hands on' familiarity with the business. The absorption from insurance-funded biomass growth would be allocated to firms which had suffered misfortune with their own TAOs on the basis of conventional insurance claim procedure, with frequent claimants facing higher insurance premia (or loss of 'no claims bonus') in later years.

Measurement Issues

Having seen that the FCCC appears to be well adapted to putting GREENS into operation we now turn to consider the first of two areas where a great deal of work needs to be done in the 1990s phase of 'getting ready'. However, it may be noted that much of the work relating to measurement questions is not special to GREENS, but will arise anyway from implementing the existing FCCC commitment on North (i.e. OECD) Parties, involving sinks as well as sources and a target date in the year 2000. For the conceptual complications of relating the dynamic reality of net emissions to the static snapshot of a date-specific target, alluded to in Chapter 7, fall well short of the problems raised by the rigour of definition needed to monitor an international commitment.

On grounds of greater verifiability, we decided – as does the FCCC – to work in terms of targets – or a commitment – specified as a reduction of actual net emissions relative to emissions in 1990. But it will be remembered that a uniform commitment specified in this way would penalise high-growth developing countries more than it does slowing down developed countries (since a 20 per cent cut on 1990 emissions is obviously going to be harder to achieve if economic activity has doubled between the time the commitment was agreed and the time it is due to be fulfilled).

Of course, measuring net emissions is more difficult than measuring gross emissions in the obvious way that the first encompasses the second. To measure net emissions you have to measure gross emissions anyway and, additionally, measure absorption. It was to the measurement of gross emissions of carbon dioxide that much technical expertise was devoted in negotiating earlier versions of the FCCC, prior to its last-minute transformation. It is relatively straightforward to get a verifiable handle on gross emissions from commercial fuel consumption by using standard production and trade statistics and established assay procedures on the technical characteristics of commercial fuels.

However, a more difficult problem is presented by the informal energy sector. This arises mainly, but not exclusively, in the traditional societies to be found in South countries where, although the consumption of refined kerosene can easily be identified, the trade in charcoal carted into urban areas goes substantially unrecorded, and where the rural use of fuel-wood is probably unmeasurable. These were amongst the difficulties that preoccupied experts and officials in struggling towards the FCCC against the June 1992 deadline.

Given that gross emissions measurement of carbon dioxide has been studied in detail, we here mention briefly the problems of measurement of other greenhouse gases and move on to the additional question raised by the transformed FCCC, as presented at Rio, that is the measuring of absorption. Since carbon dioxide is, at present, the only greenhouse gas that can be absorbed economically, through the process of sustainable biomass fuel production, we will not say anything about absorption of other greenhouse gases, but will conclude this section with some brief remarks about measuring the 'net absorption' impact of technology transfer, and measuring an exploration moratorium.

Measuring gross emissions of methane and nitrous oxide

The measurement of carbon dioxide emissions is relatively easy since it is intrinsic to any combustion process that the tonnage of carbon in fuel is converted, with near to 100 per cent efficiency, to a corresponding tonnage of carbon dioxide – if you measure the tonnage of fuel burned, and have a chemical assay of the fuel, then you have the answer. Measuring emissions of methane and nitrous oxide, the next two most important anthropogenic long-lived greenhouse gases, is more difficult in principle because their production is the outcome of inefficiencies in processes where the emission of these greenhouse gases is not intrinsic.

If the digestion of animals worked better, flatulence would not occur and methane emissions would fall. If rice paddies were fertilised by compost produced in biogas producers, with the methane output used as renewable fuel, methane emissions would fall. If methane were drained from coal seams in advance of mining it could be piped away and used, rather than escaping to atmosphere through the mine's ventilation system. If nitrogenous fertilisers were fully absorbed into the plants which they are intended for, such fertilisers would not contribute to nitrous oxide emissions. If nitrogen could be kept out of the fuel-oxygen chemical reaction that we call combustion, and which occurs in vehicle engines, then transportation would not be an important source of nitrous oxide emissions.

Measurements of these anthropogenic emissions is, then, going to depend upon a painstaking enumeration of all the processes where they arise, the average inefficiency involved in each such process, and the level of activity of each process in each country. Claims that reductions in such emissions have been achieved will depend upon demonstrating that new technology is being used that reduces the inefficiency concerned, and accountability as regards the extent to which the new technology is being used. All this is possible, but a lot more troublesome than multiplying tonnage consumption of coal by 0.75, of oil by 0.85, of gas by 0.75 and of fuel-wood by 0.52 (see Table 4.3).

Scientific work is in hand aimed at modifying the digestive microbial population of ruminants, but having modified your cow, it is another matter to ensure she stays modified and to document the proportion of more efficient microbes in the national stock of cows. The problems involved in diverting, say, South-East Asian rice producers to the use of pre-digested fertilisers may be eased by the consequent availability of a village biogas supply, but that does not mean they will be easily solved, or that the proportion of villagers who go to the trouble of collecting biomass wastes for the digester and then distributing the digested fertiliser will be truthfully told. However, what needs to be done is conceptually straightforward and we do not need to enter into the huge volume of technicalities that relate to measuring the relevant process inefficiencies.

Measuring the absorption of carbon dioxide

Since commitments, and policies negotiated to achieve them, are relative to a 1990 datum, their measurability requires definition of what happened, or may be supposed to have happened, in that year.

Base year absorption will have been affected by a few projects around the world which already – and rightly – loom large in the eyes of their sponsors as models of environmentally conscious carbon dioxide-absorbing behaviour. In the Netherlands,[4] local opposition to the construction of a thermal power station was assuaged by the replanting of an area of tropical land with new tree cover, and a similar arrangement applied in California,[5] with El Salvador the receptor of reafforestation. In the UK a £30m tree planting programme is in hand[6] whilst conservation reafforestation plays a significant role in New Zealand, both as a response to global warming and to restore soil stability to overgrazed hill country. And Brazil, of course, produces a substantial proportion of its vehicle fuels as ethanol from sugar cane,[7] while Scandinavian countries have been planting trees for carbon dioxide absorption reasons for some years.[8]

Whether or not such schemes were in being in 1990, or before, or not begun until a bit later, does not much matter from the point of view of defining a nil absorption level as the base from which to calculate future changes in net emissions. If such pioneer projects are to yield maximum benefit (in terms of fulfilment of a commitment to reduce net emissions) to their far-sighted initiators, it is necessary to count them as zero absorbers in the base year, say 1990. For the calculation of a percentage reduction in net emissions takes the form:

[(Emissions minus Absorption in base year)
  minus
(Emissions minus Absorption in target year)]
  all times 100, and all divided by
(Emissions minus Absorption in base year)

For instance, base year emissions of 20 and target year emissions of 22, with base year absorption of nil and target year absorption of six, yields a reduction in net emissions of

$$[(20 - nil) - (22 - 6)] \times 100 / (20 - nil) = 20 \text{ per cent}$$

Clearly, any number larger than nil (for the mathematical pedant any number between zero and 20) for absorption in the base year diminishes the percentage reduction in net emissions after the base year, which hardly seems a fair reward to those far-sighted countries that began early. Thus net emissions in the base year equal gross emissions in the base year.

Having thus, definitionally, removed any basis for controversy as regards base year absorption, it remains only to define a measurement of absorption in the target year, or in whatever other year after the base year may be under consideration. Here we have two dimensions to the problem. Firstly, one of legal identification as to what particular activities count as absorption activity and, secondly, one of technical measurement of the rate of absorption achieved by the activity when it has been identified.

Identifying absorption activities has as its primary requirement that the absorption be anthropogenic. Just because mother nature grows trees all over Siberia, there seems to be no reason that Russia can claim that as an offset against its profligate coal fossil fuel use (Figure 4.1 and Table 8.1). But there is much human activity which absorbs carbon dioxide and which would be going on in any case. Horticultural, silvicultural and agricultural cropping generates biomass in tonnages far exceeding the tonnages of commercial product. Bagasse residues from cane sugar production form a substantial energy supply in sugar refining, as do timber residues in paper pulp production. All of these activities provide a residence time for carbon out of the atmosphere (from which it is taken through the photosynthetic process of plant growth).

However, the short cycle shifting of carbon in and out of the atmosphere in horticulture and agriculture does nothing to arrest the build-up of carbon dioxide in the atmosphere due to the burning of fossil fuels. This is because, after a short time, the carbon is returned to the atmosphere when the corn stubble is burned, or when wastepaper is incinerated, or when the agricultural wastes are otherwise allowed to oxidise, rot or decompose. Such a short-term cycle has neither provided significant long-term carbon storage nor impacted on the net increase of carbon dioxide due to the accumulated burning of fossil fuel over time.

There indeed lies the clue as to which anthropogenic absorption should count against net targets and which should not. Cultivated non-annual biomass which is intended eventually be burned usefully as fuel, in whole or in part, can be counted as absorption and as a contribution towards a net emissions target. Otherwise biomass production does not count towards measured absorption. Here the notion of 'useful burning' means burned for a useful (commercial) purpose for which other fuels – presumably fossil fuels – would be required were the biomass not being used in substitution for them.

But it is necessary also to account for its eventually being used as fuel (or for 'making coal'), and to deduct it from measured net absorption if it is not, since it is only if the biomass produced during the absorption (growing) process is in fact used in those ways that it impacts on the cumulative process of shifting carbon from underground into the atmosphere. If, on the other hand, it is disposed of less carefully, it makes no contribution to slowing the build-up of carbon dioxide in the atmosphere – and if allowed to decompose anaerobically, produces methane, a worse greenhouse gas, albeit shorter lived.

We have excluded annual crops since, when these residues are burned usefully, they add simultaneously and equally to both emission and absorption in the target year in question, yielding nil net emission. This would be *per contra* the substitute for fossil fuels which would have produced emissions without an absorption offset. Thus the incentive to use such residues from annual crops arises automatically from the operation of the TAO, but the need to record them does not arise, an administrative convenience.

In the case where such residues from annual crops are not burned directly, but are processed to more refined fuels, say, ethanol, it would be the timing of the production process that would implicitly count for simultaneous emission and absorption (but actually could simply be ignored as just explained) even though only a part of the carbon would be emitted at that time, as an inefficiency of the process, with the larger proportion of the carbon not emitted until the ethanol is retailed to a final consumer. This would be consistent with the workings of the TAO in relation to fossil fuels, where it is the wholesale transaction that gives rise to the TAO, with retailers' and consumers' inventory hold-up ignored.

Deliberate and casual biomass fuel production are both included in principle but need to be distinguished. The definition would obviously include the deliberate production of fuel-wood, which we took as the basic backstop technology for fuel raw material production within a sustainable energy system. And, for the avoidance of doubt, as the lawyers say, it would not include the production of biomass which is burned uselessly, from an energy cycle perspective, as in the case of firing corn stubble, however agronomically desirable such stubble burning may be.

Since the deliberate production of fuel-wood by intensive techniques would be a new activity, save for minor experimental trials in the 1980s, its identification is a simple matter and the monitoring of absorption as it occurs, say over the three-crop nine-year growing cycle illustrated in Figure 7.1a, is practicable. Otherwise there is potential for slippage where intention is involved. Suppose a country claims that it intends to collect its agricultural residues – say the prunings from orcharding – and use them for fuel, but in the end uses them in its traditional manner, say by burning to waste or by ploughing them in. Two approaches may be considered.

One would be to require some evidence of a break with traditional practices of proof of the genuineness of intentions. For instance by way of legal contracts to supply the residues, when they become available, as fuel, or by way of the installation of capital equipment – say a biomass digester – designed to utilise the residues. However, it is an approach which is likely to become burdened with a multiplicity of different cases presenting an administrative nightmare.

Alternatively, all new non-annual planting could simply be measured for absorption on a provisional basis, with confirmation in relation to what actually is burned usefully (and therefore actually does displace fossil fuel burning) when it is burned. This is an approach which would have practical advantages given the technical problems of assessing the quantity of carbon absorbed each year by a developing perennial crop or fuel-wood plantation.

And it is an approach which coincidentally overcomes the difficulty in measuring gross emissions from traditional fuel-wood supplies which do not pass through the formal commercial system. From the point of view of net emissions measurements, such traditional practices, if in equilibrium with natural growth, simply cancel out, adding a net zero to the base year figures and another net zero to the target year figures. (That is except for the extent to which traditional fuel practices, but conducted in the context of a rising population trend, result in natural forest disequilibrium with loss of natural forest cover and other vegetation. However, that is part of the separate problem of measuring losses in natural biomass due to changes in land use, to which we will come.) Thus, in some respects the measurement problem is made easier by considering net rather than gross emissions, even though net measurements in principle require two things to be measured rather than one.

'Permanent' trees, not planted for fuel-wood purposes, remain to be considered. How should we take account of long-term reafforestation and other tree growing undertaken for dual purposes, i.e. partly for commercial and or amenity purposes and partly to contribute to carbon dioxide absorption. In creating a stock of carbon in some other place than the atmosphere, and taking carbon from the stock of carbon in the atmosphere in order to do it, such developments can be regarded as a very direct response to a 'stock pollution' problem.

Of course, the rate of absorption per hectare is only about one-third the rate achievable with intensive fuel-wood production methods so that, eventually, as the value of land rises due to competition between food growing and afforestation, such planted 'permanent' tree cover will be reduced in favour of short rotation fuel-wood production. So reafforestation cannot be a long-term solution to a situation where the atmospheric stock is being augmented by a flow from the underground stock of fossil fuels. There is simply not enough land to continue the process, which, as was argued in Chapter 4, is what gives rise to the need to establish a renewable fuel-carbon cycle.

Nor would there be a market for the huge volume of timber that would very soon be produced as a consequence of absorbing four to six billion tons of carbon annually. Nevertheless, a short-term boost to the planting of trees – whether for eventual cropping for conventional timber purposes, for tree crops, for animal fodder, for wind shelter belting, or for land conservation and amenity purposes – can help an absorption programme get off to a flying start since it imposes no adaptive requirements upon the commercial energy system. Eventually the trees will be cut down, or fall down, and if not used as fuel or for 'coal making', go into commercial or natural processes of use and degradation that will see their carbon content return to the atmosphere without the benefit of displacing fossil fuel use in the process.

If used eventually for fuel they will, at that stage, incur a TAO and their carbon content enter into the renewable carbon/energy cycle in the same way as purpose grown fuel-wood plantations. Thus it is the extent to which such long-term planting does not, eventually, lead to a fuel cycle input that renders long-term, multiple purpose tree planting problematical. Here the answer seems to be to include long-term plantings in the absorption measure, but at reduced quantum having regard to the slower pattern of absorption, and on a conditional basis subject to proviso that they are specifically registered with a monitoring agency, and with an obligation on the country that takes credit from such absorption to account for the eventual disposal of the woody biomass when the tree eventually comes down.

When the tree is felled, be it to make way for intensive fuel-wood production or for any other reason, that part of the biomass that is not usefully burned then gets deducted from that country's absorption measure in the later year. A similar principle is equally applicable in relation to dual purpose intensive wood production, where one possibility is to slightly lengthen the coppicing cycle – say to five years – and to use the resulting larger proportion of heavy tree trunk (compared with the high proportion of tops, twigs and branches produced by shorter coppicing cycles) for commercial pulp production.

This treatment is, then, very similar to the treatment of short and medium-term cycle agricultural crops, the main difference being that, with the very long life cycle of conventional tree growing, more care is needed with assessing year to year absorption. Otherwise rather large cumulative errors would arise, resulting in large corrections when the true weight of biomass entering the commercial fuel system is eventually measured after felling and extraction of the higher quality fractions that would go to the conventional timber trade. The allocation of responsibility, as between firms and countries, would require careful consideration in relation to such very long timescale processes.

The difference between the useful burning of residues from conventional forestry operations on the natural stock of trees and the useful burning of part or all of the biomass from registered 'permanent' trees is that the former counts for (self-cancelling) emission and absorption at the time it is usefully burned whereas the latter counts for absorption at the time it is putting on weight in the growth process, but to the extent it is not usefully burned after felling, counts for a deduction from the absorption measure in the year of felling and only counts for emission to the extent it is actually burned. Of course, in either case, the amount of biomass that enters the fuel cycle incurs a further TAO, to be discharged in a later growth cycle.

Non-energy aspects of net emissions are raised by mention in the previous section of the felling of 'permanent' trees – whether begun under an absorption programme, and registered as such with a monitoring agency, or of older vintage, possibly natural forest. Alterations of land use, be it the notorious burning off of tropical forest to make way for inefficient cattle ranching, or the more exigent clearing of forest to provide settlement space for ballooning population, or the ploughing up of pasture for cereal and other food crop production, all result in a shift of above and below ground biomass carbon into or out of the atmosphere.

Harking back to the idea that Russia can hardly expect to claim credit for the good work that mother nature has immemorially been doing in Siberia, we recognise that its simplistic appeal lies in the presumption of natural balance. Whether that is scientifically valid in the long term is dubious – certainly it is a fluctuating balance in the ultra long term as evidenced by recurring phases of glaciation, the ice ages. But if the claim of this book, that the carbon dioxide level in the atmosphere is controllable, is to hold water, maybe even to the extent of counteracting undesirable acts of nature, then all aspects of anthropogenic impact on the carbon balance need to be considered, including the pattern of land use.

Clearly changes in land use brought about by human action, such as tropical forest clearance, and their impact on the carbon balance, fall within the scope of the FCCC Article 2 objective. However, there is no presumption that all land use changes add to emission: in some cases they may add to absorption. It is an aspect of the problem which will be contingent upon future research and we come to consider research directions later in this chapter. But as regards measuring net emissions, one research outcome should be a properly and verifiably specified measure of net emissions resulting from land use changes brought about by human action, with a view to its inclusion in the total measure of net emissions.

The technical problem of measuring carbon dioxide absorption

Having identified what needs to be measured, it remains to be seen how to measure it. On this there is much less to be said here – and a great deal of research to be done hereafter, in order to implement the North's existing commitment. A response to the measurement problem must start from recognising that we do not have the data upon which to base a measurement of anthropogenic absorption, that is to say absorption which is deliberately engineered in response to a policy instrument such as the TAO. *A fortiori* a data base for measuring absorption in 1990 does not exist, which is an additional reason for ascribing zero absorption to the base year.

Absorption on a year to year basis by growing trees of different species in different conditions and under different quick rotation methods is not known with the degree of accuracy that is needed for the validation of absorption measurements. A firm may discharge its TAO by planting a given cultivar in a nine-year cycle over a given hectarage. But that does not ascertain what is absorbed in a specific target year in the particular country where the hectarage lies. The kind of data base which is required (in so far as it is measurable at all, i.e. we must of necessity ignore fuel gathering in traditional societies, relying instead on measurements of changes in land utilisation) arises in relation to medium and long-term absorption processes, such as short rotation and conventional tree growing.

For the absorption measurement problem boils down to knowing about the carbon dioxide absorption behaviour of specific tree-growing processes. Unfortunately this presents a problem. A great deal is known about the growing characteristics of conventional tree crops, both in the tropics and elsewhere, and also about commercial timber growing in temperate regions where the very limited experience of growing timber trees deliberately (as opposed to felling natural forests) has been acquired. And there is, as explained in Chapter 4, experimental and trial experience of short rotation, intensive fuel-wood production sufficient to support the thesis of this book – not only in New Zealand, but in the USA, Scandinavia, the UK and elsewhere. But that is a far cry from the detailed experience of replicated trials with different species in different places, and with different planting and cropping practices, to yield statistically secure estimates of the carbon absorption characteristics of alternative ways of meeting a TAO.

For what is required, as a basis for conveniently substantiating claims of carbon dioxide absorption, is a statistically reliable method for looking at trees, particularly looking at them from above, and being able to estimate the tonnage of biomass contained in them. For that to be possible with the novel, short rotation, systems envisaged for fuel-wood production – as it is with conventional forestry – requires the great many replications mentioned to be assessed on the ground by physical measurements of height, girth and weight on the felling of sample trees, etc. on a year to year basis and compared with simultaneous overhead photographic evidence. Such detailed evidence can then be fed into computerised scanning of satellite surveillance records to provide estimates of absorption in different areas that have been registered as the sites of carbon dioxide absorption schemes.

Eventually, as the fuel-wood comes to be cropped and to enter into the commercial energy system, it will become physically measured in the course of conventional accountancy and assay procedures. The actual absorption can then be compared with the estimated figures used during the growth process, and appropriate adjustments made to the accumulation of estimates previously used as provisional figures for the meeting of national targets and for the discharge of TAOs.

Thus, there will need to be a massive research and development programme in relation to selected intensive tree-growing procedures over the next decade to demonstrate the statistical reliability of the absorption measurements. Indeed, a concern may develop over too restrictive a focus on particular species and rotation patterns which acquire an early reputation for high absorptive capability, to the neglect of other dimensions of sustainability, including the preservation of biodiversity and amenity values.

'Net Absorption'

In Chapter 7 we dealt with the problem presented by potential inefficiencies on the emissions side of the net emissions reduction objective by introducing the idea of 'net absorption'. The problem arose because between-country equity requires that consumers in low per capita income economies be called on to pay for a lower TAO than in better-off countries. Thus firms in such countries have a lower incentive to engage in economising behaviour, so that low-cost opportunities for reducing emissions by increased energy efficiency would go begging unless firms with high TAOs could take them up, in lieu of paying for actual absorption.

For example, to elaborate our previous case in Chapter 7, suppose a Japanese firm had acquired a TAO to absorb 100,000 tons of carbon as a result of lifting one million tons of coal in Australia and using it to produce steel in Taiwan where the TAO rate on the 750,000 tons of carbon in the coal might be 13.3 per cent. Suppose it goes to the CoP and says:

The cheapest way we can absorb 100,000 tons net of carbon equivalent is to install a high efficiency biogas plant to replace a dozen old bio-digesters in a small town near Nanking. This will result in 2,500 tons less methane leaking away and the use of 8,000 less tons of coal in the area, per annum. How does this count towards the discharge of our TAO? We think that, over the nine-year (3 x

3) coppicing cycle of the standard absorption process we will have accomplished the equivalent of absorbing (2,500 x 2) + (8,000 x 0.75) = 11,000 each year, or 100,000 over 9 years.

What the CoP thinks will obviously depend upon guidelines it will have developed regarding the relative weighting to be given to different greenhouse gases (the firm's view that it is two in the above case of methane might not square with the scientific judgement reached by the CoP. Guidelines would also be needed regarding the weighting to be applied to claimed 'net absorption' in the distant future, such as might arise with a very long-lived project like a hydro-electric scheme.

And the CoP may take the view that many of the old bio-digesters would have been replaced in any case, since that is what the information communicated under Article 12 had led it to expect. Or maybe more detailed information on China's energy planning, communicated under the non-binding Agenda 21 statement of intent, also agreed at Rio, would suggest that the firm's proposals are completely redundant under plans for large-scale regional biogas production.

Not that such a mistake would be likely, given Japanese industry's reputation for gathering and using information effectively. What emerges, as regards the question of net absorption, is that claims for TAOs to be discharged in this way could only be accepted in relation to 'net absorption' projects in countries that were Parties. As Parties, such countries would have furnished the CoP with sufficient information, regarding the expected pattern of their energy sector development, for a judgement to be made as to the difference the project was going to make to what would be going ahead without the project.

Problems of strategic behaviour could arise. China might put forward an energy plan that under-played expected efficiency gains and over-played expected demand growth, so that it would be very easy for firms to find ways of discharging their TAO by 'net absorption' with China accordingly attracting more than its fair share of technology transfer. The response would have to be reliance on proficiency in the CoP's secretariat and on the achievement of appropriate negotiating etiquette. In reality a central secretariat receiving detailed information from a large number of countries is in a very strong position to ask questions, which arise naturally in the course of comparing one country's plans with another.

Ultimately, persistent strategic behaviour by one country or another would result in scepticism towards 'net absorption' proposals in that country, when they were submitted by firms, in the country where they were incurred, for approval as discharge of the firms' TAOs. Obviously a great many detailed questions arise from the 'net absorption' concept, enabling technology transfer to count towards the achievement of net emissions reduction commitments, but they require continuing research.

What is clear is that, particularly during the earlier phase when most absorption would go on in the North, the 'net absorption' concept provides a powerful incentive for drawing South countries into the GREENS strategy, and thereby extending the operation of the TAO, albeit at very low levels in the South, onto a global basis.

The exploration moratorium

Whether the FCCC is a suitable vehicle within which to negotiate the debt restructuring/exploration moratorium aspect of GREENS is a moot point. In so far as the concept involves a debt-for-environment swap, with debt a brake upon development of any sort, it would seem to be the natural forum. And *a fortiori* for sustainable development, given that the latter is presumably more difficult for developing nations, or it would be the sort of development that would take place anyway, without need for the FCCC. Moreover the Article 7 responsibility of the CoP to seek financial resources for the purposes of the Convention, together with the Articles 2 and 3 statements of objective and principles, would appear to give it standing in the matter.

However, the creditor nations are accustomed to handling debt questions through other agencies, and a bid by the CoP to take over this area of international discourse might be looked at askance. Furthermore the CoP has plenty to do in the coming years without engaging in the debt issue – some of which is revealed in the detailed questions that need answering before net emissions of greenhouse gases can be measured sufficiently well even to know whether the modest target to which North countries are now committed is being attained. Probably a question of timing is involved. If the more traditional agencies cannot negotiate a satisfactory resolution of the Third World debt problem in the years immediately ahead, the CoP may find itself forced to become involved at the end of the century in order to break up a log jam in which South Parties were blocking progress in implementation pending a settlement of the issue – maybe by collateral threat of collective default, as mentioned at the end of the last chapter.

But supposing a moratorium were agreed, either globally or by way of a series of bilateral or regional deals of the kind which Article 11 specifically accommodates, then the CoP's role is relatively straightforward. Compared with measuring emissions of methane and nitrous oxide, with measuring absorption, and with establishing a basis for accommodating 'net absorption' into target achievement, keeping track of the globe's proven fossil fuel reserves, and identifying from whence came particular tonnages of fossil fuels onto the market, is child's play. Given the huge volume of data related to energy planning which will already be at the CoP's fingertips on account of its other data-gathering and performance-measuring responsibilities, the answer would in all likelihood already be on file.

Sustainability Questions

The second major area for work in the 1990s' phase of 'getting ready' is concerned with being sure that the biomass option is not a false trail. For long-term reliance on woody feedstock, or other biomass, as the raw material basis for the transformation of the world's commercial energy system onto a sustainable basis raises more fundamental questions than those of economic impact and technological practicability, which we have shown to be not very difficult, or the more difficult problems of political economy which are attributable to conflicting national interests, either actual or perceived. These more fundamental questions relate to the sustainability of the biomass-based system, supposing that it is put in place.

For it serves much less purpose to achieve a transformation to a renewable fuel system if the biomass production system involved is itself unsustainable in some way. In the long term we have envisaged that biomass production will become linked with more advanced technologies for capturing solar energy, as a renewable source of carbon for synthesising portable fuels for transportation uses for as long as a demand continues.

But if biomass production is itself subject to sustainability problems, it can only provide a temporary respite from climate change worries and it might be more sensible to focus effort on the more advanced technologies even though, unlike biomass technology, they are far from commercially ready. On the other hand, if the climatological evidence becomes increasingly alarming of possible truly horrid surprises, even a temporary respite may provide the stitch in time to keep the fabric of commerce together until the more advanced technologies are available or until major adaptations have been made to, for instance, the distribution of global population.

Each of the sustainability questions we shall look at is fit subject for a book in itself and the comments in the following pages are firstly to suggest that none of them presents so obviously insurmountable a difficulty as to nullify the trouble of reading this book[9]* and, secondly, to point the way to a work programme for the CoP's Subsidiary Body for Scientific and Technological Advice.

Energy efficiency and energy analysis
This topic is not to be confused with the modelling of the energy supply system which is needed to quantify the dynamics of market penetration of biomass fuel driven by the net emissions commitments of Article 4

through the TAO mechanism. That is the kind of work exemplified, in the case of New Zealand, in the Appendix and the globalisation of which was called for in Chapter 7. The need for it is recognised in the Agenda 21 statement of intent and the information and communication provisions of the FCCC are apt to the purpose. We are here concerned with a more fundamental aspect of a biomass energy system.

The overall energy efficiency of the biomass system, including processing the raw material into the portable and convenience fuels required in the market, is a question to be addressed through energy analyses of the various processes involved. Energy analysis[10] is a procedure in which the intermediate inputs to every production activity are enumerated in terms of their energy content so that, despite the complexities of the interlocking production system, the basic energy implications of every final output can be determined.

For instance a pint of delivered milk in a glass bottle involves process energy in the glass (related to the number of times it gets reused before it is broken), electricity energy in the milking machine, portable fuel in the delivery vehicle, say diesel powered, food energy inputs for the working time of the farmer, delivery worker and other people involved in the supply process, various energy inputs into providing and maintaining the cow, the milking machine, the delivery vehicle, the electricity and diesel fuel supply systems (related to the proportion of their working life spent on delivering the milk) and so on. Of course, milk goes into the production of all the inputs just mentioned, so a complex 'input-output' calculation is involved, for which the techniques are well established even if the data base is somewhat sketchy.

Each of the applications technologies that were mentioned in Chapter 4 – that is the use of biomass in combined cycle gas turbine electricity generators, its simple gasification for process heat or, with greater elaboration, for synthetic reticulated gas supplies and the three main technologies for converting biomass to portable fuel (ethanol by aerobic fermentation, the 'backstop' technology of this book, anaerobic fermentation to methane gas, entailing CNG transport fuel technology, and pyrolysis to methanol) – needs to be studied from this perspective. That there is no *a priori* reason to suppose that seriously adverse results would arise is no reason to assume the outcome.[11*]

In addition the basic coppicing production process, harnessing the ambient solar energy into a combustible fuel must be considered in energy analytic terms. The cost basis for the calculations that underlie the results for New Zealand given in the Appendix are for air-dried timber delivered over a 20 km radius (sufficient, with 50 per cent ground coverage, to supply a plant producing over 100 million gallons of ethanol per year, or a 500MW power station operating at 50 per cent load factor, allowing for the inefficiencies in each process). This distance is not so great as to suggest that an energy analysis would – with fuel for transport the major component, even if, as it should be, the fuel is own-produced ethanol – significantly detract from the positive energy balance.[12]

Nor are the applications technologies in any obvious way dependent on unusually energy-intensive inputs. The inefficiency of these applications processes are somewhat conservatively taken into account in the calculations done for New Zealand – for instance 33 per cent thermal efficiency for electricity generation, despite the higher figures quoted for gas turbine generators, and ethanol conversion data for a small prototype design. All in all, there seems to be little reason to expect that the out-turn of energy analysis investigations of the GREENS alternative energy system would be likely to throw up significantly adverse results. But, as the cautionary result with sugar cane ethanol suggests, that does not mean the work does not need to be done.

Agronomic sustainability

The sustainability of any farming system relates mainly to its dependence on non-renewable inputs or its creation of wastes that accumulate to unacceptable levels. The principal non-renewable input is, obviously, the land upon which the farming is done, discussed below under soil conservation.

An aspect where fuel-wood farming may serve to allay a different kind of sustainability concern is as regards the increasing proportion of the natural photosynthetic production that is appropriated by human activity of one sort or another – a proportion that has been put as high as 40 per cent.[13] Although that figure is in some ways not wholly meaningful – for instance it includes natural biomass lost as a result of desertification, which is by no means wholly caused by human action – the effect of fuel-wood biomass production is of course to increase the total photosynthetic product.

For the present it is too soon to say in what directions research might take agronomic technique in the pursuit of pure gain in biomass tonnage. Specific fertilisers, pesticides and weed killers can each be imagined which might cause irreversible damage to the land, to neighbouring land used for other purposes, or to water run-off. One point to note is that traditional farming practice is not wholly without fault in relation to these criteria, including its dependence on highly energy-intensive artificial fertilisers and the damage to streams and rivers caused by high levels of nitrogen.

Rather than rely on pesticides, genetic engineering can produce clones that are resistant to common insect pests. An alternative approach is to manage fuel-wood production in a way that mimics the complexities of natural ecosystems and successional sequences. For instance advantage can be taken of the regular cropping process of coppicing to inter-plant a variety of annual, possibly nitrogen-fixing, species in the first year of regrowth of the fuel-wood crop for subsequent *in situ* mulching.

The work that has been done with short-rotation woody crops in the last decade has not thrown up any notorious problem and, on the positive side, the possibilities of combining energy cropping with other outputs, be it woody wastes as the by-product of conventional forestry, bagasse by-product from sugar production, or novel systems of inter-cropping, two-tier farming, or combined forage and energy production, remain largely unexplored.

Soil conservation

Soil conservation values are an important side benefit of conventional reafforestation schemes, whether or not undertaken to absorb greenhouse gases (with standing timber acting as a 'sink' for carbon absorbed from the atmosphere rather than, as with coppicing, part of a continuing fuel production process). This is because a major environmental concern in relation to past high country timber extraction is the subsequent erosion of mountain topsoils no longer protected from rainfall impact by the forest canopy, and no longer tightly bound by healthy tree root structures.

In high country, where steep gradients encourage the gathering of fast flowing and highly destructive streamlets, soil run-off with recently bared land can be 100 to 200 times as rapid as with the previous forest cover,[14] with large volumes of rich soil and humus carried to sea and lost – quite apart from flash flooding of low-lying areas due to the shorter hold-up and sudden descent of high country rainfall. Such events are related to localised weather excursions from normal, which are predicted with increased frequency as a result of global warming.

In relation to intensive fuel-wood cropping using the coppicing technique in less steep terrain, it may be noted that minimal soil disturbance occurs with the harvesting operation. The accumulation of leaf mould, loess and animal detritus over a nine-year coppicing cycle can be expected to enrich the soil – a particularly valuable effect where arable land has been subject to degradation from intensive cereal cropping, inorganically fertilised. Where no foodcrops for human consumption are involved, another route to soil enrichment is the use of fuel-woodland for sewage disposal, with consequential retention of nutrients and humus otherwise disposed to the sea (at risk of coastal pollution), enhanced growth rates for the fuel-wood, and the saving of sewage pollution and/or disposal costs.

It is not yet known how long the coppice cycle can be extended in the case of intensive fuel-wood production, but ancient European coppices (traditionally maintained for the sustainable, low intensity, production of fencing materials) have histories of hundreds of years. Nor can it yet be said whether, when replanting becomes necessary, the old stumps are best left in the ground or lifted.

As with conventional crops, nitrogen levels can be sustained by interplanting with nitrogen fixers, such as acacias (which can, incidentally, also be coppiced). Artificial phosphorus and potassium requirements are negligible in New Zealand experience – indeed, deep-rooted trees serve to lift these minerals from deeper in the soil. In general it would seem that, with reasonable management, fuel-wood cropping can lead to an enhancement rather than a degradation of soil values.

Hydrology

Hydrological aspects such as ground water and irrigational effects of fuel-wood production are evidently, from the preceding paragraphs, intimately related to soil conservation. High biomass productivity requires ample water supply which is why tropical rainforest regions that have in the past been destroyed seem likely to have the long-run competitive advantage in the business – after they have been recovered from the inefficient subsistence farming, or low intensity cattle ranching, or scrub reversion to which they have mostly gone.

Typically three-quarters of the rain falling on a tropical forest is returned to the atmosphere by tree action, with only a quarter finding its way into river systems and back to the oceans.[15] Indeed, transpiration of water to the atmosphere characterises all plant life, with some tree species, e.g. poplars, being typically more thirsty than others. This is an aspect that has led to the abandonment of arid and semi-arid regions as of potential interest in the US Short Rotation Woody Crops Programme. On the other hand, the opposite problem arises in western New South Wales. There, as previously noted, the salinity of rising ground water presents a problem precisely because of past clearing for pasture of the primordial eucalypt cover, and consequential reduced transpiration and increased downflow and the flooding of deep salty strata, thus raising the water table.

Ecological diversity

If the overall purpose of the GREENS concept, controlling climate change, is kept in view, its ultimate impact in this area of concern must be beneficial. If GREENS proves to be the only effective response to global warming that is available at acceptable cost, as seems *prima facie* likely to be the case, then it will be the salvation of ecological diversity rather than its graveyard. For it is the natural ecosystems upon which wildlife depends which, above all, are most exposed to threats from global warming. Mankind's agricultural, pastoral and even silvicultural activity on the soil may, with foresight and better models of the global climate system, be capable of being moved sufficiently rapidly to keep pace with global warming (though it is possible to foresee high criticality for the human food chain, particularly in impoverished and densely populated tropical and semi-tropical regions). However, there is no way that one can imagine in which the rich diversity of natural habitats can migrate fast enough under natural processes, or that any human intervention is likely to be available to do the trick on a significant scale. It seems, therefore, that precious habitats and ecological niches are likely to be wiped out on a large scale under business as usual scenario forecasts of climate change.

At the more detailed level of local impact, the development of fuel-wood production, interspersed with the existing often monocultural pattern of farming activity, in itself represents increased plant species diversity. Within the coppices, diversity of cultivars and species provides an insurance against disease as well as being required for nitrogen fixing. The extent to which the triennial cycle of harvesting would allow small wildlife to find a niche is hard to prejudge although some increase, including the reappearance of pheasants, has been noted in some localities in British experiments.[16]

However, land for fuel-wood production is likely to come in part not from underutilised cropland but from the reuse of forest land taken for commercial purposes, or in response to population pressures. Here there must be hope of a slowing up of forest destruction as economic prosperity facilitates a more settled lifestyle and as produced timber (possibly jointly produced with fuel-wood) displaces production from indigenous forest. As far as biodiversity is concerned, the planned use of land for these purposes, leaving connected areas of forest untouched to facilitate migration and other movements of native fauna, must be a component of policy.

The outcome on biodiversity may also be expected to depend, in part, on success with extending coppicing practice beyond the 3 x 3 years lifetime that has so far been experienced. A 30 (or 100) year coppice, harvested to the ground only in part at each harvest, would permit wildlife to migrate locally. Traditional coppices form an important haven for wildlife in Europe. Sporting interest, including the hunting of small animals and birds, are an important amenity value in some UK fuel-wood experiments.[17]

Competition with food production

The availability of land has been discussed in general terms in Chapter 4 and, for the present, has been passed over to the outcome of empirical work. The problem of competition with food production and other uses of land is, however, more complex than that question of basic fact. We already hear complaints from the South that the North's demands that land be set aside for wildlife reserves, and for the scientific and tourism values associated with conservationist objectives, run counter to the development needs of the South.

Cash crops, be they tropical fruit for airborne transport to markets in the North, or tourism services to travellers from the North, may sequester land from traditional use through legal mechanisms which indigenous groups, with uncommercialised subsistence lifestyles, are powerless to resist even if they can understand what is happening.[18*] To reinforce that process with demands for vast additional tracts of land to be given over to fuel-wood or other biomass production runs the danger that yet more millions of landless poor will be deprived of the means of subsistence. That danger is the panic aspect of the panic and derision alluded to in Chapter 1. It is what underlies the phasing of the energy system transition described in our Chapter 4 scenario, with the initial emphasis for biomass production in temperate regions.

Yet that same delayed impact in the South delays also the developmental benefit to the South which is needed as the *quid pro quo* for their participation in policies to deal with global warming. In part an immediate benefit can be provided, for those South countries that want to make such a deal, by the proposed debt relief/exploration moratorium trade-off, and in part by the 'net absorption' concept, but more rapid access to the absorption activity may be sought by some South countries wanting to boost their economies through invisible exports of pollution clean-up services. Here the cadre of extension workers mentioned earlier in this chapter must play a part in ensuring that income does indeed trickle down to those whose needs for additional cash to purchase necessities, got previously through subsistence lifestyles, are greatest. Adaptation of unsustainable traditional lifestyles and the development of a cash economy must go hand in hand with the changing pattern of land-use and new directions of commercial activity.

A more rational allocation of activity could see the North concentrating on biomass energy cropping, with the production of less bulky and more easily transported foodstuffs shifting to the South. But that is to begin to traverse ground which we have had to leave outside the scope of this book, that is to say the links between energy cropping and the long, drawn out Uruguay Round of GATT negotiations on agricultural trade.

Social impacts

If the spread of energy cropping from the North to the South provides the cash income needed to enable the South to engage in food production which is more land-conservative than traditional methods, there can be hope that the circle be squared as regards producing both more food and new fuel-wood production from the land in existence. The need is to link energy cropping with a transition from traditional nomadic slash and burn food production technology.

Modern medicine has multiplied populations in the South without multiplying the means of food production. It is traditional lifestyles that are unsustainable in the face of reduced infant mortality, with cash inflows from pollution clean-up providing the potential for escape from a cycle of over-grazing, land degradation and malnutrition. Romantic admiration for the hardihood of the people and the intricacy of their subsistence code of conduct provides no milk for a malnourished infant. Where groups can be maintained with dignity in the traditional pattern, there is scientific and cultural value in doing so if the peoples involved – unlike most, when offered the choice – accept willingly what is involved.

The art of managing the transition to a cash economy lies in devising strategies which provide meaningful options to the individuals affected, preserving their dignity, and making use of the local skills and knowledge that are available. 'The main ingredients of success are for outsiders to go in quietly, with ears and eyes open, and to have the humility and patience to learn, change course if need be, and take a long-term approach.'[19]

Nevertheless, the bad reputation of plantation agronomy may nowadays be ill-deserved, based as it substantially is on the writings of West Indian analysts informed by the peculiarly bitter experience of their isolated island economies in the colonial era. Many of the critiques of plantation agronomy have had to be modified in the light of unfortunate experience with land reform and of estate nationalisation and of happier modern developments in the context of political independence, such as the NES (nuclear estate with smallholding) pattern of plantation management.[20]

In relation to this question, and similar questions of good practice and sustainability discussed above, global action must be assumed to be taken within the context of guidelines for each type of land for every Party to the FCCC, monitored in the field as a condition of TAO fulfilment. Essentially the small print of the TAO contract document would require acceptance of sustainability guidelines, and failure to comply would constitute contractual default thus attracting penalties in the country where the TAO originated. Such a framework for GREENS would require the international agency to provide monitoring and technical assistance services adequate to protect peoples in transition from a subsistence economy against exploitation in the context of a market-oriented and international organised trade in absorption obligations, on a scale adequate to handle the global warming problem.

Formidable though that task is, like the problems of political economy discussed in Chapter 8, this overview of sustainability questions is hopeful – some readers will feel overhopeful. However, it has been seen that these questions do not point simply in one direction. A flexible approach to implementing GREENS, sensitive to local physical and social conditions, is both more likely to gain acceptance and more certain to produce benefits – which can be not only in terms of eventually reduced carbon dioxide levels, but also in a variety of other directions having to do with the D of UNCED and, in particular, the R of GREENS.

A land capability survey

These various sustainability questions boil down to building a land capability data base, where capability is to be read in the broad sense of the physical, chemical, biological, ecological, anthropological, technological and economic analysis of what could be, rather than what has been. Obviously 'what could be' is dependent on what investment is made in the land to sustain and improve it by sophisticated management based upon an interdisciplinary and holistic analysis of the possibilities. That investment is limited not by the few billion dollars annually at the disposal of the CoP through the financial mechanism of the FCCC (starting off with the $1.3 billion interim finance from the World Bank's GEF) but, ultimately, by the several hundred million dollars annually that flow through the commercial fuel supply business.

This primary compilation, needed to place GREENS on a secure footing and, more fundamentally, for securing a sustainable future for an increasingly populous globe, by establishing exactly – or, more likely in the first instance, roughly – what the earth's surface is sustainably capable of carrying in the context of current and foreseeable technological knowledge, is not the same as knowing how it is used now. The earth's surface is nowadays under constant surveillance from outer space as a side benefit of the technological progress stimulated by Cold War rivalry. The advances in commercial geographical information systems (GIS) using satellite imagery and remote sensing, whilst remarkable in comparison with only five years ago, use a fairly primitive version of that technology. Military quality surveillance can, it is said, resolve detail down to a six-inch paint can, whereas commercial GIS can barely distinguish an individual tree.[21]

This does not prevent the GIS picking up an enormous amount of fascinatingly detailed information, such as the spread of plant disease related to the different light reflectivity of healthy and diseased plants. But, even if it employed military quality hardware, the information yielded could only be related to how the land is being used, not to how it might be used. Without doubt, existing use is an important initial indicator of sustainable land capability – presumptively a lower bound indicator, but not necessarily so in particular situations of currently unsustainable land-use practices.

However, that does not resolve the critical area of doubt regarding the thesis advanced in this book, that is to say the question of whether the land which, in Chapter 4 it was argued, appears *prima facie* likely to be available, actually is available and capable, on a sustainable basis, of carrying the biomass production we have envisaged. For, although an important lower bound indicator, knowledge of existing use tells us nothing about the upper limit of sustainable use. Here what is needed is an extension of existing pilot schemes[22] for soil and terrain (SOTER) survey to a comprehensive coverage, together with 'ground truthing' of the capability of more promising areas with regard to their potential for intensive biomass production.

Of course, such ground truthing includes not only the absolute capability of a particular stretch of terrain, but its capability conditional upon existing and future population carrying requirements, and the potential of indigenous populations and social systems to adapt to and benefit from commercialised demands for fuel-wood production. The exercise of ground truthing thus involves a simultaneous integrated approach to the development of human and biological capital. That is to say, the acquisition of knowledge related to the enrichment of soil potential through its sustainable management for fuel and food production and the build-up of soil fertility and output through the application of that knowledge. That means a lot of research in the years immediately ahead.

A Smoother Road Ahead

Finally we turn to considering how, with the benefit of last minute revision of the FCCC, progress after the Earth Summit may turn out to be easier than the somewhat rocky road to Rio. Just how difficult that was, and just how suspicious the less well-off countries are of the developed world's increasing preoccupation with environmental concerns, is illustrated by the Prime Minister of Malaysia's remarks quoted in Chapter 1. The belief that environmental concern is a ploy by the North to maintain the South in a permanent economic subjugation is also a legacy of the dependency theories mentioned in Chapter 1 – theories which the recent history of Third World debt does little to discredit.

These theories articulate an observable reality of long-term economic disadvantage brought about in no small degree as a side effect of happenings in developed world financial markets which were directed – in so far as any direction was involved – at different objectives. As we have seen, the surplus of investment funds in the long period of low-growth inflation (stagflation) generated by OPEC's enforcement of a withdrawal of spending from the global economy, led to unwise Third World projects which then became loaded with escalating interest rates as developed countries adopted counter-inflationary policies.

However, the eventual focus of the FCCC negotiators on net rather than gross emissions not only provides the prospect of an effective remedy to the global warming problem (and at acceptable cost as far as North countries are concerned) but also, for South countries, a vehicle for development rather than an impediment to it, as implied by the GREENS acronym. Thus the outcome of dealing with the problem in the manner advocated in this book is the opposite to the Prime Minister's apprehensions.

In any case, the scenario presented at the end of Chapter 4 does not display long time lags out of concern for political sensitivities but because such are the time lags involved in anything so vast as the diffusion of a new energy technology through the energy supply system, especially when the technology involves biologically-determined delays such as the time-to-grow needs of the coppicing technique.

The initial focus on surplus temperate land was also driven by the initial need (pending further development of biomass to liquid fuel technologies) to substitute mainly for coal in the furnace fuel market, and by the reality that the bulk of that market is in temperate zones. Prior to that, however, technology transfer that raises the efficiency of existing (fossil) fuel utilisation in the South will result from the rationalisation of emissions reduction activity through the operation of the 'net absorption' concept, thus paving the way for greater acceptance of a need for the South to take a small share in the overall global commitment. For, although focussed mainly on the big coal-rich countries like India and China, some benefit from the net absorption/technology transfer mechanism arises wherever fossil fuel is consumed, i.e. throughout the South. And the swap – an exploration moratorium in return for debt cancellation – is much easier for South countries, where the prospect of successful exploration is much less than in the coal-rich countries.

Thus the flow of resources to the South which is looked for, though possible under the GREENS concept, is not essential for reducing net carbon dioxide emissions for 10 or even 15 years. Obviously it is greatly to be hoped that it begins sooner, that leaders such as Prime Minister Dr Mahathir bin Mohamed will be eagerly seeking the location of pollution clean-up schemes on their own territory – and that their countries will be benefiting from the job opportunities and relaxation of balance of payments constraints on their energy system development that can result thereby – from the mid-1990s on.

This would see the likely growth of bilateral and regional relationships to the mutual advantage of the parties or groups of parties involved. The economic strength of developed countries would thus be linked with willingness in the more progressive amongst other countries.

Thus can a combination of economic power and partial consensus see the GREENS concept implemented as and where it is politically possible to do so, with other countries climbing on the bandwagon as its direction of progress become more clearly apparent.

The CoP's role in all this would be facilitatory, firstly as a clearing house for the accumulation of research information needed for the build-up of the data base used both for on-going (Bayesian) reassessment of the problem and for the CoP's monitoring role (and no doubt acting as a 'public good' research organisation in its own right) and, secondly, brokering the growth of mutual interest arrangements related to net targetry implemented through the TAO or equivalent arrangements. Incidental to such work would be a watchdog role on behalf of the global environment, having regard to the concerns which have been discussed earlier in this chapter and providing both expertise in relation to those concerns and guidelines for the conduct of such mutual interest activity.

In this sense of fostering a transition to a new valuation of nature's role in the commercial achievement of material well-being, the research and training programme which is needed for the implementation of the GREENS concept may be more important and fundamental in its impact than any specific commitments on net emissions reductions, either at Rio or subsequently by the CoP. In that case the work of the CoP will be a fitting outcome, somewhere down the road from Rio, of a United Nations Conference on Environment and Development in which the E and the D are coherently integrated rather than adventitiously thrown together by political pressures.

Notes

1. Pearce, D., 1991; Nordhaus, 1991; Manne and Richels, 1992; Mors, 1991; von Weizsäcker and Jesinghaus, 1992.

2. Although it is the means of discharging policy as far as the Parties are concerned, the TAO or 'net TAO' is a burden on firms. So some sort of registration and accountancy activity is needed, as with any system in which 'bads' are traded. This is because owners of 'bads', unlike owners of conventional marketed goods, have an incentive to lose the 'bad' – if ownership of a good confers benefits which are reflected in the price people are willing to pay for it, ownership of a 'bad' confers disbenefits, reflected in the price paid to a subcontractor to take the 'bad' over. Clearly, if the 'bad' can somehow be 'lost', there is a windfall profit to be shared between the primary owner and successive subcontractors.

3. The TAO sets up governments as principals in relation to energy firms, as the agents of policy, an appropriate jurisdictional relationship, whereas a system of carbon taxes (whether or not dedicated to renewable fuel activity) sets up governments as agents, in relation to some bureaucracy of an international agreement as principal, a relationship for which no enforceable jurisdictional basis can exist. The International Court at the Hague can provide determinations as to whether a Government is conforming to agreements which it has made, but it cannot enforce these determinations.

4. Dijk et al, 1993.

5. Munroe, 1991.

6. Sims, 1993.

7. Goldemberg et al, 1992.

8. Willebrand and Verwijst, 1992.

9. Obviously my perspective is coloured by the experience I draw on in writing this book, which leaves me far from expert in many of the areas touched upon in this section. The reader will no doubt preserve a healthy scepticism. I remark only that many of his questions, like those which I raise, will hopefully be answered in the course of the programme of research and development that this book calls for in the 1990s as a key component in the necessary process of getting ready through 'learning by doing'. For an alternative view, see Cantor and Rizy, 1991, who take a commercial management perspective.

10. Thomas, 1977.

11. For instance, the inefficiency in the backstop ethanol process that was noted earlier is sufficient, if reliance is placed upon energy-oriented intensive sugar cane feedstock, to sink the technology from this energy analytic perspective. Depending on the assumptions that are made, net energy output may even be negative, with more energy used producing the fuel than is contained in it. However, with woody biomass feedstock the outcome is more satisfactory, with an overall delivery in the ethanol product of 80 per cent of the solar energy captured by photosynthesis anticipated from end-century developments of this technology.

12. Hall et al, 1993, Table 7.

13. Vitousek et al, 1986.

14. Enquete-Kommission, 1990, pp.505-15.

15. Enquete-Kommission, 1990, pp.458-63.

16. Fremantle, 1992.

17. Environmental Resources Ltd., 1988.

18. The market place loses the validation it derives from the freedom of the individual to trade, or to choose not to, when disparities of wealth result in the poor of one country having no power to secure even their most essential needs against the spending of the rich from another country. The problem arises from the same lack of a mechanism for achieving equity between nations that motivates Uzawa's proposal (Chapter 8) for allocating a carbon tax on the basis of national per capita income.

19. Leach and Mearns, 1988, p.40.

20. Tiffen and Mortimore, 1990, p.81.

21. Bouwer, 1990, p.154.

22. Baumgartner, 1990, p.520.

10. A Summing Up

We began this book by claiming that we would demonstrate that a practicable long-term strategy for dealing with global warming is available and that people could take hope that a collaborative effort worldwide to set that process in train need involve no more, in the remaining years of this century, than 'getting ready', i.e. taking the steps needed in order to be prepared for whatever action may turn out to be necessary.

Later in Chapter 1 it was stated that these steps for 'getting ready' involve firstly a great deal of on-the-ground research into land capability worldwide and into the planning of a transformation based on already available technologies of mankind's commercial energy activities and, secondly, a great deal of action research on pilot schemes in different locations around the world, which initially needs only a very low level of policy application. These activities, which we eventually came to discuss in Chapter 9, comprise a global 'learning by doing' programme in the course of which will be accumulated the knowledge base required to deal with global warming, as quickly as need be, in the opening years of the next century. This knowledge base comprises pure and applied scientific results in such fields as the earth sciences, hydrology, agronomy, economics, social anthropology, energy technology, land use planning, etc., together with the development of human capital, in terms of trained workers and institutional structures, that will be needed in greater or lesser degree if the climatologists tell us that we have indeed got a global warming problem. If they tell us that there is nothing to worry about after all, most of the knowledge will in any case find useful applications as and when fossil fuels and other natural resources, including indigenous forest cover, become scarcer.

It will come as no surprise to the inverately cynical that an academic should be making proposals for a massive research effort. I defend myself by pointing out that the most successful country in the last quarter of this century – Japan – has got where it has by a deep respect for knowledge and its rational application – most notably in redeploying its productive capacity into new and profitable fields with an organising capacity that leaves its competitors trailing.[1]* Our long-term strategy for controlling global warming does, indeed, take a leaf from the Japanese book in that it also envisages a market-oriented redeployment of activity in the supply and use of energy services worldwide that is organised rather than left to the fumblings of the invisible hand.

We are now in a position to review how far the claims of this book have been met, which we do by summarising and commenting on Chapters 2 to 9 seriatim, and to draw some conclusions.

In Chapter 2 we considered the scientific nature of the problem. We saw that the atmosphere upon which life on earth depends is quite fragile. Fragile in the sense that the enormous fluxes of energy that pass inward from the sun and outward to outer space can change its condition very substantially if some minor change in the environment alters the balance of transmission, reflection and absorption of those energy flows. In recent times quite minor volcanic episodes have had noticeable effects whilst prehistory has featured cold phases (ice ages) of which a recurrence would be catastrophic.

It is the level of carbon dioxide concentration in the atmosphere that is of concern, or possibly some combination of the level and the length of time for which the level is sustained above normal. Over the last 50 years, a business as usual industrial scenario has taken the atmosphere into a regime which, in the period which is known about, is without precedent as regards the high level of carbon dioxide which has already been reached and as regards its rate of change.

The record, over the last 160,000 years for which there is good scientific information, shows a very close association between climate change and changes in the level of carbon dioxide in the atmosphere. The timescale should be emphasised: a global climate system change that takes a century to complete has happened in the twinkling of an eye as far as geological history is concerned. It may be hoped that a 100 years or so excursion into greatly above-normal carbon dioxide levels, brought about by a phase of industrial dependency upon intensive use of fossil fuels, will be over before the more catastrophic possible responses of the system have time to develop.

The nature of the dynamics of complex non-linear systems (which is how the global climate system and its interactions with the biosphere are classified from an analytic point of view) is such that the passage of time means an increasing possibility of a sudden and quite possibly severely damaging – maybe even catastrophic – change of climate regime. Feedback processes may become unstable under parameter shifts induced by levels of carbon dioxide forced ever more rapidly and ever further away from any that are known to be stabley compatible with the climate that supports a developed pattern of civilisation. It may be that a better understanding of the scientific evidence will eventually lead to a time-constrained target specified as a need to return to a particular level of carbon dioxide in the atmosphere by a particular date.

Nothing else of a scientific nature is known about global warming with any degree of certainty. In particular two crucial dimensions of the problem, climate dynamics and the carbon cycle, are very poorly understood from a quantitative point of view. At least 25 per cent of the net anthropogenic emission of carbon dioxide is unaccounted for. Global climate models vary by a factor of three as regards the impact on average temperature that is most likely to result from the forecast increases in the level of carbon dioxide.

It should be noted that the improved global climate models that may be expected in the future are not certain to show a clear need for a time-constrained target of the kind suggested above. Indeed, given the nature of non-linear dynamic systems, it may be doubted whether the models will ever match up to the problem of telling us, for sure, whether the climate system is prone to unforeseeable 'jumps' or not. Thus the development of these models even to the limits of their capability may do nothing to resolve the current policy uncertainties.

However, we do know enough to be certain that these possibilities cannot be ruled out. Nor can we rule out the possibility that some regime change has already begun and is currently masked by the transitory effects of vulcanism, by changes in the solar 'constant' and/or the more lasting, but maybe not everlasting effect, of polar melting. Thus failure to take a precautionary stitch in time may impose severe burdens on future generations. On a worst case scenario it may leave them with no world that can be lived in.

Chapter 3 was concerned with how to take policy decisions about important and unique problems under conditions of uncertainty or even ignorance regarding important dimensions of the problem. It was suggested that one of the reasons that policy on global warming is in a muddle is that research is based on inappropriate cost-benefit analysis (CBA) that imposes currently – possibly permanently – unattainable data requirements and provides confusing signals to policy-makers.

By contrast, the regret approach, yielding a measure of 'social objection', does provides an appropriate way for thinking about once-and-for-all decisions in an uncertain world – once-and-for-all in the sense that what we do for the next two decades determines the choices available in 2010. Of course, policy can evolve as research provides new information and, indeed, deciding appropriate research directions constitutes an important aspect of policy.

As with any analytic procedure, whether computerised or not, the 'garbage in, garbage out' dictum applies. However, one needs only to assume a finite possibility of an adverse, possibly catastrophic, climate jump, to see that plausible orders of magnitude for the cost of emergency policies begun late, point clearly towards an active emissions reduction policy, in the short to medium term, especially if the cost of such a precautionary policy is low.

Such a conclusion emerges intuitively from a concern for future generations and the main function served by the regret/objection approach developed in Chapter 3 is that it enables such concerns to be formalised in an operational manner. It thus provides an appropriate alternative methodology to the familiar cost-benefit analysis (CBA). It says 'get into the bomb shelter when you hear the air-raid warning'; CBA says 'let's stand around talking about the costs and benefits of getting into the shelter as opposed to not doing so'.

CBA has provided the operational basis for environmental policies in many areas but gives little guidance in relation to global warming policy since it imposes impossible data requirements and is designed to be used in situations in which risks can be pooled over a large number of projects. But we have only one atmosphere. And to wait for knowledge of the 'damage function' (the relationship between carbon dioxide emissions and the expected cost of the damage that results) may cause the opportunity for cheap remedial action to be lost.

Chapter 4 provided a technological basis for dealing with global warming through a transformation of the industrial energy system away from the reliance on fossil fuels which has given rise to the problem. The timescale for such a transition process is 20 to 25 years, with the remainder of the 1990s devoted mainly to preparation and 'learning by doing'. Within the period, prospective economic growth in the South means that the transition must cover both developed and other countries to be effective. Rich nations cannot deal with global warming on their own.

Conventional projections of energy demand were assumed, with slower growth in developed countries and more rapid growth in other countries. It was assumed that increased efficiency, together with increased use of ambient energy technologies, both within the energy supply system and under the control of final consumers, will be brought about by rising prices. This results in approximately constant demand for fuel raw materials in the North.

Three technologies, all basically proven and available now, provide a backstop technology system for the transition. These are:

(1) intensive biomass production using short rotation tree-cropping techniques such as coppicing of selected fast-growing species;

(2) combined cycle gas turbine technology for power generation at higher efficiency and in smaller units than conventional modern thermal power stations;

(3) biomass fermentation technology to produce ethanol, a portable transport fuel.

The application of these technologies could see the end of coal mining, save possibly for isolated special applications, and a major slowing down of oil depletion within the period. This would be accomplished by increased use of natural gas in existing installations and the development of fuel-wood gasification for retrofitting existing plant where natural gas is unavailable and/or direct fuel-wood firing for new furnace installations, including a less centralised electricity generating system located in fuel-wood production areas. Where fossil fuels are too difficult to replace, the alternative of 'making coal' (or at least initiating the process) takes the form of the controlled burying of biomass.

Tropical and semi-tropical countries provide the most naturally efficient venue for biomass production but the technological transformation should begin in temperate regions to avoid unacceptable impacts upon traditional land use and social patterns. While sufficient land to meet all demands may well exist in temperate regions, tropical countries can eventually realise their competitive advantage and enhance their economic growth through 'invisible exports' of pollution clean-up services together with the adoption of the up-to-date and energy-efficient, biomass-based technologies. A side benefit would be new ways of earning a living, with improved material rewards, in lieu of existing subsistence patterns which have seen so much destruction of tropical rainforest.

This backstop technology system could provide a transition to more advanced sustainable technologies which are expected to become technologically proven and/or economic after the next two decades. These include steam injection and intercooling developments of the combined cycle gas turbine generator (for which biomass is a technically superior fuel), photovoltaic electricity, fuel-cell powered automobiles and eventually, perhaps, a hydrogen-based energy system in which carbon (and therefore carbon dioxide) has no place. *A propos* the hydrogen system, however, its portability may be more easily achieved by chemically attaching hydrogen to biomass-derived carbon than by other techniques that have been proposed. Such further technological transitions may become necessary as population growth raises demand for land needed for recreational and food-growing purposes, and as the sun's ambient energy increasingly has to be collected in the deserts or, perhaps, in outer space rather than by growing plants.

Chapter 4 concluded with a qualitative scenario describing one possible pattern of development for the global energy system over the next few decades.

Chapters 5 and 6 were mainly an exposition of those parts of economics which are needed to understand policy on global warming – needed because economics is accepted to be the main language of policy-making. The first of these chapters explains the basis of 'invisible hand' theorising which leads economists to look for market outcomes as the benchmark against which proposals for policy intervention have to be measured. The market, in principle, delivers an outcome in which nothing is wasted so that more for me means less for you and more of one good – say pollution abatement – means less of another, say guns or butter. A geometric explanation is offered, showing how the invisible hand's success in achieving social 'bliss' depends upon shaky assumptions regarding the nature of technology.

The market outcome depends also upon the distribution of spending power, with a different 'bliss' equilibrium resulting from each conceivable pattern of ownership of the means of production, and of consequential income. Leaving aside Marxian concerns with distribution and Keynesian concerns with macro-economic failure, a variety of possible reasons why the invisible hand may fail to work very well are explained, with particular attention to externalities, public goods and imperfect competition *vis-à-vis* the global warming problem and its inter-connections with the energy sector.

The problem of responding to market failure is considered in the light of the 'second best' theorem which demonstrates that there is no general rule for improvement in an imperfect world (so that 'more market' policies may result in worse outcomes). In the energy sector, which may be treated as a natural economic unit with strong internal links, indicative planning methods may be useful as an information sharing process that can help avoid such mistakes. For instance, long lead time investments in coal-fired power stations could be avoided with good information available about the future supply of biomass for fuelling combined-cycle gas turbine plant (and in relation to forecasts of electricity demand based more securely than on the wishful thinking of power engineers).

With environmental pollution there should, in principle under 'second best' theory, be an efficient level of pollution tax which results in the optimal level of pollution clean-up – i.e. where the benefit from further clean-up just balances its cost, so that further clean-up is not worthwhile. The possibility of the so-called property rights approach yielding this result is shown to be implausible in the face of transactions costs problems.

Chapter 6 went on to dismiss the possibility of the efficient taxing of pollution on grounds of informational difficulties which are two-fold. First may be a state of substantial ignorance regarding the costs of pollution damage, e.g. ignorance derived from a chain of weak links as regards the effect of carbon dioxide emissions in the atmosphere; the effect of those emissions on climate; the impact of climate on human activity and the natural ecosystem; and regarding how to value such effects. Secondly, much of the information regarding the last of these links requires the truthful disclosure of privately held information by agents who, at best, have negligible interest in its accuracy, and often a direct interest in its inaccuracy.

In the absence of useful information about the damage function, a rather coarse variety of economics is needed, in which the 'least-cost theorem' shows that a policy is better if it results in the cost of abatement, per unit of reduced pollution – say per ton of carbon dioxide emitted – being the same for all emitters. It is applicable when the target level of abatement to be aimed for has to be decided by experts rather than by economic analysis that sets the marginal cost of response against the marginal benefit of damage avoided, as perforce is in practice the case with most pollution problems.

A variety of conventional policy instruments – non-market-oriented command regulation, and market-oriented taxation or tradeable emissions permits – were considered in relation to the least-cost theorem, with the first shown to be inefficient. For instance, a mandatory reduction of carbon dioxide emissions by 20 per cent is more easily achieved in copper smelting, which just needs heat, than in steel making where some carbon is needed in the process; so it is better to achieve more of the emissions reduction in the copper smelting industry than in steel.

The special problems for economic theory raised by carbon dioxide pollution arise because it is the level of carbon dioxide that matters, and possibly for how long the level persists above normal. This means:

(a) that it is net emissions that matter, i.e. gross emissions minus absorption from the atmosphere, so that both emitting and absorbing activity are open to policy intervention; and

(b) that the problem becomes essentially dynamic in nature, since the level is the result of net emission rates, possibly changing rates, and the length of time for which emission persists.

It is, of course, point (a) which makes the renewable technologies of Chapter 4 so much more powerful a response to the global warming problem than simple taxes on gross emissions – or equivalent schemes for tradeable gross emissions permits – which have so far preoccupied policy analysts; point (b) raises difficulties for economists who are mainly trained in comparing the static equilibria of the invisible hand. Various tools of the trade for analysing time-dependent economic problems (including the discounting of cash flows using compound interest) were presented and the significance of the rate of interest used in policy choices explained.[2*]

The essentially dynamic nature of the global warming problem carries advantages in the sense that earlier policy errors can be corrected as part of a framework for taking account of new information as it becomes available from research, be it research on global climate models, on energy technology, or on land use and related matters. However, the credibility of policy requires it to be 'time-consistent', with its secular adjustment done in an announced manner which is surprise free, save for surprises due to nature. This calls for the maximum certainty in the effect of policy, with the minimisation of so-called agent-principal uncertainty. None of the conventional policy instruments does well under this requirement.

Finally, we reviewed briefly the body of economics known as macro-economics which deals *inter alia* with such failings of the system as Keynesian unemployment. It provides the framework within which the economic responses to global warming can best be analysed, although the state of the subject is inadequate for the task. It was suggested that some economists' analyses have suffered from a carry over of micro-economic habits of thought to their macro-economic analysis of the problem, although the major errors arise from an inadequate specification of appropriate, but currently largely unused, energy technologies in the macro-economic models.

Having sketched the necessary background in economics we resumed the elaboration of our long-term strategy in Chapter 7 by describing the Tradeable Carbon Absorption Duty (TAO), a policy instrument which is designed to overcome the difficulties of conventional instruments. Under the TAO, energy firms are motivated by market forces to adopt biomass as the basic sustainable energy raw material over the opening decades of the next century.

Energy sellers at the wholesale level are required to absorb some proportion of the carbon that is emitted when their product is used by the purchaser, or to contract with other firms to carry out this duty. The tradeability of the duty, i.e. that it can be discharged by third party contractors, means that the cost per ton of carbon emitted is the same for all emitters, thus achieving economic efficiency in terms of the least-cost theorem.

Although equivalent in steady state equilibrium to tradeable permits with absorption offsets, its impact is more direct. The regulatory nature of the absorption duty means that energy firms have no management discretion as to whether to undertake absorption offsets. This circumvents the agent-principal problem (save for problems with monitoring performance, which are no less present with offsets). Furthermore, energy firms become owners of biomass fuel raw material which has zero opportunity cost to them and will therefore be used by them in preference to non-zero cost supplies of traditional fossil fuels. Of course the use of the biomass is not free as it involves a further TAO to grow more biomass. But the use of fossil fuels involves both the TAO and the cost of mining the fossil fuel.

Such a policy cannot be implemented at a high level overnight and the dynamic time path for implementation, and for consequential carbon dioxide absorption and the assimilation of the use of biomass in the global energy system, provides the context for defining what is meant by a net target in a dynamic sense. Under New Zealand conditions (and starting in 1991, when the analysis was done) a target of 20 per cent net reduction by the year 2000 determines a dynamic path that adds an average of about 10 per cent to raw material energy costs over 25 years (peaking at about 17 per cent in 2005 and falling to zero by 2015), and eventually secures a 70 per cent reduction in net emissions. This may be compared with the

100 per cent tax which has been considered necessary in the USA to achieve a 20 per cent reduction in gross carbon dioxide emissions by 2020.

After some discussion of the meaning to be attached to a net emissions reduction target in a dynamic context, we consider the equity aspects by addressing the South's concern that the global warming problem has been caused by the North and should be dealt with at the North's expense. In relation to that problem an equity principle proposed by Uzawa (Uzawa, 1992) is taken up, that is to say that the target level of emissions reduction (net emissions reduction in keeping with the GREENS concept) should be related in different countries to the per capita income of the country concerned. Thus a higher level of TAO would be incurred by using a barrel of oil in Japan than if it were used in China.

As South countries improve their standard of living – in part by exporting pollution clean-up services through contracting to discharge the TAOs of energy wholesalers from developed countries – their level of TAO will rise towards that of the developed countries, with the burden becoming shared more equally. In the meantime, 'from each according to their ability'.

Different levels of TAO in different countries leads to the need to refine the TAO into a net TAO, a Tradeable Net Absorption Obligation which can be discharged either by paying for additional absorption or by paying for increased efficiency and less emission in regions where the level of TAO is low. Under this 'net absorption' approach an energy firm could either pay for growing more trees, in say the Philippines, or could pay for equipment to raise the energy efficiency of a Chinese steel mill, thus reducing the steel mill's greenhouse gas emissions.

Under this regime the energy efficiency of all plant, whether in the North or the South, would be raised to the point where further reductions in emissions would be more expensive than paying for more absorption, so that the least-cost theorem would apply equally to reductions in emissions and to increases of absorption.

Finally the question of costs is considered, firstly in a micro-economic consideration of the market for carbon fuels, from which it appeared that the value of coal in the ground would be greatly reduced by the implementation of GREENS, and secondly from a macro-economic perspective. However, the multiplier effects resulting from absorption activity in Third World countries suggest that the burden of dealing with global warming may turn out to be not a burden at all, but a boon (not to mention a boom).

So far so good: it has been seen that a transformation to sustainable energy technology is practicable, subject to the land capability question, and that the economics are not daunting and can be conveniently managed through the TAO. Indeed, expenditures in the 1990s would be relatively minor and, providing the need for a precautionary approach is accepted, the formidable problems of political decision making seem worth tackling. Of course they cannot be solved within the covers of a single book and in Chapter 8 I aspire only to provide an understanding of the difficulties involved and to suggesting some hopeful directions.

The difficulties arise from differences between national interests, despite the common interest in avoiding environmental catastrophe. To the general problem presented by the need to deal with global warming in a way that does not impede development in the South are added particular difficulties. Firstly, some countries in the South, for example India and China, are well-endowed with fossil fuel reserves and some are not (a state of affairs that obtains also in the North, to a lesser degree). Secondly, the Third World debt problem hangs over hopes for any sensible change in the relationship between North and South.

Data were presented showing that very large reserves of coal are located in only a small number of countries, which were not the same as the heavily indebted countries. Thus the two difficulties are separated – and, indeed, the problem of the heavily indebted countries seems one that requires specific remedies involving those countries and their creditors.

But the generality of South countries are suffering indebtedness on terms that are inequitable, having arisen as an inadvertent consequence of actions taken by their creditors for domestic reasons. There the possibility of a generalised debt-for-nature swap seems possible, providing it does not impair the development prospects of the South. Such a swap could take the form of moratorium on further fossil fuel exploration, voluntary by the North, but in return for the restructuring, and possible eventual cancellation, of some proportion of outstanding commercial debt in the South. The implication of such an arrangement would be the adoption of sustainable energy technology as the existing reserves are used up.

Technology transfer in these areas would occur automatically through the actions of firms discharging TAOs incurred mainly in the North. North consumers (rather than North governments) would be paying for the development of sustainable energy technology in the South, as the South escapes renewed debt constraints through invisible exports of pollution clean-up services. Energy firms would continue to be operating profitably, but using different technology under the incentives provided by the TAO.

Clearly the achievement of a general settlement of this nature is not going to come about as a sudden transformation in the behaviour of nations. But, in the meantime, there is no need for the application of the GREENS concept to hang fire. Many countries may, like New Zealand, find it beneficial – or at worst least costly – to achieve modest net emissions targets by the year 2000 using renewable biomass technology within their own borders. Such modest targets may be on a trajectory to ambitious achievements a decade or so later. Or if global warming ceases to be a worry, the relatively small initial acreage of fuel-wood plantings can find a commercial outlet as conventional timber after being allowed to grow to maturity.

Alternatively, many countries may, like Brazil has done, adopt biomass as an escape from a balance of payments constraint on their growth prospects, and some countries may opt for bilateral arrangements subject to reciprocal trading arrangements. These prospects depend on the claims made for these technologies being shown to be true from experience. All of this will constitute a learning-by-doing process which, the proof of the pudding being in the eating, will either draw in more participants until there is effective political will for a global settlement or reveal that some other remedy for global warming must be used, if a remedy still seems to be needed.

Chapter 9 was concerned with the institutional problems of implementing a comprehensive programme of transition to Global Redevelopment with Energy Environment Sustainability in the context of the FCCC agreed on at the Earth Summit, the content of which was briefly described and claimed to be broadly amenable to the implementation of GREENS through the future work of the Conference of the Parties (CoP).

However, there is an unavoidably political dimension to how it would work, the degree of which is minimised by the incorporation, through the TAO, of the subsidiarity principle into the working of GREENS. Governments would have to combine to ensure, through the monitoring activity of the CoP, that the TAOs are properly discharged by firms, in accordance with appropriate sustainability criteria embodied in the TAO contract. The levels of the TAO in different countries, broadly aligned with Uzawa's equity principle, would constitute policies pursued by those countries in pursuit of targets agreed through negotiations under the aegis of the CoP.

The political sensitivity of such monitoring and investigation activity is met by several aspects of the proposals which have been developed in this book. Firstly, as outlined in Chapter 4's scenario, initial progress with GREENS would be in developed temperate countries. Secondly, the move into tropical South countries would be by invitation – possibly stimulated by the prospect of debt relief – as they came to appreciate the economic advantages of emulating the advanced biomass energy technology path being adopted in developed countries. Thirdly, under the TAO mechanism, the remedy for default would not lie in country-to-country diplomacy, but country-to-firm relationships (in the country of origin of the TAO) of a normal regulatory type. Fourthly, countries would be assisted by the enforcement agency in achieving their net emission target by securing the effective discharge of the absorption duty laid on energy firms.

Thus the enforcement agency, in securing good behaviour by firms, would work to become perceived as the benevolent agent of technology transfer and progress towards sustainable development, rather than being heavily intrusive. Success in its dual role must derive from learning by doing in pilot schemes in the 'getting ready' phase of the 1990s, so that any mistakes would mostly be made in North countries. An expanding acceptance of transparency may be hoped for from the development of a high standard of negotiating etiquette in the work of the CoP, as has been the case with previous examples of international co-operation (Schelling, 1992).

The technical problem in measuring net emissions boils down to measuring absorption, given that the problem of measuring gross emissions was resolved before the FCCC could be signed. As for the difficulty that arises with measuring gross emissions in the informal sector, in particular with fuel-wood systems in traditional societies, this is much simpler in the context of net emissions since such activity, involving the burning of biomass fuel, can be regarded as essentially self-cancelling as regards net emissions.

Thus the problem is to measure absorption in the formal (market) economy. This involves defining what is to be included and then measuring what has been defined. As regards definition, biomass growth to be included as absorbing should be registered with an enforcement agency as planted for commercial biomass energy purposes on a medium or long-term basis. Annual crops used partly or wholly as fuel would count for absorption and emission simultaneously (as regards annually reported data), and equally, and therefore require no separate absorption measurement. Fuel-wood and conventional afforestation count for absorption whilst they grow, with eventual deduction to the extent that conventional timber is eventually not used for fuel purposes.

For actually measuring the absorption achieved by growing fuel-wood, and by conventional forestry, a major research exercise is required in the 1990s to establish the statistical properties of alternative coppicing cycles (and, to a lesser extent, conventional forestry) with different species grown in different soils and climates. Such research would also help develop the human capital resources needed for a GREENS-style technological transformation of commercial energy activity early next century. The objective, as regards measurement, would be to be able to rely on satellite observation as the main basis for global statistical coverage, with 'ground truthing' on a random basis as a check on the reliability of the satellite data and as a check against misreporting by firms as regards the discharge of their TAOs.

The measurement of emissions of greenhouse gases other than carbon dioxide (with absorption nil under current or likely technology) also presents a considerable problem for research, as does an adequate response to concerns regarding the agronomic sustainability of a biomass fuel system, and the need to resolve the land capability question. Thus the business of 'getting ready' calls for a massive programme of research as the first priority on the road from the Rio Earth Summit.

As markers for such research, Chapter 9 dealt, in less detail than they deserve, with a spectrum of concerns regarding water, soil, ecosystemic and socio-anthropological sustainability. While intensive biomass production has the potential to do great harm or great good depending on how it is carried out, it was concluded that there is no *prima facie* reason why mankind's currently unsustainable forcing of net carbon dioxide emissions should not be followed by a sustainable forcing of the planet's rate of biomass production. In some ways it would even be a reversion to the land coverage pattern that predated the industrial revolution, involving the restitution of degraded savannah that cannot support a rising population on the basis of traditional pastoral practices.

In Conclusion

My purpose in writing this book has not been simply to inform the reader and to influence public opinion in relation to the global warming problem, but also to bring its message to the attention of those involved in formulating policy. At the time I was preparing the first draft, I communicated my conclusions to the administration in Washington because it seemed that it is was there that misunderstandings as to the nature of the problem were greatest. The letter ran as follows:

Dr John H. Sununu,
Chief of Staff,
The White House,
Washington, DC, USA.   November 1991

Dear Dr Sununu,

Coming across your Profile in April's *American Scientist*, it seemed that not only is the USA on its own amongst developed countries in its 'no regrets' position on global warming, but that you alone are holding the line on that policy.

I am trained as an engineer and as an economist and have spent most of my working life on energy policy questions. Like you, I am in favour of economic growth and reject solutions that adversely affect the quality of life for billions of people. It worries me that environmentalists muddle up a legitimate concern about the sustainability of our industrial economic system with anti-growth, sometimes anti-capitalist, sentiment.

Yes, you are right in believing that the Global Climate Models are hopelessly inadequate for predicting what is happening to our climate system. But I rather doubt whether any model ever will do the job. Nor, for that matter, is our understanding of the global carbon balance all that good, though the prospects of improvement in that area seem better.

I had the good fortune, during a recent sabbatical, to sit in on a lecture course about non-linear dynamic systems. Of course, not every non-linear system displays chaotic dynamics, but there seems to be a strong possibility that the long-run climate system does, and if it does, prediction is impossible – the system can be divergent from initial conditions too close together for the difference to be measurable.

This means we need to look at ways of taking rational decisions in circumstances of genuine uncertainty, even ignorance, of the way in which nature is delivering our future. When I was a child we did not need a good model of Hitler's strategic thinking in order to make for the shelters when we heard the air raid sirens.

Were the world how most economists believe it to be, such precautionary decision-taking might lead us into the painful choices which the environmentalists wish on us. Fortunately most environmentalists and economists have, through ignorance of energy technology, got it wrong. The solution to the global warming problem which I outline in this book is more likely to have a positive rather than a negative impact on the living standards of today's billions, and certainly improves prospects for next century.

Essentially, energy firms are given an incentive to move, over the next three decades, from a fossil fuel-based system to a more or less equal cost renewable biomass basis. Unfortunately there doesn't seem to be a global economic model which is designed to show the impact of acquiring energy raw materials from Third World wage earners rather than from Third World rentiers (the existing Middle Eastern oil-producing countries), as is implied by this solution. However, attempts to replicate it on a version of the IMF's MULTIMOD are not discouraging.

The conclusions reached within these pages are as follows:

1.   It is the level of carbon dioxide in the atmosphere – or quite possibly for how long an above-normal level is maintained – that is of concern.

2. Therefore it is net emissions that matter, with increased absorption just as effective a line of solution as reduced gross emissions.

3. In a situation of extreme, and possibly permanent, uncertainty about the effect of above-normal levels, precautionary measures should be undertaken until shown to be unnecessary, even if they are expensive.

4. But they are not expensive, unless the weight of evidence regarding three well-known technologies is wrong. These involve absorbing carbon dioxide by growing biomass.

5. The quantities involved are so great that they can only be disposed of by being used as raw material for a renewable energy system, replacing fossil fuels.

6. A two to three decade timescale is required for these technologies to diffuse inexpensively into the mainstream of the global energy economy, by the end of which period more advanced renewable technologies will probably begin to penetrate the market.

7. It would be wrong to simply sit back and await the more advanced technologies since, firstly, they may take longer than hoped for to develop and, secondly, if nature turns out to have nasty surprises in store, a stitch in time can save nine.

8. Within the timescale, growth in LDCs' energy use will result in a doubling of emissions unless global collaboration is achieved. The biomass technologies give a competitive advantage to LDCs located in hot, wet climates.

9. Economic theory has little useful to contribute beyond the 'least-cost theorem' for achieving net emissions abatement targets efficiently: this is incorporated in the proposal for Tradeable Carbon Absorption Duties[3*](TCADs) which combine the effectiveness of 'command and control' regulation with an efficient market-oriented mechanism for achieving the required result.

10. LDCs' collaboration requires compensation for not using their known coal reserves. A scheme for Fossil Fuel Abstention Rewards targets that objective.

11. A combination of the two measures, TCAD and FFAR, can achieve a result of mutual advantage for an effective majority of nations. A subsidiary advantage could be a substantial reduction in the Third World debt problem as part of a global deal securing LDC collaboration.

12. The forthcoming UNCED cannot be expected to reach agreement on these lines but we may hope for a Framework Convention which gives explicit recognition to the net emission concept, and which provides machinery for international monitoring and technical assistance programmes.

13. Specifically, a commitment to a massive 'ground truthing' of GIS data to establish our understanding of land capability and a commitment to a major training programme in the bio-technical and other skills required for the realisation of the globally co-ordinated programme which may, towards the end of this decade, be recognised to be necessary.

14. The most formidable obstacles to securing an atmosphere made safe for our grandchildren appear to be political rather than technical or economic.

Yours etc....

Looking back on this letter, I would now wish it to have made two more points. On reflection I also gave up the idea of the FFAR on two grounds – firstly, the heavily indebted nations are not usually the same as those which are well-endowed with coal resources, so that debt relief could not be used as an incentive to them. And, secondly, there were problems of policy consistency over time as between the short to medium-term impact of debt relief and long-term weaning away from cheap coal. So in this book it is argued that debt relief, and the related moratorium on exploration, should find a place in easing the transition to sustainable energy technology of the generality of South countries which are not well advanced down the fossil fuel road.

The first of the two additional points is that the US has been right to emphasise, during the FCCC negotiating process, that the effect of all greenhouse gases together, rather than just carbon dioxide, needs to be taken into account. However, since control of global warming entails policy measures directed at net rather than gross emissions, and since carbon dioxide is the only greenhouse gas that we know how to absorb, this throws more rather than less weight on being ready to transform the energy system towards a biomass basis if climatological research continues to predict a serious risk of severe global warming.

Secondly, the lead times for such a process are very long and the time remaining to begin the relatively low-cost process of 'getting ready' may be correspondingly short. As a consequence it is important that there is now an FCCC in being, fortified by the inclusion of the USA amongst its signatories. However inadequate it may be as regards the targets currently adopted, they can be renegotiated by the CoP without the need to go through the ponderous business of setting up another UNCED. In the event, the USA not only signed the FCCC but was eventually the first major power to ratify. In environmental matters, it may be that nothing became the Bush Presidency better than the ending of it. Perhaps it can be hoped that such wiser counsels will prevail in the White House during the Clinton Administration and it successors.

Notes

1. It is said that, if you want to find out about the New Zealand economy, go to Tokyo, not to Wellington – and much the same could be said for all but a handful of other countries.

2. Issues of intergenerational equity, such as are central to our concern for sustainability, are involved, with the interests of future generations served by low social discount rates which result in high investment for the future and lower rates of depletion of exhaustible resources. Higher growth – and more rapid depletion of resources – does not follow from such higher public investment, where the purpose is to conserve resources. In fact it squeezes out growth generating resource using private sector investment – a low discount rate for policy decisions can thus be an instrument for balancing growth and sustainability.

3. This is the earlier name for what I subsequently called the Tradeable Absorption Obligation – see Chapter 1, note 8.

Appendix: The New Zealand Case

Policy Targets in New Zealand

Successive New Zealand governments have adopted targets for CO_2 emissions reduction of 20 per cent by the years 2005 and 2000. As we saw in Chapter 7, the notion of a net target immediately raises dynamic questions since biomass takes time to grow, quite a long time in the case of some tree species under natural conditions. The calculations described below are based upon the known technology for coppicing eucalypt species, as in Chapter 7. Thus a policy to sequester 100 per cent of the approximately 100 tonnes (t.) of carbon contained in 116t. of crude oil is taken to require the growing of 192t. of trees at the rate of 21.3t. per year for nine years, yielding three 64t. crops in years three, six and nine after year 0 in which the oil is burned. It is assumed that the means of disposal of the woody biomass crop is entirely as an energy raw material input to the commercial energy system.

For the reasons discussed in Chapter 7, all the implementation policies considered below assume a gradual build-up of the policy level with overshoot of any particular target level in the years following the target year. Such overshoot is consistent with an assumption that targets represent progress towards a higher level of achievement as regards reducing CO_2 emissions.

The six policy cases for which results have been calculated relate to three possible definitions for each of the two targets mentioned:

(a) policy level (TAO percentage) in force in 2000 or 2005.
(b) percentage of current emissions that is absorbed in 2000 or 2005.
(c) percentage of 1988 net emissions that is emitted in 2000 or 2005.

The Basecase

The 1988 starting point for the calculations is summarised in the first table on p.280:

This starting point is unusual, in relation to the global picture of Table 4.1, in a number of ways which make it more difficult for New Zealand to achieve its targets. Firstly, there is a very high proportion of hydroelectric supply but with no large, easily exploited hydro potential left; this means that it is difficult to substitute conveniently for fossil fuels in electricity production. Secondly, the Maui gasfield is fairly large by

	Coal	Oil	Gas Bio and Geoth.	Hydro	Electricity	
Industrial	35	20	36	15	41	of which 80 per cent
Transportation	0	99	33*	0	0	hydro and 20 per cent
Convenience	8	8	12	6	53	thermal with
Electricity	7	–	55	–	–	30 per cent average
Synthetic gasoline	–	–	55	–	–	generation
Total	50	127	161	21	94	efficiency

*Of which 29 synthetic gasoline and 4 compressed natural gas (CNG).
Figures are in petajoules.

world standards, and huge in relation to New Zealand's needs. As a consequence, it is used for bulk energy applications, making the displacement of fossil fuels, by biomass, less saving of emissions than the global average. This is compounded by an official unwillingness to renegotiate the Maui contract, leaving a rather small area of furnace fuel substitution until the contract begins to run down after 2005. Consequently, the more costly process of ethanol production and substitution in the transportation market, which is the largest sectoral demand for any kind of fuel in the New Zealand market, has to begin earlier than it would, on average, in the rest of the world.

The following tables provide a description of the basecase, with prices and costs calculated as explained in the section below that deals with the costs of the policies.

Basecase Fuel Prices in $NZ per GJ ($NZ millions per PJ)

DATE	1991	1992	1993	1994	1995	1996	1997
Coal	1.5000	1.5000	1.5000	1.5000	1.5000	1.5000	1.5000
Oil	5.1900	5.3872	5.5919	5.8044	6.0250	6.2539	6.4916
Gas	2.5000	2.5000	2.5000	2.5000	2.5000	2.5000	2.5000

DATE	1998	1999	2000	2001	2002	2003	2004
Coal	1.5000	1.7000	1.9000	2.0000	2.0000	2.0000	2.0000
Oil	6.7383	6.9943	7.2601	7.5360	7.8224	8.1196	8.4282
Gas	2.5000	2.5000	2.5000	2.5000	2.5000	2.5000	2.5000

DATE	2005	2006	2007	2008	2009	2010	2011
Coal	2.2000	2.5000	3.0000	3.0000	3.0000	3.0000	3.0000
Oil	8.7484	9.0809	9.4259	9.7841	10.1559	10.5419	10.9424
Gas	2.5000	2.5000	2.5000	2.5000	2.5000	2.5000	2.5000

DATE	2012	2013	2014	2015	2016	2017	2018
Coal	3.0000	3.0000	3.0000	3.0000	3.0000	3.0000	3.0000
Oil	11.3583	11.7899	12.2379	12.7029	13.1856	13.6867	14.2068
Gas	2.5000	2.5000	2.5000	2.5000	2.5000	2.5000	2.5000

DATE	2019	2020
Coal	3.0000	3.0000
Oil	14.7466	15.3070
Gas	2.5000	2.5000

Basecase Quantities (PJ x 10³)

DATE	1991	1992	1993	1994	1995	1996	1997
Coal	0.0490	0.0490	0.0490	0.0490	0.0490	0.0490	0.0490
Oil	0.1270	0.1270	0.1270	0.1270	0.1270	0.1270	0.1270
Gas	0.1610	0.1610	0.1610	0.1610	0.1610	0.1610	0.1610

DATE	1998	1999	2000	2001	2002	2003	2004
Coal	0.0490	0.0560	0.0680	0.0710	0.0710	0.0710	0.0730
Oil	0.1270	0.1270	0.1270	0.1270	0.1270	0.1270	0.1270
Gas	0.1610	0.1540	0.1420	0.1390	0.1390	0.1390	0.1370

DATE	2005	2006	2007	2008	2009	2010	2011
Coal	0.0870	0.0870	0.0870	0.0870	0.0870	0.0870	0.0870
Oil	0.1270	0.1365	0.1545	0.1550	0.1550	0.1550	0.1550
Gas	0.1230	0.1040	0.0680	0.0670	0.0670	0.0670	0.0670

DATE	2012	2013	2014	2015	2016	2017	2018
Coal	0.0870	0.0870	0.0870	0.0870	0.0870	0.0870	0.0870
Oil	0.1550	0.1550	0.1550	0.1550	0.1550	0.1550	0.1550
Gas	0.0670	0.0670	0.0670	0.0670	0.0670	0.0670	0.0670

DATE	2019	2020
Coal	0.0870	0.0870
Oil	0.1550	0.1550
Gas	0.0670	0.0670

Basecase Fuel Costs: Use Plus Refinery Costs ($NZ billions)

DATE	1991	1992	1993	1994	1995	1996	1997
Coal	0.0735	0.0735	0.0735	0.0735	0.0735	0.0735	0.0735
Oil	1.2306	1.2557	1.2817	1.3087	1.3367	1.3658	1.3959
Gas	0.4025	0.4025	0.4025	0.4025	0.4025	0.4025	0.4025

DATE	1998	1999	2000	2001	2002	2003	2004
Coal	0.0735	0.0952	0.1292	0.1420	0.1420	0.1420	0.1460
Oil	1.4273	1.4598	1.4935	1.5286	1.5649	1.6027	1.6419
Gas	0.4025	0.3850	0.3550	0.3475	0.3475	0.3475	0.3425

DATE	2005	2006	2007	2008	2009	2010	2011
Coal	0.1914	0.2175	0.2610	0.2610	0.2610	0.2610	0.2610
Oil	1.6826	1.8538	2.1516	2.2140	2.2717	2.3315	2.3936
Gas	0.3075	0.2600	0.1700	0.1675	0.1675	0.1675	0.1675

DATE	2012	2013	2014	2015	2016	2017	2018
Coal	0.2610	0.2610	0.2610	0.2610	0.2610	0.2610	0.2610
Oil	2.4580	2.5249	2.5944	2.6665	2.7413	2.8189	2.8996
Gas	0.1675	0.1675	0.1675	0.1675	0.1675	0.1675	0.1675

DATE	2019	2020
Coal	0.2610	0.2610
Oil	2.9832	3.0701
Gas	0.1675	0.1675

Basecost = ($NZ billions)

DATE	1991	1992	1993	1994	1995	1996	1997
Cost	1.7066	1.7317	1.7577	1.7847	1.8127	1.8418	1.8719

DATE	1998	1999	2000	2001	2002	2003	2004
Cost	1.9033	1.9400	1.9777	2.0181	2.0544	2.0922	2.1304

DATE	2005	2006	2007	2008	2009	2010	2011
Cost	2.1815	2.3313	2.5826	2.6425	2.7002	2.7600	2.8221

DATE	2012	2013	2014	2015	2016	2017	2018
Cost	2.8865	2.9534	3.0229	3.0950	3.1698	3.2474	3.3281

DATE	2019	2020
Cost	3.4117	3.4986

Policies

The policies to be considered are all directed at the basecase obtained by projecting these 1988 figures forward, allowing for substitution by coal and oil as the Maui contract quantities decline. Information about future trends in the New Zealand energy sector has not been conveniently available since 1986 when the regular publication of an energy planning information series was discontinued. Accordingly, the results presented below are supported by the assumption that 'energy management' (i.e. an officially sponsored programme to encourage increased efficiency of energy conversion and end use) will be effective in holding bulk energy demands constant at the levels reported for 1988. This is equivalent to assuming that a combination of economising behaviour and ambient energy technologies will hold the energy requirement for burnable fuels constant. On that basis, we have the equivalent of the middle line of figure 8.1, top panel.

The policies relate to the years 2000 (Policies 1, 2 and 3) and 2005 (Policies 4, 5 and 6). Policies 1 and 4 relate to a policy percentage rising at 2.5 per cent p.a. from 1993 and 2 per cent p.a. from 1996, and held steady once the level of 20 per cent is reached, thus resulting in asymptotic progress towards an eventual steady state outcome of 20 per cent sequestration. Policies 2 and 5 (commencing, as do Policies 3 and 6, in 1993 and 1996 respectively) build up to levels of sequestration in 2000 and 2005, respectively, which are 20 per cent of 'base case' emissions, (i.e. 1988 emissions adjusted for Maui gas rundown). Policies 3 and 6 build up to levels of sequestration in 2000 and 2005 which are 20 per cent of 'policy case' emissions, i.e. actual emissions induced by policy in those years. Since gross emissions are greater when the woody biomass is used for energy production, cutting back net emissions to 20 per cent of basecase emissions is a bigger cut, and can be expected to be more expensive to achieve, than 20 per cent of 'policy case' emissions.

Details of the policy profiles that achieve these results are given in Table A.1. Table A.2 shows the build-up (and falling off) of costs related to each policy and Table A.3 the area of land that is required. Table A.4 shows the quantity of fuel-wood produced and Table A.5 shows the reduction in net emissions relative to the initial, 1990, rate.

Table A.1 Per cent Tradeable Obligation Required in Order to Meet Various Interpretations of Targets for Net CO_2 Emissions Reduction
***bold** = target

DATE	1991	1992	1993	1994	1995	1996	1997
Policy 1	0	0	0	0	0	2.00	4.00
Policy 2	0	0	0	0	0	8.40	11.80
Policy 3	0	0	0	0	0	7.60	10.20
Policy 4	0	0	2.50	5.00	7.50	10.00	12.50
Policy 5	0	0	10.00	15.00	20.00	25.00	30.00
Policy 6	0	0	9.00	13.00	17.00	21.00	25.00

Date	1998	1999	2000	2001	2002	2003	2004
Policy 1	06.00	08.00	10.00	12.00	14.00	16.00	18.00
Policy 2	15.20	18.60	22.00	25.40	28.80	32.20	35.60
Policy 3	12.80	15.40	18.00	20.60	23.20	25.80	28.40
Policy 4	15.00	17.50	*20.00	22.50	25.00	27.50	30.00
Policy 5	35.00	40.00	45.00	50.00	55.00	60.00	65.00
Policy 6	29.00	33.00	37.00	41.00	45.00	49.00	53.00

Date	2005	2006	2007	2008	2009	2010	2011
Policy 1	*20.00	22.00	24.00	26.00	28.00	30.00	32.00
Policy 2	39.00	42.40	45.80	49.20	52.60	56.00	59.40
Policy 3	31.00	33.60	36.20	38.80	41.40	44.00	46.60
Policy 4	32.50	35.00	35.00	35.00	35.00	35.00	35.00
Policy 5	70.00	75.00	75.00	75.00	75.00	75.00	75.00
Policy 6	57.00	61.00	61.00	61.00	61.00	61.00	61.00

Date	2012	2013	2014	2015	2016	2017	2018
Policy 1	34.00	36.00	36.00	36.00	36.00	36.00	36.00
Policy 2	62.80	66.20	66.20	66.20	66.20	66.20	66.20
Policy 3	49.20	51.80	51.80	51.80	51.80	51.80	51.80

Policy 4	35.00	35.00	35.00	35.00	35.00	35.00	35.00
Policy 5	75.00	75.00	75.00	75.00	75.00	75.00	75.00
Policy 6	61.00	61.00	61.00	61.00	61.00	61.00	61.00

Date	2019	2020
Policy 1	36.00	36.00
Policy 2	66.20	66.20
Policy 3	51.80	51.80
Policy 4	35.00	35.00
Policy 5	75.00	75.00
Policy 6	61.00	61.00

Costs of the Policies

Prices are assumed to hold constant in real terms for gas until the resource is depleted. The real price of imported oil rises at 3.8 per cent per annum in line with the central assumption at the time of leading researchers. (But Manne and Richels, 1992, embodies a different assumption, which, however, does not greatly affect the outcome of the results reported here.) For coal a basecase elasticity of supply of approximately one is assumed.

Costs are expressed as a percentage of aggregate wholesale energy costs that will arise in the base case, that is a continuation of the present pattern of energy raw material inputs, adjusted for Maui rundown, and allowing for refinery costs applicable to petroleum throughout.

Costs of the different policies are calculated as the difference between the direct costs of implementing the policy (contracting for the trees to be grown at the time that CO_2 is emitted plus the costs of producing easily portable ethanol fuel from some fraction of the trees at the time they are cropped) and the savings in costs that result from a partial cut-back of the present pattern of energy raw material inputs and of conventional petroleum refining. These net costs show a peak in the year in which the policies level off (2005 for policies 1, 2 and 3, 2000 for the others). The reason for the subsequent decline in net costs is that the rising price of coal and oil results in the cost savings becoming increasingly significant in comparison with the constant real cost of fuel-wood production.

The savings realised in this way depend upon the pattern of substitution that is assumed, that is to say upon whether a given quantity of fuel-wood on the market results in less coal, less oil or less gas being used. The assumption in the calculations outlined is that initially coal and imported oil are backed out in equal proportions of the fuel-wood available and that, if coal production is thereby reduced to zero, further fuel-wood production goes equally to backing out gas and imported oil. In all cases where oil is backed out the existing refinery balance is maintained so that 25 per cent of the fuel-wood directly displaces burning oil whilst the remainder displaces portable transport fuel via an inefficient conversion process resulting in an overall increase in energy raw material inputs. It should be emphasised that, whilst these assumptions seem to the writer, who has some experience of energy policy issues, to be reasonable, they are no substitute for a properly optimised model such as might be based upon an energy sector indicative planning process as discussed on p.140 *et seq.*

Table A.2 Net Costs, as a Percentage of Estimated Wholesale Energy Costs Arising from the Tradeable Obligations of Table A.1
(negative=net cost, positive=net benefit)

DATE	1991	1992	1993	1994	1995	1996	1997
Policy 1	0	0	0	0	0	-0.68	-1.34
Policy 2	0	0	0	0	0	-2.87	-3.96
Policy 3	0	0	0	0	0	-2.59	-3.43
Policy 4	0	0	-0.89	-1.76	-2.60	-3.39	-4.15
Policy 5	0	0	-3.58	-5.28	-6.94	-8.51	-10.01
Policy 6	0	0	-3.22	-4.58	-5.90	-7.13	-8.32

DATE	1998	1999	2000	2001	2002	2003	2004
Policy 1	-1.98	-2.57	-3.15	-3.65	-4.06	-4.42	-4.76
Policy 2	-5.02	-5.93	-6.88	-7.71	-8.24	-8.84	-9.40
Policy 3	-4.23	-4.89	-5.60	-6.22	-6.56	-6.99	-7.40
Policy 4	-4.86	-5.49	-6.08	-6.55	-6.92	-7.21	-7.47
Policy 5	-11.44	-12.67	-13.86	-14.85	-15.56	-16.26	-16.91
Policy 6	-9.45	-10.37	-11.29	-12.03	-12.51	-13.01	-13.46

DATE	2005	2006	2007	2008	2009	2010	2011
Policy 1	-4.94	-4.58	-3.80	-3.69	-3.57	-3.43	-3.19
Policy 2	-9.49	-8.73	-7.16	-6.94	-6.73	-6.48	-6.04
Policy 3	-7.37	-6.72	-5.45	-5.24	-5.05	-4.83	-4.45
Policy 4	-7.56	-6.82	-4.78	-3.92	-3.07	-2.39	-1.59
Policy 5	-17.14	-15.55	-11.13	-9.34	-7.57	-6.28	-4.89
Policy 6	-13.57	-12.22	-8.64	-7.18	-5.75	-4.56	-3.15

DATE	2012	2013	2014	2015	2016	2017	2018
Policy 1	-2.95	-2.68	-1.84	-1.02	-0.20	0.53	1.28
Policy 2	-5.59	-5.10	-3.57	-2.07	-0.54	0.86	2.28
Policy 3	-4.09	-3.69	-2.51	-1.36	-0.21	0.85	1.92
Policy 4	-0.83	-0.26	0.42	1.04	1.42	1.87	2.32
Policy 5	-3.43	-2.11	-0.55	0.99	2.19	3.58	4.96
Policy 6	-1.81	-0.76	0.48	1.56	2.35	3.24	4.15

DATE	2019	2020
Policy 1	2.04	2.65
Policy 2	3.70	4.93
Policy 3	3.02	3.92
Policy 4	2.73	3.15
Policy 5	6.24	7.63
Policy 6	4.97	5.84

Depending on the particular interpretation of the target which is assumed, the cost of achieving government targets peaks at between 5 per cent and 10 per cent of bulk fuel costs for 2005 targets and between 7 per cent and 17 per cent for 2000 targets. As noted above, targets 2 and 5, related to the base case pattern of emissions, are the most expensive to achieve.

They correspond closely to the definition preferred on p.188 related to 1990 emissions. Of course, these policies also represent the most substantial progress towards whatever the climatologists may eventually tell us is the optimum, or maybe necessary, level of CO_2 reduction, as may be seen from Table 3, where the rate of sequestration is proportionate to the area planted (approximately 10 tonnes of carbon per year per hectare). All of the policies begin to show positive net savings by the year 2014, when the energy economist's central forecast is that oil prices will have risen from 18$US/barrel in 1990, at 3.8 per cent p.a., to 42$US/barrel (a figure which, in real terms, is around half the peak OPEC price of the early 1980s). Effectively this means that biomass, as an energy raw material, will be competitive with oil in about 25 years and that implementation of the GREENS concept anticipates that development by a decade or so through making users of oil pay for the growing of trees sooner than would occur under the influence of market forces. Without GREENS, coal-to-gasoline, rather than biomass-to-ethanol, would dominate, with serious environmental impacts.

On average, over the period from 1996 (1993), when tree growing begins, to 2014, the energy cost increase, as a percentage of bulk fuel costs, is as follows:

Policy 1 (2005, eventual steady state basis)   3.2 per cent
Policy 2 (2005, basecase emissions basis)   6.6 per cent
Policy 3 (2005, policy case emissions basis)   5.1 per cent
Policy 4 (2000, eventual steady state basis)   14.2 per cent
Policy 5 (2000, basecase emissions basis)   10.2 per cent
Policy 6 (2000, policy case emissions basis)   8.0 per cent

These figures may be compared with figures for carbon tax-induced economisation in the use of fossil fuels of $US250 per ton of carbon (or approximate doubling of oil prices), for a 20 per cent 2020 equilibrium reduction in emissions (where 'equilibrium' is an equivalent concept to our 'eventual steady state' basis (Manne et al, 1990b)) and of $US460 per ton of carbon to induce an equilibrium emissions reduction of 50 per cent by 2030 (Whalley et al, 1990).

Table A.3 Area of Land Required to Meet the Tradeable Obligations of Table A.1 Using Intensive Coppicing Technology (sq km) – cf NZ Forest Area 72,000 sq km, 44,000 sq km, other 53,000 sq km

DATE	1991	1992	1993	1994	1995	1996	1997
Policy 1	0	0	0	0	0	14.0	42.0
Policy 2	0	0	0	0	0	58.7	141.3
Policy 3	0	0	0	0	0	53.1	124.5
Policy 4	0	0	17.5	52.4	104.9	175.0	262.8
Policy 5	0	0	69.9	174.8	314.7	491.2	703.9
Policy 6	0	0	62.9	153.8	272.7	420.8	597.8

DATE	1998	1999	2000	2001	2002	2003	2004
Policy 1	83.9	140.5	212.4	299.2	400.9	517.6	649.6
Policy 2	247.6	379.9	539.3	724.6	937.0	1176.0	1442.6
Policy 3	214.0	323.4	453.7	603.6	774.1	964.7	1176.0
Policy 4	368.5	493.4	639.1	804.3	971.8	1141.6	1314.8
Policy 5	953.3	1244.9	1580.9	1959.1	2312.8	2676.7	3052.8
Policy 6	803.9	1043.3	1317.9	1625.5	1905.5	2192.2	2487.3

DATE	2005	2006	2007	2008	2009	2010	2011
Policy 1	785.7	921.8	1055.7	1190.7	1326.2	1462.8	1601.0
Policy 2	1685.1	1929.3	2171.5	2417.4	2666.2	2919.4	3177.3
Policy 3	1360.2	1545.0	1727.2	1911.3	2096.5	2284.2	2474.3
Policy 4	1494.9	1675.4	1834.0	1975.3	2097.7	2201.8	2287.7
Policy 5	3449.2	3852.3	4215.0	4545.3	4840.5	5102.3	5331.9
Policy 6	2797.0	3110.1	3389.4	3641.5	3864.4	4057.9	4221.0

DATE	2012	2013	2014	2015	2016	2017	2018
Policy 1	1740.6	1881.4	2005.8	2117.9	2219.6	2306.8	2379.2
Policy 2	3440.4	3708.1	3947.2	4166.2	4368.7	4545.8	4697.2
Policy 3	2667.3	2862.7	3035.5	3192.6	3337.1	3462.2	3567.6
Policy 4	2355.0	2402.2	2425.6	2431.7	2441.7	2450.0	2456.5
Policy 5	5528.0	5683.0	5790.6	5862.6	5939.9	6011.2	6076.4
Policy 6	4353.6	4451.9	4509.8	4539.4	4573.8	4603.5	4628.6

DATE	2019	2020
Policy 1	2436.8	2478.6
Policy 2	4825.4	4926.2
Policy 3	3653.3	3717.3
Policy 4	2461.8	2465.7
Policy 5	6134.8	6183.2
Policy 6	4650.6	4668.6

Table A.4 Woodfuel Produced (millions of tons)

DATE	1991	1992	1993	1994	1995	1996	1997
Policy 1	0	0	0	0	0	0	0
Policy 2	0	0	0	0	0	0	0
Policy 3	0	0	0	0	0	0	0
Policy 4	0	0	0	0	0	0.1049	0.2098
Policy 5	0	0	0	0	0	0.4196	0.6294
Policy 6	0	0	0	0	0	0.3776	0.5455

DATE	1998	1999	2000	2001	2002	2003	2004
Policy 1	0	0.0839	0.1678	0.2518	0.4233	0.5995	0.7727
Policy 2	0	0.3525	0.4951	0.6378	1.1463	1.4516	1.7496
Policy 3	0	0.3189	0.4280	0.5371	0.9756	1.2094	1.4369
Policy 4	0.3147	0.5255	0.7367	0.9485	1.2752	1.6108	1.9400
Policy 5	0.8392	1.4784	1.9059	2.3354	3.2280	3.9222	4.6042
Policy 6	0.7133	1.2662	1.6073	1.9496	2.7030	3.2547	3.7951

DATE	2005	2006	2007	2008	2009	2010	2011
Policy 1	1.0333	1.2993	1.5649	1.8500	2.1158	2.3683	2.6600
Policy 2	1.4208	2.8858	3.3493	3.8756	4.3512	4.8022	5.3507
Policy 3	1.9986	2.3527	2.7046	3.1039	3.4614	3.7980	4.2082
Policy 4	2.2797	2.6301	2.9788	3.3608	3.7130	3.9304	4.2082
Policy 5	5.3505	6.1052	6.8608	7.7289	8.5242	9.0367	9.7107
Policy 6	4.3830	4.9751	5.5656	6.2412	6.8540	7.2414	7.7537

DATE	2012	2013	2014	2015	2016	2017	2018
Policy 1	2.9289	3.1882	3.4890	3.7667	4.0328	4.2354	4.4389
Policy 2	5.8440	6.3218	6.8982	7.4225	7.9279	8.3326	8.7365
Policy 3	4.5730	4.9241	5.3489	5.7310	6.0964	6.3856	6.6738
Policy 4	4.4476	4.5548	4.7239	4.8515	4.8378	4.8642	4.8880
Policy 5	10.2956	10.6078	11.0883	11.4720	11.5377	11.7336	11.9044
Policy 6	8.1911	8.4027	8.7324	8.9867	8.9925	9.0794	9.1643

DATE	2019	2020
Policy 1	4.6432	4.7585
Policy 2	9.1431	9.3949
Policy 3	6.9633	7.1360
Policy 4	4.8982	4.9139
Policy 5	12.0014	12.1611
Policy 6	9.1993	9.2574

Table A.5 Reduction in Net Emissions Relative to 1990 Emissions
*bold = target years for 20 per cent reduction by successive governments

DATE	1991	1992	1993	1994	1995	1996	1997
Policy 1	0	0	0	0	0	0.22	0.67
Policy 2	0	0	0	0	0	0.93	2.24
Policy 3	0	0	0	0	0	0.84	1.98
Policy 4	0	0	0.28	0.83	1.67	2.54	3.70
Policy 5	0	0	1.11	2.78	5.00	6.86	9.77
Policy 6	0	0	1.00	2.44	4.33	5.84	8.27

DATE	1998	1999	2000	2001	2002	2003	2004
Policy 1	1.33	1.12	0.50	1.29	2.52	3.98	5.43
Policy 2	3.93	4.32	4.96	7.18	9.42	12.53	15.83
Policy 3	3.40	3.50	3.75	5.49	7.21	9.71	12.30
Policy 4	5.15	5.74	6.00	7.75	9.68	11.62	13.37
Policy 5	13.26	15.53	*18.33	22.98	26.60	30.82	34.99
Policy 6	11.17	12.81	14.83	18.55	21.30	24.62	27.83

DATE	2005	2006	2007	2008	20.09	2010	2011
Policy 1	05.16	08.02	11.99	13.56	15.12	16.72	18.26
Policy 2	*16.33	20.46	25.71	28.50	31.38	34.39	37.26
Policy 3	12.12	15.55	20.10	22.19	24.33	26.56	28.66
Policy 4	13.63	17.00	21.18	22.63	23.79	24.95	25.69
Policy 5	37.77	43.77	50.28	53.64	56.55	59.05	60.16
Policy 6	29.59	34.52	40.08	42.63	44.79	47.00	48.44

DATE	2012	2013	2014	2015	2016	2017	2018
Policy 1	19.88	21.53	22.83	23.99	25.00	25.93	26.63
Policy 2	40.33	43.51	46.01	48.31	50.39	52.30	53.74
Policy 3	30.90	33.22	35.01	36.65	38.12	39.46	40.48
Policy 4	26.22	26.73	26.72	26.53	26.72	26.80	26.84
Policy 5	61.08	62.37	62.27	61.97	62.95	63.35	63.74
Policy 6	49.56	50.65	50.78	50.29	50.82	50.96	51.04

DATE	2019	2020
Policy 1	27.08	27.49
Policy 2	54.25	54.90
Policy 3	41.19	41.82
Policy 4	26.91	26.93
Policy 5	64.31	64.48
Policy 6	51.26	51.33

Suggested Further Reading

Bibliographical details of works mentioned below are included in the list of References that follows.

The scientific background for most of Chapter 2 is accessibly described in Fred Pearce's *Turning Up the Heat*, which is copiously referenced. *Greenhouse New Zealand*, by Jim Salinger, gives a 'downunder' and more recent perspective. Diligent reading of either the *New Scientist* or *Scientific American* will keep the reader abreast of developments in this active field. The wonders of Chaos, including non-linear dynamic systems, are well described in *Chaos: Making a New Science* by James Gleick.

For Chapter 3, the theoretical basis of cost benefit analysis is lucidly outlined in Richard Layard's introductory essay in the book of readings on Cost Benefit Analysis in the Penguin series of readings in economics. The regret concept is widely used in management decision theory, e.g. the text *Introductory Management Science* by G.D. Eppen et al.

State of the art coverage of alternative energy technology, together with a more elaborate scenario for a renewables-intensive global energy future than could be advanced in Chapter 4, is to be found in *Renewable Energy Sources for Fuels and Electricity*, edited by Thomas B. Johansson and others. *Sustainable Biomass Energy* by Philip Elliott and Roger Booth is also useful and very easy to read. The technology and political economy of petroleum are covered respectively in *Petroleum Refining for the Non-technical Person* by W.L. Leffler and *Opec: Twenty-five Years of Prices and Politics* by Ian Skeet. An earlier period is covered by Peter Odell's *Oil and World Power* and Anthony Sampson's *The Seven Sisters*.

For Chapters 5 and 6, Michael Common's *Environmental and Resource Economics: an Introduction* provides a thorough grounding with a slightly sceptical flavour. It does not require any mathematics beyond very simple algebra and has the advantage, as far as our topic is concerned, of a substantial focus on energy questions. A complementary book, more neo-classical in flavour, is *The Economics of Energy* by Michael Webb and Martin Ricketts, which covers environmental aspects but requires both a little calculus and a more formal background in basic economics. *Blueprint for a Green Economy* by David Pearce et al. provides a non-technical survey of the issues raised for economic thinking by the heightened level of environmental concern evidenced through the Earth Summit.

None of these have much to say on macroeconomics, for which this book has, perforce, not provided a layman's guide, in parallel with the bulk of Chapters 5 and 6 in relation to neoclassical microeconomics. Perforce since there is very little of a non-controversial nature to be said about a discipline which has been singularly unsuccessful at analysing the malaise of market economies over the last quarter century. A recent survey of different schools of thought is *A Modern Guide to Economic Thought* edited by Douglas Mair and Anne Miller. Turning to the application of theory in Chapter 7, a convenient survey of macroeconomic studies is *The Macroeconomic Consequences of Controlling Greenhouse Gases: a Survey* by Gianna Boero et al. Another convenient source designed for a non-professional readership is the UNEP Report on Greenhouse Gas Abatement Strategies, a report on a project led by Michael Grubb.

But, in relation to Chapters 7 and 8, there is no economic writing which is up to date in the sense of being abreast of the FCCC's recognition of 'sinks' along with 'sources', or which encompasses the alternative technology possibilities outlined in Chapter 4. *Buying Greenhouse Insurance* by Alan Manne and Richard Richels advances the precautionary 'learn then act' approach advocated in this book, but from a more conservative technological perspective. Rudiger Dornbusch and James Poterba's edited volume records the Rome Conference of 1990, which saw the economics profession set off in the wrong direction (with the notable exception of Uzawa's paper, which not only advanced the equity concept adopted in this book, but also treated sinks alongside sources). William Cline's *The Economics of Global Warming* argues for effective action, but on the basis of conventional CBA and with only brief mention of biomass fuel possibilities. Nevertheless, it contains a wealth of detailed information. His chapter on international strategy is an excellent back-up to Thomas Schelling's essay referred to in Chapter 8, which, although it appears in a professional journal, is also highly readable.

However, neither of these draw the connection with the Third World debt problem considered in Chapter 8, for which the admirable work of the German Bundestag's Enquete-Kommission can be consulted (1990, English translation) in the context of an excellent chapter on the indirect causes of tropical deforestation. One cannot speak too highly of the excellent work of this Commission, as elaborated in the four volumes it has published on various aspects of the climate change problem. *Beyond Interdependence* by Jim MacNeill et al. and Morris Miller's *Debt and the Environment* provide more specialised background. Cheryl Payer's *Lent and Lost* provides a critique of the conventional analysis of development lending, whilst the articles in the *Economist's* 1991 survey provides an up-to-date establishment view on the work of the World Bank and IMF.

The documents of the Earth Summit, including the FCCC, are available through United Nations outlets. So far as I know, there is as yet no published material to supplement the first part of Chapter 9 on the possible *modus operandi* of the Convention, with the converse applying to the latter part: the wealth of literature on development policy and problems, large parts of which are relevant to the issues raised in this book, is an embarrassment of riches. The World Bank's World Development Report for 1992, *Development and the Environment*, provides an excellent survey of the somewhat elitist conventional wisdom and an invaluable statistical base. With its bibliographical note it is also a convenient entry point into the literature, in which I cannot claim to be deeply read. I mention here firstly the existence of dissenting, counter-elitist views, as advanced for example in the *Ecologist* edited by Edward Goldsmith, and, secondly, just a few sources which I found helpful. These include *Beyond the Woodfuel Crisis* by Gerald Leach and Robin Mearns, *Theory and Practice in Plantation Agriculture* by Mary Tiffen and Michael Mortimore, and Frank Ellis's *Peasant Economics*. I got a glimpse into the physical science of land use sustainability from *Soils and the Greenhouse Effect* edited by A.F. Bouwman from the proceedings of a scientific conference initiated by the Netherlands and of hydrological and water resource aspects from the similar type of work edited by Solomon et al. from Canada.

References

Ahmad, Syed, 1991, *Capital in Economic Theory*, Edward Elgar, Aldershot, England and Brookfield, Vermont.

Anderson, Dennis and C.D. Bird, 1992, 'Carbon Accumulations and Technical Progress', *Oxford Bulletin of Economics and Statistics*, 54(1).

Anon., 1992, 'Briefing: Inorganic oil', *Geology Today*, 8(5).

Arrow, Kenneth J., 1962, 'The Economic Implications of Learning by Doing', *Review of Economic Studies*, 29.

Arrow, Kenneth J. and R.C. Lind, 1970, 'Uncertainty and the Evaluation of Public Investment Decisions', *American Economic Review*, 60, and in Layard, 1972.

Arrowsmith, D.K. and C.M. Place, 1990, *An Introduction to Dynamical Systems*, CUP, Cambridge.

Atkinson, T.C., K.R. Briffa and G.R. Coope, 1987, 'Seasonal Temperatures in Britain During the Past 22,000 Years, Reconstructed Using Beetle Remains', *Nature*, 325.

Baumgartner, M.F., 1990, 'A Global Soils and Terrain Database: a Tool to Quantify Global Change', in A.F. Bouwman (Editor), 1990.

Baumol, William J., 1977, *Economic Theory and Operations Analysis*, Prentice-Hall International, London and New Jersey.

Baumol, William J. and W.E. Oates, 1971, 'The Use of Standards and Prices for Protection of the Environment', *Swedish Journal of Economics*, 73.

Beardsley, Tim, 1991, 'Tracking the Missing Carbon', *Scientific American*, 264/4.

Blinder, Alan, 1988, 'The Challenge of High Unemployment', *American Economic Review, Papers and Proceedings*.

Boero, Gianna, R. Clarke and L.A. Winters, 1991, *The Macroeconomic Consequences of Controlling Greenhouse Gases: a Survey*, HMSO, London, (Summary, Department of the Environment, London).

Bouwman, A.F., 1990, 'Remote Sensing Techniques', in A.F. Bouwman (Editor), 1990.

Bouwman, A.F. (Editor), 1990, *Soils and the Greenhouse Effect*, Wiley, Chichester, and New York.

BP Statistical Review of World Energy, Annually, Corporate Communications Services, British Petroleum Company, London.

Bradford, David F., 1975, 'Constraints on Government Investment Opportunities and the Choice of Discount Rate', *American Economic Review*, 65/5.

Broecker, Wallace S., 1987, 'Unpleasant Surprises in the Greenhouse?', *Nature*, 328.

Broecker, Wallace S. and T-H Peng, 1992, 'Interhemispheric Transport of Carbon Dioxide by Ocean Circulation', *Nature*, 356.

Brundtland Commission, 1987, *Our Common Future*, OUP, Oxford and New York.

Cantor, R.A. and C.G. Rizy, 1991, 'Biomass Energy: Exploring the Risks of Commercialization in the United States of America', *Bioresource Technology*, 35.

Cheung, S., 1973, 'The Fable of the Bees', *Journal of Law and Economics*, 16.

Cline, William R., 1992, *The Economics of Global Warming*, Institute for International Economics, Washington, DC.

Coase, Ronald H., 1960, 'The Problem of Social Cost', *Journal of Law and Economics*, 3.

Common, Michael S., 1988, *Environmental and Resource Economics*, Longmans, London and New York.

Common, Michael S. 1991, Australian National University, personal communication.

Crowley, Thomas J. and G. R. North, 1988, 'Abrupt Climate Change and Extinction Events in Earth's History', *Science*, 240.

Darmstadter, Joel, 1991, 'Estimating the Cost of Carbon Dioxide Abatement', *Resources*, 103, Resources for the Future, Washington, DC.

Dean, Andrew and P. Hoeller, 1992, *Costs of Reducing CO_2 Emissions: Evidence from Six Global Models*, Economics Department Working Papers, No. 122, OECD, Paris.

Department of Transport and Department of the Environment, 1992, joint evidence to the Royal Commission on Environmental Planning, HMSO, London.

Dijk, D., J. van der Kooij, F. Lubbers and J. van den Bos, 1993, *Response Strategies of the Dutch Electricity Generating Companies towards Global Warming*,

Conference on Thermal Power Generation and the Environment, Hamburg, September.

Dornbusch, Rudiger, and J.M. Poterba (Editors), 1991, *Global Warming: Economic Policy Responses*, MIT Press, Cambridge, MA, and London.

Dosi, Giovanni, 1984, 'Technological Paradigms and Technological Trajectories: The Determinants and Directions of Technical Change and the Transformation of the Economy', in Christopher Freeman (Editor), *Long Waves in the World Economy*, Frances Pinter, London and Dover NH.

The Economist, weekly, London.

The Economist, October 12, 1991, *Sisters in the Wood: a survey of the IMF and the World Bank*.

The Economist, May 30, 1992, *Sharing: a survey of the environment*.

Elliott, Philip, and R. Booth, 1990, *Sustainable Biomass Energy*, Shell Selected Papers, Shell International Petroleum Company, London.

Energy Technology Support Unit, *Arable Coppice: Energy for Tomorrow, a Farming Alternative for Today*, Renewable Energy Enquiries Bureau, ETSU, Harwell.

Enquete-Kommission, 1989, *Protecting the Earth's Atmosphere: Interim Report of the Commission of Inquiry of the 11th German Bundestag*, English translation, German Bundestag Publication Section, Bonn.

Enquete-Kommission, 1990, *Protecting the Tropical Forests: Second Report of the Commission of Inquiry of the 11th German Bundestag*, as above.

Enquete-Kommission, 1991, *Protecting the Earth: Third Report of the Commission of Inquiry of the 11th German Bundestag*, as above (2 Volumes).

Environmental Resources Ltd, 1988, *An Assessment of the Environmental Effects of Energy Forestry*, ETSU B 1166, Energy Technology Support Unit, Harwell.

Eppen, G.D., F.J. Gould and C.P. Schmidt, 1987, *Introductory Management Science*, Prentice-Hall International, Englewood Cliffs, NJ.

FAO, Annually, *Production Yearbook*, Rome.

FAO, Annually(a), *Forest Products Yearbook*, Rome.

Fremantle, Sidney W., 1992, Department of Energy, personal communication.

Gleick, James, 1988, *Chaos: Making a New Science*, Penguin Books, Harmondsworth, England.

Goldemberg, Jose, L.C. Monaco and I.C. Macedo, 1992, 'The Brazilian Fuel-Alcohol Program', in Johansson et al (Editors), 1992.

Goodland, Robert, A. Juras and R. Pachuri, 1992, 'Can Hydroreservoirs in Tropical Moist Forest Be Made Environmentally Acceptable?', *Energy Policy*, 20(6).

Gore, Senator (now Vice-President) Al, 1992, *Earth in the Balance: Ecology and the Human Spirit*, Plume (Penguin Books USA Inc), New York, NY.

Grabowski, Henry G., 1990 'Innovation and International Competitiveness in Pharmaceuticals', in Arnold Heertje and M. Perlman (Editors), *Evolving Technology and Market Structure: Studies in Schumpeterian Economics*, University of Michigan Press.

Grubb, Michael J., 1989, *The Greenhouse Effect: Negotiating Targets*, Royal Institute of International Affairs, London.

Grubb, Michael J. and ten others, 1992, *UNEP Greenhouse Gas Abatement Costing Studies, Phase One Report*, UNEP Collaborating Centre on Energy and Environment, Risø National Laboratory, Denmark.

Hall, David O., 1990, 'The Importance of Biomass in Balancing CO_2 Budgets', Paper to Conference on Biomass for Utility Applications, Tampa, FL, 23-25 October.

Hall, David O., H.E. Mynick and R.H. Williams, 1990 and 1991, *Carbon Sequestration versus Fossil Fuel Substitution*, PU/CEES Report No. 255, Princeton University. (Also in *Science and Global Security*, 2, 1991).

Hall, David O., F. Rosillo-Calle, R.H. Williams and J. Woods, 1993, 'Biomass for Energy: Supply Prospects', pp.593-653 in Johansson et al, 1993.

Hamakawa, Yoshihiro, 1987, 'Photovoltaic power', *Scientific American*, April.

Harrison, David, 1988, *The Sociology of Modernisation and Development*, Unwin Hyman, London.

Hoel, Michael, 1991, 'Efficient International Agreements for Reducing Emissions of CO_2', *The Energy Journal*, 12(2).

Hoeller, Peter, A. Dean and M Hayafuji, 1992, *New Issues, New Results: the OECD's Second Survey of the Macroeconomic Costs of Reducing CO_2 Emissions*, Economics Department Working Papers, No. 123, OECD, Paris.

Holtham, Gerald and A. Hughes Hallett, 1987, 'International Policy Cooperation and Model Uncertainty', in R.C. Bryant and R. Portes (Editors), *Global Macroeconomics: Policy Conflict and Cooperation*, Macmillan/International Economic Association/Centre for Economic Policy Research, London.

Hotelling, Harold, 1931, 'The Economics of Exhaustible Resources', *Journal of Political Economy*.

Houghton, Sir John, 1990, *Foreword, Scientific Assessment of Climate Change: the Policymakers' Summary of the Report of Working Group 1 to the IPCC*, WMO/UNEP, Geneva.

Houghton, Richard A. and G.M. Woodwell, 1989, 'Global Climate Change', *Scientific American*, 260/4.

Hubbard, Harold M., 1991, 'The Real Cost of Energy', *Scientific American*, April.

Ingham, Alan, and A. Ulph, 1990, 'The Economics of Global Warming', mimeo, University of Southampton.

IEA (International Energy Agency of the Organisation for Economic Co-operation and Development), *Energy Prices and Taxes*, Quarterly, IEA/OECD, Paris.

INL (Intergovernmental Negotiating Committee) 1992, *United Nations Framework Convention on Climate Change*, Chairman's final draft, 8 May, United Nations General Assembly A/AC.237/L.14.

IPCC, 1992, *Climate Change: the IPCC 1990 and 1992 Assessments*, IPCC, Geneva.

Johansson, Thomas B., H. Kelly, A.K.N. Reddy and R.H. Williams (Editors), 1993, *Renewable Energy Sources for Fuels and Electricity*, Island Press, Washington, DC.

Johansson, Thomas B., H. Kelly, A.K.N. Reddy and R.H. Williams, 1993a, 'Renewable Fuels and Electricity for a Growing World Economy: Defining and Achieving the Potential', in Johansson et al. (Editors), 1993.

Johansson, Thomas B., H. Kelly, A.K.N. Reddy and R.H. Williams, 1993b, 'A Renewable Intensive Global Energy Scenario', in Thomas B. Johansson, H. Kelly, A.K.N. Reddy and R.H. Williams (Editors), 1993.

Jones, Hywel, 1975, *An Introduction to Modern Theories of Economic Growth*, McGraw-Hill, New York.

Kellogg, William W., 1991, 'Response to Skeptics of Global Warming', *Bulletin of American Meteorological Society*, 74.

Kerr, Richard A., 1992, 'Greenhouse Science Survives Skeptics', *Science*, 256, 22 May.

Kerr, Richard A., 1992a, 'Greenhouse Uncertainties: Adjusting the Heat', *Science*, 256, 22 May.

Lachmann, W., 1992, 'Social Aspects of the Market Economy: the Case of Germany', staff seminar, Massey University Economics Department.

Lakatos, Imre, 1970, 'Falsification and the Methodology of Scientific Research Programmes', in his 1978, *Philosophical Papers, Vol 1*, CUP, Cambridge.

Lamarre, Leslie, 1991, untitled article, *EPRI Journal*, April/May, US Electric Power Research Institute, Palo Alto, California.

Larson, Eric D., 1991, *A Developing-country-oriented Overview of Technologies and Costs for Converting Biomass Feedstocks into Gases, Liquids and Electricity*, PU/CEES Report No. 206, Princeton University, NJ.

Layard, Richard, 1972, 'Editorial Introduction', *Readings in Cost Benefit Analysis*, Penguin Education, Harmondsworth, England.

Leach, Gerald and R. Mearns, 1988, *Beyond the Woodfuel Crisis*, Earthscan, London.

Leffler, W.L., 1985, *Petroleum Refining for the Non-technical Person*, Pennwell, Tulsa, OK.

Lind, Robert C., 1982, 'A Primer on the Major Issues', in Robert C. Lind et al. *Discounting for Time and Risk in Energy Policy*, Resources for the Future, Washington, DC.

Lindzen, Richard S., 1990, 'Some Coolness Concerning Global Warming', *Bulletin of American Meteorological Society*, 71.3

Maclaren, J. Piers, 1993, New Zealand Forest Research Institute, personal communication.

MacNeill, Jim, P. Winsemius and T. Yakushiji, 1991, *Beyond Interdependence*, OUP, New York and Oxford.

Mair, Douglas and A.G. Miller, *A Modern Guide to Economic Thought*, Edward Elgar, Cheltenham, England.

Manabe, S. and R.J. Stouffer, 1988, 'Two Stable Equilibria of a Coupled Ocean-Atmosphere Model', *Journal of Climate*, 1.

Manne, Alan S. and R.G. Richels, 1992, *Buying Greenhouse Insurance – the Economic Costs of CO_2 Emission Limits*, MIT Press, Cambridge, MA, and London.

Marland, Gregg, 1988, *The Prospect of Solving the CO_2 Problem through Global Reforestation*, DOE/NBB-0082, National Technical Information Service, Springfield, VA.

Meadows, Donella H., D.L. Meadows, J. Randers and W.W. Behrens III, 1972, *The Limits to Growth*, Earth Island, London.

Miller, Morris, 1991, *Debt and the Environment*, United Nations, New York and Geneva.

Ministerial Declaration, 1990, Second World Climate Conference, WMO, Geneva.

Mohamed, The Honorable Dato Seri Dr. Mahathir bin, 1991, Transcript of Speech to Group of 15, Second Summit, Caracas, 27 November, Press Liaison Division, Department of Information, Malaysia.

Morisette, Peter M., and A.J. Plantinga, 1991, 'The Global Warming Issue: Viewpoints of Different Countries', *Resources*, 103, Resources for the Future, Washington, DC.

Mors, Matthias, 1991, *The Economics of Policies to Stabilize or Reduce Greenhouse Emissions: the Case of CO_2*, Economics Papers (Internal Paper No. 87), Commission of the European Communities, Brussels.

Moulton, Robert J. and K.R. Richards, 1990, *Costs of Sequestering Carbon through Tree Planting and Forest Management in the United States*, US Department of Agriculture Forest Service, General Technical Report WO-58.

Munroe, Tapan, 1991, *Sustainable Energy Development and the Role of Energy Utilities,* International Energy Workshop, IIASA, Laxenburg, Austria, June.

Myers, Norman, 1989, 'The Greenhouse Effect: a Tropical Forestry Response', *Biomass*, 18.

Norby, Richard J. and E.G. O'Neill, 1991, 'Leaf Area Compensation and Nutrient Interactions in CO_2-enriched Seedlings of Yellow Poplar', *New Phytologist*, 117.

Nordhaus, William D., 1990, 'Count Before You Leap', *The Economist*, 7 July.

Nordhaus, William D., 1991, 'To Slow or Not to Slow: The Economics of the Greenhouse Effect', *The Economic Journal*, 101.

Norris, Minister of Transport, 1992, opening speech to Passenger Transport Forum Conference on Public Transport and New Urban Developments.

Odell, Peter R., 1974, *Oil and World Power: Background to the Oil Crisis*, (Third Edition), Penguin Books, Harmondsworth, England.

Payer, Cheryl, 1991, *Lent and Lost: Foreign Credit and Third World Development*, Zed Books, London and New Jersey.

Pearce, David, 1991, 'The Role of Carbon Taxes in Adjusting to Global Warming', *The Economic Journal*, 101.

Pearce, David, A. Markandya, and E.B. Barbier, 1989, *Blueprint for a Green Economy*, Earthscan, London.

Pearce, Fred, 1989, *Turning Up the Heat*, The Bodley Head, London.

Ravel, A. and V. Ramanathan, 1989, 'Observational Determination of the Greenhouse Effect', *Nature*, 342.

Read, Peter, 1990, 'Global Warming: Why Mrs. Thatcher Should Be More Ambitious', *National Westminster Bank Quarterly Review*, November.

Read, Peter, 1991, *Practicable Achievement of New Zealand's CO₂ Emissions Target*, Paper to Fifth IIASA Meeting of the International Energy Workshop, Laxenburg, Austria. (Available as Economics Discussion Paper, Massey University)

Read, Peter, 1991a, 'GREENS: A Policy Response to Global Warming', *National Westminster Bank Quarterly Review*, August.

Read, Peter, 1992, *Global Warming and Tradeable Absorption Obligations*, paper to New Zealand Association of Economists, Conference, Waikato University, August. (Available as Economics Discussion Paper, Massey University).

Read, Peter, 1992a, 'The Political Economy of a Biomass Energy Response to Global Warming GREENS', *International Journal of Global Energy Issues*, 4(4).

Read, Peter, 1993, *Efficient and Effective Economic Instruments: A Reappraisal of the Economics of Climate Change*, Sixth IIASA Meeting of the International Energy Workshop, Laxenburg, Austria.

Salinger, Jim, 1991, *Greenhouse New Zealand: Our Climate Past Present and Future*, Square One Press, Dunedin, New Zealand.

Sarmiento, J.L. and E.T. Sundquist, 1992, 'Revised Budget for the Oceanic Uptake of Anthropogenic Carbon Dioxide', *Nature*, 356.

Schelling, Thomas C., 1992, 'Some Economics of Global Warming', *American Economic Review*, 82.

Schneider, Stephen H., 1987, 'Climate Modeling', *Scientific American*, May.

Sen, Amartya, 1970, 'Editorial Introduction', *Readings in Growth Economics*, Penguin Books, Harmondsworth, England.

Simonis, Udo E., 1992, 'Cooperation or Confrontation: How to Allocate CO₂ Emissions Reductions between North and South?' *Law and State*, 46, Institute for Scientific Cooperation, Tübingen.

Sims, Ralph E.H., 1993, personal communication.

Sims, Ralph E.H., P. Handford and T. Bell, 1990, *Wood Fuel Supply and Utilisation fron Short Rotation Energy Plantations*, Agronomy Department, Massey University, Palmerston North, New Zealand.

Sims, Ralph E.H., P. Handford, J. Weber and R. Lynch, 1991, *The Feasibility of Wood-Fired Power Generation in New Zealand*, Faculty of Agricultural and Horticultural Sciences, Massey University, Palmerston North, New Zealand.

Singer, Fred., 1991, *The Washington Institute for Values in Public Policy*, presentation to International Energy Workshop, IIASA, Laxenburg, Austria.

Skeet, Ian, 1988, *OPEC: Twenty-five Years of Prices and Politics*, CUP, Cambridge.

Solomon, S.I., M. Beran and W. Hogg, 1987, *The Influence of Climate Change and Climatic Variability on the Hydrologic Regime and Water Resources*, IAHS Press, Institute of Hydrology, Wallingford, England.

Sutton, W.R.J., 1992, Tasman Forestry Ltd, personal communication.

Tans, Pieter P., I.Y. Fung and T. Takahashi, 1990, 'Observational Constraints on the Global Atmospheric CO₂ Budget', *Science*, 247.

Tasker, Alison, 1992, 'Branching Out', *Review: Quarterly Magazine of Renewable Energy*, ETSU, Harwell, and DTI Editorial Office, London.

R.H. Texeira and B.J. Goodman (Editors), 1991, *Ethanol Annual Report, FY1990*, US Department of Energy, Washington, DC.

Thomas, John A.G., 1977, *Energy Analysis*, Westview Press, Boulder, CO.

Tietenberg, Tom H., 1988, *Environmental and Natural Resource Economics*, Scott Foreman and Co., Glenview, IL.

Tiffen, Mary, and M. Mortimore, 1990, *Theory and Practice in Plantation Agriculture*, Overseas Development Institute, London.

Trabalka, J.R., J.A. Edmonds, J.M. Reilly, R.H. Gardner and L.D. Voorhees, 1985, 'Human Alterations of the Global Carbon Cycle and the Projected Future', in J.R. Trabalka (Editor), *Atmospheric Carbon Dioxide and the Global Carbon Cycle*, US Department of Energy, DOE/ER-0239, Washington, DC.

Turco, Richard P., O.B. Toon, T.P. Ackerman, J.B. Pollack and C. Sagan, 1983, 'Nuclear Winter: Global Consequences of Multiple Nuclear Explosions', *Science*, 222.

UK Department of Energy, Annually, *Development of the Oil and Gas Resources of the United Kingdom, ('the Brown Book')*, a report to Parliament by the Secretary of State for Energy, HMSO, London.

UK Department of Energy, Annually, *Digest of United Kingdom Energy Statistics*, HMSO, London.

Uzawa, Hirofumi, 1990, 'Global Warming Initiatives: the Pacific Rim', in Dornbusch and Poterba (Editors), 1991.

Vidal, John, 1992, 'The Big Chill', *The Guardian*, 19 November.

Vitousek, Peter M., P.R. Ehrlich, A.H. Ehrlich and P.A. Matson, 1986, 'Human Appropriation of the Products of Photosynthesis', *BioScience*, 36/6.

von Weizsäcker, Ernst U. and J. Jesinghaus, 1992, *Ecological Tax Reform*, Zed Books, London and New Jersey.

Waring, Peter, 1992, New Zealand Industrial Research Ltd., (formerly Department of Scientific and Industrial Research), personal communication.

Watson, Andrew, 1992, 'Conveying that Sinking Feeling', *Nature*, 356.

Webb, Michael G., and M.J. Ricketts, 1980, *The Economics of Energy*, Macmillan, London and Basingstoke.

Williams, P.B., 1991, 'The Debate over Large Dams', *Civil Engineering*, August.

Williams, R.H. and E.D. Larson, 1993, 'Advanced Gasification-based Biomass Power Generation and Cogeneration', in Johansson et al (Editors), 1993.

Willebrand, Eva and T. Verwijst, 1992, *Willow Coppice Systems in Short Rotation Forestry: the Influence of Plant Spacing and Rotation Length on the Sustainability of Biomass Production*, abstract 05.37 in 7th European Conference on Biomass for Energy and Environment, Agriculture and Industry, October, 1992, *Abstracts and Proceedings*, Granducato Viaggi, Via Masaccio 12b/r, 50132 Firenze - Italy.

World Bank, 1992, *Development and the Environment: World Development Report 1992*, OUP, New York.

Wright, L.L. and A.R. Ehrenshaft, 1990, 'Short Rotation Woody Crops Program: Annual Progress Report for 1989', (Draft, April 1990), *Environmental Sciences Division Publication No. 3484*, Oak Ridge National Laboratory, TN.

Index